global

advanced teacher's book

Frances Watkins

Macmillan Education
Between Towns Road, Oxford OX4 3PP
A division of Macmillan Publishers Limited
Companies and representatives throughout the world

ISBN 978-0-230-03332-0

Written by Frances Watkins

First published 2012

Designed by eMC Design Limited
Cover design by Macmillan Publishers Limited

Please see Coursebook for photo credits.

Teacher's Resource Disc
Illustration by Stephen Dew and Celia Hart

Motion clips kindly supplied and licensed from: BBC; BBC Motion Gallery; Blip TV; Getty

Minimum System Requirements:

Windows XP SP3: 300 MHz
Windows Vista: 1 GHz
Windows 7 – 1 GHz
Mac OS 10.5 – 867 MHz
Mac OS 10.6 – 1.5 GHz
Mac OS 10.7 – 2 GHz

Available RAM: 128 MB
Screen resolution: 1024 x 768 pixels

Audio card and speakers to access audio components.

Web browser support:
Windows – Internet Explorer 7 and above, Firefox, Safari, Opera 9 or above
Macintosh – Safari, Firefox, Opera 9 or above

Adobe Shockwave Flash browser plugin v10 or above is required to view video components.

Microsoft Word is required to open the included .doc files.

Adobe Acrobat Reader is required to open the included .pdf files.

help.macmillan.com

Printed and bound in Thailand

2016 2015 2014 2013 2012
10 9 8 7 6 5 4 3 2 1

Contents

Coursebook contents map

EV – **Extend your vocabulary** P – **Pronunciation** W – **writing**

Components for the learner

Coursebook
see pages viii–xiii

eWorkbook
see pages xiv–xv

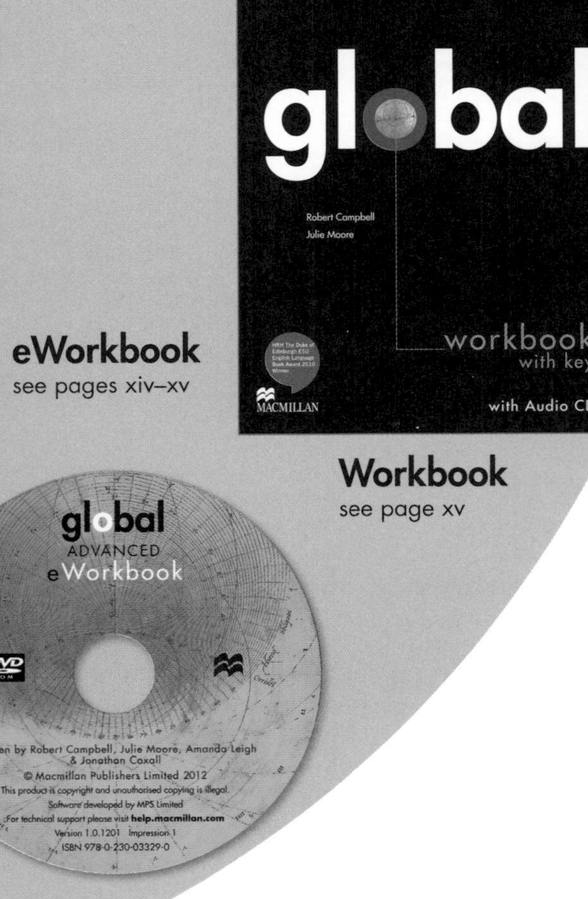

Workbook
see page xv

Components for the teacher

Teacher's Book & Teacher's Resource Disc

see page xvi

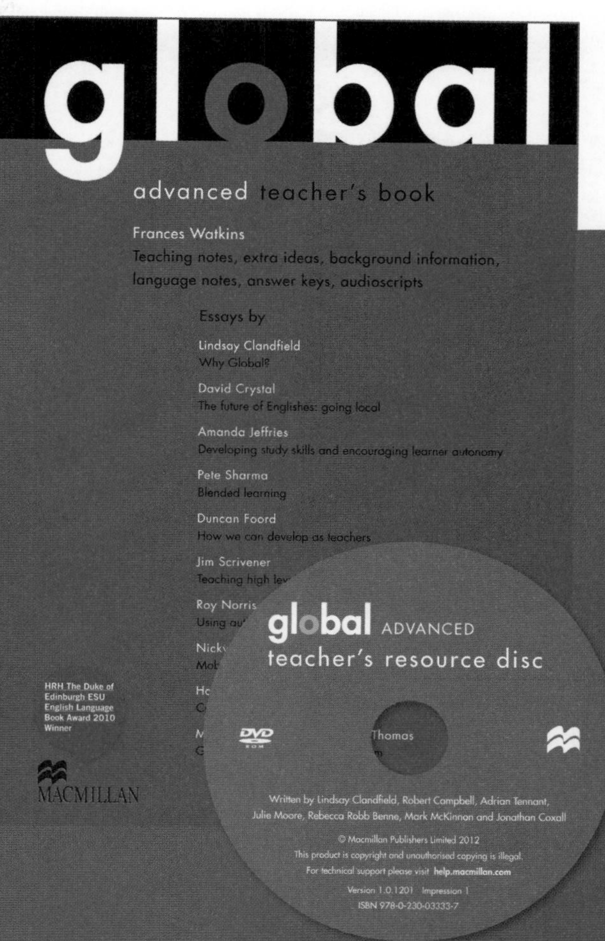

Class Audio CDs

see page xvii

Global Website

see page xvii

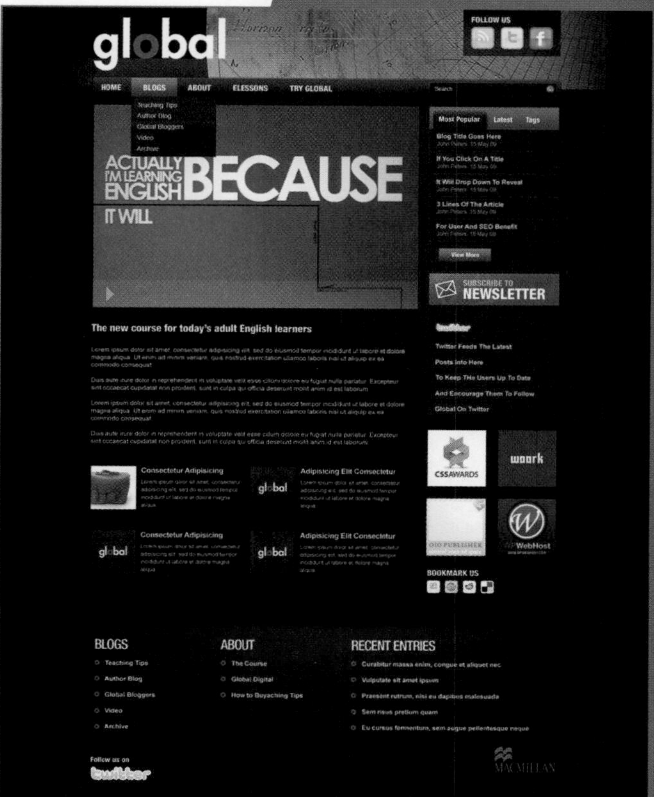

Global Digital

see pages xviii–xix

Coursebook: lessons 1 and 2 of a unit

Unit structure

Each unit is divided in six two-page lessons. The first four lessons are the core part of the unit. The last two lessons include additional material (eg Study skills, Writing). In this unit, the first two lessons are about trade, the next two lessons are about commerce.

Headings

Clear headings throughout the book show what you are teaching at each stage of the lesson.

Grammar practice

Grammar practice is highly contextualised and meaningful, often in texts that provide additional information about the topic of the lesson. Many grammar practice exercises are designed in a similar way to the reading texts.

UNIT 6 **Trade & Commerce**

Part 1

Listening
The Silk Road

Extend your vocabulary
change and exchange

Pronunciation
List intonation

Grammar
The passive

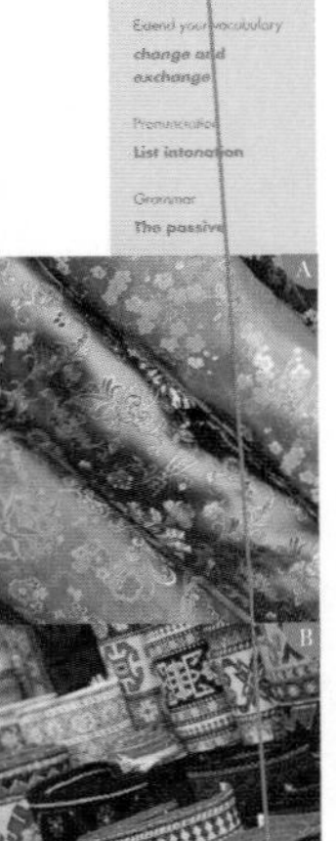

Listening

1 Work in pairs. Discuss the questions.

- Which countries or areas are your country's main trading partners? What items or commodities do you import from them, and how are they transported to your country?
- What do you know about the trade route known as the 'Silk Road'? What images does it conjure up for you?

2 2.36–2.40 Listen to someone talking about different aspects of the Silk Road, and match each section 1–5 to one of the pictures.

3 Work in pairs. Look at the pictures and discuss what you can remember about each section. What were the most interesting facts that you learnt?

4 Work in pairs. Can you remember which items in the box were traded from East to West, and which from West to East? Listen to sections 3 and 4 again to check your ideas.

algebra astronomy compass ginger glass gunpowder linen paper-making porcelain printing press saddles shipbuilding silk spices wool

5 2.41 Listen to the final part of the talk and answer the questions.

1. What else was exchanged on the Silk Road as well as goods?
2. What does the speaker say about the links between the Silk Road and globalisation?
3. How is the Silk Road being used today?

6 Would you be interested in going on a modern Silk Road tour? Why / Why not? What would be the highlights or downsides of such an experience?

Extend your vocabulary – *change and exchange*

1 Delete the noun that does not normally collocate with the verb.

1. **exchange** contracts / addresses / views / your hair style
2. **change** trains / house / gear / the subject
3. **swap** places / roles / currency / comics
4. **switch** lanes / sides / smiles / channels

2 Using some of the collocations, tell a partner about …

1. details of things that you have done in the last week, month or year.
2. things you have never done.

Pronunciation

1 Read the following sentences from the listening passage, and discuss with a partner whether your voice goes up or down on the words and phrases in italics.

1. Silk was ideal for overland travel as it was *light*, easy to *carry* and took up little *space*.
2. They also faced the ever present threat of *bandits*, not to mention *wars*, *plagues* and *natural disasters*.
3. Caravanserai were used not only by traders and *merchants*, but also by *pilgrims*, *missionaries*, *soldiers*, *nomads* and *urban dwellers*.

2 2.42 Listen to check your answers. Then practise reading the sentences with the audio.

3 Work in pairs. Compile lists for two of the following categories:

- scarce commodities or resources
- items or commodities that are often illegally traded
- items that are currently in great demand in retail outlets
- things you can buy in your local street market

4 Read your lists and compare them with another pair.

Grammar

1 Read the sentences in the grammar box and do the tasks below.

a. *The Silk Road* ***consisted*** *of an extensive network of land and sea routes.*
b. *Many important scientific and technological innovations* ***were transported*** *to the West.*
c. *When the silk arrived in Europe it* ***was made into*** *luxury goods.*
d. *Caravanserai* ***were used*** *not only by traders and merchants, but also by pilgrims, missionaries, soldiers, nomads and urban dwellers.*
e. *By the end of the 14th century, its importance* ***had*** *greatly* ***diminished****.*
f. *Today the Silk Road* ***is again being used*** *by traders.*

1. Which sentences contain an active verb form and which a passive verb form?
2. Choose the correct alternative:
   - use *an active / a passive* verb form when the main focus of the sentence is the *doer* of the action (or *agent*)
   - use *an active / a passive* verb form when the main focus of the sentence is the *action* or the *object* of the action
3. Complete the rule:
   - to form the passive, use the appropriate form of the verb ________ + the ________
   - Which of the passive sentences mention an agent? Why is an agent not mentioned in the other passive sentences?

2 Complete the text with an appropriate active or passive form of the verb.

Trade (1) ________ (*conduct*) between different groups or societies since prehistoric times. The earliest trade (2) ________ (*probably / consist*) of forms of barter, in which goods (3) ________ (*exchange*) without using a medium of exchange such as money. Later, currency (4) ________ (*introduce*) to facilitate a wider exchange of goods and services. The importance of international trade (5) ________ (*increase*) in recent decades, and trade organisations such as the EU and NAFTA (6) ________ (*establish*) to promote trade between member countries. Nowadays, trade (7) ________ (*increasingly / carry out*) with few restrictions within countries; however, trade blocs (8) ________ (*may / regulate*) international trade by means of quotas and restrictions. Tariffs (9) ________ (*usually / impose*) on imports, and some form of taxation (10) ________ (*may / also / impose*) on exports. However, it is unlikely that completely free trade (11) ________ (*ever / establish*) in the future or that forms of taxation (12) ________ (*completely / disappear*).

3 Work in pairs. Think of two or three commonly traded items or commodities (eg wheat, coffee, oil, cars, electronic goods). Write passive sentences about the past, present and future of the commodities using some of the words below and a range of verb forms.

design discover export grow import introduce invent manufacture trade use

4 Read your sentences to another pair without mentioning the names of the items. Can they guess what you have written about?

5 Work in small groups. Tell your group about an important contribution that your country, or another country you know, has contributed to the world. This could be:

- an art form
- a commodity
- a custom
- an invention
- an institution
- a manufactured item
- a religion or philosophy
- a technique

Ask and answer questions about each contribution.

Grammar focus – explanation & more practice of the passive on page 142

Contents sidebar

Content is summarised on every spread so you can see at a glance what the lesson is about.

Pronunciation

A focus on sounds, stress and intonation is included at regular intervals in *Global*. Pronunciation is integrated into the language points of the lesson. The aim is for students to achieve international intelligibility.

Grammar explanations

Short grammar explanations are provided on the page, with a cross reference to further explanation and practice at the back of the book.

Speaking

A wide variety of speaking tasks are presented in the book.

Many speaking tasks include an element of choice (students can choose from different tasks or questions). This gives the teacher and students flexibility and can be used in mixed ability classes.

Developing critical thinking

Reading tasks and discussion questions for texts encourage reflection and critical thinking.

Literary texts

Short extracts from modern literature are included, with information about the author and the book.

UNIT 6 **Trade & Commerce**

Part 2

Speaking
Freedom and slavery

Reading
The Long Song

Vocabulary
Ways of looking

Speaking

1 Look at the pictures, and with a partner discuss their connection with trade.

2 2.43 Read some quotations about freedom and slavery, and complete each one with a suitable word, as in the example. Then listen to compare your ideas with the original quotations.

1 The moment the slave resolves that he will no longer be a slave, his fetters fall. Freedom and slavery are mental *states*. (Gandhi)
2 The danger of the past was that men became slaves. The danger of the future is that men may become ________. (Erich Fromm)
3 The history of men's ________ to women's emancipation is more interesting perhaps than the story of that emancipation itself. (Virginia Woolf)
4 I disapprove of what you say, but I will defend to the death your ________ to say it. (Voltaire)
5 To be free is not merely to cast off one's chains, but to live in a way that respects and enhances the freedom of ________. (Nelson Mandela)
6 Freedom is never voluntarily given by the oppressor; it must be demanded by the ________. (Martin Luther King)
7 Governments need ________ to protect them against their enslaved and oppressed subjects. (Tolstoy)
8 Everything can be taken from a man but one thing; the last of the human freedoms – to choose one's ________ in any given set of circumstances. (Viktor Frankl)

NORTH AMERICA
EUROPE
sugar, coffee, cotton, tobacco
copper, cloth, glassware
CUBA
JAMAICA
slaves, indigo
AFRICA
SOUTH AMERICA

3 Which quotation do you like best, and why? Choose two or three of the quotations to discuss with a partner.

- How far do you agree or disagree with the ideas, and why?
- Can you think of any real current or historical situations to which they could be applied?

Reading

1 Read extracts from *The Long Song* by Andrea Levy. What is the relationship between Caroline, Godfrey and July? Do you think the story takes place *before*, *during* or *after* the emancipation of the slaves? Why?

2 Which of the underlined words refer to …

- facial expression?
- sounds?
- movement?

3 Guess the meaning of each of the highlighted words.

4 Find evidence in the text for the following statements.

1 Caroline does not initially understand Godfrey's refusal to serve her.
2 July was surprised by Godfrey's reaction.
3 Godfrey starts behaving like the master.
4 Caroline resists Godfrey's refusal to help.
5 Caroline realises that their roles have been reversed.

5 Which of these words could describe the characters' attitudes, and why?

aggressive arrogant controlling defiant loyal self-confident submissive timid

1 In what way(s) could Caroline be 'like a fish newly landed from the water' (last paragraph)?
2 Which of the characters, if any, did you sympathise with? Why?

Vocabulary

1 Read two sentences from the text. Which of the verbs in bold has a literal meaning, and which could have both a literal and a metaphorical meaning?

*Godfrey **stared at** the sack, the small trunk and the cloth valise …*

*And Godfrey, **looking down on** the missus, sucked loudly on his teeth …*

2 Work in pairs. Decide whether each of these multi-word verbs has a literal meaning, a metaphorical meaning or both.

look after look away look back on look forward to look into look on look out for look round look up look up to

3 Work in pairs. Read texts 1 and 2 below. Guess the meaning of the underlined words. Then check your ideas with a dictionary.

1 Lucy opened the kitchen door and peered inside the room. In the darkness, she could just make out a figure standing next to the fridge. She switched on the light and glimpsed James just about to eat a slice of the chocolate cake she had baked earlier in the day. When James caught sight of her standing in the doorway, he refused to look her in the eye. She glared at him. 'What on earth were you doing?' she snapped.

2 David sat gazing at the bill in disbelief, and frowning. 'There must be some mistake', he gasped and tried to catch the waiter's eye. Charles glanced at his watch. 'I'd better be going,' he mumbled, and quickly made his way out of the restaurant.

4 Write a few sentences describing a scene in which two people meet and there is some conflict. Include …

- a description of the way they looked at each other.
- their facial expressions.
- what they said.

5 Read your scenes to other students, paying attention to the past tense endings. Which scene do you like best, and why?

The Long Song

'Hurry along, Godfrey. Pick up these things', Caroline said. Godfrey stared at the sack, the small trunk and the cloth valise that stood between him and the missus. His missus, with an exasperated sigh, indicated again the items she wished Godfrey to transport.

But Godfrey, still scratching his head, said, 'You wan' me put these on the cart and take you into town?'

'Of course, into the gig. And I am in a hurry to be gone'.

'So you wan' me lift them into the gig and then drive you into town?'

'Godfrey, do not play the fool with me. You know I must go to town for my own safety until all this trouble is past. Now, let us be gone'.

And Godfrey, looking down on the missus, sucked loudly on his teeth before saying, 'Then you must pay me, missus'.

July cupped her hands over her mouth so her gasp and giggle would not escape. While all Caroline managed to utter was, 'What did you say?'.

'Me said', Godfrey began, 'that me will need payment if me is to take you into town'.

'Payment?', the missus repeated. She frowned upon Godfrey, then looked quizzically to July for some explanation of his behaviour. But July was silent – her mouth fixed with a grimace of a child in the thrill of a game.

'Don't be ridiculous, Godfrey', Caroline said, 'Now, pick up the things or I will see you punished for this'.

Godfrey sighed. He then walked past the missus into the hall and sat himself down upon one of the massa's wooden chairs. 'Then punish me, missus', he said as he lifted first one leg, and then the other, over the arms of the planter's seat and sat as if waiting for someone to remove his boots …

'Get up, get up!' Caroline jumped twice in her fury. 'Do as you are bid', then made to strike Godfrey with her closed fist. But Godfrey seized both her wrists with so tight a grip that the missus's face contorted into a wince. Her mouth fell in wordless agony as Godfrey raised himself from the chair. As he stood higher, he bore down upon the missus's wrists until the pressure of the pain impelled her to kneel in front of him. As the missus, overwhelmed by him, went limp upon the ground, Godfrey let go of her wrists.

July made a move towards the missus, but Godfrey shouted, 'Stop!'.

He sat once more and began playing with his fingernail, while Caroline Mortimer, quivering at his feet like a fish newly landed from the water, slowly lifted her head, wiped her snivelling nose upon the back of her hand, and quietly asked him, 'How much?'

Andrea Levy is a novelist who was born in London in 1956 after her parents immigrated there from Jamaica. She has written a number of widely acclaimed novels, including the prize-winning *Small Island*. *The Long Song*, published in 2010, is set in a Jamaican sugar plantation around the time of the abolition of slavery and tells the story of Godfrey and July who are slaves of Caroline Mortimer, the plantation owner.

68 Unit 6 Trade

Trade Unit 6 69

Real world people

Reading and listening texts in *Global* are about real people and the real world.

Short writing tasks

Some lessons end with a short writing task to give students the opportunity to develop fluency in writing as well as speaking.

Informal language

Informal language and idioms are introduced and discussed throughout *Global*.

Coursebook: lessons 3 and 4 of a unit

Balance of skills

Each lesson has a balance of skills work and language work.

Vocabulary

At advanced level students need to be able to recognise features such as register and formality, and to distinguish between words with similar meanings.

Topics and texts

Topics and texts are chosen to appeal to the learners' intellectual curiosity. Texts are authentic, with information about the real world. Attractive and stylish design makes the text more attractive and motivating to read.

UNIT 6 Trade & Commerce

Part 3

Reading & Speaking
Bangalore

Listening
Ideas for India's future

Vocabulary
Problems

Speaking
Tackling problems

Reading and Speaking

1 Work in pairs. Look at the industries in the box. Which are the main sources of income in your city or area? Are these industries growing or declining? Give reasons for your answers.

agriculture finance fishing forestry IT manufacturing mining service industries tourism

2 Read three different descriptions of Bangalore on page 71, a modern industrial and commercial city in India. Decide what sort of text they are (factual, descriptive, narrative, literary or persuasive, etc) and where you might find them. What words and phrases in the texts tell you this?

3 Read again and answer the questions.

1 What is the main industry in Bangalore?
2 What are the positive points about the city that each author puts forward? What words does the author use to describe them?
3 In text A, how does the author describe the transition taking place in Bangalore?
4 Is the author optimistic about the city's future?
5 What basic problem is the city faced with? What is the cause of this?

4 Find words in the texts that mean:

1 develop into (text A)
2 very poor area of a city (text A)
3 waste substances (text A)
4 friendly (*formal*) (text B)
5 very interesting (text B)
6 pleasant and comfortable (*formal*) (text B)

5 Work in pairs. Discuss the questions.

- What overall impression of Bangalore do you get from these texts?
- If you were going to Bangalore (on business or as a tourist), what aspects of the city would you be interested to learn more about?

Listening

1 Read the definition of the word *outsourcing*. Can you think of any examples of outsourcing in your country? What are the advantages and disadvantages of this type of arrangement?

outsourcing BUSINESS: an arrangement in which work is done by people from outside your company, usually by a company that is expert in that type of work.

2 2.44 Listen to an Indian entrepreneur talking about India's IT (information technology) and BPO (Business Process Outsourcing) industries. How has increased demand ultimately affected India's outsourcing business?

3 Listen again and answer the questions.

1 What do companies typically outsource?
2 Why did India's IT-BPO sector become a world-leading industry in the 1990s?
3 What has the increased demand for outsourcing in India led to?
4 What have some British and American companies begun to do?
5 How have Indian companies begun to adapt to changes in the outsourcing destination?

4 The growth of the IT-BPO sector in India was very much linked to English. What role does English or other foreign languages play in the main industries in your country?

Vocabulary

1 Choose the correct word to complete the phrases from the listening. Which of the phrases refer to a problem? Which refer to dealing with a problem?

1 For companies, ***becoming / getting*** *rid of* these tasks means lower costs.
2 This has kept ***pushing / pulling*** *up* the cost of salaries.
3 Infrastructure in these areas has not been able to *keep* ***speed / pace*** *with* growth.
4 There have been some attempts to *find a* ***way / path*** *round* these issues.
5 India has *become a* ***sacrifice / victim*** *of its own success.*

2 Look at the adjectives (1–3) that can collocate with *problem*. Match them with the correct meaning (a–c). Do the same with the verbs (4–8) and meanings (d–h).

1 major — a urgent
2 pressing — b very difficult
3 intractable — c very big

4 pose — d lessen
5 tackle — e find a solution to
6 alleviate — f make worse
7 exacerbate — g deal with
8 solve — h present

3 Complete the dialogues with the correct form of phrases from exercises 1 and 2.

A: It's a(n) (1) ________ problem. It's at the root of the nation's troubles. It's why we're not (2) ________ with other countries.
B: But it's difficult to see how it can be (3) ________ or even (4) ________ in some way. Unfortunately, I can't see any (5) ________ it.
A: The fact that child poverty still (6) ________ a huge problem in some European countries is a scandal. The EU need to (7) ________ this now.
B: Absolutely. I think what is vital is recognition that it's a(n) (8) ________ problem. More has to be done immediately to make sure it isn't (9) ________ any further.

Bangalore

A When I drive down Hosur Main Road, when I turn into Electronics City Phase 1 and see the companies go past, I can't tell you how exciting it is to me. General Electric, Dell, Siemens – they're all here in Bangalore. And so many more are on their way. There is construction everywhere. Piles of mud everywhere. Piles of stones. Piles of bricks. The entire city is masked in smoke, smog, powder, cement dust. It is under a veil. When the veil is lifted, what will Bangalore be like?

Maybe it will be a disaster: slums, sewage, shopping malls, traffic jams, policemen. But you never know. It may turn out to be a decent city, where humans can live like humans. A new Bangalore for a new India. And then I can say that, in my own way, I helped to make New Bangalore.

B What do you call a congenial, captivating, cosmopolitan confluence of software and shopping malls, electronics and environment friendliness, salubrious climate and cleanliness, modern outlook and old worldliness, precision engineering and pubs? You call it India's best city for business. It is also called Bangalore.

C City and capital (since 1830) of Karnataka (formerly Mysore) state, southern India. One of India's largest cities, Bangalore lies on an east-west ridge in the Karnataka Plateau in the south-eastern part of the state. Pleasant winters and tolerable summers make it a popular place of residence, but water supply for its increasing industrial and domestic needs is a problem, because its 914 mm of annual rainfall is inadequate and there are no rivers nearby.

From the late 20th century the city became a centre of high-technology industry, and a number of large multinational technology corporations opened offices there. In addition, major domestic firms such as Infosys and Wipro established headquarters in the city.

Speaking

1 Look at these issues and decide which three are the most problematic in your country. Make notes on the problems in these areas.

- employment and job creation
- benefits, social security and health care
- pre-school childcare
- education
- higher education
- infrastructure
- cities / urban policy
- rural areas
- environment

2 Work in small groups. Discuss the problems you have noted down. How are they being tackled? How successful are these measures? How else could the problems be tackled?

Listening

Every lesson has a reading or listening text. Listening texts are supported by different tasks for gist and specific listening. The listening texts in *Global* include a variety of genres, including lectures and presentations as well as interviews and dialogues.

Texts

Texts are either information rich or excerpts from literary texts, modern and classic, with background information about the book and the author provided to give students extra cultural information. Many of the literary texts are also on the class audio, so students can read and listen to them.

Support for tasks

Useful phrase boxes provide support for main spoken and written tasks.

Glossary

Many texts include a short glossary of difficult words.

UNIT 6 Trade & Commerce

Part 4

Speaking
Investments

Reading
The new golden age

Extend your vocabulary
gold and golden

Grammar
Cleft sentences

Speaking

1 Look at the following eight things that people invest in. Which do you think are the safest investments? Rank them in order from 1 (safest investment) to 8 (riskiest investment).

art   bank accounts   collectables   gold   government bonds   land   property   stocks

2 Compare your answers with a partner, giving reasons for your opinions. Try and agree on the three safest investments.

Useful phrases

- can be *risky / tricky / high-risk*
- *isn't going to hold its value / will depreciate*
- is dependent on *supply and demand / the state of the economy / fashion and trends*
- *is a safe bet / low-risk / guaranteed to*
- will *hold its value / appreciate in value / show a profit / give a good return of interest*
- *offers protection against inflation / can provide income*

Reading

1 Read *The new golden age* and choose the best summary of the article.

- After a long absence, gold is popular again now.
- Gold is popular now, but it always has been for many reasons.
- The popularity of gold is misguided.

2 Match the words in bold in the text to the definitions below.

1 apparently unimportant (though actually important)
2 easy to press into different shapes
3 things that can be bought and sold
4 increasing quickly by a large amount
5 existing now as a modern example of something or someone from the past
6 laughing at
7 uncontrolled activity or excitement
8 passion

3 Read again. Decide if the statements are true (*T*), false (*F*) or the text doesn't say (*DS*).

1 The price of gold always rises in moments of crisis.
2 It is important to distinguish real gold from imitations.
3 Gold contains small quantities of toxic material.
4 Gold represents much more than a simple metal.
5 Transmutation is the process by which gold is converted into base lead.
6 The author views bankers as modern alchemists.
7 Gold will be worth less in the future.

4 Answer the questions, giving reasons for your answers.

- The reading text was written in 2010. Do you think gold is still as important now?
- Do you agree with the author that gold is more than just a valuable metal?

Extend your vocabulary – *gold and golden*

The adjective *gold* means 'made of gold':
People are investing in gold jewellery.
The adjective *golden* can mean 'gold in colour':
He has lovely golden hair.
Golden can also mean 'successful':
We're living in a new golden age.

1 Is *gold* or *golden* the correct word in these sentences?
   1 She's the company's ________ girl at the moment.
   2 He just missed out on the ________ medal.
   3 They were the ________ years of jazz.
   4 There are miles and miles of ________ beaches.

2 *Golden* can also be used in fixed phrases with different meanings. Cross out the words below which do not collocate with *golden*. Use a dictionary to help you. What do the other phrases mean?

address   anniversary   dream   handshake   oldie   opportunity   remark   rule

3 Use two of the collocations and make sentences to show their meaning.

The new golden age

Gold is more valuable than ever. But what inspires our **lust** is more than mere money – gold speaks to something elemental in all of us.

The price of gold is rising, both **mocking** and relieving the gloom and **turmoil** of a worldwide recession. The world market price of this valuable metal is **shooting up** faster and more than most other **commodities**. This always happens. It did when the world turned fearful of terrorist attacks and when the dotcom bubble burst. In uncertain times it is gold that the hard-headed and stony-hearted financial gamblers invest in.

Gold has been used as currency for more than 5,000 years.

Through the centuries efforts have been made to ensure its genuineness – using official stamps and symbols. It is soft and **malleable**. When alloyed with other elements its density changes and you can get a whole range from reddish orange to white. Talented artisans and craftsmen have been inspired by it and worked it to make objects of eternal beauty, treasured and desired by humans through the world, through the ages.

'Gold is just a metal.' Yes and no. What this **mere** metal represents is meanings far beyond high price tags – emblematic, metaphorical, literary and emotional meanings.

It is in the heads of old alchemists that the most important symbolic aspect of gold is to be found. The idea of turning base lead into noble gold, a transmutation, took many into the clouds of fantasy. In their pursuit of gold, what they were also pursuing was the 'elixir of life'. They didn't find it. High-flying financial gamblers and investment bankers were **latter-day** alchemists, making fantastical promises. They couldn't turn paper into gold. So the people only trust the real stuff now, an act of faith. Its value depends on how much people believe in it. Millions clearly do. What will be fascinating is to see what comes next in this new golden age and whether the shining yellow hope people are clutching will turn to straw.

Glossary

the dotcom bubble *(noun)* – the rapid increase in value of the shares of internet (.com) companies and their subsequent crash at the end of the 1990s
alloy *(verb)* – combine two or more metals

Grammar

1 Look at the two sentences. Decide which phrase in bold is being emphasised in the second sentence. Then read the grammar box.

More than mere money inspires our lust.
What inspires ***our lust*** *is* ***more than mere money****.*

To emphasise information in a sentence we can use sentences beginning with:

- *It is / was* … (+ relative clause)
  It is gold that financial gamblers invest in.
- *What* + clause + *is / was* (+ clause / noun phrase)
  What will be fascinating is to see what comes next.
  What they were also pursuing was the 'elixir of life'.
- in a *What* clause, the auxiliary *do / did* can also be used to emphasise actions
  What the bankers did was make fantastical promises.

2 Rewrite the sentences to emphasise the words in italics. Use the word in bold.

1 The most precious of all metals is *gold*. **it**
  ________ is the most precious of all metals.
2 I really hate *how gold makes people greedy*. **what**
  ________ how gold makes people greedy.
3 He could never resist *the sight of gold*. **was**
  ________ the sight of gold.
4 *The price of gold* went up. **that**
  ________ went up.
5 The alchemists experimented *with turning base lead into gold*. **did**
  ________ with turning base lead into gold.

3 Complete three of these sentences with your own ideas.

- All I really want is …
- What annoys me most …
- The first time I saw … was …
- What the world needs now is …
- It is … that causes most problems.

Grammar focus – explanation & more practice of cleft sentences on page 142

Yasmin Alibhai-Brown is a well-known journalist originally from Uganda. She has worked for many major English newspapers and writes on issues relating to race, immigration and multiculturalism.

Extend your vocabulary

Regular *Extend your vocabulary* boxes draw on language in the unit and help students gain a deeper word knowledge. Word families, easily confused words and different ways of expressing concepts are covered in these sections throughout the book.

Grammar focus

Grammar focus sections at the back of the book provide reference and extra practice.

Coursebook: extra material at the end of a unit

Function globally

Every unit includes a *Function globally* section. This contains frequent functional and situational language that is immediately useful outside the classroom.

Global English

Every other unit contains an extra reading lesson, called *Global English* featuring a text by David Crystal, which provides interesting information about the English language.

Global voices

Every other unit contains a listening section featuring authentic and unscripted recordings of a wide range of native and non-native speakers of English, which expose learners to real English as it is being used around the world today.

6 Function globally negotiating

Warm up

1 Work in pairs. What would you do and say in the following situations?

- You have a ticket for a plane, and at the check-in desk you are told that the flight is fully booked.
- You open your bank statement and find that you have been charged for going overdrawn for a few hours.
- You are the manager of a wholesale business and you want to persuade a retailer to switch their custom to you.
- You are interested in buying a second-hand car, but the price is too high.

2 Have you ever been in a similar situation? What happened?

Listening

1 2.45–2.48 Listen to four conversations and match each one to a situation from the Warm up section.

1 What is the outcome in each case?
2 How similar were the people's reactions to your own ideas?

2 In which of the conversations did you hear the following, and what is the speaker referring to?

1 It didn't clear in time.
2 This is the one I've got my eye on.
3 45 is pushing it.
4 Surely those few hours shouldn't have incurred such a hefty fine?
5 You won't budge on that at all?
6 We could do 50.
7 We can throw in some cover.
8 There is availability.

Language focus

1 Read some sentences in which people are making an offer or concession, and complete each one with a word or phrase from the box.

absolutely the best | acceptable | could | if you can | if you like | prepared to | then I can | what I can do

1 ________ is upgrade you. Would that be ________?
2 Tell you what. ________ bring the price down, ________ place a firm order.
3 OK, I'm ________ throw in this radio, and I'll knock ten euros off.
4 We ________ offer you a credit note ________.
5 I'm afraid that's ________ we can do.

2 Read the responses below. Which express …

a acceptance? b refusal?
c indecision or a desire for further concessions?

1 Is that your final offer?
2 That sounds like a good compromise. I'll take it.
3 I'll leave it, thanks.
4 Fantastic, it's a deal.
5 I'm going to have to think about it and get back to you.
6 It will have to do I suppose.
7 Is there anything else you can do for me?
8 I'm afraid that wouldn't be viable for me.

Pronunciation

1 2.49 Listen and complete the sentences. What is the function of the missing word(s)? Say the sentences.

1 But you ________ it's not my fault?
2 You ________ into overdraft.
3 Well, that ________ good.

2 2.50 Listen and repeat the sentences you hear, adding an auxiliary verb.
You said you'd deliver them today.
You did say you'd deliver them today.

Speaking

Choose two opening lines, and improvise a conversation with a partner. What concessions did you obtain?

- I just wanted to talk to you about my overdraft limit.
- I bought this scarf here last month, and I was wondering if I could have a refund?
- I really like it, but I'm afraid it's beyond my price range.
- I'm sorry, but I asked for a non-smoking room.

74 Unit 6 Function globally

Global voices

Warm up

Do you think customer service in shops and restaurants is good where you live? Think of a recent example to support your opinion. Then discuss in pairs.

Listening

1 2.51 Listen to Marion from The Netherlands and Scott from England discuss customer service in different countries. Decide if these statements are true (*T*) or false (*F*) according to the speakers.

1 Marion thinks there are great differences between The Netherlands and England.
2 Marion thought it was unusual for the shop assistant to ask her if she needed help.
3 Scott felt that he was ignored in the mobile phone shop.
4 Both Scott and Marion think that some customer service is too much.

Marion, The Netherlands — Scott, England

2 2.52 Now listen to Lilian from Kenya and Dominika from Poland talk about their experiences in shops in England. Answer the questions.

1 What does Lilian say about customer service in Kenya?
2 What did Lilian want to buy? Did she get it in the end?
3 Who has the better experience?
4 What difference did Dominika see between customer service in England and in Poland?

Lilian, Kenya — Dominika, Poland

Language focus: stance markers

1 Stance markers are words or phrases that mark a speaker's attitude or point of view. Look at the examples below. What is the stance marker in each one? How does it affect the meaning of the sentence?

… but sadly this is not extended to the, to the low-class citizens. You literally walk inside the door and then you get five people come up to you …

2 Match the phrases in A to phrases with similar meanings in B.

A	B
frankly	obviously
basically	in fact
actually	luckily
thankfully	to be honest
clearly	fundamentally

3 Work in pairs. Prepare a two line dialogue between a customer and a shop assistant. Try to incorporate one of the words from exercises 1 or 2 into your dialogue.

Speaking

1 Look at the following example of an English customer service questionnaire. Do you have similar things in your country? Evaluate the customer service in a shop you know by giving each statement below one of the following ratings: excellent, good, average, poor.

- Staff greeted you and offered to help you.
- Staff were friendly and cheerful.
- Staff answered your questions.
- Staff showed knowledge of the products / services.
- Staff were polite throughout.

2 Compare with a partner. Do you think these questionnaires …

- are a good idea?
- are useful?
- have any effect on customer service?

Global voices Unit 6 75

Listening

Students hear conversations in various situations which help contextualise the language and provide a model.

Putting it into practice

This is followed by a choice of speaking activity so that students can put the new language to use immediately.

Extended speaking

Each *Global voices* page ends with an extended speaking task, allowing students to personalise the language.

Writing

Each unit focuses on a specific writing skill and a language point, presented within a particular genre. Learners' critical ability is developed by reading, analysing and correcting one aspect of a model writing text.

Linking ideas

At advanced level, each unit focuses on ways students can link their ideas to develop their writing skills.

Study skills

Developing effective study skills and strategies is an essential part of language learning. The Study skills section in each unit focuses on a particular skill or strategy.

6 Writing emails

a Dear Anne

Thank you for your interest in our apartment. Yes, it is possible to snorkel off the local beaches, not to mention many other beautiful beaches nearby. You can see pictures of **all these** on our website. I am not an expert on snorkelling or water sports, but my husband Goran knows a lot about **such matters** and will be happy to give you advice!

Kind regards

Ivana

b Dear Anne

Thank you for your enquiry. In fact, we have two apartments, namely Villa Gemma and Villa Maria. **The former** is unfortunately not available for **the period you mention**, but we have availability for Villa Maria **at that time**. The weekly rate is 645 euros (in other words, slightly higher than for Villa Gemma, but it is a larger apartment and has recently been completely refurbished). Please visit our website for more details about **the accommodation**. We require a 15% deposit in advance (ie 96 euros) and the balance is due on arrival.

Kind regards

Ivana

c Dear Ms Petrovic

I have seen your apartment (Villa Gemma) on the Holiday Croatia website and am writing to enquire whether it is available for the period 19–26 July. We are four adults (two married couples, to be precise), and non-smokers. Also, could you please confirm the price, and your payment arrangements?

Best wishes

Anne Le Tissier

d Hi Ivana

Just a quick mail to say a big thank you to you and Goran for your kindness and hospitality during our stay in Croatia. It was great meeting you and we had a brilliant time. We'll certainly recommend Villa Maria to all our friends and hope to be back again very soon!

All the best

Anne

e Dear Anne

Further to our phone call, I can confirm that Villa Maria is reserved for you from 19–26 July. I would be grateful if you could now complete the booking by making a deposit **as discussed**, either by cheque, through the Cashbookers website or via a bank transaction. I look forward to hearing from you soon.

Kind regards

Ivana

f Dear Ivana

Thanks for your mail regarding Villa Maria. We are very interested in **this apartment**. Just one query – we are all keen on water sports (snorkelling in particular) and are ideally looking for a place near a good snorkelling beach. Is it possible to go snorkelling near the apartment?

Best wishes

Anne

Reading

1 Read a series of emails and put them in the correct chronological order. What was the outcome of the correspondence?

2 Without looking at the emails, what can you remember about ...

1 Anne and her friends?
2 Villa Maria?
3 payment?
4 the local area?
5 Ivana and her family?

Writing skills: cohesion

1 Look at the phrases highlighted in the text. What does each one refer back to (in the same email or a previous email)?

2 Choose the correct or more natural alternative to complete the sentences.

1 There are two courses, namely Spanish A and Spanish B. The former is for complete beginners, while *the latter / the next* is at elementary level.
2 *As I promised / As promised*, I attach a visa application form for you to complete. Could you please return *this / that* at your earliest convenience?
3 Unfortunately, we have still not received the form. *This / That* means that we cannot process your application, so could you please forward it to me asap?
4 *Further / Farther* to our conversation, I have decided to cancel my order.

Linking ideas: clarification and emphasis

1 Read the emails on page 76 again and find expressions used to give clarification and emphasis.

2 Read the email below and delete the incorrect alternative.

My flight arrives in the early hours, at 2.25am (1) *to be precise / in particular*. I'd therefore be grateful if someone could meet me at the airport, or (2) *ideally / in other words / preferably* book me a taxi. There is no transport available at that time (3) *or rather / not to mention / to say nothing of* the fact that I will be exhausted. I'd like to request a ground floor room for my mother. She finds it difficult to walk far (4) *let alone / ie* climb stairs. I'd (5) *particularly / especially / precisely* like a quiet room, as during our last visit we were kept awake by noise – traffic (6) *for the most part / ideally / in particular*.

Preparing to write

With a partner, decide on one or more transactions that you would like to correspond about, eg enrolling on a course, booking a ticket or renting a flat or room.

A semi-formal email

- *I am writing / Just a quick email* to *enquire about / whether ... / thank you for ...*
- *Thank you / Thanks* for your *email / reply / enquiry*
- *I would be grateful if you could / Can you please* send *me details of ... / let me know ...*
- *I am attaching / Please find attached* a booking form
- *(Kind / Warm) Regards / Best wishes / (All the) Best / Many thanks / All for now*

Writing

Work in pairs. Using email conventions, you should each write an initial enquiry about the transaction you chose in *Preparing to write*, and pass the sheet of paper to your partner. Your partner should then write a reply to the enquiry. Continue the correspondence until the transaction is complete.

Study skills

Learning language in context

1 Read a suggestion on how to extend your knowledge of English. With a partner, discuss which of the suggestions, if any, you already follow.

A good way to extend your knowledge of English at advanced level *is to* study language as it occurs naturally in real (spoken or written) texts. Here is a useful *procedure to follow*:

- ★ Choose a text that interests you or that is *relevant to* your work or study, or one that you have already studied in class.
- ★ Read or listen to the text until you understand it fully.
- ★ Underline (or note down) any words, phrases, collocations and parts of sentences that you find interesting or useful, and that you would not normally use.
- ★ Record the new language in your vocabulary notebook, including the original sentence.
- ★ *Extend your knowledge* of the new items by looking them up in a learners dictionary or collocations dictionary. Add any useful information to your notebook.
- ★ Use the new language in a sentence to help you remember it.
- ★ Read through your vocabulary notebook *on a regular basis*; *the more often* you study something, *the better* it goes in.

2 Look again at the above section and notice the words and expressions in italics. The first two of these could be recorded as follows:

A good way to ... is to ...: A good way to make friends is to join an English class.

follow a procedure: adhere to, comply with, follow, go through, use a procedure (*Macmillan Collocations Dictionary*) If you follow the safety procedures when you dive, you are unlikely to suffer a serious accident.

3 Write a record for the other words and phrases. Then compare ideas with a partner.

Writing models

Texts are often based on authentic pieces of writing from international students at advanced level, reflecting the interests of a worldwide audience, and providing a realistic model within their capabilities.

Preparation

Structured preparation tasks, useful language and paired activities guide students towards production of a final piece of writing.

Global review

Revision is crucial for language learning. At advanced level, the Teacher's Resource Disc contains review activities that cover the main grammar and vocabulary points of each unit.

eWorkbook

Comprehensive component for self-study

The *Global* eWorkbook represents an evolution in self-study materials for learners. Within a rich multimedia environment it provides a wealth of resources for the learner, enabling them to continue their studies at their own pace, and in their own time.

Language Work

The eWorkbook contains a wide range of activities which allow for extra practice and review of the language presented in the Coursebook. These activities cover all aspects of language learning. Grammar, Vocabulary, Listening and Pronunciation practice activities are available both as fully interactive activities and in a printable pen-and-paper format. There are also worksheets to practise reading and writing skills.

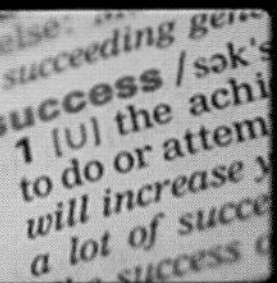

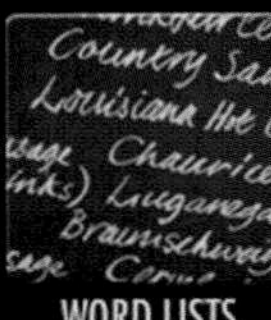

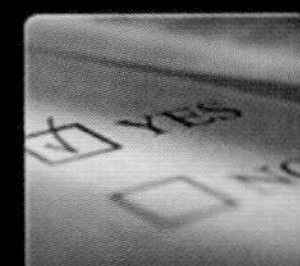

Tools for reference and support

The eWorkbook offers all the support the learner may need. For instance, links to the Macmillan Dictionary Online, Word lists per unit and grammar help organised by topic. The Writing tips section includes information on general aspects of writing, such as spelling, punctuation, paragraphing, etc.

Learning on the Move

The *Global* eWorkbook provides a wide variety of authentic extra listening and video materials supplied in commonly used file formats, so learners can load them onto their portable music and video players and study and review 'on-the-go'.

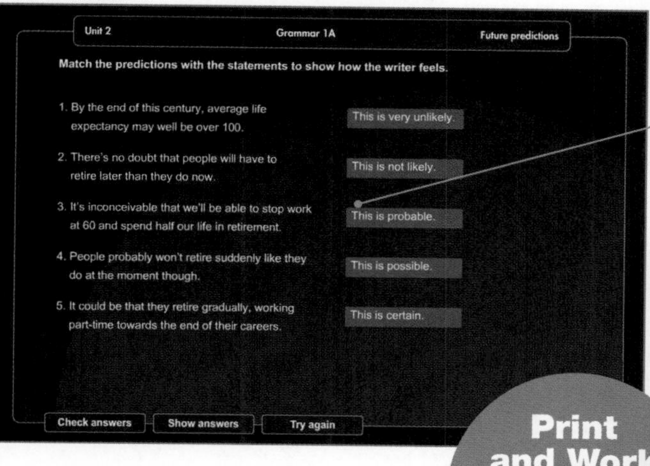

Show answers
Try again

Interactive activities

Meaningful practice.

Video

Extracts from BBC and other programmes as well as original videos that can be downloaded and used on the move.

And one piece of advice was to start with a story.

Print and Work

For those who prefer to work offline.

2 Light & Dark

Grammar 1A
Future predictions

Match the statements a–e with the predictions 1–5 to show how the writer feels about these predictions.

1. By the end of this century, average life expectancy may well be over 100.
2. There's no doubt that people will have to retire later than they do now.
3. It's inconceivable that we'll be able to stop work at 60 and spend half our life in retirement.
4. People probably won't retire suddenly like they do at the moment though.
5. It could be that they retire gradually, working part-time towards the end of their careers.

a. This is certain.
b. This is probable.
c. This is possible.
d. This is not likely.
e. This is very unlikely.

Grammar 1B
Future predictions

Are these sentences correct or incorrect? Circle your answer.

1. By 2050, scientists will be finding a cure for the common cold.
   • correct • incorrect
2. In thirty years' time, doctors will be using gene therapies to cure or prevent many conditions.
   • correct • incorrect
3. Sadly, there seems little likelihood that malaria will be eradicated in the near future.
   • correct • incorrect
4. I won't probably see an end to cancer in my lifetime.
   • correct • incorrect
5. Future medical advances undoubtedly will be limited by economic and ethical issues, not by scientific knowledge.
   • correct • incorrect
6. There's no doubt that the gap between rich and poor in terms of healthcare will continue.
   • correct • incorrect

Grammar 2A
Narrative tenses

Choose the best verb phrase to complete the story. ... your answer.

Anna had been in Athens for about three months when she decided to find an apartment of her own. (1) *She was staying / She'd been staying* with a friend, Zoe, in a rather dark, dingy basement apartment. Zoe (2) *had done / did* her best to make her feel welcome, but it just wasn't the Mediterranean lifestyle (3) *she's imagining/ she'd imagined.* So when she (4) *visited / has visited* the little top-floor apartment in Kolonaki with its roof terrace ... the square, she (5) *was falling / fell in* ... As the agent opened the door and ... spring sunshine (6) *had been str...* through the full-height wind... area in a warm golden light ... a little more than (7) *she p...* spend, but she (8) *was put...* and then.

Grammar 2B
Narrative tenses

Complete the story with the ... verbs in brackets.

It was early June and Anna (1) ______ in the apartment for a couple of month... (2) ______ (*begin*) to realise the draw... her new home. When she (3) ______ (*move*) in back in the spring, the weather (4) ______ (*be*) rather like a British summer, comfortable warm and bright. Now as the Greek summer got into full swing, the temperature (5) ______ (*rise*) day by day and her top-floor apartment with its floor to ceiling windows (6) ______ (*catch*) the full glare of the sun for most of the day.

This morning, she (7) ______ her roof terrace over... It (8) ______ (9) ______ (*soon / hav...* some sha...

Global Advanced eWorkbook © Macmillan Publishers Limited 2012

The Print and Work feature of the eWorkbook is also available in a printed workbook format.

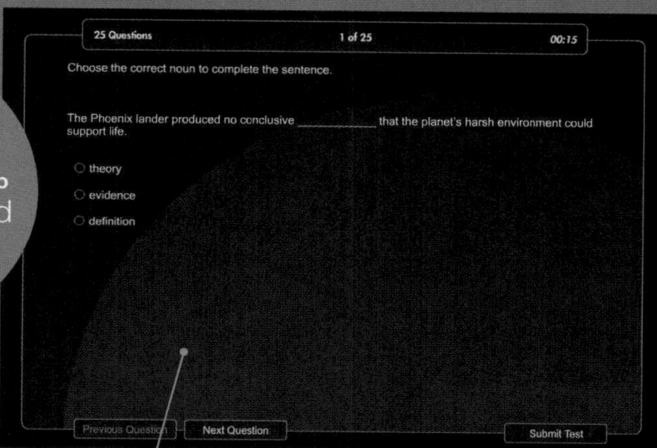

25 Questions
1 of 25
00:15
Choose the correct noun to complete the sentence.
The Phoenix lander produced no conclusive ________ that the planet's harsh environment could support life.
theory
evidence
definition
Previous Question
Next Question
Submit Test

Listening

Comprehensive listening section, with tracks that can be downloaded and used on the move.

global
ADVANCED
eWorkbook
Using commas
Using exclamation marks
Using colons
Using semi-colons
Using brackets and dashes
Using apostrophes
Giving examples
Adding interest: synonyms, questions and direct speech
You can use a colon to separate the first part of a sentence from a list that exemplifies or expands on the point made.
Bertie comes across as a complex figure: a son who feels inferior to his father, a kind father to his own children, a true friend and a great King to the country.

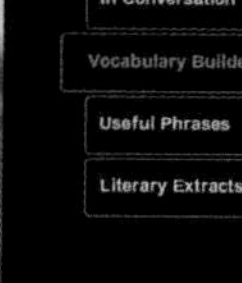

LISTEN ON THE MOVE

In Conversation
Vocabulary Builder
Useful Phrases
Literary Extracts

Collocations for going online
Emotional reactions
Prefixes
Describing the quality of light
Real and metaphorical light
Energy
Feelings
Sounds
Ways of describing fear
Travel experiences
numbers
quiet and silent

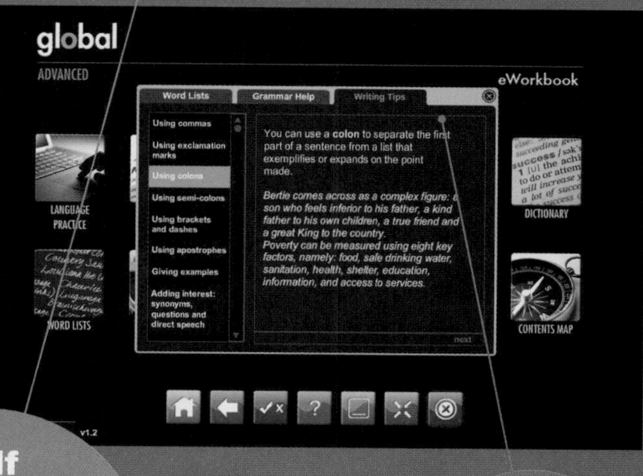

Self assessment

Test generator and Common European Framework checklists for self assessment.

Tools

Comprehensive tools for self study.

Teacher's Book

David Crystal: The future of Englishes: going local

When people talk about 'global English' they are usually referring to the common features which identify the variety we call standard English. Increasingly, however, attention has been drawn to the regional features which differentiate one part of the English-speaking world from another. So today we happily talk about British, American, Australian, South African, Indian, and other 'Englishes', and studies are accumulating of the way these varieties make distinctive use of pronunciation, orthography, grammar, vocabulary, and discourse. Much of the distinctiveness resides in the area of lexicology, the linguistic domain which most closely reflects cultural identity, and dictionaries have been compiled of the distinctive lexicons encountered in these regions.

It does not take long before these lexicons reach many thousands of words. When a country adopts a language as a local alternative means of communication, it immediately starts adapting it, to meet the communicative needs of the region. Words for local plants and animals, food and drink, customs and practices, politics and religion, sports and games, and many other facets of everyday life soon accumulate a local wordstock which is unknown outside the country and its environs. When someone in South Africa says 'The bakkie had to stop at a red robot', we need to know that a bakkie is a truck and a robot is a traffic-light. There are thousands of such words in a dictionary of South African English. And other parts of the English-speaking world display the same kind of creativity.

This seems to be the pattern, as English becomes a local alternative language. When a group of people in a country switch into English, for whatever reason, the subject-matter of their conversation inevitably incorporates aspects of their local environment. They talk about the shops, streets, suburbs, bus-routes, institutions, businesses, television programmes, newspapers, political parties, minority groups, and a great deal more. They make jokes, quote proverbs, bring up childhood linguistic memories (such as nursery rhymes), and recall lyrics of popular songs. All this local knowledge is taken for granted, and used in sentences without gloss. Visitors who hear such sentences, or read them in local newspapers, need to have them explained. Conventional dictionaries will not help, for they do not include such localisms, especially if the expressions are encyclopedic in character (referring to local people, places, institutions, and suchlike).

Every English-speaking location in the world has usages which make the English used there distinctive, expressive of local identity, and a means of creating solidarity. From this point of view, notions such as 'Swedish English' take on a fresh relevance, going well beyond traditional conceptions of English spoken with a Swedish acc… English displaying interference from Swedish grammar. Swedish English, for e… I define as the kind of English I need to know about when I go to Sweden, oth… I will be unable to converse efficiently with Swedish speakers in English. It w… be amazingly useful to have a glossary of the English equivalents of Swedish… references, but I know of none. This seems to be a neglected area for any la…

We need regional cultural dictionaries or glossaries. It is something every… do, and something to which everyone who learns English can contribute. … an hour or so to accumulate a list of dozens of culturally specific items. A… these are written down, in the style of a glossary, it has an interesting effe… participants. They feel they have somehow made the English language the… suspect such projects also add greatly to their linguistic confidence and sel… no-one else in the world knows their home-grown variety of English as we… And they can take pride in the fact that they have added their own small pie… global jigsaw puzzle that comprises the English language.

xiii Essays

UNIT 1 Fact & Fiction

Part 1

TEACH GLOBAL THINK LOCAL Lead-in

Provide a model for the first activity by giving students three facts about yourself, plus another one which is false. Simply tell the students, or write the facts on the board for students to guess. Try to make the facts interesting but believable, eg *I won a national award for badminton at the age of 15.* Let them ask you up to 12 questions, to find out more.

Speaking and Pronunciation (SB page 6)

1 Put students in pairs, but avoid putting together students who know each other really well. Encourage them to ask up to 12 questions to help identify which is the incorrect 'fact', as in the *Lead-in*. Early finishers can join in with another pair. As students are working, listen out for any personal facts which are interesting and could be shared in whole-class feedback session at the end.

2 To flow neatly into this pronunciation focus, use one of the examples from exercise 1, eg *I thought the third fact was incorrect, but actually it was the second one.* Put it up on the board and elicit the stressed words. Do the same for the two new sentences.

3 1.01 Ask students to pay particular attention to the …ssed words when listening. In pairs, students read out …tences. You could raise the challenge and ensure … really natural here by focusing on other … aspects too, such as weak forms, eg *was* …g, eg *but actually*. Check that students are …lly naturally /ˈæktʃuəli/ or /ˈækʃəli/.

…student, but actually he's the teacher.
…om Spain, but in fact I'm from Mexico.

…ences is also significant and worth …ther at the board stage (Exercise …3). At the end of both clauses, …ate this is new information:
…ut actually he's a teacher.

… similar adverbs, are also …cate to a listener that a correction …y, drill this in class and / or respond …cise 5, SB page 6.

…mple here, particularly if you have …r rather embarrassing, eg *One day, … put my bag on the floor so I could look at … saw a suspicious woman walk away with …fter her and grabbed the bag. Then I realised it … in actual fact, it contained her new shoes.* Then … work together in pairs, eg *I thought you were about …ut actually you're over 30.*

Reading (SB page 6)

TEACH GLOBAL THINK LOCAL Pre-reading activity

Read out the following questions and ask students to write short answers:

Where's the first place you'd go to find the following items? If you'd look on the internet, say which website(s).

a) a recipe b) a fact for a piece of research c) some information on the planets d) some gardening information e) how to play a new sport.

Let students compare their ideas in small groups.

This reading text describes the nature of user-generated content, such as that found in Wikipedia, and discusses the source and quality of the material in comparison to more traditional providers of knowledge.

1 Students discuss the questions in groups, and then briefly as a class. If/when Wikipedia is mentioned, write it up on the board.

2 First elicit what students know about the Wikipedia website, without commenting yourself. Then students read the six facts and locate the false information. Let them compare their ideas in pairs or groups. Elicit the correct answer, with supporting reasons, if possible.

Statement 6 is false.

3 Hold up the article (SB page 7) for all to see, and read the heading aloud. Elicit what the heading might mean. Give students the gist task, telling them how long they have to read, eg 3–6 minutes (depending on your group). At the end, let them compare answers before taking swift feedback.

2 (*Surely the only way of achieving a coherent overview is to invite experts to sift through the content and judge what is quality and what is not? … expert knowledge, which remains invaluable today.*)

4 Show students where the lines go by holding up the book and referring to paragraphs A-D in the text. Students work independently, but check in pairs. Write the answers on the board for students to self-check.

1 C 2 A 3 D 4 B

Fact & Fiction Unit 1 3

Teach Global Think Local

The Teacher's Book includes comprehensive teaching notes with answer keys and audioscripts, and detailed background and language notes. It also provides 'Teach Global Think Local' ideas: extra activities that can be adapted to individual teaching situations.

Specialist essays

The Teacher's Book features a number of specialist essays, each focusing on a different aspect of language teaching. These have been written by a range of well-known and award-winning guest ELT authors and teacher trainers, and will be of interest to teachers of all levels of experience.

Teacher's Resource Disc

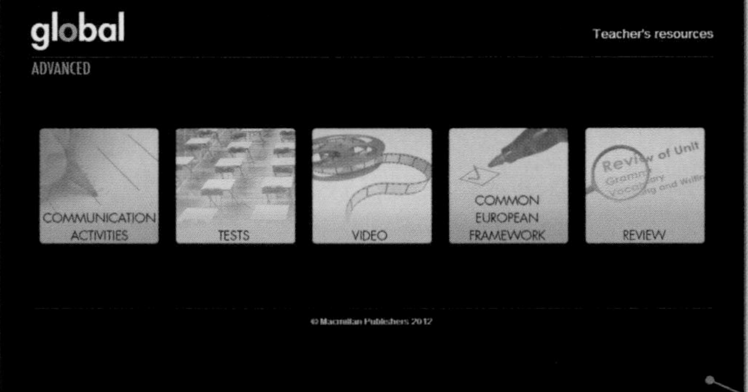

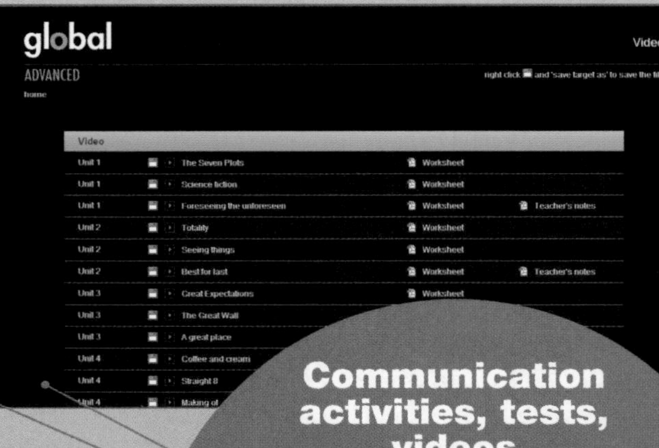

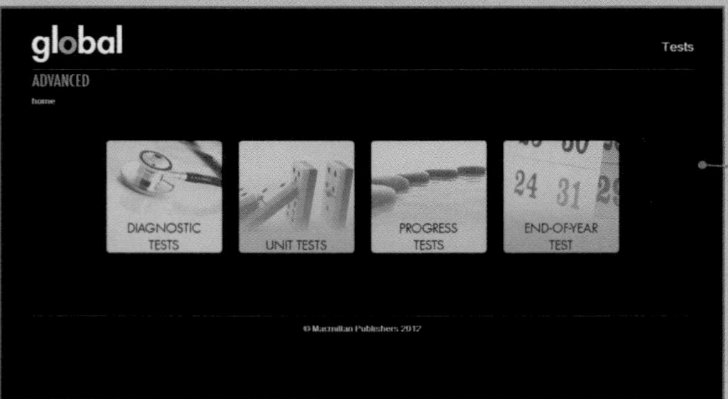

Communication activities, tests, videos

The Teacher's Resource Disc includes printable communication activity worksheets that practise areas of language from the Coursebook units and printable communication activity worksheets to do at different stages of the course. In addition, it provides a wide range of tests (diagnostic, progress tests, end-of-year test, etc) and additional video clips and video worksheets for the teacher.

Class Audio CDs

The *Global* Advanced class audio is contained on three CDs. They include the listening material from the Coursebook and recordings of the literary extracts featured in the book.

Website

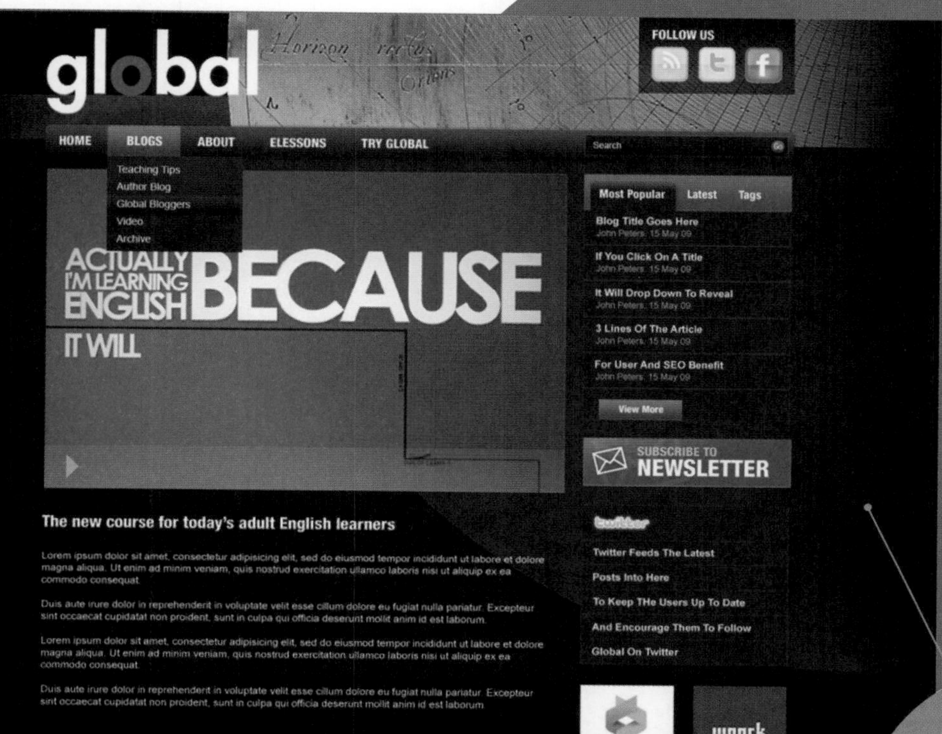

The *Global* website consists of an author blog, teaching tips, extra resources and much more.

www.macmillanenglish.com/global

Global Digital

Enhancing the teaching experience in the classroom

Global Digital is a digital component designed for classroom use. It can be used with an interactive whiteboard or with a computer and projector.

The Digital Book

The Digital Book allows the teacher to access and display an interactive version of any page from the Coursebook in front of the class. All of the relevant audio, video and reference materials are instantly accessible right on the page.

3 Work in pairs. Compile lists for two of the following categories:

- scarce commodities or resources
- items or commodities that are often illegally traded
- items that are currently in great demand in retail outlets
- things you can buy in your local street market

4 Read your lists and compare them with another pair.

Grammar

1 Read the sentences in the grammar box and do the tasks below.

a *The Silk Road **consisted** of an extensive network of land and sea routes.*
b *Many important scientific and technological innovations **were transported** to the West.*
c *When the silk arrived in Europe it **was made into** luxury goods.*
d *Caravanserai **were used** not only by traders and merchants, but also by pilgrims, missionaries, soldiers, nomads and urban dwellers.*
e *By the end of the 14th century, its importance **had greatly diminished**.*
f *Today the Silk Road **is again being used** by traders.*

1 Which sentences contain an active verb form and which a passive verb form?
2 Choose the correct alternative:
- use *an active / a passive* verb form when the main focus of the sentence is the *doer* of the action (or *agent*)
- use *an active / a passive* verb form when the main focus of the sentence is the *action* or the *object* of the action

3 Complete the rule:
- to form the passive, use the appropriate form of the verb ________ + the ________
- Which of the passive sentences mention an agent? Why is an agent not mentioned in the other passive sentences?

2 Complete the text with an appropriate active or passive form of the verb.

Trade (1) ________ (*conduct*) between different groups or societies since prehistoric times. The earliest trade (2) ________ (*probably / consist*) of forms of barter, in which goods (3) ________ (*exchange*) without using a medium of exchange such as money. Later, currency (4) ________ (*introduce*) to facilitate a wider exchange of goods and services. The importance of international trade (5) ________ (*increase*) in recent decades, and trade organisations such as the EU and NAFTA (6) ________ (*establish*) to promote trade between member countries. Nowadays, trade (7) ________ (*increasingly / carry out*) with few restrictions within countries; however, trade blocs (8) ________ (*may / regulate*) international trade by means of quotas and restrictions. Tariffs (9) ________ (*usually / impose*) on imports, and some form of taxation (10) ________ (*may / also / impose*) on exports. However, it is unlikely that completely free trade (11) ________ (*ever / establish*) in the future or that forms of taxation (12) ________ (*completely / disappear*).

3 Work in pairs. Think of two or three commonly traded items or commodities (eg wheat, coffee, oil, cars, electronic goods). Write passive sentences about the past, present and future of the commodities using some of the words below and a range of verb forms.

design discover export grow import introduce invent manufacture trade use

4 Read your sentences to another pair without mentioning the names of the items. Can they guess what you have written about?

5 Work in small groups. Tell your group about an important contribution that your country, or another country you know, has contributed to the world. This could be:

- an art form
- a commodity
- a custom
- an invention
- an institution
- a manufactured item
- a religion or philosophy
- a technique

Ask and answer questions about each contribution.

Grammar focus – explanation & more practice of the passive on page 142

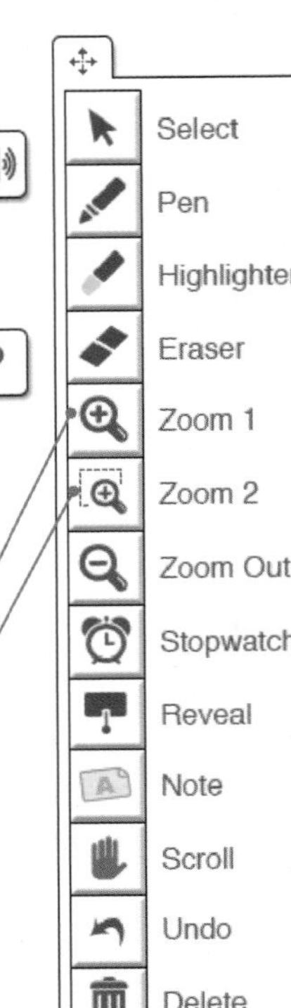

Navigation pane

The navigation pane allows you to select a page from anywhere in the book.

Zooming in and out

The Zoom tools allow you to zoom in either on predefined areas or any part of the page that you choose.

Toolbox

The toolbox provides a number of tools which enable you to interact with the Digital Book page.

The Teacher's Area

The Teacher's Area can be used to create your own material either before or during the class. You can insert and edit text and images, add links to pages from the Digital Book and insert audio and website links.

Navigation pane

The navigation pane displays thumbnails of the pages you have created in the Teacher's Area.

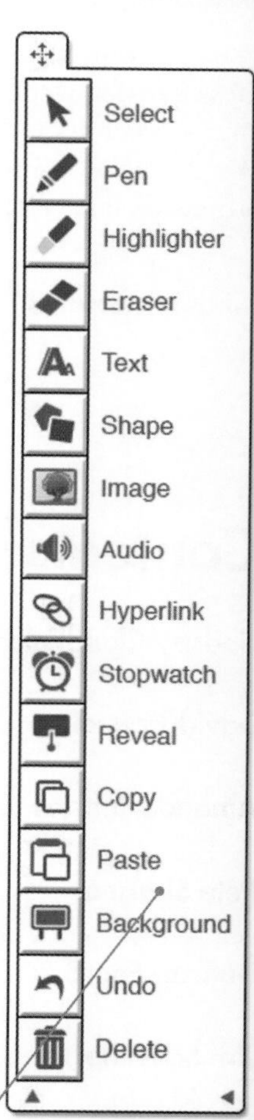

Games section

The games section provides interactive game templates to which you can add your own content.

Toolbox

A toolbox which includes some different tools from the ones for the Digital Book enables you to make annotations and create and edit materials.

Introduction

Ideas about language teaching, like languages themselves, are subject to change. For much of the twentieth century different 'methods' were presented as the best way to learn or acquire a new language. Some argue that we are now 'beyond methods', or in a 'post-method' condition in the twenty-first century. However, suggestions and approaches, useful tips, techniques and advice for good teaching practice are still as important as they ever were.

We know that language teachers often like to be informed of the newest developments in our field. With current technology we know more about the English language than ever before. Additionally, we as teachers are harnessing technology and the internet in new and exciting ways that help us help our students in ways we could not have imagined twenty years ago. And yet, there are some things that remain the same in the classroom.

What follows are a series of short essays, each written by experts in the field. The aim of these essays is to provide you, the language teacher, with up-to-date information about your subject matter. Like the material in *Global* itself, they are thought-provoking pieces. We also believe that learning more about what we do is extremely useful for our ongoing professional development. We hope you find them useful.

Lindsay Clandfield

Contents

Lindsay Clandfield: Why *Global*?

Every book is a product of its times. Nowhere is this truer than in educational materials. Notions of how people learn, of what they learn and of what is important are shaped by the world around us and the period we live through. What then, are the times that have shaped *Global*?

We live in an era of fast communication. More and more people are gaining access to internet and quicker communications technology. This means that we are writing and reading more than before, be it emails, text messages, blogs or web pages. Language learners need to work on quick and unplanned writing (writing for fluency) just as they do for speaking.

We live in an era of information. New technologies enable us to communicate more and with more people, but they have also made more and more information available than ever before – and it is available faster. Much of this information is still in English. Students need to be able to access information and assimilate it quickly.

We live in an era of uncertainty. Precisely because so much information is out there, we are often unsure what is accurate and what is opinion or even misleading. To succeed in an information-rich world one has to learn how to discern, analyse and evaluate what one sees or hears. Fostering critical thinking skills has long been an important goal of educaton.

We live in an era of global English. One of the most important realisations in the field of English Language Teaching of the past decade or so is that English is an international language, spoken all over the world, by people with different accents and different 'Englishes'. A learner is just as likely, if not more likely, to use his or her English with another non-native speaker as with a native speaker.

Given all this, the goals of *Global* are threefold:

1 For your students to **learn English**. This, as for any language course, is the primary goal of *Global*, which reflects modern developments in language teaching and learning. There is a strong lexical focus as well as a complete grammar syllabus, language presentation and practice is highly contextualised with many opportunities for personalisation, and there is plenty of meaningful communicative practice which in *Global* extends to mean writing as well as speaking fluency. *Global* includes a wide variety of reading and listening genres and practises a range of reading and listening skills. With the addition of sections to develop functional language, writing and study skills and review language, we are confident this course provides your students with the tools to become competent users of the language.

2 For your students to **learn through English**. The texts and topics of *Global* are selected so that in every lesson you and your students will be learning something new. We have chosen material that is thought-provoking, interesting, intelligent and above all, real. We have also included tasks that encourage students to examine the information they receive critically, and to find out more about a topic if they are interested. Unlike many other courses, texts and topics steer away from the light human interest or celebrity-related story. We use real world information from a wide variety of domains and the power of literature to unlock students' self-expression.

3 For your students to **learn about English**. This course also includes a focus, through extra reading and listening activities, on the English language as a subject itself. What is it? How is it changing? What kinds of English are appearing around the world? What are the implications of this? We believe these are important questions, worthy of being touched on in the language class. It is why we asked the foremost world expert author on these matters, David Crystal, to contribute to this new and innovative thread of *Global*.

Lindsay Clandfield is the lead author of *Global*. Originally born in England, Lindsay grew up in Canada. He began his teaching career at the Autonomous University of Chiapas in southern Mexico. He has taught in Canada, Mexico, the UK and Spain where he currently resides. Lindsay has received prestigious awards for his contributions to English language teaching, including two awards from the English Speaking Union (ESU) which he received at Buckingham Palace from the Duke of Edinburgh. Lindsay has given workshops and conferences to teachers in over thirty countries.

David Crystal: The future of Englishes: going local

When people talk about 'global English' they are usually referring to the common features which identify the variety we call standard English. Increasingly, however, attention has been drawn to the regional features which differentiate one part of the English-speaking world from another. So today we happily talk about British, American, Australian, South African, Indian, and other 'Englishes', and studies are accumulating of the way these varieties make distinctive use of pronunciation, orthography, grammar, vocabulary, and discourse. Much of the distinctiveness resides in the area of lexicology, the linguistic domain which most closely reflects cultural identity, and dictionaries have been compiled of the distinctive lexicons encountered in these regions.

It does not take long before these lexicons reach many thousands of words. When a country adopts a language as a local alternative means of communication, it immediately starts adapting it, to meet the communicative needs of the region. Words for local plants and animals, food and drink, customs and practices, politics and religion, sports and games, and many other facets of everyday life soon accumulate a local wordstock which is unknown outside the country and its environs. When someone in South Africa says 'The bakkie had to stop at a red robot', we need to know that a bakkie is a truck and a robot is a traffic-light. There are thousands of such words in a dictionary of South African English. And other parts of the English-speaking world display the same kind of creativity.

This seems to be the pattern, as English becomes a local alternative language. When a group of people in a country switch into English, for whatever reason, the subject-matter of their conversation inevitably incorporates aspects of their local environment. They talk about the shops, streets, suburbs, bus-routes, institutions, businesses, television programmes, newspapers, political parties, minority groups, and a great deal more. They make jokes, quote proverbs, bring up childhood linguistic memories (such as nursery rhymes), and recall lyrics of popular songs. All this local knowledge is taken for granted, and used in sentences without gloss. Visitors who hear such sentences, or read them in local newspapers, need to have them explained. Conventional dictionaries will not help, for they do not include such localisms, especially if the expressions are encyclopedic in character (referring to local people, places, institutions, and suchlike).

Every English-speaking location in the world has usages which make the English used there distinctive, expressive of local identity, and a means of creating solidarity. From this point of view, notions such as 'Swedish English' take on a fresh relevance, going well beyond traditional conceptions of English spoken with a Swedish accent, or English displaying interference from Swedish grammar. Swedish English, for example, I define as the kind of English I need to know about when I go to Sweden, otherwise I will be unable to converse efficiently with Swedish speakers in English. It would be amazingly useful to have a glossary of the English equivalents of Swedish cultural references, but I know of none. This seems to be a neglected area for any language.

We need regional cultural dictionaries or glossaries. It is something every region can do, and something to which everyone who learns English can contribute. It takes only an hour or so to accumulate a list of dozens of culturally specific items. And when these are written down, in the style of a glossary, it has an interesting effect upon the participants. They feel they have somehow made the English language their own. I suspect such projects also add greatly to their linguistic confidence and self-esteem, for no-one else in the world knows their home-grown variety of English as well as they do. And they can take pride in the fact that they have added their own small piece to the global jigsaw puzzle that comprises the English language.

David Crystal is honorary professor of linguistics at the University of Bangor, and works from his home in Holyhead, North Wales, as a writer, editor, lecturer, and broadcaster. He read English at University College London, specialised in English language studies, then joined academic life as a lecturer in linguistics, first at Bangor, then at Reading, where he became professor of linguistics. He received an OBE for services to the English language in 1995. His books include *The Cambridge Encyclopedia of the English Language* and *The Stories of English. Just a Phrase I'm Going Through: my Life in Language* was published in 2009.

Amanda Jeffries: Developing study skills and encouraging learner autonomy

Learner autonomy can be defined as the ability of a learner to take charge of their own learning, not only by learning specific strategies or study skills but also by developing an entirely new attitude to learning. A truly independent learner of English is aware of their learning needs and goals, can reflect on how they learn, has a positive and proactive attitude to language-learning, and can make the most of learning opportunities both in and out of class.

Study skills are strategies and approaches that can lead to more effective learning. The *Global* series follows a comprehensive study skills syllabus covering metacognitive strategies (thinking about, planning, and evaluating learning) and affective and social strategies (monitoring your attitude to learning and working with others) as well as dictionary and reference skills. It also develops specific strategies for learning and practising listening, speaking, reading, writing, vocabulary, and grammar more effectively. All learners are different and research suggests that effective learning depends on choosing the right strategy, or combination of strategies, for the task, the learning context, or the particular individual.

Why deal with learner autonomy in class?

Most teachers recognise the importance of learning effectively, but many have reservations about doing learner training or learning awareness activities in class: 'It wouldn't work with my group'; 'There's already too much to do in class'; or 'I wouldn't know where to start'. It is important to remember, however, that a focused and independent learner is not only more efficient but also more motivated. Moreover, learner autonomy activities provide a valuable extra practice opportunity.

How can I help my learners to develop these skills?

You may find some of the following suggestions useful in your teaching situation.

- Include short regular learner training slots in your timetable, so that your learners get used to the idea of study skills as a key part of their learning.
- Offer students a 'menu' of possible strategies for, say, planning an essay, or memorising vocabulary to help them choose the strategy that works best for them. Comparing ideas in pairs or groups can also suggest new and useful ideas. Suggest they try out a new strategy for a week and report back on how effective they found it.
- When doing class activities, share your aims with your students and suggest useful strategies; for example, explain that you are asking them to read primarily to understand the gist of a passage and offer good gist reading tips.
- Ask students regularly to note down or discuss how well they have learned and what they have enjoyed or found puzzling, and make resolutions for how to improve.
- Find out how your students learn. You could ask them to write you a short letter about their progress and write back with suggestions!
- Make students aware of the range of practice opportunities and materials available – in a library or study centre, online, or in the media. Students can also keep a record of work outside class that they can discuss with you.
- More advanced groups might find writing learner diaries a good way to reflect on their learning styles and preferences.
- Above all, show you are convinced that developing good learning habits is a valuable learning focus – that way, your own attitude is more likely to rub off on your students.

Amanda Jeffries teaches university students and works on teacher development programmes in Oxford. She has contributed to the Macmillan *Straightforward* and *New Inside Out* series. She has written the writing, study skills and review pages for the *Global* series, and is the co-author of *Global Advanced*.

Pete Sharma: Blended learning

The term 'blended learning' is a 'buzz' term, yet one that means different things to different people. The 'classic' definition of blended learning is a course consisting of traditional 'face-to-face' language lessons, combined with 'distance learning', ie the opportunity to study 'beyond the classroom'. Such a course can provide many benefits for language learners.

In our book *Blended Learning*, we suggest a broader definition, taking blended learning to mean a combination of classroom teaching and the *appropriate* use of technology. Technology such as an interactive whiteboard can be used inside the classroom to enrich the learning experience. In addition, the students could have 24/7 access to their interactive learning materials, allowing them to study at anytime, anywhere.

Principles

Whichever definition is used, new technology has had a major impact on language teaching and learning. We describe four key principles for successfully integrating technology into language teaching:

- Differentiate the role you play as a teacher, and the role the technology is playing. For example, the teacher can clarify 'fuzzy' areas of grammar. The interactive exercises on a CD-ROM could then offer extra practice in 'crisp' areas of language, with students receiving feedback from the computer.
- Teaching should be principled. In other words, there should be a sound pedagogical reason for using the technology.
- The technology should complement and enhance what the teacher does. It is not a replacement for the teacher.
- 'It's not what it is, but what you do with it.' The interactive whiteboard in itself is just a 'tool'. It is how teachers actually use it, to help provide engaging language lessons, which can lead to better learning outcomes.

Integrating technology into language courses

There are many ways to integrate technology into a language course. A teacher can:

- support their face-to-face teaching with a Virtual Learning Environment, a web based platform which learners can access at any time. The VLE can be used, for example, to post language feedback for students to study after a class discussion.
- run 'learner training' sessions to show students how to benefit from the digital material in the eWorkbook at the back of their coursebook. For instance, you can download the audio files to their mp3 players to allow learning 'on the go'; use the 'QuickFind' feature on their electronic dictionary, and download the free interactive version of the phonemic chart from the web.
- use technology before a class. Before a fluency lesson, email students a pre-discussion reading task to get them thinking about the topic.
- use technology during a class. If you use an interactive whiteboard, you can save the electronic flip-charts you create. This allows you to build up a bank of personalised digital materials including photographs and sound files to support each of the coursebook units.
- use technology after a class. Students focusing on writing can collaborate together to produce an essay using a wiki, a website which contains editable web pages.

If teachers continue to provide pedagogically sound and interesting lessons, and allow the technology to support learning both inside and outside the classroom, then a blended learning approach can certainly enrich the language learning experience of students.

References

Barrett, B and Sharma, P *Blended Learning* – using technology inside and beyond the language classroom (Macmillan, 2007); Jones, C (1986) 'It's not so much the program, more what you do with it: the importance of methodology in CALL' System 14 / 2, 171-178

Pete Sharma is an associate Lecturer at Oxford Brookes University, UK. He has written books on technology in language teaching, and is co-author of *Blended Learning: using technology in and beyond the language classroom* (Macmillan 2007). Pete is a Director of Pete Sharma Associates, which runs training in educational technology: www.psa.eu.com. He has edited the CALL Review, the newsletter of the Learning Technologies SIG of IATEFL, and blogs on technology at: www.te4be.com.

Duncan Foord: How we can develop as teachers

Development means change and change is inevitable. You are not the same teacher (or person) you were a year ago. Working with a new coursebook, new students and colleagues, taking part in in-service training, preparing classes – all of these challenging elements of your day-to-day routine have changed you. You are always developing, you just have to decide how.

Our choices are framed by the culture we live in, the school we work in, government policy, students' expectations and so on. Some schools may encourage and support teacher development, others less so, but you will always have choices to make about how you teach and how you deal with challenges inside and outside the classroom. Focus on what you can do rather than what you can't.

Guiding principles

Just like a lesson, your working life needs some aims to guide your choice of development activities, your development plan, if you like. Here are six which I like.

- Take an interest in my students.
- Enjoy teaching.
- Take on challenges.
- Manage stress.
- Balance work and home life.
- Share my enthusiasm with others.

Give your teaching a 'developmental twist'

Here are some ideas for practical activities which are easy to integrate into your teaching routine and not time-consuming.

- **Get feedback** from your students. Five minutes before the end of the lesson ask the students to write on a piece of paper three things they liked about the class and one thing they didn't like, or a 'suggestion' if they prefer. Thank your students and collect the papers in. In the next class (or via email) respond to the comments.
- **Make a short video** of your class. For this you need a small hand-held camera or mobile phone with video. Get a colleague or student to video your class for about 5–10 minutes. Watch the video afterwards more than once. The first few times you will be cringing at your appearance and mannerisms! After that you will notice more interesting things about your choice of language, gestures and facial expressions and get a good idea how your students see you.
- **Try activities out first.** Before you use a speaking activity, try it out with a colleague. Afterwards assess how much time you needed, whether the instructions were clear, if you needed preparation time, what language you used, whether your students would find it easy or difficult and what help they might need. Adjust your lesson plan accordingly.
- **Break your routine.** This can be a very good way to help you understand your teaching better and add an element of surprise and fun to your classes. For example, let one of your students become the teacher for ten minutes and you become a student, move the seating arrangement, supplement the coursebook text with one you find which will particularly interest your students …
- **Create a staff 'sharing board'.** This is a place where you can share materials and teaching ideas with your colleagues. Once it catches on, the board will help build staff rapport as well as provide a source of interesting lessons and save you preparation time.

Duncan Foord is the Director of the teacher training institution OxfordTEFL. He is responsible for teacher training and development in the company and teaches on Trinity Certificate and Diploma courses in the Barcelona centre. He is co-author (with Lindsay Clandfield) of *The Language Teacher's Survival Handbook* (It's Magazines, 2008) and *The Developing Teacher* (Delta Publishing, 2009) winner of the Duke of Edinburgh ESU English Language Award 2009 for Best Entry for Teachers.

Jim Scrivener: Teaching high level learners

High level learners are successful learners

In many schools you might find lots of elementary and intermediate learners but significantly fewer high level learners. To get to be upper intermediate or advanced you have to progress past the infamous Intermediate plateau, that level of competence where you know enough to cope and where you start wondering if it's worth making more effort for what seem to be limited extra gains.

This suggests that those who make it to higher classes are, by definition, successful language learners. They have the mind-set, skills and personality that have enabled them to be successful at a very difficult task: learning English well. They are a tiny percentage of the much wider range of people who originally started out learning English.

High level classes are still mixed ability classes

Because schools tend to have fewer high level classes, there is often a tendency to squash all supposedly high students together – so one class can sometimes encompass a range from upper intermediate to advanced. Even the term *advanced* can encompass a surprisingly wide variation from 'I just passed my Intermediate exam' through to 'I lived in the US for five years'. The Common European Framework subdivides 'advanced' into two levels: C1 and C2 – and these make up a third of its level scheme!

Teacher worries

For the teacher, a higher level class may cause some additional worries, especially concerning the teacher's own language awareness and skills: 'Might they know more about English than me?' 'Are they going to ask me impossible grammar questions?' 'Will they show up my weaknesses?'

In terms of teaching techniques, there may also be concerns. High level students have enough language, confidence and experience both to understand you when you speak and to state their own opinions clearly and precisely. Teaching them requires a different approach than the one you may have used at lower levels.

A few teaching suggestions

- **Work with them.** High level teaching is collaborative. Language questions will arise that are exciting and challenging for everyone – students and teacher. Find a way to revel in these and 'swim around' in the problems – rather than feeling that you need to have all the answers instantly at your fingertips. Encourage learners to take part in an exploration rather than being merely passive listeners and followers.
- **Be open about what you don't know.** Acknowledge your own uncertainties. The alternative of covering up your ignorance and trying to pretend that you do know something you don't is a strategy that learners quickly see through.
- **Make sure there is tangible learning in each lesson.** A frequent complaint from high level students is that they don't feel they have learnt enough in an individual lesson. This may be to do with an equation of learning solely with 'new things'. Keep some minutes at the end of a lesson to raise awareness about what has been done and achieved. Explicitly point out new vocabulary, grammar and pronunciation issues as well as growth in skills.
- **Hit the pace.** Advanced learners can sometimes be very fast – and can easily get bored – but they can also be very slow, really trying to understand something challenging and going to great lengths to make sure they get it right. As far as possible take your pace from the students in class. Follow their pace rather than lead. Be prepared for sudden, dramatic shifts in pace – and go with them.
- **Get them to teach.** Actively involve learners in teaching – eg doing a presentation on a topic or running parts of the lesson.

Jim Scrivener is Head of Teacher Development for Bell International based at Bedgebury School in Kent, UK, where he developed and runs the Online DELTA course. He is the author of *Learning Teaching* (Macmillan), *Oxford Basics Teaching Grammar* (OUP) as well as the Teacher's Books and Portfolios for the *Straightforward* coursebook series (Macmillan).

Roy Norris: Using authentic material with high level students

An important role of the teacher of English at higher levels is to encourage students to supplement their coursebook with regular exposure to authentic materials, that is, materials which have not been specifically written or simplified for learners of English. Thanks to technology, a wealth of authentic material including newspapers and magazines, radio and TV programmes, is readily available to the student in his or her own home. With very little time and effort, teachers can help students access that material and incorporate it into their learning programme.

Why encourage students to use authentic materials?

There is simply not enough time in the classroom to give learners the amount of contact with language they require in order to become true advanced users of English. No matter how good the coursebook, higher level students will always need more – much more – written and spoken input. It is essential that they engage with a wide range of language used naturally in a variety of contexts; exposure to different Englishes, registers and lexical fields will help them broaden their vocabulary, gain a feel for the language and its structures, and become better readers and listeners. It will also provide valuable preparation in the knowledge and skills they require for any English examinations they intend to take. Encouraging students to work with authentic materials outside of the classroom empowers them; it enables them to take more control of their learning, with decisions concerning the choice of materials handed over to them, rather than imposed on them. They can explore topics which genuinely interest them, and learn not just the language but *through* the language. This level of autonomy is clearly a great aid to motivation.

Where can students find authentic material?

Students may have access to printed newspapers and magazines, books, cable and satellite television programmes and DVDs. But perhaps the biggest source of material is the internet. For reading material, a site such as www.onlinenewspapers.com/ has links to a whole world of newspapers including *The Australian* and *The Jamaica Observer*. Typing the name of an interest area together with the word 'magazine' into a search engine (eg *tennis + magazine* or *film + reviews + magazine*) provides a huge number of further possibilities. For listening material, the BBC site www.bbc.co.uk/podcasts is an excellent source, but general sites such as www.podcastdirectory.com/countries/ or www.mikesradioworld.com will give access to further UK and non-UK podcasts and English language radio programmes from around the world.

What activities can students do with the materials?

First of all, set up a regular reading programme whereby students read a different text of their choice at home, say, once a week. Encourage them to read a range of text types (eg articles, blogs, reviews, interviews) on a variety of topics. You can then set aside time in class for oral feedback in pairs or small groups; students outline the content of their texts, summarising any opinions expressed in them, and then discuss the issues involved. Students preparing for an examination can devise tasks (eg multiple choice or multiple matching activities) for their classmates based on the text they have read. Additionally, they can pick out and record collocations and other chunks of language they find interesting in a text, or cohesive devices they might be able to use in their own writing. A regular listening programme is also advisable. You can set generic tasks for students to carry out, depending on the type of podcast they listen to. For radio phone-in programmes, summarise the main points the speaker is making; for reviews, note down what the speaker(s) liked and did not like about a particular film; for TV and radio news bulletins, describe the main items and any opinions expressed. Initially, students could all listen to the same podcast, but since one of the aims is greater student autonomy, the more choice they have the better.

Roy Norris has been involved in language teaching for over 25 years. He taught French and German for five years in an English comprehensive school, before changing to a career in ELT. He has worked as a teacher and teacher trainer in Lithuania and Spain, where he now lives. He is the author of *Ready for FCE* and *Straightforward Advanced*, and co-author of *Direct to FCE* and *Ready for CAE* (all published by Macmillan).

Nicky Hockly: Mobile learning

Mobile learning, or mLearning, refers to any learning that takes place on a handheld (or 'mobile') device. Mobile learning is not just about mobile phones (or 'cellphones'). Tablet computers (such as the iPad), pocket computers (such as the Apple iTouch), small laptops (often called netbooks), e-readers (devices which allow you to read electronic books), MP3 players (for audio) and MP4 players (for video) – even handheld gaming devices – are all potential mLearning devices.

Mobile learning outside the classroom

Mobile learning is often referred to as 'learning on the go'. Students can download learning materials onto their handheld devices, and access them while on the move, or during 'down time' – for example, while travelling on the train to work, while waiting for a bus or a dentist's appointment, even while lying on the sofa after work! Downloadable learning materials can be found on the internet, or may come with a coursebook. You'll have noticed that *Global* has a 'Listen on the Move' section, consisting of downloadable audio files, which students can put on their mobile devices and listen to outside of the classroom. *Global* also has a 'Watch' section, with downloadable videos for students. Organisations such as the British Council have downloadable podcasts and other learning materials for language learners on their respective websites. Some materials are specially created 'apps' (applications, or small programs) for smart phones such as the iPhone, Blackberry or Android phone. Typical English language learning apps include word, grammar and pronunciation games, or audio and video podcasts. Podcasts may be linked to social media sites where students can interact with podcast characters and practise their English. Tell your students what is available for their mobile devices, encourage them to experiment with using apps in their free time, and get them to report back to the class on what they have used and how useful they have found it. You might find it's contagious, and other students start to try out apps too!

Mobile learning inside the classroom

Learning with mobile devices does not have to take place exclusively outside the classroom. Some schools provide class sets of mobile devices, such as wi-fi enabled pocket computers or netbooks, which teachers can integrate into classroom work. For example, imagine that you are working with your students on creating a tourist guide to your city. The students use the class set of mobile devices to search the internet for information on different topics in small groups (sights, food, festivals and traditions, history, etc). They can even interview and record tourists in the street with their devices, and take photos! The students then use the devices to create multimedia presentations of their topic, including video, audio, photos and text. All the topics are then collated into a multimedia guidebook, which is put online. The flexibility and portability of a mobile device makes it an excellent potential learning tool. Buying a class set of handheld devices is also much cheaper than equipping an entire computer lab for a school.

Sharing mobile learning resources with students

Nowadays many students have their own mobile devices, at least in the form of a mobile phone. Pointing your students to mobile resources encourages them to use their own devices for out of class language study. Although studying English on their mobile devices may not be every student's idea of a good time, it's about offering them choices. Mobile devices are here to stay. Mobile resources are available and increasingly ubiquitous, and as teachers, it's our job to let our students know about the options. It's up to us to help our students use them to support their own English language learning, whether inside the classroom or outside.

Nicky Hockly is Director of Pedagogy of The Consultants-E, an online teacher training and development consultancy. An EFL teacher and teacher trainer since 1987, she is author of numerous articles on teaching methodology and training. Her published books include *How to Teach English with Technology* (Pearson Longman), awarded the 2008 Ben Warren International House Trust Prize, and *English as a Foreign Language for Dummies* (John Wiley Publishing), both co-written with Gavin Dudeney. Her latest book, *Teaching Online* (Delta Publishing), was co-written with Lindsay Clandfield. She is currently working on books on digital literacy, and on mobile learning.

Hall Houston: Critical thinking

What is critical thinking?

Critical thinking is a subject that has drawn much attention in education circles during the past few decades. In its simplest form, it involves the examination of arguments and supporting evidence in texts such as discursive essays, research papers, and editorials.

Critical thinking skills refer to a basic set of skills which have many applications. These include looking at more than one side of an issue, creating arguments with relevant support, judging the arguments and support in a piece of writing, avoiding bias, spotting logical fallacies, and solving problems.

Why bring critical thinking into the classroom?

Students can benefit in various ways from training in critical thinking skills particularly at higher levels when they have the degree of fluency that may be demanded for these kinds of activities. There are three main reasons for bringing critical thinking into the classroom:

- Working with critical thinking skills can motivate students to reflect more on a text and connect on a deeper level with a piece of writing. This provides more opportunities for focus on form and negotiation of meaning.
- Critical thinking skills are important for students in any academic setting. They allow students to participate more fully in discussions and debates, and improve their academic writing skills.
- Critical thinking skills are helpful in everyday life. Students will get more out of texts they encounter on a daily basis, such as advertisements, news articles and editorials, ultimately helping them to become more informed consumers and citizens.

Ways that teachers can do this

Teachers who want to emphasise critical thinking in their lessons should remember that critical thinking doesn't mean being 'a critic' in the sense of being cruel and harsh in the expression of one's opinions. Examining an argument involves more than pointing out its flaws. It also entails identifying the strengths of the argument. The following are a variety of ways to foster critical thinking skills in class:

- **Reading critically** Students read an essay or an editorial that expresses a point of view, then summarise all the arguments and supporting facts.
- **Listening critically** As in the previous exercise, but using a listening text.
- **Language analysis** Students look for phrases authors use to make their arguments. They also consider other phrases that could be used.
- **Deconstructing the coursebook** Students identify three things they like about their coursebook, and three things they think should be changed or improved. They read out their lists and specify reasons for their choices.
- **Judging an advertisement** Students look at an ad from a magazine or a TV commercial and comment on what they like and don't like about it.
- **Public speaking** Students prepare and give short speeches, presenting a position and supporting evidence, followed by feedback from classmates.
- **Debating** Students learn the basics of debating and debate an issue in class.
- **As part of creative work** Critical thinking is closely tied with creative thinking. They support each other and overlap in some ways. Therefore, when assigning students creative work, such as writing a short story or building a website, plan time for creative thinking (producing new ideas and shaping the final product) and critical thinking (judging the final product and suggesting improvements).

Critical thinking doesn't need to be perceived as an extra element in a lesson. It can be integrated with skills work to make a richer, more memorable language learning experience.

Hall Houston teaches undergraduate students at Kainan University in Taoyuan County, Taiwan. His practical articles on language teaching have been published in periodicals such as *It's for Teachers*, *Modern English Teacher*, and *English Teaching Professional*. His first book, *The Creative Classroom: Teaching Languages Outside the Box*, was published in 2007. His most recent book, *Provoking Thought: Memory and Thinking in ELT*, is a resource book for teachers that covers five main areas: thinking, memory, creativity, critical thinking, and expressing thought in writing.

Martina Pavlíčková and James Thomas: Global issues and the ELT classroom

What do I have in common with people on the other side of the planet and how do my decisions affect them? Whose opinions carry the most weight in today's world and what power relations are in play? What lies behind my own beliefs and perspectives? Am I able to see the lens through which I look at my world? How do I react when I encounter a difference and why?

Such questions are at the core of global education. The primary objective is to lead students towards an understanding of today's fast-changing, interconnected world and of their place in it. While it is necessary to have some knowledge about distant parts of the world, it is above all the exploration of what links us to other people and places – socially, environmentally, politically, economically and culturally – that allows us to make informed choices and take responsibility for our actions.

Since such understanding is a personal matter, the importance of confronting our own belief system is recognised as the starting point. Focusing on our inner worlds enables us and our students to track how our knowledge and opinions have been formed, what contexts underpin them, and to acknowledge their partiality and incompleteness. Without understanding ourselves we cannot understand each other.

Given that our exposure to the media, information sources and other people reshapes our thinking, this is an interactive process. And in the information age, we are more than ever before not only consumers but producers of information – in the classroom as much as anywhere. As teachers, we can support interaction by choosing procedures such as mind-mapping, debates, reflective prose composition and dramatic representations which help students to cumulatively construct new knowledge, which in turn leads to a higher level of information processing and response. At the same time as engaging students and giving them language production opportunities, these activities help develop their sense of cooperation, critical thinking and empathy, as well as valuing and respecting diversity – the keys to living in a complex, globalised world. From a language learning perspective, the more advanced a learner's lexical, syntactic and pragmatic competences are, the more they are likely to derive from engaging in such activity.

Bringing the world into your classroom

Since global education is about how we look at the world around us, it is a new mode of enquiry that we bring to the classroom, not new things. Asking our students to generate new questions about old topics helps them see things differently, identify parallels and links, causes and consequences. Watch your class's mind expand and their eyes open wide as you elicit a mindmap on what lies behind their mobile phone, a T-shirt, a photo.

Two heads are better than one. In a world where it is increasingly recognised that groups can achieve more than individuals, collaborative skills are more valuable than a competitive, survival of the fittest mentality. Choose activities and methods that support cooperation and develop empathy, where students listen to each other and move forward together, even in an environment of agreeing to differ.

Take the bull by the horns. There are conflicts going on not only in remote corners of the world, but in our students' worlds also, and the communicative, collaborative and interactive classroom can be a suitable venue to air them. In learning the language that is required to deal with contentious issues on personal, local and global levels, students also acquire coping strategies.

Two swallows don't make a summer. Given the rich diversity of the world in which we live, and students' awareness of the differences between people, lifestyles and living conditions, there is no need to dumb them down with generalisations. In terms of personal development and language learning, there is much to be gained from having students recognise their own stereotypes and consider how they have been formed.

Based in Brno, Czech Republic, **Martina Pavlíčková** and **James Thomas** are the co-editors and co-authors of the teachers resource book *Global Issues in the ELT Classroom* which was awarded the 2010 Cambridge ESOL International Award for Innovation at the British Council ELTons ceremony. Martina teaches adults young and old, writes materials and runs workshops for teachers on Global Education for the Czech NGO Společnost pro Fair Trade. James is head of ELT teacher training at the Faculty of Arts, Masaryk University. In addition to teacher training courses, he teaches academic writing, ICT for ELT and is constantly experimenting with practical corpus-based approaches.

Teaching notes

UNIT 1 Fact & Fiction

Coursebook			
Unit 1	**Language**	**Texts**	**Communication skills**
Part 1 SB page 6	Extend your vocabulary Collocations for going online	Reading *Six Wikipedia 'Facts'* *Is Wikipedia part of a new 'global brain'?*	Speaking & Pronunciation Personal facts Writing An online encyclopedia entry
Part 2 SB page 8	Grammar Present simple and continuous for facts and trends	Reading & Speaking *The world's most adventurous museums* Listening Interview about museums	
Part 3 SB page 10	Vocabulary & Pronunciation Emotional reactions	Listening *The Arabian Nights*	Speaking Fiction and stories Writing A story
Part 4 SB page 12	Extend your vocabulary Prefixes Grammar Ellipsis	Reading *Just science fiction?* Listening Reacting to a question	
Function globally SB page 14	Making plans and arrangements Listening to people making arrangements to meet Inviting and making firm arrangements Future forms		
Global English SB page 15	English: just the facts? Discussing the evolution of words connected to technology		
Writing SB page 16	A job application Writing skills: formal letter conventions Linking ideas: addition Giving personal information		
Study skills SB page 17	Setting goals		

Additional resources	
eWorkbook	Interactive and printable grammar, vocabulary, listening and pronunciation practice Extra reading and writing practice Additional downloadable listening and video material
Teacher's Resource Disc	Communication activity worksheets to print and photocopy, review material, test, and video with worksheet
Go global Ideas for further research	**Fact** Ask the students to do some internet research on a museum in the country where they live and to make a short presentation of what it offers and how it helps to attract visitors. **Fiction** Ask the students to research the origins of a famous folk story from their country on the internet. Ask them to find out who wrote it, who for, what was the historical context and why it is still famous in modern times.

Part 1

TEACH GLOBAL THINK LOCAL Lead-in

Provide a model for the first activity by giving students three facts about yourself, plus another one which is false. Simply tell the students, or write the facts on the board for students to guess. Try to make the facts interesting but believable, eg *I won a national award for badminton at the age of 15.* Let them ask you up to 12 questions, to find out more.

Speaking and Pronunciation (SB page 6)

1 Put students in pairs, but avoid putting together students who know each other really well. Encourage them to ask up to 12 questions to help identify which is the incorrect 'fact', as in the *Lead-in*. Early finishers can join in with another pair. As students are working, listen out for any personal facts which are interesting and could be shared in whole-class feedback session at the end.

2 To flow neatly into this pronunciation focus, use one of the examples from exercise 1, eg *I thought the third fact was incorrect, but actually it was the second one.* Put it up on the board and elicit the stressed words. Do the same for the two new sentences.

3 **1.01** Ask students to pay particular attention to the stressed words when listening. In pairs, students read out the sentences. You could raise the challenge and ensure they sound really natural here by focusing on other pronunciation aspects too, such as weak forms, eg *was* /wəz/ and linking, eg *but_actually.* Check that students are pronouncing *actually* naturally /ˈæktʃuəli/ or /ˈækʃəli/.

1 I thought he was a student, but actually he's the teacher.
2 She thought I was from Spain, but in fact I'm from Mexico.

Language note

The intonation of these sentences is also significant and worth pointing out. Highlight this either at the board stage (exercise 2) or after listening (exercise 3). At the end of both clauses, there is a falling tone to indicate this is new information:

I thought he was a student, but actually he's the teacher.
↘ ↘

The word *actually*, and other similar adverbs, are also prominent: such words indicate to a listener that a correction is forthcoming. If necessary, drill this in class and/or respond to their actual use in exercise 5, SB page 6.

4 Give a personal example here, particularly if you have one that is amusing or rather embarrassing, eg *One day, I was shopping and I put my bag on the floor so I could look at something. Then I saw a suspicious woman walk away with my bag. I ran after her and grabbed the bag. Then I realised it wasn't mine; in actual fact, it contained her new shoes.* Then students work together in pairs, eg *I thought you were about 25, but actually you're over 30.*

5 Give an example to start with, eg *This is Samir. He's a history student. He says he's written a book, but in fact he hasn't.* While students are working in new pairs, monitor, focusing on whether their pronunciation sounds natural. To round off this stage, get a student with good pronunciation to give one or two examples to the whole class. This can help to raise the profile of good pronunciation.

Reading (SB page 6)

TEACH GLOBAL THINK LOCAL Pre-reading activity

Read out the following questions and ask students to write short answers:

Where's the first place you'd go to find the following items? If you'd look on the internet, say which website(s).

a) a recipe b) a fact for a piece of research c) some information on the planets d) some gardening information e) how to play a new sport.

Let students compare their ideas in small groups.

This reading text describes the nature of user-generated content, such as that found in Wikipedia, and discusses the source and quality of the material in comparison to more traditional providers of knowledge.

1 Students discuss the questions in groups, and then briefly as a class. If/When Wikipedia is mentioned, write it up on the board.

2 First elicit what students know about the Wikipedia website, without commenting yourself. Then students read the six facts and locate the false information. Let them compare their ideas in pairs or groups. Elicit the correct answer, with supporting reasons, if possible.

Statement 6 is false.

3 Hold up the article (SB page 7) for all to see, and read the heading aloud. Elicit what the heading might mean. Give students the gist task, telling them how long they have to read, eg 3–6 minutes (depending on your group). At the end, let them compare answers before taking swift feedback.

2 (*Surely the only way of achieving a coherent overview is to invite experts to sift through the content and judge what is quality and what is not? … expert knowledge, which remains invaluable today.*)

4 Show students where the lines go by holding up the book and referring to paragraphs A–D in the text. Students work independently, but check in pairs. Write the answers on the board for students to self-check.

1 C 2 A 3 D 4 B

5 Students work in pairs, but try to mix stronger with weaker students to provide useful support. Students are likely to be able to work out the meaning of the items both from context and from an understanding of both individual parts of the phrases. In feedback, draw attention to the fact that, in context, *peer review* is the only verb; the others are nouns.

1 anything written online by amateurs
2 ordinary people recording events
3 give opinions on the ideas of other people like you
4 the combined, generally-accepted knowledge of many individuals
5 researched and verified content
6 ordinary people whose interest and level of knowledge is comparable to that of professional experts

TEACH GLOBAL THINK LOCAL

Mixed ability

If early finishers are interested in the text, they can record these and other useful collocations, compounds or lexical phrases of interest in the text, eg *any chosen subject, knowledge pool, a small proportion*. Let them compare their findings.

6 Ask students to read the statements and choose the word or phrase that best expresses their opinion. In pairs, students then compare and discuss their ideas. For this type of opinion-based activity, encourage students to give at least one reason to support their responses.

Extend your vocabulary – collocations for going online (SB page 7)

Books closed. Quickly write up the nouns and ask students to supply the verbs which go with all of them, eg ______ *a website / web page / blog*. Be prepared to accept possible additional verbs if you do this. Students then work in small groups to discuss the questions given. If the students have their gadgets with them, allow them to quickly show their partners for real, eg a recent upload. Share any interesting points as a whole class.

Writing (SB page 7)

Write the three topics up on the board to focus students' attention. Explain the task. Tell students they need to write the first one (or two) paragraphs for their entry.

1 Tell students that, very importantly, like all genuine Wikipedia authors, they should read the instructions. Then refer to the two questions. Particularly if you have weaker students, ensure you leave them enough time to digest this dense text. Let students check answers in pairs and have a whole-class feedback session, if you wish.

1 neutrality and accuracy
2 a neutral point of view: presenting all points of view where appropriate
verifiable accuracy: providing references by citing verifiable, authoritative sources

2 If students are writing their introductions in class and without access to the internet, they will probably not be able to verify their evidence by giving references. Tell them that they can invent references, as appropriate. If necessary, give more guidance here. See *Language note*.

Students should look at their partner's work, paying close attention to the two criteria. They should then ask their partner at least two questions about the content.

Language note

When students write their Wikipedia introductions, they should avoid writing subjective descriptions. Provide some poor examples at a relevant point, eg *It's a friendly town, the most beautiful in the region*. Elicit alternatives, eg *Most people say that X is a friendly town; it is considered by many to be the (one of the most) beautiful in the region. According to the writer X, it was 'a heavenly place, full of unexpected surprises of nature …'*

TEACH GLOBAL THINK LOCAL

Homework extra

For homework, ask students to continue writing at least two more paragraphs. Remind them that they can use the internet, but that they must not plagiarise. If appropriate for your students, you could tell them how to reference (internet) sources, which is likely to be useful at this level. They need to include the name of the organisation or author; date of publication; title of article (underlined or in italics); web address; date viewed, eg The United Nations (2011) *World Demographics*. www.un.org (8 January 2012).

Part 2

TEACH GLOBAL THINK LOCAL Lead-in

Books closed. Dictate the words from exercise 1, leaving out *historical artefacts*. If students do not know the words, they should try to guess the spelling. At the end, students work in pairs to a) clarify the meaning of any unknown words and to b) guess what type of place they all refer to.

Reading and Speaking (SB page 8)

1 After students have discussed the questions, check pronunciation of any difficult words, eg *exhibit* (highlighting the silent letter here). Ask *Which of you like visiting museums?* Elicit recommendations of museums worth visiting.

2 Put students in groups of four. To focus them, write the names of the four museums on the board: *Museum in the Clouds; Chichu Art Museum; Museo Subaquático de Arte* and *Pitcairn Island Museum*. Elicit why these museums might be special / what they specialise in, without supplying answers. Give students a few minutes to read the information about their corresponding museum and answer the questions. Provide dictionaries for optional use. Warn students that they will not be able to look at their text at the reporting stage; they should try and remember or take notes if necessary.

A Museum in the Clouds
1 paintings and sculptures of the Dolomite mountain range (from the private memorabilia of pioneering climber Reinhold Messner)
2 It is over 2,000 metres above sea level.
3 to celebrate the thrills and challenges that adventurers face on that range (possibly to provide an incentive to climb, or to commemorate Reinhold Messner's achievements)

B Museo Subaquático de Arte
1 65 life-size sculptures by British sculptor Jason de Caires Taylor
2 It is below the sea and visitors must scuba dive to the site.
3 to encourage marine life to develop, and to encourage travellers to reflect upon their impact on the coast

C Chichu Art Museum
1 artwork by artists such as Claude Monet, Walter De Maria and James Turrell
2 The entire exhibition is below ground and there is a 400 square metre garden above ground.
3 to encourage visitors to explore man's relationship with nature

D Pitcairn Island Museum
1 Polynesian artefacts
2 It's on a volcanic outcrop in the South Pacific. It's a 30-hour, $4,000 boat trip from the island of Mangareva.
3 Not stated – perhaps to bring tourism and revenue to the island, or to provide a record of the island's history as the population is so small

Background note

For students reading text D, the *Bounty* was a British ship, made famous by the mutiny of its crew members in 1789, against their apparently cruel captain. The mutineers then sailed to Tahiti. Later they settled with the native islanders on the nearby, hidden island of Pitcairn in 1790 (named after the crew member who first spotted it). The islanders still bear the names of the mutineers, and speak a dialect that is a mixture of eighteenth-century English and Tahitian.

3 Students describe their museum and listen to descriptions of the others. Monitor as they discuss the two questions. Conduct a whole-class feedback session if students are interested in the topic.

Listening (SB page 8)

This listening is an interview with Professor Ken Arnold, an expert from a London museum, in which he talks about the nature and history of museums.

1 Before students start discussing the statements, tell them that they need to justify their opinions, even if they believe the statement is true.

Background note

The Renaissance was the period in Europe between the 14th and 16th centuries when there was increased interest in ancient Greece and Rome, which produced new developments in art, literature, science, architecture, etc.

2 **1.02** Play the recording pausing after the first paragraph to elicit the answers. Then play the rest of the interview. Let students compare answers before you check them with the class. Monitor and establish how they did. Be prepared to replay (part of) the recording, if necessary.

1 F (*... in recent years attendance at many museums has in fact risen steadily.*)
2 F (*... museums are increasingly appealing to young adult audiences*)
3 T
4 T
5 T
6 F (same function but for more people)
7 T
8 F (*although they'll look and function differently*)

1.02

A: So, Professor Arnold, are people still going to museums today?

B: Yes, well, more than ever in fact, so more people are going to public cultural institutions these days than are going to sporting venues, and in recent years attendance at many museums has in fact risen steadily.

A: So, what sort of people are they? Is the audience for museums changing?

B: Well, it can be hard to tell actually, but I think museums are increasingly appealing to young adult audiences … A number of museums have also experimented with the idea of opening up in the evening, and some have found themselves absolutely crowded with youngsters looking for I suppose what is for them a different but fun night out. So at Wellcome Collection, our biggest audience sector has ended up being in the years 20 to 30.

A: So, tell us something about the history of museums. Where have they come from?

B: Well, modern museums really started in the Renaissance and as you know, the Renaissance was a time when there was a massive blossoming of interest in the idea of knowledge, particularly gathering facts, and using scientific investigation and discovery to create knowledge and actually some historians have gone so far as to argue that museums helped establish the very notion of knowledge being based on evidence.

A: Can you explain a bit more by, what you mean by 'knowledge based on evidence'?

B: Well, I guess what I mean is this idea of facts that were publicly visible, that they were verifiable by anyone who wanted to question them so museums in this respect were particularly important because they provided places where this sort of factual evidence – so specimens and samples from parts of the world almost unknown to Europeans or, on the other hand, examples of extraordinary craftsmanship and ingenuity that very few people could see, all of that could be gathered together, it could be ordered, it could be made available for scientific study. And the important thing is, done in public.

A: Can you give us some examples of those kind of specimens gathered in these early museums?

B: Yeah, well, almost every Renaissance museum had a unicorn's horn. Lots and lots of them had human flesh which was believed to have medical properties. And then some of the first examples of what were then exotic fruits were brought into museums, so the very first banana in England arrived in a museum in the early 17th century.

A: Fascinating. What about now? I mean, we have the internet, we have so many other sources of knowledge now. What place is there now for museums?

B: Well, actually as far as I'm concerned, museums can still effectively perform the same sort of function, but now not just for a few people – it's for everyone, and that function is creating and engaging knowledge through experimental projects. So, for example, you can put on an exhibition about skin … and you can bring together the scientific knowledge of how skin works – it's the biggest organ in our body – but also all the ideas that artists and historians have put together about the same topic. So through temporary exhibitions as well as through live events which museums play host to, I think museums hold up this notion of ideas for inspection, and this not so much by presenting dry information, through factual knowledge in books, but rather, really, sort of emotionally-charged facts, facts that you can, you can almost feel in your stomach.

A: And finally, do you think there'll still be museums in 100 years? And if so, what do you think they'll look like?

B: Yes, I'm pretty sure there will be museums. I'm sure in some respects they'll look and function very differently, though often, it's in ways that we simply can't tell at this stage. They'll look different in ways that we can't predict.

TEACH GLOBAL THINK LOCAL

Listening extra

There are some other interesting facts in the text which students may not have focused on in the initial listening(s). To highlight these and provide additional listening practice, write up the following nouns: *a unicorn's horn, human flesh, a banana, a skin exhibition*. Replay the whole recording, or you could just play it from the third question: *Can you give us some examples …?*

3 Let students read the interview extracts first, before replaying the interview. If necessary, pause and/or replay the relevant point.

1 *well*; *in fact*; *in fact*
2 *actually*
3 *Well, I guess what I mean*
4 *Well, actually as far as I'm concerned*

4 Students work in pairs. Tell them that the expressions could be used more than once.

1 all of them could start an answer
2 *I guess what I mean is*; *As far as I'm concerned*
3 *in fact*; *actually*

5 Give students a few moments to digest, choose and consider the questions, then put them in pairs. Monitor as they are talking and pick up on any points of interest, either topic or language-related, for later feedback.

Grammar (SB page 9)

1 First of all, ask students to work in pairs to discuss the main uses of a) the present simple and b) the present continuous. Then let students work individually on the matching task, before comparing answers swiftly in pairs. Conduct a whole-class feedback session.

a an established fact
b a habit or routine
c a trend or new development
d a temporary situation

2 In pairs, students match the adverbial words and phrase with the rules. When checking, elicit any other examples they can think of, eg (in group 2) *usually, normally*.

1 rule c (a trend)
2 rule a (a fact)
3 rule b (a routine)
4 rule d (a temporary situation)

Language note

When the present continuous is used with adverbs of indefinite frequency like *always*, *forever*, *constantly* or *repeatedly*, the events described are often, though not always, negative or unwanted, eg *he's forever leaving a mess all over the house; she's constantly nagging me to get a puppy*. Although the present simple is also possible here, the continuous aspect emphasises the idea of repetition of unplanned actions. Note that when spoken, the adverbial is also stressed: *They're always talking about moving abroad.*

Verbs normally considered 'state verbs' such as *love*, can occasionally be used in the continuous, to give extra emphasis to the current moment, eg *I'm thinking it's going to fail* (= that's what is in my head right now).

Nowadays, verbs like *love* and *like* are sometimes used colloquially in the present continuous form, eg *I'm loving this cake! It's delicious.*

3 Let students make their choices independently, then discuss their answers and reasoning in pairs. In feedback be open to discussion as there are sometimes grey areas. Make sure that your feedback is clear, using terms like *typically* or *usually*, with good examples.

1 *are becoming* (a change)
2 *work / am working* (fact or temporary situation)
3 *provide* (fact – has gone on for a long time)
4 *is trying* (a temporary activity – not a permanent state of affairs)
5 *being reduced* (trend)
6 *is always trying* (emotional connotation) / *always tries* (habit); *don't have* (state verb – this is revision, but alluded to in the rule)
7 *is sounding* (continuous dynamic meaning of state verb)

4 In pairs, students complete the sentences. Remind them before they start that the adverbial can be more than one word. Check answers in a whole-class feedback session.

Suggested answers

1 At the moment / At present (*currently* is possible, but note it is usually mid-position); *have* is present simple because it is a state verb
2 rarely / normally
3 forever / always / currently
4 In general / Nowadays
5 increasingly

Language note

Depending on their first language, some students may be tempted to use the word *actually* to mean *currently* or *now*. Be prepared to clarify that this is a false friend.

5 Choose one example as a class and elicit some true sentences about it. Invite different students to write up their sentences on the board to help focus them. Then students work on the other topics on their own. Monitor as they work, assisting individuals with problem areas where appropriate.

6 Put students into groups of three to read, listen and discuss their sentences. As well as asking about evidence, they should also state whether they agree or disagree with the writers' statements.

G Grammar focus

Refer students to the language summary on present simple and continuous for facts and trends on page 132.

You can use exercises 1–3 on page 133 for:
a) extra practice now, b) homework or c) review later on.

The answers are on page 162 of this Teacher's Book.

Part 3

TEACH GLOBAL THINK LOCAL Lead-in

Bring in a novel that you have read. Show students the cover. Tell them about the book and why you like it, and encourage them to ask questions. Encourage similar conversations, either as a whole class or, if possible, in small groups.

Speaking (SB page 10)

1 In pairs, students classify different types of books as fiction / non-fiction. Elicit an example, eg biography, to get them started. If students seem to find this difficult, give some alternatives, eg a memoir, a thriller, etc.

TEACH GLOBAL THINK LOCAL Mixed ability

For early finishers, be prepared to put additional questions on the board, such as: *Where and when do you usually read? How do you read? (quickly, slowly) Where do you get your books from? How do you choose a book? Do you prefer a paper copy or an e-book?*

2 You could approach this via a brainstorm: first, either as a class or in groups, students say what they think the main ingredients of a good story are. Then they look at the list and select the six most important features on their own, before comparing their choices.

You could take feedback after question 2. Then have students do question 3 and share their story summaries with the whole class.

Listening (SB page 10)

This listening is the opening of the story of the *Arabian Nights*.

1 After the students have read *The Frame Story*, ask one of them to read it aloud. Discuss the questions.

a shorter story which is part of a longer, main story

Background note

The *Arabian Nights* is a collection of stories, which have their roots in ancient and mediaeval folklore and literature, including Indian, Persian and Arabic oral traditions. Whilst the stories were only written down (in Arabic) in the 14th century, the fables were circulating for centuries earlier. At times, the characters begin to tell their own story to other characters, providing a story within a story. The version here comes from a new translation by Malcolm and Ursula Lyons.

2 **1.03** As you start the listening, check how to pronounce the characters' names. Also clarify the meaning of *vizier* (n) /vɪˈzɪə(r)/ (an important government official in some Muslim countries in the past).

Shahrazad and Dunyazad are sisters, and daughters of the vizier. The vizier is employed by the king. Shahrazad marries the king (we assume).

1.03

The Arabian Nights

Long ago, in the islands of India and China, there was a king called Shahriyar. He ruled over the lands, treating his subjects with justice and enjoying the affection of them all until one day the news reached him that his wife had been unfaithful to him. The king was furious, and overcome with rage and sorrow, he killed both his wife and her lover. And from that day on, he developed a deep hatred for all women. He would order his vizier to bring him a young girl every night, marry her, and after their wedding night he would kill her. The story continues …

This led to unrest among the citizens; they fled away with their daughters until there were no nubile girls left in the city. Then, when the vizier was ordered to bring the king a girl as usual, he searched, but could not find a single one, and had to go home empty-handed, dejected and afraid of what the king might do to him.

This man had two daughters, of whom the elder was called Shahrazad and the younger Dunyazad. Shahrazad had read books and histories, accounts of past kings and stories of earlier peoples, having collected, it was said, a thousand volumes of these, covering peoples, kings and poets. She asked her father what had happened to make him so careworn and sad, quoting the lines of a poet:

Say to the careworn man: 'Care does not last, And as joy passes, so does care.' When her father heard this, he told her all that had happened between him and the king from beginning to end, at which she said: 'Father, marry me to this man. Either I shall live or else I shall be a ransom for the children of the Muslims and save them from him.' 'By God.' He exclaimed, 'you are not to risk your life!' …

Shahrazad listened to what her father had to say, but she still insisted on her plan, and so he decked her out and took her to King Shahriyar. Shahrazad had given instructions to her younger sister, Dunyazad, explaining: 'When I go to the king, I shall send for you. You must come, and when you see that the king has done what he wants with me, you are to say: "Tell me a story, sister, so as to pass the waking part of the night." I shall then tell you a tale that, God willing, will save us.'

Shahrazad was now taken by her father to the king, who was pleased to see him and said; 'Have you brought what I want?' When the vizier said yes, the king was about to lie with Shahrazad, but she shed tears and when he asked her what was wrong, she told him: 'I have a young sister and I want to say goodbye to her.' …

Later that night, the king agreed to Shahrazad's request and Dunyazad was sat by her bedside …

They then sat talking and Dunyazad asked Shahrazad to tell a story to pass the waking hours of the night. 'With the greatest pleasure,' replied Shahrazad, 'if our cultured king gives me permission.' The king was restless and when he heard what the sisters had to say, he was glad at the thought of listening to a story and so he gave his permission to Shahrazad.

Shahrazad said: 'I have heard, O fortunate king, that a wealthy merchant, who had many dealings throughout the lands, rode out one day to settle a matter of business with one of them …'

Morning now dawned and Shahrazad broke off from what she had been allowed to say. 'What a good, pleasant, delightful and sweet story this is!' exclaimed Dunyazad, at which Shahrazad told her: 'How can this compare with what I shall tell you this coming night, if I am still alive and the king spares me?' 'By God,' the king said to himself, 'I am not going to kill her until I hear the rest of the story,' and so they spent the rest of the time embracing one another until the sun had fully risen.

3 In pairs, students try to remember the order in which the events happened. Monitor to see how they are doing, as this will affect when you replay the recording.

4 At an appropriate point, replay the recording, for students to either complete the task or check answers. Encourage them to mention the reasons behind the events.

Correct order

- f (because the king had them executed)
- d (because he had helped the king who had killed a lot of young women / because he couldn't fulfil the king's wishes to bring him a young woman)
- a (to be a ransom for the people)
- b (because he wanted to marry her)
- e (to ask her to tell them a story to save them)
- c (the king was restless and agreed to listen)
- g (to hear the rest of the story)

5 Give students one minute to consider their answer. If they seem animated by the task, put them in groups to discuss it; otherwise handle it as a class.

6 Remind students why the King repeatedly let Shahrazad live another day: he was gripped by her stories. Refer back to the text *A good story*. Let students reflect on a story they think would be equally gripping, and the reasons why. Invite them to report back to the class.

TEACH GLOBAL THINK LOCAL Speaking extra

You could let students work in small groups to actually recount their stories. They should start by saying: *The story I have chosen is* … or, if appropriate, *Once upon a time …* Allow some planning time in class, or let them prepare at home. Ask them to use notes rather than a script and to speak for up to three minutes.

Vocabulary and Pronunciation (SB page 11)

1 As a lead-in to this activity, you could jumble the words in each of these two sentences. With students' books closed, dictate one word at a time from the first sentence but out of order, being careful not to miss out or repeat a word. Then do the same with the second sentence. After students have put the words into the correct order, instruct them to locate the adjectives and answer the question. Write the examples on the board, under the headings *Gradable* and *Ungradable Adjectives* and elicit other examples.

surprised is gradable

Language note

Most adjectives are gradable, that is, they can be measured or modified with words like *very* or *less* and have comparative and superlative forms, eg *big, pretty*. In contrast, ungradable adjectives cannot be modified in the same way. They classify nouns, eg *married, alive, impossible, handmade.* You cannot say *more married* or *a little married*, for example.

2 Ask students to look at the two examples from exercise 1. Write the relevant clauses up on the board and circle the words before the adjectives: *somewhat* and *absolutely*. Elicit what type of words these are (adverbs which modify the adjective). Then ask students to complete exercise 2 on their own, before whole-class feedback.

1 b 2 a 3 c

3 Students complete the exercise alone, then check their answers in pairs. Write up the answers on the board, or project them, for students to self-check.

Incorrect alternatives

1 angry	3 shocked	5 pleased
2 upset	4 puzzled	

4 Elicit the possible answers to stress pattern 1. In pairs, students work on the remaining ones.

1 shocked; pleased
2 enraged; incensed; upset; distraught; appalled
3 angry; speechless; puzzled; baffled
4 bewildered; delighted; euphoric
5 overjoyed
6 furious; heartbroken; horrified; mystified
7 devastated

5 1.04 Students listen to the answers. If appropriate, drill the more difficult words, eg *distraught*, *bewildered*. Then, in pairs, students read out the sentences. They should place the main stress on the adjective itself, although the adverb is also clearly stressed. Model this first yourself, eg *The king was absolutely furious to learn of his wife's betrayal.*

6 Write the example up on the board and ask students to transform the sentence, using the word *amazed* instead of *amazement*, eg *The vizier was utterly amazed to learn that Shahrazad had not been killed.* Ask how the sentence has changed. Above the initial example (*to his utter amazement*), write up *to his/her + adjective + noun showing reaction*. In pairs, students think up other examples. Monitor to assist, especially with collocations (see *Language note*). Elicit some examples.

Possible answers

Shahrazad realised to her great amusement that the king was enjoying her story.

The king heard to his slight annoyance that Shahrazad wanted to tell a story.

To his vague bemusement the king decided that he wanted Shahrazad to stay with him.

To his total dismay the vizier saw that his daughter was determined to see the king.

TEACH GLOBAL THINK LOCAL

Extra activity

To provide more practice of the adverbs in Vocabulary and Pronunciation exercise 2, give students some unusual situations: Say, *Imagine ... you received your exam results this morning and got excellent marks in all papers; ... you received a late birthday present through the post; ... you found a new dent in the side of your brand new car; ... you left your house this morning and saw about 40 stray dogs in the street; ... your pet hamster died last night.* Think of at least three more situations. Read the situations out and ask students to write down their immediate responses using the target language (adverb + adjective), eg *I felt totally confused.* Then students compare their reactions in groups of three.

Writing (SB page 11)

1 Remind students that it does not matter if they are unfamiliar with the original story. You may like to initially brainstorm ideas for one of the opening lines together. If possible, let the pairs write on a computer as this makes rewording easier. Give a clear time-limit for the actual story-writing. Monitor and encourage use of the new language to show emotional reactions.

2 In groups of four, students read out their stories. Encourage them to use their voice to show feeling. While listening, pick up on one or two successful examples of emotional language, if appropriate.

Part 4

TEACH GLOBAL THINK LOCAL

Lead-in

Ask students to try and define 'science fiction' in 15–20 words. Elicit some examples. Then write up this incomplete dictionary definition on the board for students to complete the missing words (given in brackets here): *books and (films) about (imaginary) future events and characters, often dealing with space (travel) and life on other (planets).*

Reading (SB page 12)

1 Ask students to think of at least three associations with 'science fiction'. Elicit some examples. Promote interest by asking the questions and eliciting examples of films and books too, particularly ones students enjoyed.

2 Do the first example together to clarify the task. Students then complete the quiz alone, before comparing answers in pairs. In a whole-class feedback session, discuss which ones they believe to be false and why. Do not confirm the answers at this point.

3 This text discusses how developments in space technology have lead to further investigations into life on other planets, and to explorations of other planetary and star systems.

Students read the text, matching the paragraphs to the statements. Give some time afterwards for students to compare answers in pairs. Write up the answers on the board and discuss any differences they may have.

1 B 2 E 3 A 4 C 5 D

TEACH GLOBAL THINK LOCAL

Mixed ability

Early finishers could start compiling a mind map® of space-related words, based on the text and also on the NASA quiz in exercise 2. Write the word *space* in a circle in the middle of the board; students come up and add associated words, eg *solar system* (n), *planet* (n), *orbit* (v), *capsule* (n), etc.

4 Students read to check the answers to exercise 2. They discuss in pairs which of the facts were the most interesting. Invite some students to share their responses with the whole class.

A, C, D are false.

5 Time taken on this discussion will depend on your students' interests. Have some extra questions ready for early finishers, eg *What do you think will happen in the next 30 years in terms of space travel? Do you believe there is life on other planets? What kind of skills does an astronaut need?*

Extend your vocabulary (SB page 12)

1 Ask students as a class to try and provide one more example for each prefix, eg ***tele****vision*, ***ultra****-cautious*, ***extra****curricular*, ***inter****act*. Then students complete the matching task. Provide a written record on the board, eg *tele = over a distance*

1 over a distance	3 beyond
2 extremely	4 between

2 Students work independently, then compare and explain their words in pairs. After doing this, they can verify that they have formed a proper word combination, checking with a dictionary or with you.

> interactive = involving communication between people or people and computers
> interchangeable
> extrajudicial
> ultra-modern
> extraordinary = out of the ordinary/very unusual
> teleshopping = shopping through special television programmes
> ultrasonic = (describing sounds) extremely high frequency

3 It's likely that your students will be familiar with most of these prefixes, so you could handle this task as a competition. In groups of three, students have two minutes to brainstorm as many words as they can for each of the prefixes. When time is up, ask how many words each group has for each prefix, then allow students to check their examples in the dictionary, if necessary. At the end, elicit the meaning of each prefix.

> anti: against
> hyper: more than usual or normal
> multi: many
> post: after
> sub: under

Listening (SB page 12)

This listening is a recording of different individuals giving their opinions on the value of space travel.

1 **1.05–1.09** Students first read the three questions, then listen to the five separate recordings. Tell students that some of the recordings are dialogues and others are monologues.

> question 2

1.05–1.09

1

A: I hope not. Well, I don't think so. I think we have some sort of duty, moral duty, to the future generations, our children, our children's children, to find out, you know, discover if we are alone in the universe or not. Or at least try to.

B: I agree. I just think that we're, you know, we're exhausting all our resources here and we need to find things further afield.

A: Exactly.

2

Don't know really. Hadn't thought about it. Suppose it's up to every generation to spend the money on the technology they think's worth spending it on. I grew up in the 60s so there was lots of space exploration stories around and it was exciting when I was a kid, but is it appropriate now? Not sure really. Don't really have an opinion.

3

A: No, I don't think so. I think it's important to find out about the things we know little about. I'd certainly go into space if I had the chance. Wouldn't you?

B: Yeah, I mean, I would too and, you know, we have got to know more about our, you know, existence, you know.

A: Exactly.

B: I mean, marine exploration, they spend a lot of money on that.

A: Yes, but space is so huge and we know so little about it.

B: Exactly, so why not spend, I mean, what is the amount they're like billions …

A: Well, it's billions, but it's got to be inconsequential to the rewards of finding out about us as the human race and our environment and how to survive.

4

Well, no, I don't think it is actually because without it, well, I think all kinds of things wouldn't have been discovered and generally speaking, you know, we need to … we need to invest in research, you know, if we want to make new discoveries and push back boundaries. Know what I mean? Because without, you know, without those kind of groundbreaking explorations we won't … we won't discover, maybe, the things that make life easier to live.

5

A: You know what, NASA had a budget of 18 billion, not million, billion dollars last year.

B: I don't believe it.

A: It's incredible. And just think, the government could have used that money to … well, help people in need for starters.

> B: Yeah, you're right, they could have. I mean, they could have put it into their international … overseas aid for a start.
> A: International development, yeah.
> B: Yeah, and education in their own country, health.
> A: Yeah.
> B: I mean, it's mad, the whole system.

2 Students listen again to establish which of the speakers agree or disagree, and their rationale. Let students compare answers before whole-class feedback.

> 1 Disagree: moral duty to future generations (to discover if we are alone); exhausting resources on Earth
> 2 Doesn't know: up to every generation to spend money on the technology they want, not sure it's appropriate today
> 3 Disagree: need to find out more about existence, human race, environment, survival
> 4 Disagrees: need to invest to make new discoveries
> 5 Agree: too much money spent, could have been used to help people in need (international development, health, education)

3 The listening provides some thought-provoking ideas. Students can either rearticulate these ideas or provide their own rationale. Elicit any new arguments and end with a class vote on the topic: *Is space exploration a waste of money?*

Grammar (SB page 13)

1 Tell students that the sentences are taken from the listening and demonstrate the feature of ellipsis. Point out the explanation below the examples. Do the first example together, eliciting what the full sentence would be. Students finish the task alone, before checking in pairs. Check the level of formality in the examples too.

> 1st rule: b (*I would **go** too*), and f (*could have **used that money …***)
> 2nd rule: a (*try to find out*)
> 3rd rule: d (***I** don't know, **I** haven't really …*)
> 4th rule: e (***Do** you know what?*)
> 5th rule: c (***Do you** know what I mean?*)
> c, d and e sound informal

2 Write up the examples on the board, and elicit the phrases that *so* and *not* substitute. See *Language note*.

> I don't think it is a waste of money.
> I hope it isn't a waste of money.

Language note

When words are replaced by other words, rather than by nothing, this is called 'substitution', as in exercise 2. Students at this level will no doubt already be using this discourse feature, even if they are doing so unconsciously.

In informal conversations, features such as ellipsis and substitution are often used both for efficiency and because there is a lot of shared knowledge so the speakers can be less explicit.

3 Students complete the exercise alone. Then, in pairs, they read out the mini interactions. Elicit which versions sound more natural (their amended versions).

> 1 B: It might be (a shooting star). Hmm, but then again it might not (be) (a shooting star).
> 2 B: I hope he isn't (going to) (go on about that again.) / I hope not.
> 3 A: (Do) you believe in extraterrestrials? B: Yes, I think I do (believe in extraterrestrials). / I think so. (You) can't believe everything scientists tell you.
> 4 A: (Do you) fancy going to see the new sci-fi film? (I) think it's still on. B: Yes, (I'd) love to (see the new sci-fi film).

4 In AB pairs, students turn to the corresponding activity. Give an example yourself and ask a student to respond using one of the phrases in their list, if necessary. Say *I think the most interesting country in the world is (China)*. Monitor and invite them to share any points of interest with the class.

TEACH GLOBAL THINK LOCAL Extra activity

For practice of substitution and ellipsis, provide this dialogue (you could also cut it up or jumble it for them to order).

A: Fancy a cup of tea?
B: Love one.
A: Sugar?
B: Please. Two.
A: Biscuit?
B: I shouldn't. Diet starts tomorrow!
A: You joking?
B: No. Not at all. It always starts tomorrow!
A: Very funny!

In pairs, students write the dialogue out 'in full'. Then they write similar dialogues. Give possible starters, eg *Want to go to the cinema this evening?* or *Hot, isn't it?*

G Grammar focus

Refer students to the language summary on ellipsis on page 132.

You can use exercise 4 on page 133 for:
a) extra practice now, b) homework or c) review later on.

The answers are on page 162 of this Teacher's Book.

Function globally: making plans and arrangements

These lessons in *Global* are designed to provide students with immediately useful functional language. They all follow a similar format.

Warm up (SB page 14)

Aim: to introduce the topic via a quick speaking task or picture work.

Tips:

- Do not over-correct here, especially in speaking activities.
- Encourage students to use as much variety of language as they can.
- Respond with genuine interest to their recommendations about places to have lunch, things to do locally, etc. This stage may well 'take off' in class.

Listening (SB page 14)

Aim: to present the functional language in context via a conversation or series of conversations.

Tips:

- Play the recording all the way through for each task (there are always two tasks). (Tracks 1.10–1.14)
- Pause the recording after each conversation.
- Encourage students to reread the audioscripts for homework, exploiting them for useful language.

1

Conversation 1

1 father and daughter
2 a family lunch
3 at her parents' house, next Sunday

Conversation 2

1 friends / partners
2 he is going to pick her up at the coach station
3 at the meeting point by the clock in the coach station, around 4.45

Conversation 3

1 professional; they work for different companies
2 have a working lunch
3 one o'clock at an Italian restaurant which she will book

2

Conversation 1

1 she's helping a friend move house
2 because her parents have arranged a big family lunch for the same day

Conversation 2

1 4.30
2 he might get stuck in traffic

Conversation 3

1 He will be in the area before one and is due in court at half past two.

1.10–1.12

1

A: Hello.
B: Hi, darling, it's me.
A: Oh, hi Dad.
B: How are you?
A: I'm really well. How are you?
B: I'm fine. Listen, erm, are you doing anything on Sunday?
A: This Sunday?
B: This Sunday, yes.
A: Yes, um, I'm actually tied up on Sunday. I've arranged to meet Sarah.
B: Oh dear.
A: I'm helping her move house.
B: Oh dear. That's a shame because we're … we're having a big family Sunday lunch.
A: Oh no, I'm sorry, Dad, I really can't, I've sort of …
B: Your Aunty Rene's coming.
A: Dad, it's been in the diary for ages and she's really relying on me.
B: Right, I understand. Listen, what about next Sunday? You doing anything then?
A: Let me see what I can do.
B: Oh that's great because Rene's down for a couple of weeks so she'll be here next Sunday and she'd love to see you.
A: And I'd love to see her, Dad. OK, well, why don't I give you a call back and, erm …
B: OK, but next Sunday is on, yes?
A: OK, Dad, next Sunday's on, next Sunday's on.
B: I'll tell your mother.
A: OK. I've got to go, Dad, erm, so I'll speak to you soon.
B: All right, darling, take care.
A: OK, love to Mum.
B: See you next Sunday.
A: OK, bye.

2

A: Hi, Rob, it's Clare.
B: Oh, hi Clare.
A: I'm still on the coach at the moment.
B: Right.

A: I wondered if you could come and pick me up?

B: Er, what, from the coach station?

A: Yeah. My coach gets in at 4.30.

B: Er, what's the time now? It's about 3.15, that gives me an hour and … er yes, yes I can pick you up.

A: Erm, where do you want to meet me?

B: Oh, um, there's a meeting point in the coach station, by the clock. Um, if you can wait there, I mean, I don't know how long it'll take me to get there and I might get stuck in traffic or whatever, but I'll be there as soon as I can.

A: You'll probably be there before me 'cause it's pretty chocka on the motorway so um …

B: OK, um, right well, I'll do my best, but I'll certainly get there by 4.45.

A: OK, brilliant, that sounds great so it's the meeting place by the clock?

B: I'll see you there.

A: All right, see you then.

B: Bye.

A: Bye.

3

A: Hello, HRP.

B: Hello, is that Joanna Evans?

A: Speaking.

B: Hello, it's Geoff Parker.

A: Oh, oh thank you for getting in touch. We need to meet up.

B: Yes, um, is tomorrow any good for you?

A: Um, yes, I'm going to be working here until … one o'clock, ten to one. I could do lunch.

B: That's … that could work actually. I'm due in court at half past two so maybe between one and two would be good for me, then it would give me time to get there.

A: We could meet, um, on the corner, that Italian?

B: That sounds fine. I was going to be in that area anyway so … what time did we say, about five past one?

A: One o'clock. I'll book it.

B: Oh that's super. Thank you very much.

A: See you there.

B: Thanks, bye bye.

3

Conversation 1

She's going with her three brothers to her dad's to celebrate his 70th birthday. They are going to have a meal in a restaurant on Saturday and probably go to a garden centre on Sunday.

Conversation 2

B is going to London for a tennis tournament and may do some gardening on Sunday; A is going to paint the bathroom, and possibly do some gardening and visit her mother-in-law.

1.13–1.14

1

A: What are you up to at the weekend then?

B: Well, on Saturday I'm going down to my dad's in the countryside, erm, where I'm meeting up with my three brothers because it's his 70th birthday, my dad, so we're going to have a lovely meal in a restaurant. And, erm, Sunday we'll probably just go to the, you know, the nursery and, you know, buy some plants for the garden.

A: Lovely.

2

A: So Ben, what are you doing this weekend? You got any plans?

B: I'm planning to go to London on Saturday. I've heard that there's a tennis tournament on so I thought I'd go and see what that's like and I might see if I can take some of my friends along. How about you?

A: Well, I think I'm just stuck at home really. We've got so many chores to do, I'm just going to basically paint the bathroom, which is getting really grotty, and after that I think if the weather is good I'll get into the garden 'cause it's looking a bit messy after the winter.

B: Oh lovely.

A: Yeah. Then I'm thinking of going and visiting my mother-in-law because I haven't seen her for a couple of weeks so I'll just check up and see how she's doing.

B: Maybe I'll do some gardening on Sunday as well if I'm free.

Language focus (SB page 14)

Aim: to draw students' attention to the items of functional language.

Tips:

- Students work alone first before comparing answers in pairs. Discuss any areas of ambiguity.
- Give students time to make a note of any new phrases they would like to remember.

1 B 2 B 3 C 4 A 5 A 6 C 7 D 8 A
9 D 10 A 11 D 12 D

Pronunciation (SB page 14)

Aim: to focus students on a particular aspect of pronunciation of the target phrases.

Tips:

- Play the recording two or three times, if necessary. (Track 1.15)
- At this level, try to promote good all-round pronunciation including stress, intonation and linking. This also raises the challenge for students.
- Use students with exemplary pronunciation to act as models to help others in the class.

1

1 up   2 up   3 down   4 down   5 down   6 down

2

yes/no information questions: voice up at end

yes/no questions where no information is requested (eg requests, offers): voice down at end

Speaking (SB page 14)

Aim: to allow students an opportunity to use this language in a meaningful, real-world context.

Tips:

- Ask two students to model the beginning of the conversation, to motivate and clarify.
- Encourage students to use the *Useful phrases*.
- Give students time to prepare this activity. Circulate and monitor carefully whilst they are talking.
- Correct sensitively, paying attention to the target language especially.
- If time, repeat the task with new pairs.
- Invite one or two students to share strong examples with the whole class to round off the activity.

Global English

These lessons in *Global* have two main goals: 1) to give you and your students interesting information about English and language in general; 2) to provide practice in different kinds of reading comprehension tasks that they are likely to encounter in future study, for example in exams.

TEACH GLOBAL THINK LOCAL

Lead-in

In pairs, ask students to name three of the following:

- varieties of English around the world
- English words related to botany or flowers
- English words related to zoology or animals
- (fairly) new words in the English language

Elicit examples. Explain that this links with the reading today.

Warm up (SB page 15)

Aim: to engage students with the topic, and highlight potentially difficult vocabulary in the text.

Tip:

- Elicit some of the difficulties involved in estimating figures relating to language.

Reading (SB page 15)

Aim: to provide students with interesting information about English, and practise reading exam skills.

Tips:

- There are two tasks. The first focuses on gist; the second is a more difficult task, similar to that of a reading exam.
- The third question raises students' awareness about a language feature.
- Challenge students to guess the answers for exercise 3 without looking at the text. Then they reread it to check. At the end, focus their attention on the suffixes, both meaning and form.
- This language is not tested or reviewed in future units, which means you have more flexibility with this material as to when and where you use it.

1

With estimates and opinions – there are too many variables and ways of describing language; various areas of language have not been described such as scientific terms; new words are entering the language all the time and old words falling out of use

2

1, 3 and 6 can be inferred from the text.

3

1 demonstrable   3 uniformity   5 tabulate

2 remarkably   4 marked

TEACH GLOBAL THINK LOCAL

Reading extra

If your learners would benefit from a quick revision of punctuation in use, ask them to locate examples of the following in the text: a comma; a question mark; an exclamation mark; a colon; a semicolon; a dash; speech marks; a hyphen; brackets. In pairs, they should then discuss why these are used in the text and if there are possible alternatives. You might also want to point out style issues – the tone is relatively informal as shown by the punctuation, eg the frequency of questions, the exclamation mark, the dashes, etc.

Speaking (SB page 15)

Aim: for students to relate the material in the reading to their own language, culture and experiences.

Tips:

- Conduct a whole-class feedback session on any points of interest.
- Discuss which of these words are the same in their first language. Ask students *Do you mind the fact that many foreign words are used nowadays?*

As you go through these *Global English* lessons in the book, don't be afraid to ask students' opinions and reactions to the information in the texts. Ask *Which do you find interesting? Do you know of similar experiences or facts in your own language or other languages?*

Writing: a job application

These lessons in *Global* are designed to provide extended writing practice. They all follow a similar format.

Reading (SB page 16)

Aim: to provide a sample text for students to analyse.

Tips:

- Books closed. Before starting, elicit the main information included in a job application letter.
- There are often two questions for these texts: one which focuses on gist and the other on specific details.
- For exercise 2, in pairs, ask students first to think of an alternative, more formal expression without looking at the text. Then they should check their own answers by reading the text again.
- Ask students *Is the style of a job application letter in your language any different from this one?*

1

1 d 2 b 3 a 4 c

2

1 *position*
2 *believe I possess*
3 *hold a master's degree*
4 *I have undertaken further*
5 *extensive*
6 *Prior to*
7 *broadened my outlook*
8 *look forward to hearing from you*

3

Students' own answers.

Writing skills: formal letter conventions (SB page 16)

Aim: to give students a chance to develop their writing through various different micro skills.

Tips:

- Clearly explain the focus and do an example of one of the questions first with the students before asking them to continue on their own.
- Let students check their answers in pairs or small groups, then correct in open class.
- Draw out some comparisons with students' first language(s), eg which conventions are similar or not.

1 F (don't include your name here, only your address)
2 T
3 F (write it after the salutation)
4 F (*Yours sincerely* with *Dear Mr / Ms Bragg*; *Yours faithfully* with *Dear Sir / Madam*)
5 T
6 F (don't use *My name is …*)
7 T
8 F (put it above your name)

Linking ideas: addition (SB page 16)

Aim: to highlight and focus on a particular aspect of language that students can use to improve their writing.

Tips:

- Do the first example together in class, then let students work through the others in pairs. Elicit some suggestions as a whole class and respond to these if incorrect, before students check with the text.
- The *not only* structure (exercise 2, SB page 17) is commonly tested in exams and one worth highlighting; it sounds sophisticated in formal written English.

1

1 In addition *to* my skills …
2 *… in **both** Italy and the UK.*
3 *… Italian as well **as** English.*
4 *… in a crisis. **Moreover**, I am creative.*
5 *… my outlook, **but** also enabled …*

2 Suggested answers

1 I not only speak Swedish, but am also fluent in Norwegian.
2 I can not only work under pressure, but I also enjoy challenges.
3 I hold not only a degree in languages, but also a diploma in translation.
4 I not only qualified as a nurse, but have also undertaken further training in midwifery.

Rule: *not only* and *also* go:

– before the nouns they are contrasting
– between the subject and a single-word verb
– after an auxiliary verb and the verb *be*
– (inversions can be used with *not only*, eg *Not only does she speak three languages, she is also learning sign language.*)

3 Suggested answers

1 I play golf. Moreover, I am a coach for the local boys' football team. (or, … moreover, …)

I not only play golf, but am also a coach for the local boys' football team.

2 In addition to being a good team player, I am a good listener.

I am both a good team player and a good listener.

3 I play the flute. In addition, I sing in the choir. (or, … the flute and, in addition, I …; or, In addition to playing the flute, I (also) sing in the choir.)

I not only play the flute, but (I) also sing in the choir.

Preparing to write (SB page 17)

Aim: to give students an opportunity to gather ideas for the writing task.

Tips:

- Allow students to brainstorm ideas in pairs or groups.
- Ask students to make notes here, but not to begin writing.
- Monitor as students are writing (exercise 1), to clarify and assist as necessary.
- Monitor as students are talking (exercise 2) and take note of any good and problematic topic-related language for later feedback.
- Encourage listeners to ask at least one question for each autobiographical fact given.

TEACH GLOBAL THINK LOCAL **Alternative procedure**

You could handle exercises 1 and 2 as a 'Guess who' activity. Ask students to complete the sentences so that they are true for themselves. They should avoid making their identity too obvious in their sentences as later their peers will have to guess who is being described. Put the anonymous sheets around the room for others to read and identify the author. If students have little job experience, you could do this as an 'idealised self' – someone that they hope to be in X years' time.

Writing (SB page 17)

Aim: to give practice in more extended writing tasks.

Tips:

- This section can be done as homework.
- Remind students to refer back to the model text.
- Suggest that they find/write an imaginary job description/advert too, to work from, if they like.
- Ask students to check their work carefully before they hand it in.
- Tell students that you will be assessing their writing using the following criteria: appropriate range of relevant vocabulary and phrases; clarity of organisation; range of grammar and syntax; appropriacy of formality and tone of the letter (confident but not arrogant or unrealistic); accuracy.

Study skills

Setting goals (SB page 17)

TEACH GLOBAL THINK LOCAL **Alternative procedure**

If students know each other fairly well, they can work in pairs. Ask each student to finish the two sentences **as if they were their partner**. Then they can show their ideas to their friend to see how close to the truth they were.

1 Ask students to work on their own. They should use at least five words to complete each sentence.

2 Invite students to share some of their reasons for learning English with the whole class. Put any useful phrases up on the board, eg *to help/advance my career prospects; to enable me to get into a university abroad*, etc.

3 Books closed. Write up the words *An advanced student is someone who (can) …* on the board. Elicit two or three possible ways to finish. Ask students to work in groups of three to think of at least five more descriptors. If they need help, put up prompts such as *pronunciation, reading, speaking, style, genres …*

Monitor and read what they have written, opening it out to the whole class if appropriate. Students then compare their sentences with those in the exercise. They rate themselves 1–3 for each statement.

4 In pairs, students discuss their positive areas and those they would like to improve. Their partner should listen to the problem areas and give at least two suggestions. You may need to model this, eg *I'm not very good at speaking confidently on some subjects in English.* Possible suggestions: *Try to research less familiar topics, to pick up useful vocabulary, before you need to use them; record yourself speaking on a given topic for two minutes, then play it back to see how it could be improved.* Elicit some problems and possible solutions.

5 Students complete the exercises on their own. Invite them to share their ideas in a whole-class feedback session.

UNIT 2 Light & Dark

Coursebook			
Unit 2	**Language**	**Texts**	**Communication skills**
Part 1 SB page 18	Pronunciation Chunking	Listening & Speaking Light in paintings Reading & Vocabulary *Cloths of Heaven* Real and metaphorical light	
Part 2 SB page 20	Grammar Future predictions	Vocabulary & Reading *The Solar Solution*	Speaking The Sun
Part 3 SB page 22	Vocabulary & Writing Sounds	Reading *Dialogue in the Dark* *An exhibition to* *discover the unseen*	Speaking Disabilities
Part 4 SB page 24	Extend your vocabulary Ways of describing fear Grammar Narrative tenses	Speaking & Listening *Through the Tunnel*	Speaking Difficult experiences
Function globally SB page 26	Agreeing and disagreeing Listening to people explaining their opinions Stating opinion		
Global voices SB page 27	Phobias *like* Describing frightening experiences		
Writing SB page 28	A story Writing skills: an email to a friend Linking ideas: time expressions		
Study skills SB page 29	Exploring collocations		

Additional resources	
eWorkbook	Interactive and printable grammar, vocabulary, listening and pronunciation practice Extra reading and writing practice Additional downloadable listening and video material
Teacher's Resource Disc	Communication activity worksheets to print and photocopy, review material, test, and video with worksheet
Go global Ideas for further research	**Light** Ask students to search on the internet for examples of poetry associated with the idea of light. Ask them to choose one they particularly like and explain why. **Dark** Ask students to find information online about support for people who are blind or partially sighted in their own countries. Ask them to report their findings.

Part 1

TEACH GLOBAL THINK LOCAL Lead-in

Write up these proverbs on the board and ask students to discuss what they understand by them and which they like:

Firelight will not let you read fine stories, but it's warm and you won't see the dust on the floor. ~Irish Proverb

Turn your face to the sun and the shadows fall behind you. ~Maori Proverb

Where there is sunshine the doctor starves. ~Flemish Proverb

Introduce the topic for the new unit: Light and Dark.

Listening and Speaking (SB page 18)

1 Students first look at the two works of art in silence and think for two minutes about the questions, before discussing them in pairs. (The answers are quite subjective. Later, students will hear an expert's view of the painting too.) If you can, research other pictures of Eliasson's light installation. Search online with the keywords: *Eliasson light installation sun.* Conduct a feedback session on some of the more interesting issues raised.

Suggested answers

1 Vermeer painting: the woman
  Eliasson installation: the yellow circle
2 Vermeer painting: foreground: table, jewellery box; background: painting (of *The Last Judgement*), curtain over window
  Eliasson installation: foreground: silhouette of person; background: walls
3 Woman is weighing her jewels on a balance; students' own answers
4 Vermeer painting: dim, faint, soft, warm
  Eliasson installation: bright, dazzling, deep, rich, warm
5 the sun / sunlight
6 Students' own answers.

Background note

Installation art is a genre which describes three-dimensional objects, usually of huge proportions. The works of art are positioned or 'installed' within a space so that they raise the viewer's awareness, inviting a response. Installations can either be temporary or permanent, in a gallery, museum or other setting; they are often site-specific, as both the work of art and the environment form part of the whole. In this way, installation art is intended to break down the division between art and life.

Olafur Eliasson is a professor at the Berlin University of Arts, where he has established the Institute for Spatial Experiments. His large installations use natural elements and he frequently collaborates with other experts such as architects, geometers, authors and engineers. The Weather Project was installed in 2003 in the Tate Modern Gallery, London, attracting over two million visitors.

2 **1.16** The listening is a description by an art expert, in which she talks about the use and effect of light in the Vermeer painting.

Let students read the two questions first, and reread the earlier questions referred to in question 1. Ask students to follow the recording with their finger poised over the picture! After listening and comparing answers in pairs, have a whole-class feedback session.

1 1 the woman's face and the balance
  2 window, mirror, table, pearls, balance, the woman's stomach
  3 The expert suggests the woman is contemplating her pregnancy against a backdrop of measuring her material wealth and the belief in a future divine judgement.
  4 dim, soft

1.16

Woman with a Balance is one of Vermeer's finest paintings. As in so many of his interiors, the mood of gentle serenity is created by light streaming into a dimly-lit room from an external source and highlighting the most important details. Here, in the top left-hand corner, you can see a soft pale light emanating from a high window where the shutters seem to be half-closed. As it passes through the orange curtain it creates a warm golden glow, contrasting with the deep shadows around it, producing a faint reflection in the mirror, and then bouncing off the grey wall opposite to fall onto the table. Then our eyes follow the light as it shimmers on the edge of the table and, on the pearls which each gleam like single drops of light and finally rest on the woman's fingers and the balance in her hand. Then it's as if Vermeer creates an invisible line that draws us up to the woman's face and then down again as she contemplates the balance. It's a timeless moment as we gaze with her at the balance in the very centre of the painting, which itself is held in the balances of light and shadow, of grey and gold, in the surrounding canvas. What is she thinking? What is the meaning of the balance in her hand? Perhaps the painting of *The Last Judgement* in the background, and her clearly pregnant stomach are there to provide clues.

3 Put students in AB pairs. Give them time to consider their work of art. Encourage them to try and answer questions 1–6 from exercise 1, page 18 (selecting question 4 or 5, as appropriate). Ensure that students do not show their work of art to their partners until you tell them to, as they need to picture it themselves first, in their own minds. (If possible, sit them back to back in their pairs.)

Pronunciation (SB page 19)

1 Write this sentence on the board. Elicit suggestions regarding the pausing and their reasons.

Woman with a balance // is one of Vermeer's finest paintings.

2 1.17 Students initially listen to the first part of the track simply to check their predictions. Then let them read the two questions before you replay this part of the recording. Elicit, then mark the intonation of the speaker's voice on the board, using a small arrow in a different colour. Also mark the stressed words.

Woman *with a* ***Balance //*** is one of **Vermeer's** **finest paintings**. ↘ ↘

3 In pairs, students predict where the pauses will be for the rest of the extract for audioscript 1.17. After listening to check, let them read the text once silently in their heads, before working in pairs.

 **1.17**

Answers

Woman with a Balance // is one of Vermeer's finest paintings. // As in so many of his interiors, // the mood of gentle serenity // is created by light streaming into a dimly-lit room // from an external source // and highlighting the most important details. // Here, // in the top left-hand corner, // you can see a soft pale light // emanating from a high window // where the shutters seem to be half-closed. // As it passes through the orange curtain // it creates a warm golden glow, // contrasting with the deep shadows around it, // producing a faint reflection in the mirror, // and then bouncing off the grey wall opposite // to fall onto the table.

TEACH GLOBAL THINK LOCAL

Homework extra

If students liked the two works of art, they could research at least six interesting pieces of information about one of the pieces, or about one of the artists. They should take notes, to report back next lesson.

Reading and Vocabulary (SB page 19)

1 Focus students on the image at the top of page 19. Ask them to think of verbs or adjectives to describe the light, eg *dazzling*, *streaming*, *dancing*, *exploding*. Refer them to the *Glossary*. Read the poem aloud, with feeling and clear phrasing, asking students to read along silently. Focus attention on the information about Yeats. Students work in pairs to answer the questions. Discuss the answers with the class. At the end, ask *So what are the cloths of heaven?* (clouds; starry night sky, etc). *How much do you think he loves this person?* (a lot).

Possible answers

1 a loved one – perhaps a lover, or a child
2 the heavens' embroidered cloths, ie the skies; his dreams
3 day and night; times such as dawn or dusk / twilight
4 The poet has offered something very precious and does not want to be hurt by having his gifts rejected or destroyed.

2 Do the first sentence together to clarify the task. Then students work independently on the exercise. They compare answers in pairs before whole-class feedback.

Real light: 5, 9
Metaphorical light: 1, 2, 3, 4, 6, 7, 8, 10

3 To facilitate the task, if necessary, point out that the parts of speech of the words in the box give a helpful clue towards finding the answers. Do the first one together and let students have a few moments working on their own. In pairs, students compare their answers.

1 help us understand better
2 understanding
3 approved
4 considering
6 signs that a situation is going to improve
7 emerged
8 informative; looked at later and in a calmer way
10 in a new way

TEACH GLOBAL THINK LOCAL

Extra activity

Many of these expressions with *light* are commonly used and useful for advanced students. If you have a monolingual group (or two or more students in your class who share the same mother tongue), then do a translation activity. Students sit in same first language pairs, then separately translate either sentences 1–5 or 6–10 from exercise 2 into their first language. After closing the books, they should pass their translations to their partner, who should translate them back into English. Then let them compare their versions with the original sentences. In a whole-class feedback session, find out if any of the *light* metaphors are similar in other languages.

4 In groups of three, students choose which topic they would like to discuss. Be prepared to motivate them with other topics, if necessary, eg politicians and their policies; a serious discussion you had with someone; somebody you used to trust, but now do not.

Part 2

TEACH GLOBAL THINK LOCAL Lead-in

In groups of three, give students two minutes to think of as many different light sources as they possibly can, including unusual sources, eg *fireflies*. Elicit some examples.

Speaking (SB page 20)

1 Students work in pairs. Write up some extra ideas, eg *What's your favourite type of summer holiday? Do you know anyone with SAD (seasonal affective disorder)? What are the dangers and benefits of sunbathing?* Skip feedback unless there is something of particular interest.

2 In the same pairs, students each read a different text and write at least three quiz-style questions. Monitor and assist while they are writing the questions.

Students first ask their questions to see if their partner knows any of the answers before reading. Then they swap texts, listen again to the questions orally and try to locate the answers as quickly as possible.

Vocabulary and Reading (SB page 20)

1 Write *solar* ______; *nuclear* ______; ______ *energy* and ______ *emissions* on the board. In pairs, students write possible collocations, before completing exercise 1. Elicit answers and check vocabulary.

Incorrect alternatives

1 fuel 2 warming 3 fossil 4 solar

2 In pairs, students should actively try to use at least one of the collocations from exercise 1 per visual on page 21.

3 This reading discusses the power of the sun and its (potentially) positive impact on the environment and on communities all over the world.

TEACH GLOBAL THINK LOCAL Reading extra

Your students may benefit from a gist task (before exercise 3). If so, ask them to read the text and write appropriate paragraph headings. Discuss the best ones.

Students initially work alone on exercise 3 without dictionaries, except at the end, to check. In pairs, let them discuss their answers. Check as a class only if necessary.

1 a Nights are long and activities are difficult without lighting. There is more sunlight in these latitudes.
b Candles are dim; kerosene is expensive, toxic and dangerous.
c Their lower consumption means panels are relatively inexpensive to produce and install.
d It enables them to work, communicate and do business more easily.
e It reduces our dependence on fossil fuels and may help stop climate change.

2 *at hand* – now available
a huge outlay – a lot of money spent at the start
the benefits of civilisation – technological advances
a staggering fact – a very surprising fact
dwindling resources – non-renewable energy resources that are slowly running out
the impending catastrophe – a huge disaster that could happen very soon

3 affluent – wealthy
inexhaustible – limitless
curtail – halt
generate – produce
dwelling – home

4 In groups of three, students discuss these points about solar power. You could show visuals by doing an internet image search.

TEACH GLOBAL THINK LOCAL Homework extra

If students live in a country where solar panels are popular, let them do some internet research. They should locate a solar panel company and find information about the installation, costs, savings, nature of the panels, etc to share next lesson.

Grammar (SB page 21)

1 Elicit some suggestions for the first gapped prediction, then let students complete the task. Then students discuss grammar questions 1 and 2 in pairs. In question 2, be ready to clarify *may well*. (Whilst *may* talks about possibility, *may well* is used to talk about something which the speaker deems more likely to happen, ie a probability.)

a could b may c might
1 possible
2 may well (more probable), will (more of a certainty)

2 Students will have encountered these verb forms before, so they can answer in pairs. Assist with concept questions and form, if necessary.

1 a is stating what will definitely happen in the year 2030
b is stating what will happen some time before 2030, so that in 2030 they will already be finished
2 a is an action that will happen once this time next year
b is a regular repeated activity that will be happening at this time next year

Language note

The future perfect is used to emphasise the **completion** of an action **before** a specified point in the future, embodying an idea of looking backwards from that point. Future time adverbials are often found with this form, eg *by, in* (X amount of time), eg *In six months' time, they'll have moved abroad.* Ask *By when? Will the action be in progress or complete?* (complete). The future continuous refers to something in progress at a specific time in the future, eg *This time next week, I'll be sitting my first exam.* Ask *Is it a specific time? When? Will it be finished or in progress?* This form can also be used to refer to events due to take place, so that other events can occur, eg *I'll be driving your way home later (so I can give you a lift).*

3 Monitor and assist as students, in pairs, discuss the options. Elicit answers and write up a clear record on the board.

Students' own answers.

1 *will* before the adverb, *won't* after the adverb

2 *in the near future*, *in the coming decades*, *in my lifetime*

4 Students read the examples and suggest other possible options for the same prediction. Allow enough time for students to express their own opinions in writing.

5 Put students into groups in which they are likely to have differing opinions, if possible. Inform them that they have at least five minutes for this activity: explain that they need to respond to and question each other. Monitor and then invite groups to comment on the most pessimistic and optimistic group member.

TEACH GLOBAL THINK LOCAL Extra activity

If your students need more specific practice of these future tenses then dictate these ideas: *food supplies; planes; cars; rich and poor; fish stocks; rubbish; BRIC countries (Brazil, Russia, India, China); me / my job.*

Write *Ten years from now* on the board. In pairs, students write 1–2 predictions for each topic. Monitor and assist as they work. Elicit some good examples. If appropriate, get them to transform their sentences, and to use some of the alternative phrases from exercise 3, page 21, eg *In 10 years' time, we'll be recycling about 70% of our rubbish.* ➛ *In 10 years' time, 70% of rubbish may well be/is bound to be recycled.*

G Grammar focus

Refer students to the language summary on future predictions on page 134.

You can use exercises 1–3 on page 135 for:
a) extra practice now, b) homework or c) review later on.

The answers are on page 162 of this Teacher's Book.

Part 3

TEACH GLOBAL THINK LOCAL Lead-in

If appropriate for your group, bring in a blindfold and without explaining why, ask students to take it in turns to be lead around the room. You could place some 'safe', unexpected obstacles and noises around, eg a cushion, tin foil on the floor or small pebbles, a paper plane flying past, a feather floating, a fan blowing, etc.

Reading (SB page 22)

1 Let students read the sentence quietly and after a pause, invite suggestions as to the meaning and significance, with example situations.

2 Ask *Have you ever heard of* Dialogue in the Dark*? Can you predict what it is about?* If necessary, point out the image of Braille on the left to help them. Read the two questions in the rubric, then give students time to read and find out. Focus particularly on the aims of the exhibition. After feedback, fire random additional comprehension questions orally to students to check understanding, eg *Where is the exhibition? Whose idea was it? Why does it aim to evoke very powerful emotions? Is the experience popular? What's special about the people it employs?*

aims of exhibition:

- to give sighted people an insight into the experience of being blind and of otherness
- to provoke a change in perspective
- to evoke in the visitors extraordinary and powerful emotions that are mentally challenging
- to effect a profound change in the quality of their human interactions

By physically experiencing or encountering situations that are new for them, visitors learn.

3 This reading is a detailed account of a sighted person's experience of when they visited an exhibition centre designed to raise awareness of being blind.

Give students about four minutes to read *An exhibition to discover the unseen* and to answer the two questions. In feedback, elicit their immediate personal reactions.

touch, smell, hearing

Students' own answers.

4 This vocabulary extension exercise might enable students to comprehend more details in the text prior to exercise 5. In pairs, encourage students to use the context rather than resorting immediately to a dictionary. At the feedback stage, further check understanding by asking for examples or by using concept check questions, eg *What sort of memento might you have from this course? When or why might you stumble?* Write useful words clearly on the board, eg *devoid of sth*, noting and drilling pronunciation too, if appropriate, eg /dɪˈvɔɪd/.

1 memento	5 devoid of
2 immersed	6 piece together
3 stumbling	7 ganging up
4 discrete	8 fumble

5 Although the task appears short, students are likely to need a few minutes to do it properly. Elicit supporting words, phrases or sentences for the first emotion as an example, then students work in pairs. Discuss the answers in a whole-class feedback session.

confusion (*disorientation does not begin to describe this unique experience; … did not make sense at first …; as my brain struggled; … I could have sworn that the sound of water clattering onto marble stones came from my left. I was dead wrong.*)

fear (*… left me feeling insecure and apprehensive.*)

interest (*… wholehearted fascination*)

sickness (*… feelings of dizziness, light nausea …*)

surprise (*what personally surprised me the most was the smell illusions*)

6 Tell students that all the sentences are true; they just need to look for 'evidence'. They should work alone, then check in pairs. Ask students if they need whole-class feedback on this – it might not be necessary.

1 *docked at the Amsterdam harbour*
2 *It was as if my senses were ganging up to compensate for the one I had left behind, …*
3 *Another strange sensation was how often I was mistaken in locating the direction sounds were coming from.*
4 *… the smell illusions I was having while immersed in this world of darkness.*
5 *… our guide thankfully brought us to a bar (pitch black, of course), where we had to fumble for our wallets and the right coins to pay for our drinks, …*

7 Ask students *Would you like to experience the exhibition which the writer described?* Encourage them to explain their reactions. Put them in pairs or groups of three to discuss the two other questions. Invite some students to share their ideas with the whole class.

TEACH GLOBAL THINK LOCAL

Alternative procedure

For exercise 7, question 1, you could ask students to actually imagine that they were the writer, having just experienced this startling exhibition.

Give each student a piece of paper and ask them to write their Braille message, using no more than three sentences. They could do this anonymously. Collect in the messages and read (some of) them out to the class.

Vocabulary and Writing (SB page 22)

1 Speculate as a whole class on possible missing words, without referring to the text. Then students read to check.

1 whooshing by	4 barking
2 chirping	5 honking
3 ringing	6 clattering

2 Students might enjoy making the sounds themselves. Put them into groups of three to work. Then check answers together.

3 **1.18** Go straight into this exercise. Replay the recording if students request it. Students work in pairs to decide which are onomatopoeic in English. When checking answers, drill the infinitives of these words, eg *pop, rumble*, using your voice to highlight the onomatopoeic quality – this will aid memorisation. For interest, elicit the equivalents are in the students' first languages, to see if they are onomatopoeic too.

1 a balloon popping	6 a mouse squeaking
2 a lorry rumbling	7 a radio crackling
3 a bee buzzing	8 a car alarm going off
4 a gate creaking	9 a camera clicking
5 a door banging	

4 In pairs, students work on this activity. Do the first example together.

Suggested answers

a fire: popping, crackling
a floorboard: creaking, squeaking
a hammer: banging
an alarm clock: going off
a pen: squeaking, clicking
conversation: rumbling, buzzing
new shoes: creaking
thunder: rumbling

5 Ask students to write a paragraph describing the sounds in their chosen situation. Draw attention to the *Useful phrases* and the *Language note*. Provide further examples and questions to clarify the latter, if necessary, eg *I saw the man cross the road; I saw the man crossing the road.* Highlight the difference in meaning here, and the link between the *-ing* form and the continuous aspect – both carry an idea of repetition and/or of an action in progress.

Give an example of your own first, to both model and motivate, eg *The car door closed with a bang; A police siren was wailing in the distance and I heard the neighbours chattering*, etc. Have them share their paragraphs with at least two other students. Monitor and invite some students to share their work with the whole class.

TEACH GLOBAL THINK LOCAL
Extra activity

If students are engaged in this topic and language and enjoy creative writing, ask them to write a poem called *Soundscape*, either in class or as (optional) homework. Provide this optional opening, which some may find useful:

I left the house,

The door clicked heavily behind me.

My feet crunched on the chalky stones as I walked down the drive.

Speaking (SB page 23)

If appropriate, ask students *Do you know anyone with any of the disabilities mentioned? What difficulties do they encounter? How does it affect their lives?* In groups of three, students discuss the different points. Monitor and pick up on any points of interest, either content or language-related, for later feedback.

TEACH GLOBAL THINK LOCAL
Extra activity

If students enjoyed the discussion in *Speaking*, and were able to empathise with some of the difficulties people with disabilities might encounter, ask them to write a (fictitious) letter to the head of their learning institution. They could brainstorm some ideas together in class. In the letter they should highlight any problems (or strengths) the centre has in relation to catering for disabled students. The letter might also include possible solutions or requests.

Part 4

TEACH GLOBAL THINK LOCAL
Lead-in

Tell students to listen to three descriptions of places and write down where they think it is, in silence.

1 *This place needs to be lit; it's always cool. It was commonly found in larger houses, especially wealthier ones. It was often used to store certain things, usually below ground.* (a cellar)

2 *This can also be lit. It can be long, it can be short, it can be wide, it can be narrow. You can use it when travelling, or when searching for something such as coal. You can sometimes see light at the end of it.* (a tunnel)

3 *It's naturally dark, as well as cool and damp or wet. Some people go there for sport. It's the home of certain animals. It's been used by people for millennia.* (a cave)

Let students compare answers in groups of three, before checking. Elicit what they all have in common: *darkness*.

Speaking and Listening (SB page 24)

1 Let students think for two minutes about one of the places, using the questions as prompts, before sharing their description with their partner. Listen to any exciting or unusual stories or descriptions as a whole class.

2 This listening is an extract from a short story by Doris Lessing on a boy's frightening but fulfilling sea adventure.

Write the title of the short story and the author on the board to focus students. In pairs, after reading the synopsis and looking at the picture, students should try to anticipate events. Invite them to comment on the nature of many of the words in the box (they are very physical, even violent; many relate to the senses of hearing, sight and touch/feeling).

Jerry is practising to dive through an underground tunnel.

Students' own answers.

3 **1.19–1.21** This is an exciting, but lengthy listening, which has been recorded onto three tracks should you wish to break the activity up. Let students read the three questions and take brief notes on them if they wish to, before closing their books. Ensure that students are focused at the start, so that they engage immediately with the listening. The story is a powerful and evocative one: some students may simply prefer to listen rather than responding in writing to the questions.

TEACH GLOBAL THINK LOCAL
Mixed ability

Particularly for less confident listeners, be prepared to use the natural breaks in the recording to allow pairs to discuss what they have heard so far. If necessary, break up the listening at the end of each track, asking questions to check they are following the gist. This is particularly important if you have less strong listeners in your group.

1 fear, horror, dizziness, panic
2 rock, roof of cave, his own fear, hard to breathe, long tunnel, lapses into unconsciousness, pain in head
3 he succeeded, but it made him afraid and tired

 1.19–1.21

Through the Tunnel

1.19

In another four days, his mother said casually one morning, they must go home. On the day before they left, he would do it. He would do it if it killed him, he said defiantly to himself. But two days before they were to leave – a day of triumph when he increased his count by fifteen – his nose bled so badly that he turned dizzy and had to lie limply over the big rock like a bit of seaweed, watching the thick red blood flow on to the rock and trickle slowly down to the sea. He was frightened. Supposing he turned dizzy in the tunnel? Supposing he died there, trapped? Supposing — his head went around, in the hot sun, and he almost gave up. He thought he would return to the house and lie down, and next summer, perhaps, when he had another year's growth in him – then he would go through the hole.

But even after he had made the decision, or thought he had, he found himself sitting up on the rock and looking down into the water, and he knew that now, this moment when his nose had only just stopped bleeding, when his head was still sore and throbbing — this was the moment when he would try. If he did not do it now, he never would. He was trembling with fear that he would not go, and he was trembling with horror at that long, long tunnel under the rock, under the sea. Even in the open sunlight, the barrier rock seemed very wide and very heavy; tons of rock pressed down on where he would go. If he died there, he would lie until one day — perhaps not before next year — those big boys would swim into it and find it blocked.

He put on his goggles, fitted them tight, tested the vacuum. His hands were shaking. Then he chose the biggest stone he could carry and slipped over the edge of the rock until half of him was in the cool, enclosing water and half in the hot sun. He looked up once at the empty sky, filled his lungs once, twice, and then sank fast to the bottom with the stone. He let it go and began to count. He took the edges of the hole in his hands and drew himself into it, wriggling his shoulders in sidewise as he remembered he must, kicking himself along with his feet.

1.20

Soon he was clear inside. He was in a small rock-bound hole filled with yellowish-grey water. The water was pushing him up against the roof. The roof was sharp and pained his back. He pulled himself along with his hands — fast, fast — and used his legs as levers. His head knocked against something; a sharp pain dizzied him. Fifty, fifty-one, fifty-two … He was without light, and the water seemed to press upon him with the weight of rock.

Seventy-one, seventy-two … There was no strain on his lungs. He felt like an inflated balloon, his lungs were so light and easy, but his head was pulsing.

He was being continually pressed against the sharp roof, which felt slimy as well as sharp. Again he thought of octopuses, and wondered if the tunnel might be filled with weed that could tangle him. He gave himself a panicky, convulsive kick forward, ducked his head, and swam. His feet and hands moved freely, as if in open water. The hole must have widened out. He thought he must be swimming fast, and he was frightened of banging his head if the tunnel narrowed.

A hundred, a hundred and one … The water paled. Victory filled him. His lungs were beginning to hurt. A few more strokes and he would be out. He was counting wildly; he said a hundred and fifteen, and then, a long time later, a hundred and fifteen again. The water was a clear jewel-green all around him. Then he saw, above his head, a crack running up through the rock. Sunlight was falling through it, showing the clean dark rock of the tunnel, a single mussel shell, and darkness ahead.

He was at the end of what he could do. He looked up at the crack as if it were filled with air and not water, as if he could put his mouth to it to draw in air. A hundred and fifteen, he heard himself say inside his head — but he had said that long ago. He must go on into the blackness ahead, or he would drown. His head was swelling, his lungs cracking. A hundred and fifteen, a hundred and fifteen pounded through his head, and he feebly clutched at rocks in the dark, pulling himself forward, leaving the brief space of sunlit water behind. He felt he was dying. He was no longer quite conscious. He struggled on in the darkness between lapses into unconsciousness. An immense, swelling pain filled his head, and then the darkness cracked with an explosion of green light. His hands, groping forward, met nothing, and his feet, kicking back, propelled him out into the open sea.

He drifted to the surface, his face turned up to the air. He was gasping like a fish. He felt he would sink now and drown; he could not swim the few feet back to the rock. Then he was clutching it and pulling himself up on it. He lay face down, gasping. He could see nothing but a red-veined, clotted dark. His eyes must have burst, he thought; they were full of blood. He tore off his goggles and a gout of blood went into the sea. His nose was bleeding, and the blood had filled the goggles.

He scooped up handfuls of water from the cool, salty sea, to splash on his face, and did not know whether it was blood or salt water he tasted. After a time, his heart quieted, his eyes cleared, and he sat up. He could see the local boys diving and playing half a mile away. He did not want them. He wanted nothing but to get back home and lie down.

1.21

In a short while, Jerry swam to shore and climbed slowly up the path to the villa. He flung himself on his bed and slept, waking at the sound of feet on the path outside. His mother was coming back. He rushed to the bathroom, thinking she must not see his face with bloodstains, or tearstains, on it. He came out of the bathroom and met her as she walked into the villa, smiling, her eyes lighting up. 'Have a nice morning?' she asked, laying her head on his warm brown shoulder a moment.

'Oh, yes, thank you,' he said.

'You look a bit pale.' And then, sharp and anxious. 'How did you bang your head?'

'Oh, just banged it,' he told her.

She looked at him closely. He was strained. His eyes were glazed-looking. She was worried. And then she said to herself, 'Oh, don't fuss! Nothing can happen. He can swim like a fish.'

They sat down to lunch together.

'Mummy,' he said, 'I can stay under water for two minutes — three minutes, at least.'

It came bursting out of him.

'Can you, darling?' she said. 'Well, I shouldn't overdo it. I don't think you ought to swim any more today.'

She was ready for a battle of wills, but he gave in at once. It was no longer of the least importance to go to the bay.

4 Students discuss their responses in pairs. Monitor and ask *What did you think of the story? Did you like how the events were described?*

5 If students seem very animated by the story, let them continue to work in pairs to maintain the energy. Write the answers up on the board so students can self-check. You could ask students to justify their answers.

before: 3, 4; during: 2, 6, 7; after: 1, 5

6 Let students refer to the audioscript on pages 154–5 to see this last line in context. They then discuss what it might mean. Elicit ideas from the class.

Suggested answers

He didn't need to prove anything anymore, he had succeeded and overcome his fear of the tunnel. The tunnel probably represents initiation (via difficult feat) into adulthood, separation from the mother, entering the world of the older boys.

Extend your vocabulary (SB page 24)

Write the word *afraid* on the board and ask students to work in groups of three to brainstorm synonyms before they do the task. At the end, check answers and also understanding of words which might be less familiar.

moderate fear: a, b, d, e   extreme fear: c, f

Grammar (SB page 25)

1 In pairs, students take turns to read out the sentences in exercise 5, page 24. Then they complete this tense-identification exercise on their own, before discussing and explaining their answers in pairs. Check answers.

1 had made
2 had been staying
3 had been going
4 were shaking, were beginning
5 put on, fitted, tested
6 would be able to go, were leaving, would shortly be going

Language note

For advanced students, this should be an opportunity to review these tenses with the possible exception of 'future in the past' which may be new to them.

The 'future in the past' refers back to events which were future at the time in the eyes of the speaker, events which had not yet happened. In English, changing the future to past avoids a potentially confusing mix of past and future forms, eg *when we last saw each other in May, you **were** going on holiday soon after* NOT *when we last saw each other in May, ~~you are going on holiday soon after.~~*

Remind students that you use the past perfect (both continuous and simple) to emphasise that something happened **before** another event. In addition to this concept, the past perfect continuous also suggests that an action is temporary, in progress (before it was interrupted) or repeated – all common characteristics of the continuous aspect – here the action is temporary and interrupted: *I'd been quietly humming to myself, when lightning struck.*

2 Students work independently to find other examples, before pooling their ideas in pairs.

finished action: drifted, felt, struggled, filled, cracked ('turned' and 'died' are not strictly finished actions in this context. They are hypothetical.)

repeated action: could see … diving and playing

continuous unfinished past action / state: was gasping, was being continually pressed, was swelling, cracking

future (in the past) action: would go, would drown

3 Students work alone again. Monitor carefully, so that you can establish where any gaps in their knowledge lie. Students should then compare and justify their answers in pairs.

1	was sitting	12	looked
2	had been renting	13	had left
3	was thinking	14	hoped
4	would soon be	15	would not do
5	(was) worrying	16	was starting / would be starting
6	had been behaving	17	did not want
7	reflected	18	was (on the verge of) going down / was about to go down / was going to go down
8	had suddenly become	19	caught
9	had changed		
10	got up		
11	walked		

4 Elicit idieas and discuss possible ways to begin the description. Remind students to start the story with a contextualising sentence, describing the background to the main event. For less imaginative students, start them off, eg *It had been hot and sunny for three weeks. Every day we'd been going down to the beach, without fail. Then one day, a foreign boy appeared out of the blue …*

G Grammar focus

Refer students to the language summary on narrative tenses on page 134.

You can use exercises 4–5 on page 135 for:
a) extra practice now, b) homework or c) review later on.

The answers are on page 162 of this Teacher's Book.

Speaking (SB page 25)

1 Be prepared to suggest situations, if necessary, eg a new job, an accident, etc. Tell them they have four minutes to prepare their story, using the guiding questions. Monitor and assist at this stage.

2 In pairs, students should listen to their partner's story and ask questions. The storytellers make a (mental) note of the questions, for the next stage.

3 In different pairs, students retell their stories, including any additional information their original partner asked about. Monitor and note any good or problematic uses of the narrative tenses for later feedback.

TEACH GLOBAL THINK LOCAL Homework extra

Ask students to write down their personal stories. If they enjoy linguistic analysis, ask them to write the story on computer using a range of tenses, and to use the *Comment* function to explain why they have used a certain form. This will enable you to identify any difficulties. Alternatively, they could write their stories on paper adding notes in the margin.

Function globally: agreeing and disagreeing

These lessons in *Global* are designed to provide students with immediately useful functional language. They all follow a similar format.

Warm up (SB page 26)

Aim: to introduce the topic via a quick speaking task or picture work.

Tips:

- Do not over-correct here, especially in speaking activities.
- Encourage students to use as much variety of language as they can.
- Pick up on any points which students seem to find interesting / controversial to raise as an issue for the whole class.

Listening (SB page 26)

Aim: to present the functional language in context via a conversation or series of conversations.

Tips:

- Play the recording all the way through for each task (there are always two tasks). (Tracks 1.22–1.24)
- Pause the recording after each conversation.
- Briefly elicit students' reactions to the three conversations (there is opportunity to discuss further in *Speaking*).
- Encourage students to read the audioscripts for homework, exploiting them for useful language.

1

Conversation 1: 4
Conversation 2: 6
Conversation 3: 5, 6

2

Conversation 1

1 A and B like it, C dislikes it.
2 original (*it's rather special; it shows the artists' state of mind, it's the chaos; anybody could have done it, but only one person did*)
3 unattractive (*it looks like my room when I haven't cleaned it for four weeks; it's just a mess*); unoriginal (*these modern exhibits … that anybody could have done and then they just put a huge price tag on it to pretend like it's a piece of art*)
4 *You know, I'm wondering the same thing, why didn't you stay at home?; Oh, come on …*

Conversation 2

1 to push the limits, to progress, to do research, to advance medicine

2 it's in our nature to create art

3 scientists, to encourage young people to work towards scientific research; artists, in order not to dissuade them from creating

Conversation 3

1 arts

2 arts subjects can be studied later in life in your own time; she could have studied something more valuable that would have got her a better job with more money

3 to create a fully rounded human being

1.22–1.24

1

A: What do you think of it then?

B: I really like it. This is why I came.

A: Yeah.

B: To see this.

A: I think it's fantastic.

B: Yeah, me too.

C: Seriously? You came to see this exhibit?

B: Yes.

A: Something like this, you know, this is really rather special.

C: It looks like my room when I haven't cleaned it for four weeks.

B: Precisely.

A: That's the point.

B: It's about …

C: If I had wanted to see that I would have stayed at home. Why would I pay money to come see this?

A: You know, I'm wondering the same thing, why didn't you stay at home?

C: Oh ho …

B: It's the fact that it shows the artist's state of mind, it's the chaos.

C: Oh it's these modern things, these modern exhibits which are … they're … anybody could have done and then they just put a huge price tag on it to pretend like it's a piece of art. This isn't art …

A: Well, the thing is …

B: … it's just a mess.

A: … anybody could have done it, but only one person did and that's what's important.

B: Absolutely. It is about somebody's idea, the originality of the piece.

C: You see, I couldn't disagree with you more. Just because something is original doesn't mean it's necessarily good.

A: Oh come on …

C: Oh come on yourself. Just because somebody went and painted a giant red line on the side of a building, nobody else may have done that, that doesn't make it art.

A: You are denying all art since the 1920s.

C: No, I'm not denying all art, but …

2

A: And, of course, there's so much choice with university courses, aren't there?

B: Yes, absolutely.

C: Yes, perhaps too much.

A: Yes, perhaps.

C: And what we really lack is people who are studying the sciences.

B: Yes, that's right, yeah.

A: Proper science is about kind of pushing the limits forward, isn't it? Whereas …

C: Yes and research …

A: … fine art could be seen as …

C: … you know that's what we need …

A: … enhancing, enriching life yeah, maybe.

C: … we need, yes.

D: Yes, but if we thought like that then in the next 20 years we're going to need to have artists, you know, if we're sort of …

B: Yeah.

D: … moving …

B: Absolutely.

E: I think a healthy balance is required.

A: But do you really think we need artists? I mean, we need scientists to help advance medicine …

C: Yes, we really do …

E: I see what you mean.

A: Do we need artists?

B: Well, we could survive without them probably, but …

C: There always will be artists.

B: Always will be, yes. It's in our nature to create art.

C: But we should be encouraging the youth of today …

B: Absolutely.

C: … to, to work towards science and research, progress.

D: I'm sorry, I'm sorry …

E: We shouldn't be dissuading them from creating.

D: I have mixed views about that because I think that, you know, we should be nurturing artists and there should be a lot more funding for them.

B: Nurturing artists and funding scientists.
C: Yes, I see what you mean.
E: And funding artists.
B: Yeah.
E: But, you know, art can't survive unfunded.
B: No.
D: Well, look at all the cuts they're making in the arts at the moment.
B: Exactly.
E: It's cutthroat.
A: Perhaps there needs to be a fine balance.
E: Yes.
D: That's certainly true.

3

A: I feel quite strongly about it. I don't think that people should study art subjects at university.
B: Really …
A: Yeah.
B: … even though you did?
A: Yeah, I think it's a waste of time quite frankly.
B: Really.
A: Yeah, I did it …
B: So you wish you'd done science?
A: Um, well, I wish I'd done something slightly more scientific … um … than what I did do. I just think that you … there's nothing that you can study on an arts subject that you can't do in your own spare time later.
B: Yes, but isn't that the problem we have? We just think that everything to do with the arts is just a leisure activity and the only thing that counts is science, you know, hard facts.
A: But, Leonie, don't you think that's true, it is a leisure activity really?
B: It's not that scientists need to read books or, you know, read literature, it's just that the humanities make you into a fully rounded human being …
A: So three years at university reading novels, that does that, do you think so because to be honest when I was at university I wasted a lot of time, I wasted a lot of time, I could have been learning something valuable …
B: I agree …
A: … that could have got me a better job, I could have made more money, I could have contributed to society.
B: Ah, but you see that's the two things, making money and contributing to society. You can contribute to society without being completely focused on making money or getting a good job straight away.
A: But it would be nice to have some money, don't you think?

Language focus (SB page 26)

Aim: to draw students' attention to the items of functional language.

Tips:

- Students work alone at first, before comparing answers in pairs.
- Students should be able to pronounce these phrases intelligibly so drill them, if necessary.
- Encourage students to highlight or make a separate note of new expressions which they would like to integrate into their speech.

1

1 h 2 g 3 b 4 a 5 d 6 e 7 f 8 c

2

1 5d; 6e 2 3b; 7f 3 2g; 4a 4 1h; 8c

3

Strong agreement:	1, 3, 7, 10
Agreement:	4, 6, 8, 12
Disagreement:	5, 11
Strong disagreement:	2, 9

Pronunciation (SB page 26)

Aim: to focus students on a particular aspect of pronunciation of the target phrases.

Tips:

- Play the recording two or three times, if necessary. (Track 1.25)
- At this level, try to promote good all-round pronunciation including stress, intonation and linking. This also raises the challenge for students.
- Use students with exemplary pronunciation to act as models to help others in the class.

1

rise fall rise across the words in italics; expresses ambivalence

Speaking (SB page 26)

Aim: to allow students an opportunity to use this language in a meaningful, real-world context.

Tips:

- Give students time to prepare this activity. Circulate and monitor carefully whilst they are talking.
- Add one or two additional related topics which you think will be of relevance to your learners, if possible, eg access to higher education for the rich vs poor students; compulsory subjects for study at school, etc.

- Correct sensitively, paying attention to the target language especially. With stronger students you could also focus on the pronunciation aspects they have just learnt.
- If time allows, ask students to repeat the task, but with a new partner.

Global voices

These lessons in *Global* are designed to provide students with exposure to authentic speakers of English from both native and non-native English backgrounds. They all follow a similar format.

Warm up (SB page 27)

Aim: to introduce the topic and highlight potentially difficult vocabulary the students will encounter.

Tips:

- Be generous in helping students with the vocabulary here, but let them try and work it out first.
- Circulate and monitor any speaking task, but be careful not to over-correct.
- Elicit how to pronounce the different phobias and then drill them.

1

1 acrophobia – fear of heights
2 hydrophobia – fear of water
3 bibliophobia – fear of books
4 claustrophobia – fear of small spaces
5 arachnophobia – fear of spiders
6 agrophobia – fear of public spaces
7 xenophobia – fear of people from other countries

2

Students' own answers.

Listening (SB page 27)

Aim: to expose students to English spoken with a variety of accents.

Tips:

- Students will need to hear the recording at least twice, if not more times, to understand it. (Tracks 1.26–1.27)
- The first time they listen, tell them you don't expect them to understand every word; some of it will be hard. This is because the text has not been scripted or graded in any way. It's what they would hear in 'the real world'.
- The first task is easier and focuses on gist, the second task is more detailed.
- Students can read the audioscript at the back of the book if you / they wish.
- It may be tempting to hunt for specific pronunciation or language errors, but we recommend against this. In real-world communication not everyone speaks perfect English all the time, not even native speakers.
- Encourage students to give their own opinions after exercise 2. Ask *Do you agree with the speakers' views?*

1

1 what they can see
2 putting the lights off when watching a scary film
3 Caroline; Giacomo doesn't like them

2

you can't see — sight is so important
you imagine things — you don't know what is happening

 **1.26**

A = Giacomo; **B** = Caroline

Giacomo (Italy), Caroline (France)

A: Why do you think so many people are afraid of the dark?

B: Well, I think that's mainly because they can't see anything, so their other senses are kind of aroused and I think that imagination can arouse from, can be aroused from only the hearing because it leaves you the door to, like, imagine much more things so I think that's the main reason why. But what do you think?

A: Yes, I think these kind of things like mainly caused by imagination, yes, because when you are in the dark you really can't see and the sight is mainly the, for most of the people the most important sense that you have and so you always, like, base your …

B: Sure.

A: … behaviour and everything like your decisions on what you see. When you are in the dark you can't really see what's happening and you don't know what can happen.

B: But don't you think that sometimes people are kind of attracted by the darkness? For example, when you watch a scary movie the tendency of most people is, like, to, to switch off the lights, don't you think? Don't you do that? When you're …

A: Yes, yes, it's true because you want to be more scared. Actually, I don't really like, personally, scary movies. Do you?

B: OK. Oh yeah, in fact when I was younger I was really after this kind of movies.

A: Really?

B: Yeah, and so I can remember that I had seen like all the horror movies from my video club.

3

a muffled sound — hear scratches
laughing out loud — distinguish a shape

1.27

B: And so I was in my room with my sister, actually in my room with my sister at the time, and so at some point I saw like the door opening, but I couldn't distinguish, like, what shape it was, it's a human one, and, and so we began to hear, like, kind of scratches against the desk …

A: Really, scratches?

B: Yes, scratches and some, like, muffled sound and we couldn't, like, really say what it was. And so my sister, like, woke in panic so she …

A: Was she screaming? Was she shouting?

B: No, no, she wasn't, but she was, like, 'Caroline stop!' because she, she …

A: She thought it was you.

B: She thought it was me and I was, like, 'Oh no, I'm not doing anything!' so basically we also began to argue about this. And so she began to, like, run at the door and she hit, like, really violently and just, like, fell on the floor. And yeah just my father like got out of the desk and he was laughing like out loud. It was really crazy and then she was pretty mad at him for one week. Yep.

A: Nice for your father, I mean, so all your fear of the dark is because of your father and that night he came into your room.

B: Yes, I think so.

A: Good.

Language focus: *like* (SB page 27)

Aim: to raise students' awareness of a particular piece of language present in the listening.

Tip:

- The objective of these exercises is awareness-raising, not production. Don't expect students to produce this language in an exercise or in conversation immediately.

1

sentence 3

2

Students' own answers.

Speaking (SB page 27)

Aim: for students to discuss the same or similar questions as the speakers in the listening.

Tips:

- The speaking tasks here are slightly more open to allow for students to explore the subject. Give them time to do this.
- Monitor as they are talking and note down good or problematic use of language. You can use this in feedback (oral or written) later on.
- As you go through the book and the *Global voices* lessons, ask students for feedback on these listening activities and their potential use of English with other people. Ask *Are they very difficult? Have you used English as a 'lingua franca' with other non-native English speakers? How did you find it? What tips do you have on understanding or making yourselves understood in an international context?*

Writing: a story

These lessons in *Global* are designed to provide students with extended writing practice. They all follow a similar format.

Reading (SB page 28)

Aim: to provide a sample text for students to analyse.

Tips:

- The first exercise is a gist reading task.
- Retelling the experience (exercise 2) not only gives oral fluency practice, it also demonstrates how much they have understood of the text. Make sure you monitor carefully.
- For exercise 3, put the appropriate paragraph numbers for each item on the board, eg *walking*: *paragraph 2* (1–6 = par. 2; 7–11 = par. 3; 12 = par. 4).
- Let students check their answers in pairs before whole-class feedback.
- Put any new lexis up on the board, eg *dangle* (v). Try to elicit other examples of the word/phrase in context.

TEACH GLOBAL THINK LOCAL **Pre-reading activity**

Put these sentences up on the board: *I had a really frightening experience as I was leaving work recently. I'd just finished my shift and I was making my way to my car. It was pitch black and rather foggy …* Ask students to do some speed-writing. Give them six minutes to continue the story. When they have finished, let them swap their stories. Invite a couple of students to share their stories with the whole class.

1

1 close: friends or family members (*can't wait to hear all your news; lots of love*)

2 a scary and embarrassing one; she thought she was being chased by a potential attacker and took refuge in a pub, but in fact the man was running after her with her car keys which she had dropped.

2

Students' own answers.

3

1	making my way	7	slipped inside
2	fumbled	8	heaving a sigh (of relief)
3	grabbed	9	stepped in
4	glanced	10	came up to
5	running for my life	11	dangling
6	yelling	12	can't wait

Writing skills: an email to a friend (SB page 28)

Aim: to give students a chance to develop their writing through various different micro skills.

Tips:

- Clearly explain the focus and do an example of one of the questions first with the students before asking them to continue on their own: this particular focus is on style.
- Let students check their answers in pairs or small groups, then correct in open class.
- Keep the pace brisk, as much of this is likely to be familiar to advanced learners.

Language note

The layout of an email very much depends on your audience and purpose. Formal emails are clearly structured and are often very similar to formal letters. Informal emails are often closer to everyday speech. There may even be no greeting or introduction, and short forms might be used, eg *Thanks for your message. See you on Sat! Don't forget the food! Fxx* The example email from Taru (SB page 28) is fairly informal, but the tone suggests they do not often write to one another.

1 Hello friend
2 I apologise for the delay in replying.
3 I trust
4 I am yearning
5 I look forward to hearing from you.
6 With thanks in advance

Linking ideas: time expressions (SB page 28)

Aim: to highlight and focus on a particular aspect of language that students can use to improve their writing.

Tips:

- Sometimes this section serves as reinforcement of language that students have encountered passively before in the unit. Make this link clear where possible.
- Let students check their answers in pairs or small groups, then correct in open class.
- Put some of the answers on the board for students to self-check for variety and efficiency, eg exercise 3.

TEACH GLOBAL THINK LOCAL Language extra

If you have a confident group, perhaps on an exam-oriented course, ask them to rephrase sentence 4 in exercise 1 starting with: *hardly, scarcely, no sooner* … These adverbials require inversions. Give examples, eg *No sooner had I closed the door than I realised I'd locked my keys inside; Scarcely had I got to the car when I saw that the window had been smashed.*

1

1 at the same time
2 after (being on the point of)
3 before
4 before

2

1 When / While I was making my way towards the car, I heard footsteps. (*While* and *as* are interchangeable in many contexts, but *as* tends to be used when we want to give less importance to the background information.)
I was making my way towards the car when I heard footsteps.
2 I was just about to phone the police when I saw that the man was getting nearer.
3 Immediately / The moment / I saw the man coming towards me, I started running.
I started running the moment I saw the man coming towards me.
4 I had hardly / just arrived at the pub when the man stepped in.

3

1 e 2 g 3 a 4 f 5 c 6 b 7 d

4 Suggested answers

1 beforehand
2 At first
3 suddenly / all of a sudden
4 immediately
5 meanwhile / in the meantime
6 Eventually / In the end
7 before long

Preparing to write (SB page 29)

Aim: to give students an opportunity to brainstorm ideas for the writing task.

Tips:

- Allow students to discuss ideas in pairs or small groups.
- Ask students to make notes at this stage, but not to begin writing.
- Refer students to the *Useful phrases*, and encourage them to integrate these into their email.
- Remind students the story within the email can be completely made-up if necessary; they can also take a story from the local/national press, if preferred, and make it their own, eg someone winning some money, a remarkable pet, etc.

Writing (SB page 29)

Aim: to give students practice in extended writing tasks.

Tips:

- This section can be done as homework.
- Remind students to refer back to the model text and encourage them to experiment with some of the target language from this section.
- Ask students to check their work carefully before they hand it in.

Study skills

Exploring collocations (SB page 29)

1 Books closed. Ask *Can you define what a 'collocation' is? Does the same thing exist in your language?* (Of course it does!).

Ask students to read the introductory paragraph to this section if they are unsure about what a collocation is.

Background note

Professor Michael Hoey is the chief adviser on the Macmillan English Dictionary Advisory Panel.

Put the three given words on the board. Elicit an example, eg *a small chance*, then let students work in pairs. Clarify that *chance* and *light* are used as nouns here, whilst *rumble* is a verb. Elicit some examples, adding them to the board. Don't worry if students are not referring specifically to collocations from Unit 2.

Possible answers

strong / good / slight / slim chance

bright / cold / dazzling / deep / dim / faint / harsh / rich / soft / warm light; light bursts in, shed light on, in the cold light of day, give the green light to, in the light of

a lorry / thunder rumbles

2 This is intended to further raise the profile of collocations and to highlight the reference sources available by providing practice in using a collocations dictionary. Let students read the example, then ask them which collocations with *darkness* are new to them. Elicit what other information is provided. Alternatively, first approach the material as in the suggestion, which highlights the need for a collocations dictionary.

TEACH GLOBAL THINK LOCAL Alternative procedure

Before students start working on exercise 2, read out this extract from a story, asking students to write it down, leaving a gap where you tap the desk.

George rubbed his eyes, and soon became aware that he was alone in the church and in (tap) darkness. The only light that (tap) the darkness came from the neon sign in the window. He was cold and weary. The darkness (tap) him again, but this time there seemed to be lights up ahead.

Students work in pairs to think of at least one or two collocations with *darkness* in each of the three gaps. Then they read and check with the collocations dictionary extract in exercise 2. Elicit answers to the two questions given in the rubric for this exercise.

adjective + noun

verb + noun

noun + verb

Other information: word combination patterns, synonyms, related prepositions, example sentences

3 Write this question on the board: *How do you learn and develop your knowledge of collocations in English?* Elicit some possibilities as a whole class. Give examples of your own preferred strategies if possible, perhaps ones you have used when learning another language. Then students read the four suggestions and discuss them. Be prepared to explain what a corpus is. See *Background note.*

Background note

The detailed information on collocations which can be found in collocations dictionaries is gleaned from feeding in natural examples of spoken and written English into a corpus on computer. If you think your students might be interested, refer them to the *British National Corpus*. This particular corpus has around 100 million words. Students at this level may find it useful to see how words or phrases are used in real-life speech or writing: http://www.natcorp.ox.ac.uk/. The user simply types in a word or phrase and is given a series of example sentences, such as those shown in a standard modern dictionary. If possible, show students an example in class, typing in the phrase: *switch on the light.*

UNIT 3

Great & Small

Coursebook

Unit 3	Language	Texts	Communication skills
Part 1 SB page 30	Grammar Relative clauses	Reading & Listening *Great Expectations*	Speaking Greatness Speaking Hopes and expectations
Part 2 SB page 32	Extend your vocabulary *great* Vocabulary & Pronunciation Numbers	Reading & Speaking *Great travel experiences* Listening Geographical sites	
Part 3 SB page 34	Extend your vocabulary *small* or *little* Grammar Compound nouns	Listening Childhood toys	Writing A small toy Speaking Collecting
Part 4 SB page 36	Vocabulary & Speaking *quiet* and *silent*	Reading & Listening *The God of Small Things*	Pronunciation Weak and strong forms
Function globally SB page 38	Narrating and responding Listening to anecdotes about childhood events Telling anecdotes		
Global English SB page 39	Indian English Discussing varieties of a language and dialects		
Writing SB page 40	An essay Linking ideas: contrast Writing skills: gathering ideas Giving a personal opinion		
Study skills SB page 41	Improving your reading efficiency		

Additional resources

eWorkbook	Interactive and printable grammar, vocabulary, listening and pronunciation practice Extra reading and writing practice Additional downloadable listening and video material
Teacher's Resource Disc	Communication activity worksheets to print and photocopy, review material, test, and video with worksheet
Go global Ideas for further research	**Great** Ask students to go online and find out about the Fibonacci sequence of numbers. Ask *In what ways is mathematics linked to patterns in nature?* **Small** Students find examples of offers from magazines, TV advertising and websites that encourage people to start collections. Then they report back on one product, saying how the product is advertised, what age group it is appealing to, and its pricing.

Part 1

TEACH GLOBAL THINK LOCAL Lead-in

Books closed. Write up the quotation at the start of Unit 3 on the board, omitting the words *great* and *greatness*. Tell students that the missing words are either a noun or related adjective (from the same word family). Let students work in pairs to try and figure it out. Elicit suggestions. At the end, elicit who they think the author might be.

Speaking (SB page 30)

Students interpret the quotation together and give examples. Invite some students to share their ideas with the whole class. Ask students what they think *greatness* actually means here.

Some people are born into families who have great wealth or are part of a royal or aristocratic family. Some have famous parents. Some are recognised for their own achievements and hard work (artists, authors, entrepreneurs). Others become important by some twist of fate and perhaps against their own inclinations.

Students' own answers.

Reading and Listening (SB page 30)

1 Write up the title of the novel on the board, or project an image of the book. Elicit any ideas about it and in particular what students think the title might mean in relation to a young man's future (Pip), who is the main character.

Background note

Great Expectations is one of Dickens' later and best-known works. It was written in 1860 and published in serial form in his weekly journal *All the Year Round*. It is partly autobiographical, and is a novel about the personal growth and development of the young protagonist, Pip, at a time when Britain and other countries were experiencing profound social and industrial change.

2 **1.28** Check students know the words *orphan* (n), *gentleman* (n), *fancy* (n), *objection* (n) and *guardian* (n) via eliciting and peer teaching; these words are necessary to understand the extract. Explain to students that Pip is a very poor, uneducated boy. Students read the questions, then read and listen to the extract. In pairs, students share answers before whole-class feedback – they may be a little distracted by the rather flowery, literary style.

Pip is going to inherit some property and he is going to be given money for his education.

In the words of the quotation, he is having 'greatness thrust upon him'.

3 Ask students what they notice about the language overall, and then the lawyer, Mr Jaggers'. Ask *Is it everyday spoken language?* Do the first example together, then students work independently. Discuss the answers as a class. Explain to students that this kind of language is harder to process for native English speakers too (as is a letter written in 'legalese'!).

1 *I am instructed to communicate to him.*
2 *… it is the desire of the present possessor of that property, that he be immediately removed …*
3 *You will have no objection, I dare say, to your great expectations being encumbered with that easy condition.*
4 *This is not for you to inquire into.*
5 *There is already lodged in my hands, a sum of money amply sufficient for your suitable education and maintenance.*

4 Let students work alone, before comparing and discussing answers in pairs. In whole-class feedback, highlight to students that Dickens is often comic: his description of the nervous Pip and the brusque lawyer is intended to be amusing.

Suggested answers

1 The first condition is that he should continue to be called Pip (*… you always bear the name of Pip.*). The second is that he should not try to find out who is helping him (*… remains a profound secret …*).
2 He is overwhelmed. His biggest dream has come true. (*My dream was out; my wild fancy was surpassed by sober reality … my heart was beating so fast … I could scarcely stammer …*)
3 His response to Pip saying he has no objection seems to indicate that he thinks Pip is very lucky and should be exceedingly grateful (*I should think not!*).

5 Elicit reactions from the class as a whole. Ask students *Who do you think gave Pip this great opportunity? Do you know of anyone whose fortunes have also changed so instantaneously and unpredictably?*

TEACH GLOBAL THINK LOCAL

Extra activity

To engage students further with the story, and to help them connect more with the forthcoming *Grammar* section, use the a–f sentences under *Grammar*. Add this additional text: *Pip is given an education and money to live on. As a young adult, to his utter surprise he finds out that his benefactor is in fact the escaped convict from his youth*. Jumble the sentences on the page and then use as a handout or a projected document. Students work in pairs to put the muddled sentences of the summary in order.

If you have the facilities, now might be a good opportunity to show the opening clip from the 1946 film – probably the best-known version. Find it on the internet by typing in the keywords: *Great Expectations David Lean film*.

Grammar (SB page 30)

1 First write an example on the board: *Pip is a young boy whose parents died years earlier*. Ask a student to come up and underline the relative clause. Then students complete the exercise independently before discussing their answers in pairs. Conduct a whole-class feedback session and be prepared to give additional examples and ask prompt questions, as appropriate.

Students may need more guidance with question 4 (see answer below) and with questions 3 and 5, where you could clarify by asking students if *a tool* (sentence c) and *the kindness* (sentence f) are subjects or objects of the verb in the relative clause (objects, which is why the relative pronoun can be omitted). At any point, if you wish, you could elicit / write up and discuss the difference between *defining* and *non-defining clauses* (or *identifying* vs *non-identifying*, if these are likely to be more familiar terms), or refer to the grammar explanation on page 136.

1 *whose, who, which*
2 *who, which*
3 It is non-defining, ie it is extra information which is not an essential part of the main sentence.
4 The fact that he has to steal from his family – it refers to the whole clause rather than to a particular word.
5 *which / that* (object)

2 This exercise focuses on prepositions in relative clauses. In pairs, students complete the tasks. Refer them to the *Language note* in relation to *whom*. Conduct a whole-class feedback session.

1 at the very end of the sentence
2 *He wants Pip to steal food and a tool with which he can take off his leg shackles.*
3 In everyday speech people use prepositions at the end of sentences. Using the preposition followed by the relative pronoun is more formal.
4 sentence c: *The name of the person <u>who</u> is your liberal benefactor*

sentence d: *That person is the person from <u>whom</u> you derive your expectations.*

whom is used in the second sentence because it follows a preposition and is the indirect object of the clause. (In sentence c *who* is the subject of the clause.)

That person is the person who you derive your expectations from.

(more formally) … *whom you derive your expectations from.*

Language note

For advanced students, your focus should be on the more challenging aspects of relative clauses, for example the style issue in relation to the use of *whom* and prepositions, as in Grammar exercise 2 above.

It may also be worth highlighting the way the clause is spoken: with a non-defining relative clause, marked by commas in the written form, the voice drops to reflect that it is 'extra' information. The clause may also be uttered at a slightly faster pace, as an 'aside'.

Note that *that* is usually used in preference to *which*, after the following words: *all, every / some / any / nothing*, eg *I'm left with nothing ~~which~~ that I first came with. That* is also preferred in superlatives, eg *This is the best ice cream (that) I've ever tasted*.

Relative clauses like sentence e in Grammar exercise 1, SB page 30, are only used with *which*, not *that* – these qualify the whole preceding clause and have a comment function. These clauses are quite common in everyday speech too, eg *I managed to finish my homework, which was a relief, I can tell you!*

3 Rewrite the first pair of sentences together. Elicit from students if the pronoun can be omitted and why (it can be omitted because it is the object of the verb in the relative clause). Then students work together before checking as a whole class. Monitor and guide students where necessary. If there are any problems, put the examples on the board to clarify.

Suggested answers

1 She was the one in my family who/whom I thought would go on to great things.
2 I let my parents down because they had high expectations for me which / that I just couldn't live up to.
3 The exam was easier than we expected, which made for a nice change.
4 Their team, whose results were consistent all year, showed great promise for the final.
5 I had a good feeling about the apartment which / that we were about to move into. / I had a good feeling about the apartment into which we were about to move.
6 I spoke to a lot of people, many of whom were disappointed about their career.

G Grammar focus

Refer students to the language summary on relative clauses on page 136.

You can use exercises 1–3 on page 137 for:
a) extra practice now, b) homework or c) review later on.

The answers are on page 162 of this Teacher's Book.

Speaking (SB page 31)

1 If you can, give a personalised example of either yourself or someone students are likely to know, such as a well-known sportsperson. If appropriate, you could suggest that they discuss their youth, eg parental expectations at school or college, etc. Give students a few moments reflection time and encourage them to try and use at least two examples of relative clauses. Your students may prefer to write the sentences down, using the target language. Monitor if students do this.

2 Students work in pairs. If you hear some interesting examples, particularly using the target language, then exploit these at the end.

TEACH GLOBAL THINK LOCAL Homework extra

Encourage students to call out adjectives that could describe Pip's feelings after his surprise encounter with the lawyer, Mr Jaggers. Ask students to continue the story, writing what happened in the story after the lawyer left. They should either write the dialogue between Pip, Joe and his sister, or describe exactly what Pip did and how he felt.

Part 2

TEACH GLOBAL THINK LOCAL Lead-in

Ask students to imagine they are going on a trip/holiday of a lifetime. Ask what three elements they would personally value the most for their ideal trip. Write up the list of options in exercise 2, SB page 32, for them to choose from, eg *accommodation, activities, food,* etc.

Reading and Speaking (SB page 32)

1 Students read and identify the text type. Invite some students to share their responses to the second question with the whole class.

It's a travel blog and would probably be found on an internet travel site.

2 Your students may find it easier to work alone initially, then to compare and check their answers in pairs. Whole-class feedback is not necessary here, unless there is a problem or query.

Montana

accommodation: a guest ranch

scenery and surroundings: a different world, natural environment and not a city (cows instead of cabs and sky instead of skyscrapers), breathtaking scenery

transport: usual method of travel is pick up truck (but author can't drive)

Switzerland

activities: cycling

food: cheese and chocolate

local people: courteous and friendly drivers

scenery and surroundings: idyllic countryside

transport: bikes

travelling companions: mother, sister and others in biking group

weather: warm but not hot, some showers

3 The aim of this exercise is to highlight some natural-sounding phrases used to talk about having totally new experiences. Challenge strong learners to see if they can fill in any of the gaps **without** looking at the text first.

1	found	4	encounter
2	got; day	5	that had
3	came	6	part

4 Encourage all students to describe a personal trip, even if it wasn't far away, or was a long time ago. They could even just describe a very positive experience in general, eg a day out; a sporting event. Ask them to use at least two of the new phrases to talk about the effect of their amazing experience. Invite one or two students to share interesting experiences at the end, encouraging listeners to react freely and ask questions.

Listening (SB page 32)

1 Students work in different pairs here to discuss the questions. Very swiftly check which is the odd one out.

The Great Depression

TEACH GLOBAL THINK LOCAL **Extra activity**

To motivate students and to change the focus, bring in two or three visuals of each of the three places in exercise 1, SB page 32. Put them around the room, like in a gallery, for students to wander around and peruse. Encourage students to write up short comments on each place, expressing their views (you give your own, as an example). Students could imagine they had just visited the places and experiment with some of the phrases from exercise 3, SB page 32.

2 **1.29–1.31** This task is designed to sensitise students to genre types. As a whole class, elicit the kind of thing that would be representative of each of the text types in the list. If you wish, you could even elicit the first one or two possible sentences to the board. Alternatively, you could find and read out some real examples, eg *This is a stunning area with lots of variety in terms of sport and suitable for the whole family* (travel agent description). Ask students to listen and make notes before checking the answers.

1 The Great Wall of China: a prepared talk by a tour guide
2 The Great Lakes: a natural history TV programme
3 The Great Barrier Reef: a description by a travel agent

1.29–1.31

1

Welcome to the Great Wall of China, one of the world's greatest national and historical sites and the longest man-made structure in the world. The Great Wall of China was built and rebuilt from the 5th century BC through to the 16th century and it was originally intended to protect the northern borders of the Chinese Empire against attacks by many different enemies.

The Wall stretches from Shanhaiguan in the east to Lop Nur in the west and along the southern edge of Inner Mongolia. Many people think it was built all in one go, but this isn't true. In actual fact it is a network, various segments were built at different times by different dynasties. The entire structure, with all its branches stretches for nearly 9,000 km. Of these 9,000 km, over 6,000 are actual wall, while nearly 3,000 kilometres consist of trenches and natural defensive barriers such as hills or rivers.

We will shortly be arriving at the most visited section of the Great Wall in Badaling. This section was built during the Ming Dynasty. Please remember to …

2

This is one of the great natural features of the North American continent and of the planet itself. The Great Lakes – a chain of lakes in east-central North America comprising Lakes Superior, Michigan, Huron, Erie and Ontario. The combined area of the Great Lakes is some 94,850 square miles or 245,660 square kilometres, covering an area exceeding that of the United Kingdom. The Lakes contain about 84% of North America's surface fresh water and just over a fifth or 21% of the world's fresh water supply. Except for Lake Michigan, the lakes provide a natural border between Canada and the United States, a frontier that was stabilised by a boundary-waters treaty in 1909.

Individually, the lakes rank among the 14 largest in the world. They played a central role in the European colonisation and development of North America and for decades have attracted people and industry; Lakes Erie and Ontario and the southern portion of Lake Michigan are now ringed with large population concentrations. The lakes have not benefited from this development, however, and have been seriously affected by pollution. In the late 20th century, both the US and the Canadian governments began to investigate methods for reversing the consequences of years of misuse of the lakes' waters.

3

The Great Barrier Reef is one of the best places to visit in the world. One thing that you may not know before you plan your trip is you've got to really think about the size of the area and also really narrow down which part of the Great Barrier Reef you might want to visit.

Did you know that there are actually over 900 islands? Not all of them you can visit, but a very large proportion of those. And the islands actually stretch over 2,600 kilometres so it's a much larger surface area than what people think. In fact, I think it actually works out at 344,400 square kilometres which is just massive. Most people don't realise that. I mean, obviously if you wanted to, you can take day trips to different islands so you don't have to choose just one. You could, for example, choose a couple of different ones which are close enough by each other. Sometimes it'll be a day trip, sometimes it's a longer trip, maybe a day or two. You can do overnights as well to visit the different islands, so that's a fantastic thing to do.

One thing to keep in mind though is that there are 2,900 individual reefs and the marine life is protected, so because of that the tours actually are only allowed to visit a small part of those areas, so before you make your choices, just really make sure you know which ones of those tours that you really want to go to.

Of course, once you make your choice you can do all sorts of activities on any of the islands. Outdoor activities are the main attraction. Snorkelling and scuba diving absolutely the principal things to do. If you are afraid you could also take the glass bottom boat.

3 Give students a moment to read through the questions before they listen again for specific information. Give them the opportunity at the end to check answers together, and also to request a replay of (part of) the listening, if necessary.

Speaker 1	
1 c	2 b
Speaker 2	
3 b	4 a
Speaker 3	
5 c	6 a

4 In pairs, students discuss the three questions. Tell them that they have at least four minutes for the discussion. Monitor and give feedback on any linguistic or content-related matters of relevance.

Extend your vocabulary (SB page 33)

1 To raise the challenge slightly, books closed, dictate the sentences in exercise 1. Ask students to individually think of synonyms for *great* in each case. Then, after comparing answers in pairs, they should do the matching exercise. At the end, ask students *Which use(s) of the word* great *do you tend to use?*

1 important	3 enjoyable
2 bigger than usual	4 enthusiastic

2 Students write two true sentences. They should read the sentences to their partner, who says which meaning the word *great* has in each case.

Vocabulary and Pronunciation (SB page 33)

1 **1.29–1.31** Give students time to say the numbers in their heads, then to check with a partner. Replay the listening for students to check their answers.

> *6,000 km* = six thousand kilometres
>
> *245,660 square kilometres* = two hundred and forty-five thousand, [pause] six hundred and sixty square kilometres
>
> *2,900* = two thousand, nine hundred

2 **1.32** Be prepared to play the recording twice if necessary as this is very intensive listening. It is important that students compare answers here, and do so orally (not just showing their papers), as this functions as a self / peer drill. You could challenge them to say the numbers faster and faster to one another. Monitor and assist, if necessary, highlighting problem numbers on the board.

> See audioscript.

> **1.32**
>
> 1 two thousand eight hundred and forty square miles
> 2 62 per cent
> 3 2:1
> 4 six point two
> 5 22 square metres
> 6 1909
> 7 a hundred thousand
> 8 three point one four
> 9 a third
> 10 one million
> 11 2020
> 12 1:5
> 13 two-fifths
> 14 five per cent

3 In pairs, students group the numbers from exercise 2, after doing an example together first. Then say *Imagine you were teaching someone of a lower level, highlight some simple rules and features on how to say numbers in English.* Give them an example, eg *When talking about ratios, you use the weak form of the word* to (2:1 = /tu:/ /tə/ /wʌn/).

areas: 2,840 sq. miles; 22 m^2	ratios: 2:1; 1:5
decimals: 6.2; 3.14	round numbers: 100,000; 1,000,000
fractions: 1/3; 2/5	
percentages: 62%; 5%	years: 1909, 2020

4 **1.33** This exercise focuses on the schwa sound. Be quite fussy in terms of their pronunciation, to raise the challenge. Break the parts down if necessary and drill. Then listen to check.

> all words in bold are pronounced with weak forms /ə/

5 Put students into AB pairs and give them a minute to read their respective rubric on pages 127 and 130 and their text, mentally saying the numbers. Warn students that, as listeners, not only do they have to listen to their partner's information carefully, but they should also take notes of the numbers, as they will need to relay the information back immediately after listening. Monitor to check they are pronouncing the numbers correctly.

TEACH GLOBAL THINK LOCAL

Homework extra

Ask students to research either the Great Fire or Great Depression (or another 'Great' if they'd prefer). They should find at least six additional facts. Tell them they will be sharing information in groups of three at the following lesson.

Part 3

TEACH GLOBAL THINK LOCAL Lead-in

If you can, bring in a sample of toys that you enjoyed playing with, or your children do/did, or alternatively a childhood photo or a picture of a similar toy. Tell students why you loved it and the different ways you would play with it.

Writing (SB page 34)

Students should keep their books closed until the *Listening* section on page 34.

1 Read the rubric to the class. Ask them to write at least three sentences about their chosen toy. If necessary, put some prompts up on the board, eg *appearance*, *your age*, *ways of playing*, *why you liked it*, *particular memories*, etc.

2 Read out one example text and elicit some possible questions for it, to find out more details. Then, in pairs, students swap texts. Encourage them to write two interesting questions to find out more information. Faster students can write an additional question. Then they return the text and questions to the writer.

3 Students rework their text to incorporate the requested information at the most logical place, if possible as part of a current sentence. Monitor and assist as they are writing. Then they show the revised text to their partner.

4 Put students into groups of three or four, but not including their original partner. They share their texts and say which toy sounds a) the most unusual and b) the most loved. Ask *Did any of you choose the same toy?*

Listening (SB page 34)

1 Now students open their books and, in pairs, discuss the toys shown and the questions.

2 **1.34–1.37** This listening involves four monologues: four people describe a favourite childhood toy.

Students need to take written notes as there are lots of details to remember. Rather than checking as a class, students work in pairs and take it in turns to talk about two toys each. If there are any discrepancies, they should ask you.

1 Slinky: like a spring, simple
Good memories: felt like it had a life of its own; made an obstacle course for it; used to race it with a friend down the stairs; loved it for its simplicity

2 Rubik's Cube®: drove him mad with frustration, so many different routes to get there (but in the end read how to do it)

3 LEGO®: huge boxful of bricks, different colours
Good memories: *just heaven*, spent hours making buildings, people, animals, cars, castles. Bad thing: mum and dad would tell him off for leaving the bricks on the floor – they would tread on it with bare feet, agony

4 yo-yo: red, wooden
Good memories: fascinated when she was a little kid, could put it in your pocket and take on boring visits, do tricks; but got a bit boring after a while

1.34–1.37

1

When I was about seven or eight, um, it was Christmas morning, I remember coming down to this great pile of presents. But that day, the one thing that captured my imagination was this red box with a slinky in it. And basically, a slinky is, um, a spring, and for some reason this thing just captivated me and we had a good flight of stairs in our house, and after lunch when all the grown-ups had gone to sleep I started playing with this thing, and just, it felt like magic that it had a life of its own tumbling down the stairs. So then I started making obstacle courses for it and it didn't matter how steep the steps were, amazingly this thing would jump from one step to the other. And I had a friend with one as well and we used to race them down the stairs. It was such a simple toy and for all the technology that you can get today there was something about this that I absolutely loved.

2

I got my Rubik's Cube® in the 80s so I must have been about 13 and I got it from a friend who couldn't do it and she passed it on to me who … I equally couldn't do it. And it was really frustrating at first because there're so many different ways to get all the different colours on the different faces, there're so many different routes to get there, that just when you think you've solved it there's one colour out and, ah, you just … drove you mad with frustration and before you knew it you'd been doing it for like an hour. But in the end I actually just read about how to do it and, you know, followed the solution and there was no mystery left at all, and actually it made you think, 'How did I find it so hard?'. Which is exactly why I think that future kids won't play with toys like this because they just won't have the concentration or the patience and they will just be able to go on the internet pretty quickly, read the solution and solve it, so, there'll be no challenge.

3

Well, when I was a child I really loved LEGO® bricks. I had a huge boxful, you know, all different colours. I mean, it was just heaven. I spent hours, probably days, making all sorts of different buildings, people, animals, cars, everything – castles, actually one of my favourites was a castle. And I just see nowadays that modern LEGO® it's … it hasn't really got the creativity. They come in kits so you kind of have to make a specific thing as opposed to just getting a box of bricks and making what you want. But it was just brilliant. The one thing that was very funny was when my mum and dad would come into my bedroom and, you know, they have bare feet or something and they'd tread on the LEGO® and it was like agony and that was something I constantly got told off for. But I just think it's something that's really stood the test of time and will probably be here forever. You know, it's so simple, you don't need batteries, you know, it promotes, you know, coordination, creativity, just everything about it is just such fun, such fun in these little different coloured blocks.

4

Oh, I had a red wooden yo-yo. I think they're all plastic or lightweight metal, aluminium or something like that now. But I remember being fascinated when I was a little kid, maybe about seven, because you could put them in your pocket and take on boring visits. And you could do tricks with them, the cradle or the swing or something I think they were called. I mean, you never played with a yo-yo for very long because they get a bit boring after a while. And when you get older they're not so interesting. But my nephew got one recently, very modern. It was all plastic with a ball-bearing system and they come back automatically and light up. I mean, is that cheating for yo-yo connoisseurs? I mean, they seem popular now. I don't know if a toy can reinvent itself further to appeal to kids in the future. I think the yo-yo has probably evolved.

3 This is another opportunity to hear the recording again, to both confirm what they heard earlier, and to focus on one part of each recording.

1 We don't know. The speaker alludes to the fact that many modern toys rely on technology, but that this was a very simple toy.
2 No, children don't have the concentration or the patience, will just go on the internet and read the solution, no challenge
3 Yes, has really stood the test of time, so simple, no batteries, promotes coordination and creativity, it's fun. But comes in kits now, make a specific thing – not as much creativity
4 Not sure, doesn't know if it can reinvent itself to appeal to kids in the future; modern yo-yos are plastic or aluminium, come back automatically, probably evolved as far as possible

4 In small groups, students compare their answers and give their opinions. Open up the questions about toys, past and future. Ask them if there are any toys around nowadays which are likely to last and why.

Extend your vocabulary (SB page 34)

1 Students should tackle this exercise alone initially. Some sentences are likely to be much easier than others, eg 1 and 2. When checking, clarify what sentences 3, 4, 5, 6 and 7 mean, asking for synonyms, alternative expressions or contexts. Elicit what part of speech the target items are, eg 1 = pronoun, 2 = adj, etc. See *Language note*.

1 little
2 small
3 small
4 small
5 little; little
6 Little
7 small
8 little
9 small

2 Students should work in pairs for this exercise. Do the first example together, eliciting both a question and a sentence in this case. At the end, elicit some examples.

Possible answers

Contexts

1 an answer to an offer of some food / drink
2 a comment about a strange coincidence, eg bumping into someone you know in an unexpected situation
3 an answer about a party or event that finished late (*the small hours* = the very early hours of the morning, approximately from 1–4am)
4 a comment about a problem with a contract (*small print* refers to the details, eg the terms and conditions, of a contract, that are usually written in smaller text)
5 a comment offering encouragement in a challenging situation
6 a comment about a secret or surprise that some people are unaware of
7 a complaint about a person's behaviour / actions making the speaker feel insignificant
8 an affectionate comment
9 a comment about size, eg of an item of clothing

Language note

Little and *small* can both be used adjectivally, but whereas *small* can be used both **before** and **after** the noun it describes, *little* is generally used **before** or **attributively**, eg *The small house ..., the house is small. The little house ...* ~~*The house is little.*~~ *Little* is also less neutral than *small*, it can carry with it different connotations, eg affection, amusement, distaste, eg *Some little man asked me to leave. It was so rude.* (distaste) *What a gorgeous little face!* (affection). *Little* is rarely used with adverbs like *very* or *quite* as it is considered ungradable; it does not have a comparative form, unlike *small*.

Grammar (SB page 35)

1 In pairs, students select the correct form of the compound nouns. At this level students are likely to know the right answer, but not necessarily why. When checking, try and get students to give / formulate some rules, to see what they know already.

1 a board game	5 a doll's house
2 a children's toy	6 the bathroom floor
3 a pack of cards	7 the front of the house
4 a chess piece	8 a lifetime's work

2 Working individually, students read the rules and find examples before checking answers in pairs. (Fast finishers can also think up additional examples.) Monitor to see how they have done; hold a quick class feedback session, if necessary.

- noun + noun: board game, chess piece, bathroom floor
- noun + *of* + noun: a pack of cards, the front of the house
- noun + *'s/s'* + noun: a children's toy, a doll's house, a lifetime's work

Language note

In compound nouns, it is often difficult even for native English speakers to know if a noun is hyphenated or not, or if it is one word or two. Generally, the more frequently co-occurring they are, the closer they are likely to be, eg *postman* but *letter box*. Remind students that a dictionary will tell them.

It might also be worth pointing out to students to generally avoid *'s* to refer to abstract nouns or inanimate objects, eg ~~the piano's stool~~ *the piano stool*, ~~the happiness's height~~ *the height of happiness*. However, the *'s* is often used with place names, which may seem quite odd to some students, eg *Italy's president*. It is also used for time expressions, as indicated in the *Grammar box* in exercise 2.

G Grammar focus

Refer students to the language summary on compound nouns on page 136.

You can use exercises 4–6 on page 137 for:
a) extra practice now, b) homework or c) review later on.

The answers are on page 162 of this Teacher's Book.

3 Let students work alone initially. Warn them that they may have to change the order of the words in brackets. Check answers with the class, inviting students to refer back to the rules, if necessary. Be prepared to clarify the punctuation rules about the apostrophe for singular and plural nouns, eg in 2 and 5.

1 box of picture books	4 charity shop
2 girls' toy section	5 three days' work
3 traces of lead	6 model planes

Speaking (SB page 35)

TEACH GLOBAL THINK LOCAL Extra activity

Put students in groups of three to brainstorm what people – adults or children – can collect. Elicit an example or two first. At the end, invite some students to share their examples; there may be some interesting and perhaps unusual ones.

1 In pairs or groups, students discuss what they collected and include details on which type, when, why, how many, how long, etc. Put these questions on the board as prompts, if necessary. At the end, invite individuals to share their information with the class. Ask *Why do you think people collect things?*

2 Ask a student to read out the magazine extract aloud. Then, in groups, students select their three questions for discussion. Monitor and pick up on any interesting language or content-related points for full-class discussion.

Part 4

TEACH GLOBAL THINK LOCAL Lead-in

Put up these three well-known sayings on the board, but don't include the final word, here bracketed:

Silence is (golden).

Be grateful for small (mercies).

Children should be seen and not (heard).

In pairs, students predict what the final words are. Elicit some suggestions before giving the answers. Ask *Do you have similar sayings in your language? What do they mean? What situations might they be used in?*

Reading and Listening (SB page 36)

1 With the full class, discuss the questions, eliciting any cultural differences. Try to elicit the following situations as contexts when silence might be a good thing: *to reflect, to plan, to calm, to appreciate, to energise, to relax*, etc.

2 **1.38** This extract describes how a boy, Estha, gradually became completely silent, and how people responded to this. Students first read the questions and then read and listen to the text. Point out the *Glossary*. Discuss answers in a feedback session.

1 We don't know why Estha is quiet, but the text says he had always been quiet and refers to a sort of evasion.
2 No, he is surrounded by noise: *a quiet bubble floating on a sea of noise*.

3 This exercise demands a closer reading. Students compare their answers in pairs, after working independently first. They will need to support their answers by referring directly to the text. Discuss answers with the class.

1 T (*… no one could pinpoint exactly … there wasn't an 'exactly when', … a gradual winding down and closing shop. A barely noticeable quietening.*)
2 F (*… Estha's silence was never awkward. Never intrusive. Never noisy. It wasn't an accusing, protesting silence …*)
3 F (*It usually took strangers a while to notice him even when they were in the same room with him. It took them even longer to notice that he never spoke. Some never noticed at all.*)
4 T (*… in Estha's case the dry season looked as though it would last for ever.*)
5 T (*… much to the initial embarrassment of his father and stepmother …*)
6 F (*… would attend to him amidst the clamouring of their other customers … gave him rusted film cans … They never cheated him. … they would transfer them to his red plastic shopping basket … and always a sprig of coriander and a fistful of green chillies for free.*)

4 Read out the three questions slowly and in a thought-provoking manner. In pairs, students discuss the questions. Be prepared to put further questions on the board for those students who run out of things to say, eg *How would a child suffer in life by not talking? How would you help a child who had this self-inflicted problem?*

Pronunciation (SB page 36)

1 **1.39** As with the focus on the schwa in Vocabulary and Pronunciation exercise 4 on page 33, this looks at weak forms, but in fluent speech. Ask students first to look at the first paragraph of *The God of Small Things* and locate the grammar words from exercise 1. Then ask them to listen. Students at this level will be very familiar with this aspect of pronunciation receptively, but may be less skilful in producing it.

Discuss how they are pronounced and drill the words within their clause / phrase chunks.

They are pronounced as weak forms
1 schwa /ə/
2 more quickly
3 more quietly
4 They are usually 'grammar' words; they make the sentence grammatically correct, but do not carry significant meaning.

2 The strong pronunciation is relatively uncommon. Encourage students to think up examples of when this might happen and elicit examples. (See answer key.)

Strong pronunciation is used when these words are being emphasised or contrasted with another word, eg *I wasn't going to the market, I was coming from the market*, or when they are at the end of a sentence.

3 It would be helpful for students to put these into context, eg *I'll see you **at** the station; I'm at work **but** I'm sick; He's **from** Paris; She's quicker **than** me; Jim gave **them** the gift and left.* Drill this, if necessary. Again try to elicit examples of when the strong form is used.

	weak	strong
at	/ət/	/æt/
but	/bət/	/bʌt/
from	/frəm/	/frɒm/
than	/ðən/	/ðæn/
them	/ðəm/	/ðem/

4 Students should first locate the small grammar words which naturally require a schwa within the indicated paragraph (beginning *Estha occupied …*). Encourage them to read and mutter the words under their breath. Check any other difficult pronunciation too. Monitor and assist.

Vocabulary and Speaking (SB page 37)

1 Tell students these are phrases to talk about being quiet and unnoticed. Respond promptly if you sense that students have no idea, letting them refer back to the text. Discuss what the expressions mean, and when you might use them.

1. background (used when someone doesn't stand out, is not very noticeable)
2. conversation; left (used when everything has been said about a topic)
3. awkward (used to describe a situation when you feel you should say something, but can't think of anything to say)

2 Students work in pairs, referring to a dictionary towards the end, if needed. Put up the answers on the board for a self-check. Point out that *quiet* in number 6 is actually a noun. Students should record in their notebooks at least four of the phrases to use in the future.

1 silent	3 quiet	5 silent	7 quiet
2 silent	4 quiet	6 quiet	8 quiet

3 This exercise focuses on meaning. Students work in different pairs to discuss possible contexts. First check their understanding of 1 (when someone is annoyed with you and ignores you), 4 (a discreet conversation that others can't hear) and 8 (some unofficial work that he prefers people not to know about).

Challenge students to write a six-to-eight-line dialogue in seven minutes. Set clear stages/timing for a) writing b) practising c) acting out. Invite one or two pairs to share some good examples. You may wish to point out afterwards that 5 (*You have the right to remain silent.*) is often used by police officers when making an arrest.

TEACH GLOBAL THINK LOCAL

Extra activity

Put students in AB pairs. B students close books and A students are the 'testers'. They read out the first four sentences from exercise 2, saying 'beep' for the italicised word in each case, eg. *Everyone fell* ***beep*** *when the head teacher entered the room*. Student B tries to provide the missing word. Then they swap roles, for the last four sentences.

Function globally: narrating and responding

These lessons in *Global* are designed to provide students with immediately useful functional language. They all follow a similar format.

Warm up (SB page 38)

Aim: to introduce the topic via a quick speaking task or picture work.

Tips:

- Do not over-correct here, especially in speaking activities.
- Encourage students to use as much variety of language as they can.
- Encourage students with entertaining situations to share these with the rest of the class. Students will later tell full anecdotes as part of the Speaking section below.

1 Suggested answers

Adult: Because I say so! Now, don't let go. We'll see.

Small child: Can I have a go? It wasn't me! That's not fair!

Listening (SB page 38)

TEACH GLOBAL THINK LOCAL

Lead-in

To help students 'connect' with the two anecdotes, put some words from each story up on the board. In pairs, students predict what happens. Tell them that both stories involve children.

<u>Story 1</u>

kite	*borrow*	*happily flying*
grandad	*photograph*	*naughty*
completely disappeared		

<u>Story 2</u>

open-air event	*hill*	*three years old*
never appeared	*terrified*	
crying	*under a tree*	

Aim: to present the functional language in context via a conversation or series of conversations.

Tips:

- Play the recording all the way through for each task (there are always two tasks). (Tracks 1.40–1.41)
- For multiple conversations pause the recording after each one.
- Invite students to respond to the two listenings, which they may find entertaining and remind them of incidents in their own childhood.

1

Conversation 1

1 pestered an older brother/cousin who was flying a kite to let him fly it; then he let it go

2 an older boy (Tom) and their grandfather who had bought the kite for Tom

3 Tom had a tantrum (lost his temper) because he had suspected Ben, the child, would let it go. The kite flew off into the air and disappeared.

4 funny (the incident); nice (kite); naughty (Ben's smile); windy day

Conversation 2

1 he ran up a hill in a park out of sight of his mother and got lost

2 his mother, lots of people attending the event therefore easy for him to get lost; someone (probably an official or someone who knew him, but this is not stated) who found him

3 the boy sat under a tree crying until he was found and returned to his panicking mother after about 15 minutes

4 big open-air (the event); small (hill); anxious, terrified, fearful (his mother); lost, tired (Alastair)

2

1 Grandad
2 Tom
3 Ben
4 Tom

3

1 let
2 about 15 minutes
3 had been looking for Emily

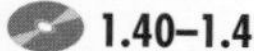 **1.40–1.41**

1

A: Did I ever tell you about that time when Ben was on Port Meadow and wanted to borrow Tom's kite?

B: No.

A: Well, it was really funny. Grandad was there and he had bought a really nice kite for the twins and they were using it because they were a bit … four years older than Ben and there was Ben aged five. Tom was very happily flying this kite. Ben said 'Can I have a go, can I have a go?' and Tom said 'No, no' and finally Grandad persuaded him, 'Oh go on you …'

B: Yeah, yeah.

A: … and Tom said 'No, he'll let go of the kite,' and Ben said 'No, I won't.' 'Grandad said you won't, will you?' 'No, no won't let go', so they handed the kite to Ben and, of course, he let go …

B: Oh no.

A: … and the kite goes flying off into the air and we have a photograph of Ben with this very naughty smile on his face after this whole incident.

B: And what happened in the end then, what happened to the kite?

A: I think Tom probably had a tantrum and said 'You see, I told you he would.' The kite disappeared somewhere because it was a very windy day, just completely disappeared.

B: Oh you must have been so annoyed.

A: Yeah, funny as well.

2

A: Have I told you about the time that we lost Alastair?

B: No.

A: We were at a big open-air event at a park in Reading. There were quite a lot of people there. Alastair was only about three years old at the time.

B: Oh no. …

A: … and we were walking along and Alastair said 'Oh Mummy, can I run up this hill and I'll meet you on the other side?'. And I thought fine, it was just a small hill, so I let him run up and I went round to meet him on the other side and I waited and he never appeared …

B: Oh no.

A: … and I … I was, you know, I started to get really anxious …

B: Yeah, bet you did.

A: … and I started looking around at the back of the hill, I went round the other way, I couldn't see him anywhere. I started asking all sorts of people, have you seen a little boy wearing whatever he was dressed in …

B: You must have been so worried.

A: I was, I was absolutely terrified and getting really fearful about what might have happened to him and … he was probably only lost for about 15 minutes, but I think it seemed like 15 hours …

B: Yeah, it must have been awful.

A: … yeah, but … um … eventually what happened was somebody did find me and ask me if I'd lost a child …

B: What a relief.

A: … and he, Ally, had got tired and lost himself in trying to find me and had gone and sat under a tree and was just crying under a tree …

B: Oh poor little thing.

A: And I was so, so relieved …

B: I bet you were, yeah.

Language focus (SB page 38)

Aim: to draw students' attention to the items of functional language.

Tips:

- Students work alone at first before comparing answers in pairs. Discuss any areas of ambiguity.
- Drill the story openers to focus students and help them to memorise them.
- Explain that some responses can be used in more than one way, depending on the intonation (and situation).
- At the end, ask students which of the target language items (the story openers and the responses) they already use when speaking English.

1 Possible answers

1 scary / frightening / awful
2 amazing / fantastic / exciting
3 sweet / lovely / cute
4 hilarious (ungradable adjective therefore only one possibility)

2

Have I ever told you …?
I had the most … experience when …
You'll never guess …
I must have told you …

3

Interest:	Yeah.
	Right.
	Uhuh.
Sympathy:	You must have been so annoyed.
	What a nightmare!
	It must have been awful.
	Oh no!
	I bet you were worried.
	Poor little thing!
Gladness:	Fantastic!
	What a relief!
	That was lucky.
Surprise:	How incredible!
	You're joking!
	That was lucky.
	Oh no!

Pronunciation (SB page 38)

Aim: to focus students on a particular aspect of pronunciation of the target phrases.

Tips:

- Play the recordings two or three times, if necessary.
- At this level, try to promote good all-round pronunciation including stress, intonation and linking. This also raises the challenge for students.
- Use students with exemplary pronunciation to act as models to help others in the class.

1 d 2 a 3 c 4 b

Speaking (SB page 38)

Aim: to allow students an opportunity to use this language in a meaningful, real-world context.

Tips:

- Give students time to prepare this activity. Circulate and monitor carefully whilst they are talking.
- Encourage students to ask questions, too, when listening (as well as using the listener responses) – questioning is a natural reaction.
- Correct sensitively, paying attention to the target language especially.
- If time, repeat the task with new pairs.
- Invite one or two students to share strong examples with the whole class to round off the activity.

Global English

These lessons in *Global* have two main goals: 1) to give you and your students interesting information about English and language in general; 2) to provide practice in different kinds of reading comprehension tasks that they are likely to encounter in future study, for example in exams.

Warm up (SB page 39)

Aim: to engage students with the topic, and possibly to highlight potentially difficult vocabulary in the text.

Tips:

- Try to elicit what these English words have in common (they are Indian English).
- Let students work in pairs to share ideas and to help energise them at this point in the lesson.

1 b 2 a 3 b 4 a

Reading (SB page 39)

Aim: to provide students with interesting information about English, and practise reading exam skills.

Tips:

- There are two tasks. The first task may only require a superficial skim read or quick scanning task (here it is a scanning task). The second is a more difficult task, similar to that of a reading exam.
- This language is not tested or reviewed in future units, which means you have more flexibility with this material as to when and where you use it.

1

Do not criss-cross on expressway; Road in curve ahead; No 2-/3-wheelers

2

1 F (loanwords from local languages, sounds and rhythms from local languages and local cultural practices all influence)

2 T (*… the evolution of a literature that proudly articulates its culture in a distinctive voice in poetry, plays, stories, and novels. When this happens, a 'new English' has truly come of age, as most clearly seen in the mature literature of American (as distinct from British) English.*)

3 T (*… India, which has had a longer exposure to English than any other country using it as a second language …*)

4 T (*No dictionary yet includes all such usages … that have grown up around the country.*)

5 F (*Gone are the days when everyone in a novel … spoke standard British English, and the same linguistic diversity is apparent in Indian cinema.*)

6 T (*We are still in an early chapter of the story of Indian English.*)

TEACH GLOBAL THINK LOCAL

Reading extra

This is a dense text with potential for further exploitation. Students work in pairs and write five to seven comprehension questions. They should ensure that the last one is a more challenging one. Put the students into groups of four, and let them swap questions. They can mark each others'.

In addition, you could ask students to locate these two sentence starters in the text: *The longer English is established in a country, the more …; Gone are the days when …* Ask students to write their own sentences about English or languages in general using these lexical phrases/patterns.

Speaking (SB page 39)

Aim: for students to relate the material in the reading to their own language, culture and experiences.

Tips:

- Monitor as students are talking and note down any problematic language, for feedback later.
- Conduct a whole-class feedback session on any points of interest.
- Highlight any problems anonymously. You may decide to do this in a written format, eg compile a handout with a collection of ten of their problematic utterances for students to correct next lesson.

As you go through these *Global English* lessons in the book, don't be afraid to ask students' opinions and reactions to the information in the texts. *Which do you find interesting? Do you know of similar experiences or facts in your language or other languages?* Some of your learners might be in your class because they are very interested in language, and these texts provide a great opportunity for you to capitalise on that motivation.

Writing: an essay

These lessons in *Global* are designed to provide extended writing practice. They all follow a similar format.

Reading (SB page 40)

Aim: to provide a sample text for students to analyse.

Tips:

- Before students start reading, focus their attention on the photo and elicit descriptions and comments.
- There are often two questions for these texts: one which focuses on gist and the other on specific details. Allow just two or three minutes to respond to the two gist questions in exercise 1.
- Let students work initially on their own, then check answers in pairs.
- Ask students *Would this genre look different in your language? If so, how?*

1

1 the laser / laser technology

2 its range of present and potential benefits

2

1 Lasers work by concentrating and focusing intense beams of light.

2 science, commerce, industry, surgery, cosmetic surgery, archaeology, criminal detection, daily life, communications, the military

3 surgery: reducing the impact of major operations; treatment for skin conditions; cutting and welding metals; CD and DVD players; laser printers and bar code scanners; fibre optic systems in computers and internet communications; targeting and detecting weapons; space exploration or maybe for production of clean, powerful energy using nuclear fusion

4 Students' own answers.

Linking ideas: contrast (SB page 40)

Aim: to highlight and focus on a particular aspect of language that students can use to improve their writing.

Tips:

- In exercise 1, do one example together in class, then let students come up with others in pairs.
- Use exercise 2 as a diagnostic one, to see how students do. Monitor as they are working and encourage them to discuss answers. In feedback, discuss the differences in syntax, style and emphasis between these words and phrases. See *Language note*.

1

However, they are best known for their applications in daily life.

They are, however, best known for their applications in daily life.

They are best known, however, for their applications in daily life.

They are best known for their applications in daily life, however.

In general, it emphasises what immediately precedes it, eg *Some people like coffee. Others, however, prefer tea.* *However* is commonly used at the start of a sentence, to contrast with the whole of the preceding sentence. It is also commonly used mid-sentence, eg after a new subject, or after the verb *be* or an adjective, and some people prefer this stylistically. Emphasis is weakened at the end of a sentence, and this position is less common. Some people consider the overuse of *however* to be poor style, so students should be encouraged to use other alternatives as well. The use of *however* to join sentences, though increasingly common, is still considered incorrect by many. It seems likely, however, that this usage will increase in frequency and become acceptable.

2

1 but / yet (*yet* implies a stronger contrast)

2 Despite / In spite of (no difference)

3 Although / Even though / While (*Even though* suggests a stronger contrast; *While* suggests a weaker one)

4 However / Nevertheless / Even so (*However* and *Even so* are stronger)

5 But / Yet (both commonly used here, especially in journalistic style, though their use to start a new sentence is often considered incorrect; *however* and *nevertheless* are also possible, but would require a following comma)

Language note

Some of these words and phrases used to show contrast are either adverbs, conjunctions or prepositions. As a result, they are followed by different syntax. *While, although, yet* and *even though* are conjunctions, so require two clauses: *Even though he was tired, he still went to the party. In spite of* and *despite* are prepositions, so are followed by noun phrases, eg *They cheated, despite the warnings. Even so, however* and *nevertheless* are adverbs, usually followed by a comma.

TEACH GLOBAL THINK LOCAL Extra activity

To focus students on the syntax, give them a single pair of sentences and ask them to transform it, using four or five different words used to show contrast, eg *She wouldn't wear her hat. It was cold.* ➛ *Although it was cold, she wouldn't wear her hat.*

Writing skills: gathering ideas (SB page 40)

Aim: to give students a chance to develop their writing through various different micro skills.

Tips:

- This type of exercise is designed to expose students to useful strategies for use when planning. Often the ideas-getting stage is the hardest for students, particularly under exam conditions.
- Encourage students to compare and discuss strategies used.
- Encourage some students to share their choices and ideas with the whole class.

Preparing to write (SB page 41)

Aim: to give students an opportunity to gather ideas for the writing task.

Tips:

- Allow students to brainstorm ideas in pairs or groups.
- Ask students to make notes here, but not to begin writing.
- Point out and encourage students to use the useful language under *Giving a personal opinion*.
- Bear in mind that this stage both prepares students with ideas for writing, and also allows them to see whether their chosen alternative is a good one. Ask *Do you have enough to discuss and therefore write about?*

Writing (SB page 41)

Aim: to give practice in more extended writing tasks.

Tips:

- This section can be done as homework.
- Remind students to refer back to the model text.
- Tell students that the questions in *Preparing to write* will provide a structure for the essay.
- Ask students to check their work carefully before they hand it in.
- If appropriate, ask students to write a second draft of their essay, after some feedback from you.

Study skills

Improving your reading efficiency (SB page 41)

1 First of all, dictate these questions: *Are you a fast reader in your first language? What about in English? Do you remember what you read, generally? Do you tend to read every word, in say a novel or article?* In pairs, students discuss these questions briefly. Then they read the list, attempting to identify the two poor strategies and explain why. Refer students to the notes on page 131 and discuss.

> Looking up unknown words: this is not a good general strategy. It may increase your vocabulary, but it will slow you down. Often you do not need to know the meaning of every word in order to understand what you need from a text, though there are some texts (eg instructions, legal documents) where you need a detailed understanding.
>
> Reading aloud slows most people down and can distract from understanding, although a few auditory readers may find it beneficial.
>
> In general, you should experiment with reading strategies to find what works best for you, as no two readers are exactly the same.

2 After students' discussion in pairs, elicit their preferences, and encourage them to give some sort of rationale.

3 Ask a student to read the text aloud. As students are unlikely to have suitable reading texts with them, you will probably have to set this for homework. These statistics (200–250 words per minute for an average native speaker) and the focus may help remind students of the importance of improving their reading speed at this level. Ask students to report back next lesson on their reading speed in a) their first language and b) in English.

UNIT 4 Theory & Practice

Coursebook

Unit 4	Language	Texts	Communication skills
Part 1 SB page 42	Vocabulary & Writing Theory and research Grammar Modals: language functions	Speaking & Reading *The Myth of Mars and Venus* Listening Communication problems	Speaking & Reading Gender differences
Part 2 SB page 44	Vocabulary & Speaking Cinema Grammar Modals of obligation Past modal forms	Reading Dogme 95	Vocabulary & Speaking Cinema Writing A manifesto
Part 3 SB page 46	Grammar Determiners	Reading *El Sistema*	Speaking Skills
Part 4 SB page 48	Extend your vocabulary Similes	Listening *Pygmalion*	Speaking Small talk Pronunciation Question tags Speaking Accents
Function globally SB page 50	Asking for clarification Listening to explanations and clarifications Asking for and giving clarifications		
Global voices SB page 51	Practice *I mean* Discussing ways to improve your English		
Writing SB page 52	A review Writing skills: writing a plan Linking ideas: extra information Describing a film		
Study skills SB page 53	Working on pronunciation		

Additional resources

eWorkbook	Interactive and printable grammar, vocabulary, listening and pronunciation practice Extra reading and writing practice Additional downloadable listening and video material
Teacher's Resource Disc	Communication activity worksheets to print and photocopy, review material, test, and video with worksheet
Go global Ideas for further research	**Theory** There are a number of websites that list film genres, for example www.filmsite.org/genres.html and www.mecfilms.com/critic1.htm. Students can research a particular genre and report to the class on the main films, most famous scenes and directors, etc. **Practice** There are a number of websites that report on the Venezuelan *El Sistema* musical training programme. As well as finding out details of how successful it is, students can find articles from newspapers questioning whether it could be successfully imported into other countries. Students can report on these commentaries.

Part 1

TEACH GLOBAL THINK LOCAL Lead-in

Write up the following sentences on the board. Ask students who they think they refer to, *men* or *women*:

Language and communication is more important to them.

They talk more about things and facts.

They choose harmony over disharmony.

They talk more about feelings and relationships.

They tend to be more competitive.

Add extras if you wish. In groups of three, ask students to discuss their views trying to justify their ideas.

Speaking and Reading (SB page 42)

The reading discusses claims made about gender differences and why the author – Oxford University professor, Deborah Cameron – disagrees with their basic tenets.

1 Students discuss the titles, and whether they have read these or similar publications. Discuss as a class.

2 Invite students to share their reactions to extract A. Ask *At this point, do you know what the author's own view is?* (Not really, so far it is a neutral presentation of ideas, apart from the use of the word *myth*, which sounds negative.)

3 Ask students to read the other extracts to find out what Cameron's views actually are. Elicit responses.

> The myth that men and women speak different languages
>
> Cameron does not agree. She says the claims are not supported by evidence based on solid research.

4 This task focuses on language which conveys the author's attitude; the connotation of certain words or phrases. At the end, ask *Now that you have read Cameron's arguments, do you agree with her or not?*

> 1 *No doubt; The reality is that*
> 2 *dogma; unquestioned article of faith; myth; does not stand up to scrutiny; mythology; trite formulas; sweeping claims*
> 3 proposition; premise; claims; hypothesis; science sound bites

5 Students work independently then compare ideas. Check answers in a whole-class feedback session.

> 1 *a myth … that women's talk is cooperative and men's competitive (research shows that both sexes engage in both kinds of talk)*
> 2 *a myth … that men and women systematically misunderstand one another (research has produced no good evidence that they do).*
> 3 *Conflicts which are really caused by people wanting different things are persistently described as 'misunderstandings' or 'communication problems'.*
> 4 *… there is potential for communication to go awry in every exchange … language is not telepathy.*
> 5 *… the idea that communication problems are the major source of conflict … does not stand up to scrutiny.*

Vocabulary and Writing (SB page 42)

1 Let students work in pairs. Clarify any new words. These phrases are particularly useful for writing argumentative essays (see SB page 88) or for formal debates.

Incorrect alternatives

1	expounds	4	is not a sweeping generalisation
2	dogma	5	questions
3	verifies	6	in theory

2 Students write about three sentences on their chosen theory, giving a sentence which elaborates or supports the initial statement, then their own opinion. If you think (any of) your students will find this task challenging, let them work in pairs.

3 Students discuss their sentences with a (new) partner. Monitor and encourage students to share their examples. Allow them to respond to each others' views if they wish.

Listening (SB page 42)

This listening extract gives Cameron's views on some example claims made by John Gray, an author of one of the self-help books. This relates to how women can communicate more effectively with men.

1 **2.01** If appropriate, start by eliciting minor examples which demonstrate that men and women think differently, eg going shopping. Let students read the questions first. At the end, ask if they need to listen again. Students compare answers before feedback.

> 1 To make requests in the form of direct questions asking the person to do something rather than questions which may be interpreted as requests for information or hypothetical questions about whether something is possible.
> 2 She dismisses it as nonsense (*patently ridiculous*) and not something a competent user of English would misunderstand.
> 3 Both people understand that these questions are requests, not merely information-gathering questions.
> 4 Her parents did not question or argue about their roles because they were understood as part of gender difference; nowadays 'pretty much everything is up for negotiation' and is therefore more likely to lead to conflict.

2.01

The Myth of Mars and Venus

In a section of his book which explains how to ask men to do things, Gray says that women should avoid using indirect requests. For instance, they should not signal that they would like a man to bring in the shopping by saying, 'The groceries are in the car': they should ask him directly, by saying, 'Would you bring in the groceries?' Another mistake women make is to formulate requests using the word 'could' rather than 'would'. 'Could you empty the trash?', says Gray, 'is merely a question gathering information.' 'Would you empty the trash?' is a request.

Gray seems to be suggesting that men hear utterances such as 'Could you empty the trash?' as purely hypothetical questions about their ability to perform the action mentioned. But that is a patently ridiculous claim. No competent user of English would take 'Could you empty the trash?' as 'merely a question gathering information', any more than they would take 'Could you run a mile in four minutes?' as a polite request to start running.

A friend once told me a story about the family dinners of her childhood. Each night as the family sat down to eat, her father would examine the food on his plate and then say to his wife something like, 'Is there any ketchup, Vera?' His wife would then get up and fetch whatever condiment he had mentioned. According to Gray's theory, he should have reacted with surprise: 'Oh, I didn't mean I wanted ketchup, I was just asking whether we had any.' Needless to say, that was not his reaction. Both he and his wife understood 'Is there any ketchup?' as an indirect request to get the ketchup, rather than 'merely a question gathering information'.

The more similar men and women become, the more they are in direct competition for the same kinds of rewards (jobs, status, money, leisure time). My parents never argued about who should take out the trash, pick up groceries, wash dishes, drive the car, or make important financial decisions. Nor were they ever in conflict about whose job came first or whose life had to be fitted around domestic commitments. These things were settled in advance by the basic fact of gender difference. [But] For many couples today, pretty much everything is up for negotiation. That has the potential to lead to arguments and conflicts.

2 Elicit students' responses as a whole class, or allow time for discussion in groups if you see students are very enthusiastic. Ask *Do you ever buy this kind of book?*

Grammar (SB page 43)

This grammar focus is on modals and their different functional uses.

1 Write up on the board *Could you lower the noise?* Elicit different purposes for this question, eg a request, a warning, a complaint, a suggestion. After students complete the exercise check answers as a class.

1 offer
2 recommendation
3 request
4 making a suggestion
5 request for permission
6 complaint about an annoying habit
7 suggestion of moral obligation
8 unenthusiastic suggestion
9 promise

2 Put up the following questions on the board: *Which is more direct? Which is more formal? Which sounds more old-fashioned?* In pairs, students discuss the alternatives in exercise 1 and share their ideas with the class.

1 More direct: *Can*; More formal / old-fashioned: *Shall*
2 No difference in register; *must* is stronger in meaning.
3 More direct: *Can*, *Will*; More formal: *Could*, *Would*. *Could* and *Would* are slightly politer forms in most contexts.
4 More direct: *Shall*; More formal: *Should*. *Should* in this context is a weaker suggestion and suggests an expectation of a less positive response.
5 More direct: *Can*, *Could*; More formal: *May*, *Might*; More old-fashioned: *Might*
6 No difference in register. Both are quite formal and suggest a complaint about an unwelcome habit.
7 More direct: *Should*, *Ought to*; More formal: *Could*, *Might*; More old-fashioned: *Might*. *Might* also suggests a lack of sympathy with the fact that the other person has not yet apologised.
8 No difference in register. *Might* is more tentative or expresses less agreement.
9 More formal: *I shall* form. *I shall;* also suggests a more emphatic statement, an offer / promise perhaps, contrary to the expectations of the other speaker.

3 Mime to students that you have a headache. Elicit what modal-related language you could use, eg *Could you get me an aspirin?* Students do the exercise. In feedback, check whether their overall intonation is appropriate and polite. See *Language note*. Respond to this accordingly by highlighting and drilling.

Suggested answers

1 Could you close the window / turn the heating up, please?
2 Shall we go to the cinema / out for a meal?
3 You might lend a hand / do the washing-up once in a while!
4 Shall / Can I give you a hand?
5 Will you / someone answer the phone?

Language note

Exercise 3 (and also the listening) touch on what is called 'the illocutionary force' of language in discourse. If a person says *I've got a headache*, it could imply: *Can you get me an aspirin? Can you leave me in peace? I don't want any food. I'm sick of this work* and so on, depending on the context. Often a listener will attempt to clarify the meaning, eg *So, you mean you're not hungry?* This indirect use of language is commonly used across languages.

Students at this level are likely to be familiar with all of these functional uses, with the possible exception of sentence 6 and also *could* and *might* in sentence 7 (Grammar exercise 1, SB page 43).

TEACH GLOBAL THINK LOCAL

Extra activity

Ask students to think of an indirect way to express sentences 1, 3, 4 and 5 in exercise 1 (SB page 43), eg *Can I get you a lemonade?* ➛ *I'm a bit thirsty*. Give them some additional requests eg *Can I borrow one of the class dictionaries to take home?* These indirect requests can sometimes be a more polite and tentative way of asking for or suggesting something.

4 In pairs, challenge students to write a short dialogue using at least three of the modals. Give them time to rehearse. Elicit some examples.

Pronunciation note

When working on modals, it is essential to integrate work on pronunciation. Misplaced stress or the use of full forms rather than weak forms, can radically change the tone. At advanced level, it is often most appropriate to deal with pronunciation reactively, when problems arise. Give attention to:

- generally in requests and suggestions, the modal is unstressed and a weak form is used, where possible.
- where the speaker wishes to highlight the function of the modal verb, the modal **is** stressed, eg *I <u>shall</u> write to you, honest!* (promise); *I <u>will</u> give your dinner to the cat if you don't come!* (second warning); *You <u>could</u> apologise!* (complaint); *You really <u>must</u> see that film!* (recommendation).

Drill different sentences to show how intonation and stress radically change the meaning, eg

Will you <u>empty</u> the <u>dustbin</u>? (polite request);

<u>Will</u> you empty the <u>dustbin</u>? (exasperated request/order).

G Grammar focus

Refer students to the language summary on modals: language functions on page 138.

You can use exercises 1–3 on page 139 for:
a) extra practice now, b) homework or c) review later on.

The answers are on page 162 of this Teacher's Book.

Part 2

TEACH GLOBAL THINK LOCAL

Lead-in

Project or write the following instructions/questions on the board, or put them around the room. (The answers are in brackets, where relevant.)

- *Name three well-known film directors.*
- *Name the actor who played Indiana Jones.* (Harrison Ford)
- *How many Godfather films were there?* (3)
- *Hum or clap the theme tune to a film and see if your partner can guess it.*
- *Name one Hitchcock film.*
- *Name three James Bond films.*
- *Who starred as Harry Potter in the films of that name?* (Daniel Radcliffe)

Vocabulary and Speaking (SB page 44)

1 If you did the *Lead-in*, then the question writing is a natural follow-on. If not, elicit one or two example questions about films. If necessary, let students work in pairs and then in groups of four.

2 As a class, quickly brainstorm different genres of film. Then, in pairs or groups, students read the descriptions and name the genres and guess the films.

1 thriller (*The Clouded Yellow*)
2 epic (*Gladiator*)
3 musical (*South Pacific*)
4 animated film (*Toy Story*)
5 costume drama (*Pride and Prejudice*)

3 Students work individually to complete the text before finishing and checking in pairs. At the end, elicit any new or problem words, putting them up on the board, together with the word class.

1 stars; nominated
2 props; sets; shot; digitally
3 Set; score
4 budget; box office; sequel
5 adaptation; screenplay; cast

4 Allow students to think about their favourite film. Write up the following pointers on the board: *film genre, main stars, basic storyline (in two sentences), where set, any awards, why you like it*. In pairs, students talk about their favourite films. Monitor and invite students to share some interesting examples, in a whole-class feedback session.

TEACH GLOBAL THINK LOCAL Writing extra

The following film-related words are often confused, even at this level: *shoot* (v), *star, cast, set, play* (all nouns **and** verbs). Ask students to try and use at least four of these words in a paragraph-long description of their favourite film, plus at least two of the other ones from the box in exercise 3. Monitor and/or take their writing in to check. Highlight good examples to put on the board, or conversely, problematic ones to help out with.

Reading (SB page 44)

1 Students read the opinions and reflect for a moment. Elicit some responses and examples of films which use lots of special effects. Ask students *Is it possible to make a film without any special effects these days?*

2 The reading is essentially the manifesto of a film movement which advocates going 'back to basics' in film-making, as a reaction to the style and expense of huge Hollywood blockbusters.

Tell students they are going to read about a very interesting angle on film-making. Ask them to write a two-line summary of the text. Let them compare their summaries. Elicit some examples.

Suggested answer

'Back to basics' – everything should be truthful, with no technical intervention misrepresenting or distorting what is presented on-screen. The theory was intended to allow directors working with small budgets to compete with Hollywood films by making a virtue out of realism.

3 This task is essentially a comprehension task, demanding that students relate and interpret the two texts. Let them compare answers in pairs before feedback.

1 Rules 1 (filmed in studio); 4 (black and white); 8 (thriller); 10 (director credited)
2 Rules 1 (filmed in different location, props used); 2 (images added digitally); 7 (set in Ancient Rome); 8 (epic)
3 Rules 1 (filmed in different location); 5 (special filters used); 7 (set during World War 2); 8 (musical)
4 Rules 1 (animated); 2 (animated so sound produced separately); 3 (action not filmed directly with camera); 8 (animated)
5 Rules 1 (used costumes / props); 7 (set in 19th century); 8 (costume drama)

More rules are likely to have been broken, eg in musicals, the soundtrack is produced separately, but the above is what can be worked out from the information given.

4 Ask students *If you were a film director, how hard do you think it would be to stick to the rules of Dogme 95 and why?* Students then read the quotation and answer the questions in groups of three. Monitor and invite some groups to share their responses with the whole class.

5 Write up the name of the film *Italian For Beginners* and ask students if they have seen it. Form AB pairs who should follow the instructions on their respective pages. Ask them to avoid writing notes, but simply to use their memory. Books closed, students compare their reviews.

Grammar (SB page 45)

1 This exercise focuses on uses of different modals and semi-modals to talk about necessity, desirability and prohibition. Do the first sentence together as an example. Students then work independently to complete the task, comparing their choices in pairs before class feedback.

Incorrect alternatives

a doesn't have to	c must	e can't
b mustn't	d should	

2 Let students reflect for a couple of minutes before completing this task in pairs. Put the answers on the board for students to self-check. Invite any questions.

1 a 2 c 3 e 4 d 5 b

3 This exercise asks students to look at the difference between so-called 'internal' and 'external' obligation. See *Language note*. Elicit the response as a whole class, including their reasoning.

1 producer: stating a rule which he has imposed – authority comes from the speaker
2 reporter: reporting something which is necessary – authority comes from elsewhere

Language note

Must is used for so-called 'internal' obligation, from the speaker him/herself. *Have to* comes from outside and is 'external', often used therefore to talk about regulations and rules. This is only a generalisation, however, and at advanced level, students should be aware of the limitations of this.

Need can be a modal verb, almost always used in the negative to talk about absence of obligation. It is used by someone in authority when giving permission, eg *He needn't go.* However, it can also be a normal lexical verb, eg *He doesn't need to go*. The meaning of *need* as a lexical verb and as a modal often overlaps.

Note that *could* is used to talk about general ability in the past, eg *Mark could run faster than me as a boy.* However, it is not used to talk about an ability limited to one time, eg *Mark ~~could~~ run faster in yesterday's race, and won.* Here, other verbs such as *be able to* or *manage to* are preferred. However, the negative *couldn't* is used to talk about both general and particular times.

4 Students work alone then compare answers before feedback. Remind them that sentence c acts like a modal, see *Language note*, but is not actually a modal verb in form.

1 d 2 f 3 a 4 c 5 b 6 e

5 Students write sentences about real things which happened in the last two weeks or so. Give some personal examples, eg *I had to eat pasta for four days on the run, because I couldn't go shopping. I should have just gone, but I had too much marking to do.* Monitor and check accuracy as they write. Before students read their sentences to each other, point out that they should ask at least two questions. Elicit examples.

Students' own answers.

G Grammar focus

Refer students to the language summary on modals of obligation and the past forms of modals: obligation and need on page 138.

You can use exercise 4 on page 139 for:

a) extra practice now, b) homework or c) review later on.

The answers are on pages 162–3 of this Teacher's Book.

Writing (SB page 45)

1 Put up the following adjectives on the board: *forbidden, prohibited, allowed, permitted, (un)acceptable*. In pairs, students think back to the *Dogme 95* manifesto, without looking, and use the adjectives to orally describe the movement's objectives. Monitor to see if they are using them appropriately.

Ask students to write a *Language Class Manifesto*. Put this on the board as a title. Elicit an example. Give students 10–15 minutes to write their manifesto. If necessary, give some prompts: *homework, correcting work, assignments (deadlines, length, plagiarism), behaviour and attitude, punctuality, exams*, etc. Encourage them to use a more natural mixture of modals and adjectives, as in the *Dogme 95* text. Monitor as they are writing, assisting on the spot, as appropriate.

2 Students sit in groups of four to share and comment on each others' manifesto.

Part 3

TEACH GLOBAL THINK LOCAL Lead-in

To lead in to the topic, ask students to finish these sentence starters.

I'm fairly skilled at / in ...

I'd like to be skilled at / in ...

My XXX (friend/relative) has an unusual skill. He/She ...

Before they start, show or tell them about something you are skilled in, if possible bringing in an example of something you have done or tools you work with, where relevant. Give some extra information about your skill, eg how and why you started, what it involves, how you do it, etc.

Give a few, wide-ranging examples of skills, eg baking, gardening, understanding people, saving money, knitting, etc, so that everyone has something to talk about. Students think for a moment or two, then discuss their sentences in groups of three, giving details about their skill.

Speaking (SB page 46)

In pairs, students discuss the first two questions about the given skills. When they have finished, invite them to share their ideas on the final bullet point. Establish what the difference is between 'collective' and 'individual' practice. Elicit what students understand by these terms. Give an example, eg *Some people like to practise meditation on their own, some prefer to do it in a group.*

Reading (SB page 46)

This text discusses the successful impact on individuals and on society of the *El Sistema* music programme. It also describes the nature of practice for the orchestra members.

1 Students should look at the two photos at the foot of the page and try to work out how they are related. Write up the words *El Sistema* and elicit what they know about it, if anything. Ask students to read and discuss the quotation and to consider how it relates to the photos. Invite some students to share their ideas with the whole class.

TEACH GLOBAL THINK LOCAL Extra activity

For a real challenge, put up the quotation, in muddled groups of words, on the board. In pairs, students have to put the words in order to make a single sentence, without looking at the Coursebook. Underline the first two words to help and tell them this quotation is Abreu's view of the value of an orchestra. Monitor and help by giving the next word(s), if necessary:

it is objective that essential and itself is a is that community comes with fundamental together the only <u>an orchestra</u> exclusive of agreeing where the feature community with the

On finishing, let students discuss what they understand by this quotation.

2 Students read the first part of the text, *What exactly is El Sistema?*, to find out if they were right. Ask students to focus their attention on the aims and achievements as they read. Let them discuss their answers and reactions in pairs before sharing their ideas with the class.

Aims:
to offer music education to children and young people, mainly from impoverished backgrounds, in order to improve their lives through music. Its primary aim is to make a positive social impact, rather than to produce accomplished musicians.

Achievements:
It has produced internationally renowned performers and conductors.

It is linked with a marked reduction in drug addiction and juvenile delinquency, and improved school attendance.

3 Let students complete this comprehension task of the remaining text on their own, before checking answers in pairs. Monitor as they are doing this, to pick up on any problems. Conduct a feedback session to discuss any differences or queries. Ensure that students support their views with evidence from the text.

1 regardless of	4 more frequently
2 in mixed ability groups	5 eliminate errors
3 teamwork	6 certain students

4 This exercise highlights new words and encourages students to work out the meaning from the context. Let them refer to a dictionary to check their answers before whole-class feedback. Then elicit the answers, focusing on the pronunciation. Many of the words are a little tricky because the stress is on the second syllable, eg *accomplished* /əˈkʌmplɪʃt/, *renowned* /rɪˈnaʊnd/, *impoverished* /ɪmˈpɒvərɪʃt/, or due to silent letters, eg *paradigm* /ˈpærədaɪm/ or consonant clusters, eg *lapses*, *accomplished*.

1 ground-breaking	5 mesmerised
2 impoverished	6 paradigm
3 accomplished	7 from the outset
4 renowned	8 lapses

5 Put students in pairs to discuss their reactions to the programme. Ask if they have heard of similar social projects, either locally or globally, musical or otherwise.

Grammar (SB page 47)

The section focuses on different determiners. (There is an additional focus in Unit 7 on articles and on quantifiers in Unit 9.)

1 First ask students what they understand by the grammatical term *determiner*, eliciting different examples onto the board. Ask them to read the Grammar reference summary on SB page 47. They then complete the exercise individually before checking answers in pairs. They should try to explain the difference in meaning between the two choices in each case. In feedback, ensure students understand the difference.

1 No	3 Every	5 either
2 Any	4 Each	6 Neither

2 Let students work on this in pairs. Discuss the answers as a class. They will probably have heard both/all alternatives, so are likely to be interested here in the difference.

1 in each case, the second alternative with *no / neither*
2 the first alternative with *any*

Language note

A determiner is a small grammar word which comes at the start of a noun phrase. The determiner tells us about quantity, possession or whether it is familiar or new information; only one determiner is generally used.

Some determiners are used in more formal contexts: *much* and *little* are preferred to *a lot of* and *not much* respectively, eg *Much trouble was caused because so little money was spent. A lot of trouble was caused because not much money was spent*. Likewise, *few* is more formal than *not many*, as is *neither* in comparison to *either*: *She liked neither of the films.*

Some and *any* have strong forms as well as weak forms, which have a different meaning, eg *Some woman gave this note to me.* (This means a particular woman whose identity is not known.) Note that the form is *some* + singular noun. A strong form of *some* can also be used to show contrast: *Some people pay rent, but others don't.* The strong form of *any* means 'it does not matter which', eg *You can open any of these parcels.*

3 Give students time to work on their own and write out the new sentences. Monitor as they are working to check their choice of determiners, clarifying as necessary. Let students compare their answers in pairs. Elicit different options accepting any grammatically correct and logical combinations.

Possible answers

1 With (some) training and time, a / any / every student can learn to play any / an / this / that instrument.
2 It is a good idea to find (a / some) regular time every / each / one day to practise.
3 No / Neither / Any / A / This / That student can make (any) (no) progress without an / another / the / instructor.
4 Neither / No practice nor effort can compensate for (a / his / that) lack of talent.
5 Every / Each / Any individual has a different learning curve.
6 You need (either / some) discipline or perseverance and preferably both to succeed.
7 It is a good idea to practise with each student so you can encourage each one and correct each one.

4 Students discuss the statements with a different partner. If time at the end, ask the class *Which of you can play an instrument? How did you learn? How much do / did you practise?*

TEACH GLOBAL THINK LOCAL **Speaking extra**

Students may enjoy discussing language learning in a similar way. Put up these statements about English on the board. Let them reflect for three or four minutes, then put students into groups of three, grouping them carefully to cater for personality types:

- *Any person can learn to speak a language well.*
- *Some people can just pick up a language really effectively, without any study.*
- *To speak a language with a convincing accent, you have to have an excellent ear and great confidence.*
- *The mastery of a language depends on the amount of time you invest.*

G Grammar focus

Refer students to the language summary on determiners on page 138.

You can use exercise 5 on page 139 for:
a) extra practice now, b) homework or c) review later on.

The answers are on page 163 of this Teacher's Book.

Part 4

TEACH GLOBAL THINK LOCAL **Lead-in**

Put up some situations on the board, eg *at a bus stop; in the dentist's waiting room; at the hairdresser's; at a party.* Put students into AB pairs. They choose a situation before A starts. They should improvise a two-minute conversation with a stranger. Warn them you will time them! Then pairs choose a different situation, with B starting. This time, time them for three minutes! Monitor and share some nice examples of conversation starters.

Speaking (SB page 48)

1 In pairs, students answer the questions about the topics. Elicit any affecting factors, eg you might discuss health if you were feeling unwell, etc.

2 In pairs or groups, students discuss these questions and share some examples of recent situations.

3 In pairs, students discuss why the 'a' responses are inappropriate. Invite suggestions and, at this point, also elicit an alternative suitable 'b' response.

1 not considered polite to disagree with remarks made as a conversation opener / to pass time (phatic conversation) and intended primarily to establish pleasant relationship / harmonious interaction
2 too limited, speaker is expected to qualify the remark and volunteer more information
3 speaker is expected to react positively.

4 **2.02** Explain to students that they only need to write a few words in each case. Elicit one or two examples, then listen to the audio to compare.

2.02

1
A: Great party!
B: Yes, fantastic.

2
A: Have we met before?
B: Yes, you look familiar – where do I know you from?

3
A: Hi, I'm Marina.
B: Hi, I'm Laura. Nice to meet you.

4
A: May I join you?
B: Please do.

5
A: Do you mind if I open the window?
B: Actually, I'd rather you didn't if you don't mind.

Pronunciation (SB page 48)

Language note

Students at advanced level are likely to have studied question tags several times already. However, even at this level, students do not use them very often, preferring other strategies, such as direct questions: *You're married, aren't you?* → *Are you married?* or simple statements for the confirmation tags: *It's a lovely day, ~~isn't it?~~* These can sound less natural, something worth pointing out to learners. It may also be worth reminding students how commonly these tags (or equivalents) are used in their own first language, where relevant. Tags are a very useful strategy for keeping a conversation going (as they demand a response).

Advanced students may still have problems hearing the difference between the two types of tags, and certainly with producing them.

1 **2.03** This exercise focuses on intonation in question tags and its effect on meaning. To raise the challenge, you could put the three sentences on the board and discuss how they (could) say them and the difference in meaning. Then listen to check.

1 down	2 down	3 up

2 Check these answers together. Then play the audio again for repetition. Focus in on students' intonation here, zooming in on accuracy and helping individuals to hear / produce rising or falling tones.

a 2 b 3 c 1

3 Get students to ask you questions first using different tags of both types (conversation openers and genuine questions), eg *We've studied this before, haven't we?* Give genuine responses to their questions. Then students continue in pairs. Monitor and provide support as needed.

4 If you did the *Lead-in*, ensure students are working in different pairs. Tell them to start with the tag question, and to carry on at least six conversational turns. If appropriate, award marks out of ten for pairs' pronunciation.

Listening (SB page 48)

1 **2.04** After students have read the information about George Bernard Shaw, check they understand the word *cockney* (a person born in East London). Set the scene before students listen: Higgins is bringing his new 'student' (the Cockney flower girl Eliza Doolittle) to a small upper-class party at his mother's house. He is intending to 'try out' his student in this environment, with her newly acquired 'posh' pronunciation. Students read the statements before listening.

1 F (*you promised not to come … go home at once*)
2 F (*I don't mean a love affair.*)
3 T
4 F (*She's to keep to two subjects: the weather and everybody's health*)
5 T
6 T

2.04

A = Mrs Higgins; **B** = Higgins; **C** = Parlour maid; **D** = Mrs Eynsford Hill; **E** = Clara; **F** = Eliza; **G** = Freddy

Pygmalion

A: Henry! What are you doing here to-day? It is my at-home day: you promised not to come. … Go home at once.

B: I know, mother. I came on purpose.

A: But you mustn't. I'm serious, Henry. You offend all my friends: they stop coming whenever they meet you.

B: Nonsense! I know I have no small talk; but people don't mind. … Besides, I've picked up a girl.

A: Does that mean that some girl has picked you up?

B: Not at all. I don't mean a love affair.

A: What a pity!

B: Why?

A: Well, you never fall in love with anyone under forty-five. When will you discover that there are some rather nice-looking young women about? … Now tell me about the girl.

B: She's coming to see you.

A: I don't remember asking her.

B: You didn't. I asked her. If you'd known her you wouldn't have asked her.

A: Indeed! Why?

B: Well, it's like this. She's a common flower girl. I picked her off the kerbstone.

A: And invited her to my at-home!

B: Oh, that'll be all right. I've taught her to speak properly; and she has strict orders as to her behaviour. She's to keep to two subjects: the weather and everybody's health – Fine day and How do you do, you know – and not to let herself go on things in general. That will be safe.

A: Safe! To talk about our health! about our insides! perhaps about our outsides! How could you be so silly, Henry?

B: Well, she must talk about something. Oh, she'll be all right: don't you fuss. I've a sort of bet on that I'll pass her off as a duchess in six months. I started on her some months ago; and she's getting on like a house on fire. I shall win my bet. She has a quick ear; and she's been easier to teach than my middle-class pupils because she's had to learn a complete new language. She talks English almost as you talk French.

A: That's satisfactory, at all events.

B: Well, it is and it isn't.
A: What does that mean?
B: You see, I've got her pronunciation all right; but you have to consider not only how a girl pronounces, but what she pronounces; and that's where …
C: Mrs. and Miss Eynsford Hill.
B: Oh Lord!
D: How do you do?
E: How d'you do?
A: My son Henry.
D: Your celebrated son! I have so longed to meet you, Professor Higgins.

2 **2.05** Tell students they are going to listen to a scene from the actual party, where Eliza meets Mrs Higgins' friends. After listening, students discuss answers in pairs, before checking. Replay the recording, if necessary.

1 She keeps to the script that Higgins has taught her.
2 Yes, until she suspects Freddy is laughing at her, when she tackles him.
3 Eliza's guard slips and she utters an expression that is unacceptable in polite society.

2.05

C: Miss Doolittle.
B: Here she is, mother.
F: How do you do, Mrs. Higgins? Mr. Higgins told me I might come.
A: Quite right: I'm very glad indeed to see you.
D: I feel sure we have met before, Miss Doolittle. I remember your eyes.
F: How do you do?
D: My daughter Clara.
F: How do you do?
E: How do you do? …
D: My son Freddy.
F: How do you do? …
A: Will it rain, do you think?
F: The shallow depression in the west of these islands is likely to move slowly in an easterly direction. There are no indications of any great change in the barometrical situation.
G: Ha! ha! how awfully funny!
F: What is wrong with that, young man? I bet I got it right. … Here! what are you sniggering at?
G: The new small talk. You do it so awfully well.
F: If I was doing it proper, what was you laughing at? Have I said anything I oughtn't?
A: Not at all, Miss Doolittle.
F: Well, that's a mercy, anyhow. What I always say is …
B: Ahem!
F: Well: I must go. So pleased to have met you. Good-bye.
A: Good-bye. …
F: Good-bye, all.
G: Are you walking across the Park, Miss Doolittle? If so …
F: Walk! Not bloody likely. I am going in a taxi.

3 Students work independently. If they ask about the meaning of any phrases, ask them to wait till the next stage.

1 up 2 off; on 3 to 4 at

4 **2.06** Students listen to check their answers. In a whole-class feedback session, clarify that *pick up a girl* usually means to begin talking to someone with the intention of starting a romantic relationship with them. Higgins uses the phrase here to refer to finding something and taking it away, as in: *I picked up a lovely old painting at the market on Saturday.* Put the phrase *pass sb/sth off as sb/sth* and *get on like a house on fire* on the board, eliciting what they mean. The simile, in particularly, is commonly used, and nowadays usually refers to a positive relationship (platonic or otherwise) between two people.

Ask students *What kind of man is Higgins?* (He is using Eliza to win a bet with a friend; he has a snobbish attitude towards Eliza, a mere flower girl and a woman!).

2.06

1

A: But you mustn't. I'm serious, Henry. You offend all my friends: they stop coming whenever they meet you.
B: Nonsense! I know I have no small talk; but people don't mind. … Besides, I've picked up a girl.
A: Does that mean that some girl has picked you up?
B: Not at all. I don't mean a love affair.

2

B: Well, she must talk about something. Oh, she'll be all right: don't you fuss. I've a sort of bet on that I'll pass her off as a duchess in six months. I started on her some months ago; and she's getting on like a house on fire.

3

B: Well, it's like this. She's a common flower girl. I picked her off the kerbstone.
A: And invited her to my at-home!
B: Oh, that'll be all right. I've taught her to speak properly; and she has strict orders as to her behaviour. She's to keep to two subjects: the weather and everybody's health – Fine day and How do you do, you know – and not to let herself go on things in general. That will be safe.

4

F: What is wrong with that, young man? I bet I got it right. … Here! what are you sniggering at?

G: The new small talk. You do it so awfully well.

F: If I was doing it proper, what was you laughing at? Have I said anything I oughtn't?

A: Not at all, Miss Doolittle.

5 Encourage students to discuss this as a whole class.

Speaking (SB page 49)

TEACH GLOBAL THINK LOCAL

Pre-speaking activity

Put up the following different accents of English on the board. Ask students if they know how any of these sound, or if they can imitate them. If you can, give some examples, or play some examples from the internet, typing in the keywords: *different English accents*. Check these in advance though – some of the clips are riddled with swear words!

*American, Australian, New Zealand, South African, Nigerian, Indian, Welsh, Scottish, Irish**

Brummy (Birmingham), Scouse (Liverpool), Geordie (Newcastle), West Country (south west of England), Cockney, Mancunian (Manchester), RP (Received Pronunciation), (British) street language.

* of course there are huge variations within these accents too, eg Northern Irish vs Southern.

Students discuss the questions in groups of three. Tell them they have about 8–10 minutes for this. Then elicit some ideas. You could bring up the point here for 'global English', one which is more neutral and not linked to a specific accent. See *Background note*.

Background note

RP (Received Pronunciation) is the form of English on which most British English language dictionaries, coursebooks and pronunciation materials are based; however, it is currently spoken in its pure form by less than 6% of the population. The term RP refers to accent and not to grammar or vocabulary. Although it derives from the accent of the southern part of Britain, it is a style of speech based on social class and not on geographical region. People used to send their children to expensive public schools or pay for 'elocution lessons' so that they would learn how to speak RP; however, nowadays many young people in England are trying to speak in a more informal way. In the past, BBC announcers used to speak with an RP accent, but nowadays modified regional accents are increasingly acceptable, even actively sought out.

Extend your vocabulary (SB page 49)

1 First elicit the simile *like a house on fire*, from Listening exercise 3. Ask students to put it into a sentence of their own. Then students work independently and compare their answers before checking in a dictionary.

1 a fish out of water	5 a leaf
2 a bear with a sore head	6 a chimney
3 a sieve	7 water off a duck's back
4 a log	

2 Students discuss the similes as a class.

3 Students select at least two similes to use in a personal situation. After three minutes to think, they work in small groups to share their experiences.

TEACH GLOBAL THINK LOCAL

Extra activity

If your students are interested in Cockney rhyming slang, show this example: *Give us your* ***bees and honey*** *or I'll shoot!* (money).

Students in pairs study the examples and decide on the meaning of the words in bold – you could display these on strips of paper around the room, so students can walk around and discuss them:

a *Get up those* ***apples and pears*** *to bed!* (stairs)

b *The girl put the money in her* ***sky rocket****.* (pocket)

c *That guy was a* ***tea leaf*** *so he spent some time in prison.* (thief)

d *He put the whole cake in his* ***north and south****.* (mouth)

e *When you have a minute to talk, just pick up the old* ***dog and bone****.* (phone)

f *Can you* ***Adam and Eve*** *it?* (believe)

g *If you're lucky, you'll get to meet the* ***baked bean****.* (queen)

h *That dog worked really hard, but now he's* ***brown bread****.* (dead)

i *It's nice and sunny. Put some cream on and brown your* ***bacon and eggs****.* (legs)

j *Don't be so silly. Just use your* ***loaf of bread****.* (head)

At the feedback stage, inform students that in Cockney rhyming slang the rhyming word is often dropped in use, eg *Get up those apples!* (stairs); *Brown your bacons!* (legs); *Use your loaf!* (head); *Give us your bees!* (money).

Function globally: asking for clarification

These lessons in *Global* are designed to provide students with immediately useful functional language. They all follow a similar format.

Warm up (SB page 50)

Aim: to introduce the topic via a quick speaking task or picture work.

Tips:

- Do not over-correct here, especially in speaking activities.
- Encourage students to use as much variety of language as they can.
- Pick up on any points which students find interesting / amusing to raise as an issue for the whole class.

Listening (SB page 50)

Aim: to present the functional language in context via a conversation or series of conversations.

Tips:

- Play the recording all the way through for each task (there are always two tasks). (Tracks 2.07–2.10)
- Pause the recording after each conversation.
- If students would like to, let them listen to the audio again, this time following the audioscript. Students often like to read and listen.
- Encourage students to read the audioscripts for homework, exploiting them for useful language.

1 Possible answers

Conversation 1: 1 at home; friends / partners or in a TV shop; shop assistant / customer; 2 how to connect a camera to the TV

Conversation 2: 1 talking on phone; friends; 2 the time of football practice

Conversation 3: 1 at sports centre; receptionist and customer; 2 the price to become a member of the sports centre

Conversation 4: 1 at a school meeting with their teacher; mother of two children, Michael and Ellie; 2 how well the children are doing at school

2

Conversation 1: 1 the back of the TV 2 push the button

Conversation 2: 1 6.45 2 6.15

Conversation 3: 1 if you join for a year 2 fill in a form

Conversation 4: 1 handwriting 2 more focused

2.07–2.10

1

A: OK, so what does this button here do?

B: OK, that actually turns the camera on right there. Once you've turned that on you're going to want to plug the cables into the back of the TV.

A: So hang on, I have to plug that cable into the … into the television?

B: Yes, right … right in the back of the television, right there. Once you've done that then you're going to need to take the television and put it to 'Input 1'.

A: Sorry, you've lost me. Can … what 'Input 1' …?

B: When you turn the television on there's a button on your remote that says 'Input' and you just keep pushing it until the picture comes up on the front.

A: OK.

B: So you don't … again you don't need to know 'Input 1', but just keep clicking it until it comes on and as long as you have it in the back then you should be fine.

A: Fantastic.

2

A: Hi, Nige.

B: Hi, Ben. You all right?

A: Yes good mate, you?

B: Not too bad thanks.

A: Good.

B: I've just had a call from Mark …

A: Yeah.

B: … he's told me … it's about footie practice on Thursday …

A: Oh right, yeah.

B: So he's changed the time of it.

A: Right … from, to?

B: It was going to be 6.45, it's now quarter past six.

A: Right, so 6.45?

B: Yeah, it was going to be 6.45, it's now quarter past six.

A: Sorry, can you speak up a bit?

B: Quarter past six.

A: Sorry, I didn't catch that?

B: Um, the footie practice is going to be at 6.15 on Thursday.

A: Oh I'm sorry mate, this is a really bad line. I can't hear what you're saying. Just something about footie practice?

B: Um, I'll ring you back in ten minutes.

A: Sorry?

B: I'll ring you back in ten minutes.

3

A: So, you want to join the gym?

B: Ahm, yes.

A: Right, well, if you want to be a monthly member, that costs £45, but if you want to be a yearly member, that's for 12 months, that's £350 and that's a much better deal.

B: Sorry, could you repeat that, please?

A: Right, for a monthly membership it's £45, for the year it's £350. Now that is the one you should really go for because you're saving yourself a lot more money that way.

B: Right … er … sorry, how much is it for the one month?

A: One month, £45, and all you have to do is fill out this little sheet of paper there, put your name at the top and all the relevant boxes, if you fill those out.

B: Sorry, I have to do what?

A: Fill in this form, and once you're a member then you can use all the facilities.

4

A: Oh well, hello, Sally, thanks for coming.

B: Oh you're welcome, hi.

A: Sorry to have kept you, we're running a bit late. Yes, about Michael and Ellie.

B: Yeah?

A: They're both doing really well.

B: Great.

A: There's no concern about Michael, it's just …

B: Oh.

A: … I'm just kind of flagging up …

B: Right.

A: … that his concentration is not quite as good as Ellie's. I mean, you might say she's doing a little bit better than him at the moment.

B: Right. Better?

A: Yes, um, simply in terms of being a bit more focused and a bit more enthusiastic about getting on with her tasks. Michael, you know, he just needs a little bit of a push now and again, um, especially with … his ability to sit down and hold a pencil and make small marks, you know, if you could encourage him, you know, perhaps to do a little bit of handwriting every day at home that would help.

B: So are you saying that he's disruptive?

A: No he's not … I'm not exactly saying that, he's not disruptive yet …

B: Because, you know, at home he's very active …

A: Yeah.

B: … but he is well-behaved.

A: Yes, it just depends …

B: He doesn't cause trouble.

A: … in a situation where we like them to sit and listen then he's finding that a bit difficult. I'm not saying there's actually a problem yet.

B: So are you saying that Ellie is basically much, much better in class?

A: Well, yes, more focused, more focused let's say.

Language focus (SB page 50)

Aim: to draw students' attention to the items of functional language.

Tips:

- Students work alone, then compare answers in pairs.
- Students should be able to pronounce these phrases intelligibly so drill them, if necessary.
- Students make a note of any new expressions.

1

What? (Note that *Excuse me?* is used in US English to ask for repetition. In British English it generally means 'I'm sorry', without question intonation. *Pardon? Say again?* and *Sorry?* are informal.)

2

a 2, 5 b 1, 3, 4, 6, 7, 8

Pronunciation (SB page 50)

Aim: to focus students on a particular aspect of pronunciation of the target phrases.

Tips:

- Play the recording two or three times, if necessary.
- At this level, try to promote good all-round pronunciation including stress, intonation and linking. This also raises the challenge for students.
- Use students with exemplary pronunciation to act as models to help others in the class.

The /t/ often seems to disappear in spoken English in mid-position. In fact, it does not disappear altogether, but is not finished, and sounds something close to a glottal stop.

Speaking (SB page 50)

Aim: to allow students an opportunity to use this language in a meaningful, real-world context.

Tips:

- Give students time to prepare this activity. Circulate and monitor carefully whilst they are talking.
- Encourage students to use the *Useful phrases* as well as some of the phrases in the *Language focus*.
- Correct sensitively, paying attention to the target language especially. With stronger students you could also focus on the pronunciation aspects they have just learnt.
- Ask students to repeat the task with a new partner.

Global voices

These lessons in *Global* are designed to provide students with exposure to authentic speakers of English from both native and non-native English backgrounds. They all follow a similar format.

Warm up (SB page 51)

Aim: to introduce the topic and highlight potentially difficult vocabulary the students will encounter.

Tips:

- Be generous in helping students with the vocabulary here, but let them try and work it out first.
- Circulate and monitor any speaking task, but be careful not to over-correct.

Listening (SB page 51)

Aim: to expose students to English spoken with a variety of accents.

Tips:

- Students will need to hear the recording at least twice, to understand it. (Tracks 2.12–2.15; 2.16–2.17)
- Tell students you don't expect them to understand every word because the text has not been scripted or graded in any way.
- The first task is easier and focuses on gist, the second task is more detailed.
- Students can read the audioscript at the back of the book if you / they wish.
- It may be tempting to hunt for specific pronunciation or language errors, but we recommend against this. In real-world communication not everyone speaks perfect English all the time, not even native speakers.

1

Katsuya: 2, 6 Carolina: 1, 3 Miguel: 5, 7 Rod: 4, 8

2.12–2.15

Katsuya, Japan

I think probably not the easiest, but the most fun to learn was the pronunciation because, um, every time I find a phrase that I can't pronounce properly, um, I repeat saying the phrase while I am having a shower, like, you know, just singing a song in the shower room and stuff.

Carolina, Argentina

So I started learning English at high school, but I actually, I haven't studied formally English. I tried to pick up words and phrases from TV shows in English or from movies and … but as I am a scientist we are currently exposed to articles written in English and we usually go to conferences in which the official language is English so you get the chance to practise a lot to, I mean, you need to, to find a way to express and to tell others about your work. You have to communicate your results so that's a really good opportunity to keep your level of English.

Miguel, Portugal

Well, I have been learning English since I am 12 and I studied one year abroad in Finland and all the university lessons were taught in English so I had to adapt and improve my English. It was really a necessity. If I have free time I tend to watch movies without subtitles because that way I am obliged to catch the accent and any vocabulary I may not know.

Rod, Gabon

Well, I started learning English at an early age when I was, since secondary school around the age of 12 years old, as you I mean. And I was really passionate in foreign languages, especially English, and tried to speak the language instead of speaking my native language, which is French, I mean, which is French. And I also use very much books in English, try to read, even if I didn't really understood what was going on in the book, but I use it at least to acquire new vocabulary, new words.

2 Suggested answers

Rod: Engage in conversation with native speakers if possible, watch TV

Carolina: Speak without thinking about making mistakes. If you try to be perfect you will be embarrassed, so relax and experiment.

 **2.16–2.17**

Rod: Well, I would certainly encourage them, certainly encourage learners of English to go and engage in conversation with a native speaker if they can, if they can, I mean, if they possibly can do that. If they can't do that then use as much as possible, I mean, things like BBC, all the stuff you know which is really interesting.

Carolina: Start speaking in English without thinking about the mistakes you might make. Because if you want to be perfect you will never speak English. I mean, you will never dare to speak English, you will be embarrassed and you won't do it and I think that you have to experiment and you have to try to relax and just let it, let it be and that's the best way of improving your English level in my opinion.

Language focus: *I mean* (SB page 51)

Aim: to raise students' awareness of a particular piece of language present in the listening.

Tips:

- The objective of these exercises is awareness-raising, not production.
- Ask students if they already use *I mean*, or what 'corrector' they usually use, eg *Sorry, I should say*, etc.

Speaking (SB page 51)

Aim: for students to discuss the same or similar questions as the speakers in the listening.

Tips:

- The speaking tasks here are slightly more open to allow for students to explore the subject. Give them time to do this.
- Monitor as they are talking and note down good / problematic use of language. You can highlight this in feedback (oral or written) later on.
- If this topic is relevant for your students, why not ask students to make a group poster based on ideas from *Speaking*, giving suggestions on how to improve.
- As you go through the book and the *Global voices* lessons, ask students for feedback on these listening activities and their potential use of English with other people.

Writing: a review

These lessons in *Global* are designed to provide students with extended writing practice. They all follow a similar format.

Reading (SB page 52)

Aim: to provide a sample text for students to analyse.

Tips:

- At this stage of the lesson merely ask students to read the text and extract the information.
- Give students a limited time to complete the gist task, eg 2–4 minutes.
- If you wish, ask for their views on the review and whether they'd like to see the film or not.
- At the end, ask students to look back and find four words or phrases that they would like to 'steal'.

TEACH GLOBAL THINK LOCAL

Pre-reading activity

Ask students to discuss how good they are at speaking publicly (whether in their first language or English). They should rate each aspect out of 5, where 5 = *extremely difficult for me* and 1 = *not a problem at all for me*.

- *Maintaining a good volume*
- *Speaking fluently, without hesitation*
- *Sounding convincing and passionate*
- *Connecting with the audience*
- *Keeping talking for long enough*
- *Sounding coherent*

In pairs, they discuss when they last spoke publicly. At the end, ask how important it is for famous people to be able to speak effectively in public.

1

The reviewer clearly thought highly of the film (*moving and thought-provoking; brilliant and memorable film that should not be missed*) Probably 9 or 10 out of 10.

Writing skills: writing a plan (SB page 52)

Aim: to give students a chance to develop their writing through various different micro skills.

Tips:

- Explain that this is basically an organisation template for writing a book / film review.
- Work through the example first with the students before asking them to continue on their own.
- Let students check their answers in pairs or small groups, then correct in open class.

1

Paragraph 1 b theme c genre d context

Paragraph 2 b plot

Paragraph 3 b acting c message d recommendation

Linking ideas: extra information (SB page 52)

Aim: to highlight and focus on a particular aspect of language that students can use to improve their writing.

Tips:

- Tell students that this focus is aimed at helping them to write more sophisticated sentences.
- Look at the example first with the students before asking them to continue on their own.
- Let students check their answers in pairs or small groups, then correct in open class.

TEACH GLOBAL THINK LOCAL

Extra activity

To practise techniques for making writing more sophisticated, ask students in pairs to break down the first sentence into at least six individual facts / sentences, eg *The film is called The King's Speech; it won four Oscars®*, etc. Then they close their books and rebuild it back into one complex sentence. You could do this either at the start or the end of this section, depending on your students.

1

2 four Oscars® (in brackets)
3 King George VI (clause contained between commas)
4 the film (phrase preceding the noun, followed by a comma)
5 the 1920s and 1930s (followed by a comma)
6 his stammer (between en rules / dashes)
7 an unorthodox speech therapist (contained between commas)
8 Bertie (followed by a comma)
9 a complex and multifaceted figure (following a colon)

Language note

You may wish to point out that the punctuation of extra information follows conventions:

At the start of a sentence: followed by a comma or colon

In the middle: contained within commas, brackets or dashes

At the end: preceded by a comma, colon or dash.

2

a 1, 5, 6, 8   b 2, 4, 7, 9   c 3

3 Possible answers

1 The writer of the screenplay, David Seidler, had a stammer as a child.
2 Released in January 2011, the film was widely praised by critics. / The film, which was released in January 2011, was widely praised by critics.
3 *The King's Speech* received numerous awards: Oscars®, BAFTAs and Golden Globes®.
4 King George was crowned in 1936, when his brother, King Edward VIII, abdicated. / King George, whose brother King Edward VIII abdicated, was crowned in 1936.
5 King George, whose daughter was Queen Elizabeth II, was a shy man.
6 The film, starring Colin Firth, Geoffrey Rush and Helena Bonham Carter, is set in the period before World War II.
7 Bertie, played by Colin Firth, was a complex figure. / Bertie, (who was) a complex figure, was played by Colin Firth.

Preparing to write (SB page 53)

Aim: to give students an opportunity to brainstorm ideas for the writing task.

Tips:

- Ask students to make notes here, but not to begin writing.
- Refer students to the phrases in *Describing a film* and encourage them to integrate these into their review.
- Ask students to refer back to *Writing skills: writing a plan* on page 52 to help structure their work coherently.

Writing (SB page 53)

Aim: to give students practice in extended writing tasks.

Tips:

- This section can be done as homework.
- Remind students to refer back to the model text.
- Ask them to choose a film that they actually liked.
- Tell students that their work will be read by other students who will select the film they'd most like to see, based on the most compelling review.
- Remind students to check their work carefully.

Study skills

Working on pronunciation (SB page 53)

1 Before students choose, ask them to think of a non-native English speaker who has really good English pronunciation. Ask *What do you think makes them sound so good? Do you know how they achieved this high level?*

2 From the alternatives in exercise 1 students choose their **target** pronunciation and discuss this in pairs.

3 Here students are encouraged to reflect on micro-aspects of their pronunciation. Be prepared to tell them about phonological areas you consider important for certain individuals.

4 After the pair discussions, as a class brainstorm some useful suggestions. Be ready to inject one or two of your own preferred reference materials here too.

5 Students discuss these questions in groups. Assist as necessary. Elicit answers to the last question.

a) vowels: top left quadrant
b) diphthongs: top right quadrant
c) consonants: bottom half
Value: to be able to read dictionary pronunciation transcriptions, to help record and learn pronunciation of new vocabulary, to identify and work on key sounds

TEACH GLOBAL THINK LOCAL

Extra activity

Find out how familiar your students are with the phonemic chart. Ask them to use phonemics to write out a word or phrase describing their reaction to the phonemic chart. They should write it in their notebooks first, and you can check it, before they write it on the board, for everyone to see! eg /ɪts ˈfæbjələs ən aɪ lʌv ɪt/.

6 If you have the facilities, show them the pronunciation app, highlighting how it can help their pronunciation.

UNIT 5 # Heroes & Villains

Coursebook			
Unit 5	**Language**	**Texts**	**Communication skills**
Part 1 SB page 54	Speaking & Vocabulary Heroism and personal qualities Vocabulary Expressions with *stand* and *give*	Reading & Listening *Gilgamesh*	Speaking & Vocabulary Heroism and personal qualities
Part 2 SB page 56	Vocabulary World problems Extend your vocabulary Abbreviations and acronyms for international organisations Grammar Present perfect simple and continuous	Listening & Speaking Unsung heroes/World Vision volunteers	Listening & Speaking Unsung heroes/World Vision volunteers Writing News reports
Part 3 SB page 58	Vocabulary & Speaking *Crimes and punishments*	Reading *Piracy* Listening & Speaking Piracy in Somalia	Vocabulary & Speaking *Crimes and punishments* Listening & Speaking Piracy in Somalia Pronunciation Word stress
Part 4 SB page 60	Extend your vocabulary Ways of describing bad people Grammar Participle clauses	Reading *The nature of evil*	Speaking Stanford experiment
Function globally SB page 62	Managing conversations Listening to people exchanging stories Interrupting and changing the topic of conversation		
Global English SB page 63	Linguistic heroes and villains Discussing the protection of minority languages		
Writing SB page 64	A report Writing skills: paragraph structure Describing facts and figures		
Study skills SB page 65	Register awareness		

Additional resources	
eWorkbook	Interactive and printable grammar, vocabulary, listening and pronunciation practice Extra reading and writing practice Additional downloadable listening and video material
Teacher's Resource Disc	Communication activity worksheets to print and photocopy, review material, test, and video with worksheet
Go global Ideas for further research	**Heroes** Students should look up the website of one of the international organisations discussed on page 57. They should report on the aims of the organisation, how it is organised, what it does and any major achievements. **Villains** There are a number of websites, such as http://www.simplypsychology.org/milgram.html that report the infamous Milgram Study, which was an experiment to look into how far ordinary people would go to obey orders. Students find out what the study was about, and its main findings. You could have a class follow-up discussion on the ethics of conducting such experiments.

Part 1

TEACH GLOBAL THINK LOCAL Lead-in

Go into class with three prepared descriptions of heroes your students are likely to know, either ancient or modern. Project the descriptions or read them out, asking students to write down who they think it is, in pairs, silently. At the end ask who guessed correctly. Then students work in pairs to do the same thing for others in the class (two descriptions per pair).

1 *He spent over 25 years in prison, mainly on an island, and became president of his country after his release* (Nelson Mandela).

2 *She is the daughter of a general. She spent years under house arrest and became a symbol of resistance to her country's leaders. She won the Nobel Peace prize* (Aung San Suu Kyi).

3 *He was an Indian lawyer who organised peaceful resistance to British rule in India* (Mahatma Gandhi).

Speaking and Vocabulary (SB page 54)

1 Students brainstorm some heroes in their culture – these could include lesser known people, or local heroes. In feedback, encourage students to explain succinctly why their chosen people are considered 'heroes'.

TEACH GLOBAL THINK LOCAL Alternative activity

Books closed. Put students in groups of three or four, and sit them in small circles. Write on the board *A hero is someone who …* Elicit one suggestion of a hero's characteristics / personality traits. The first person in the circle should finish the sentence at the top of an A4-sized paper, then fold it over and pass it on (so that the next person cannot see), and so on. They should try to do at least two rounds with the paper, and possibly three, so that each person writes at least two separate ideas. Encourage students to be original. At the end, they all read their list. They should cross off any entries that repeat the same idea and then share their original ideas with the whole class.

2 If you did not do the *Alternative activity* above, elicit one or two characteristics of a hero. Then ask students to read the list, discussing whether these characteristics are appropriate for their own heroes. Invite students to share any points of interest, eg if any of their own heroes possessed different or additional qualities.

At an appropriate point, put on the board any new lexical items which might be useful for advanced learners, eliciting where possible, eg *face danger; welfare; follow / have strong moral principles, betray sb; a sense of mission; modest; do sth for the sake of sth/sb else.* Note the part of speech and highlight appropriate collocations or prepositions. Check students' understanding by asking for examples or contexts.

3 In pairs, ask students to check their understanding of the nouns and to point out where the stress falls on each word. They should check meanings and the word stress by using a dictionary (let them check the stress at this point, before they say the words again). Allow ample time for the challenge of this exercise. Monitor to see how they are doing. If there are pronunciation problems, ask a student who is saying it correctly to model it.

1	courage	6	loyalty
2	selflessness	7	single-mindedness
3	self-confidence	8	perseverance
4	integrity	9	conviction
5	self-sacrifice	10	humility

4 Do an example together, eg *courage* → *courageous.* Warn students that not all of the nouns have corresponding adjectives. Let them check with each other, then in the dictionary. Early finishers should write the answers on the board, also marking the stress. They can drill the rest of the class, if appropriate (warn them before they do so). At the end, elicit and discuss other heroic qualities, writing any new and useful words on the board.

5 Initially students work alone to write a response to this statement, supplying a possible reason. Then students discuss their opinions in groups of three. Open this discussion up if students appear interested.

Reading and Listening (SB page 54)

1 Talk through the two questions here as a class. Project up, or read out the dictionary definition of *epic*: *a long poem, book or film that tells a story about ancient people, gods and events from the past.*

Possible answers

Literature: *The Iliad*, *The Odyssey* (Homer), *Don Juan* (Lord Byron), *Don Quixote* (Cervantes), *Shogun* (Clavell), *The Grapes of Wrath* (Steinbeck)

Films: *Lawrence of Arabia*, *Ben-Hur*, *Schindler's List*, *Cleopatra*

2 Write up *Gilgamesh* on the board and elicit what students know about it, if anything. Refer them to the images on pages 54–55 and ask them to make predictions. Then students read the introduction on page 54 and discuss answers in pairs and finally with the whole class. Draw their attention to the picture of one of the stone tablets on page 55.

1 It's one of the oldest works of literature in the world.

2 fiction, based on fact (Gilgamesh was a historical figure)

3 protagonist / main character (*Its hero, Gilgamesh …*); also 'hero' because of his actions (*he battles monsters …*)

3 2.18 Write the two characters' names up: *Gilgamesh* and *Enkidu*. Ask *They are a few metres from the monster Humbaba's den. How do you think the men feel?* Let students read and listen to the extract. Then students respond as a class to the questions.

They both do.

4 Give students a few moments to tackle this task individually, if necessary with a dictionary, before they compare answers in pairs. Elicit some possible responses, helping with and drilling pronunciation, if appropriate.

1 courage, perseverance, single-mindedness, loyalty, self-confidence
2 physical experience: *arms feel weak; your legs tremble; his mouth went dry; his legs shook, his feet were rooted to the ground*
emotion: *Their blood ran cold; Dread surged through Gilgamesh; terror flooded his muscles; his heart froze; I feel haunted. I am too afraid to go on.*

5 In pairs, locate the relevant parts of the poem before checking the answers orally.

1 *we will make a lasting name for ourselves, we will stamp our fame on men's minds forever*
2 *If we help each other and fight side by side we will make a lasting name for ourselves; Two intimate friends cannot be defeated.*
3 *Why, dear friend, do you speak like a coward? What you just said is unworthy of you.*

6 Students reflect for a couple of moments on the statements before discussing in pairs. Raise the question of it being a male view in a whole-class discussion.

Vocabulary (SB page 55)

1 This exercise focuses on multiword verbs and idioms with the verbs *give* or *stand*, all of which are commonly used. Ask students to initially cover the synonym box and to substitute the italicised phrases for a synonym, using a word in their first language if they can't think of one in English. Do the first one together as an example.

When they have finished, ask students to uncover the words in the box. Put any unknown words on the board, with the word class, and elicit the meaning from students who know. Finally, students work in pairs to do the matching task. Check answers and ask students concept questions as necessary, eg *Have you ever stood up to anyone? What was the situation?* Bear in mind that many of these words have radically different meanings, just by changing the particle. A board record would be a useful summary here. See *Language note*.

1	confront	5	compromise
2	abandon	6	obstruct
3	remain firm	7	defend
4	make concessions	8	be loyal to

Language note

Put up a board record like this, eliciting as much of the information as you can from your group. This chart reference can be a memory aid and give clarity:

give	***stand***
Multiword verbs	
give up sth	*stand up to sth/sb*
give in (to sth/sb)	*stand up for sth/sb*
	stand by sb/sth
Phrases	
give way	*stand your ground*
	stand in the way of

2 Look back at sentence 1 in exercise 1 and elicit / point out what is meant by 'contrast'. The meaning here is to contrast expectations between the information in the adverbial or noun clause and the information in the clause it is dependent on. Elicit the word or phrase that expresses the contrast in this example (*no matter how much*). In pairs, students complete the exercise. You might want to point out that these are general rules and that there are exceptions.

1 regardless of; irrespective of
2 however / wherever, etc; no matter how / what / where, etc

3 Ask two different students *Do you agree that you should always stand up to bullies, no matter how much they threaten you? Why? / Why not?* Ask them to rate the statement 1–5. Then students do the same independently for the other statements, before working in groups of three to discuss them. In this way, students will be drilling themselves on the target language. Monitor and take note of any problems, particularly in relation to the target phrases, for later feedback.

Part 2

TEACH GLOBAL THINK LOCAL Lead-in

Dictate these questions: *What voluntary organisations do you know? What kind of voluntary work can people do? Why do you think people volunteer? Have you ever volunteered?* Students discuss these questions in groups of three.

Listening and Speaking (SB page 56)

1 Focus students on the headline and elicit what *unsung* means in this context, highlighting the fact that this is a collocation: *unsung hero*. Then elicit the responses to the questions, referring them to the visuals.

local volunteers who gave their time and energy to help people without recognition or seeking recognition

TEACH GLOBAL THINK LOCAL Extra activity

Take this opportunity to focus on the style used in newspaper headlines. Ask students how this differs from a normal sentence. In pairs, ask them to make it more grammatical. Invite a couple of students to write up the sentence on the board: *'Some local volunteers are the unsung heroes of the flood relief,' says an international development charity.*

2 Do the first example together, before students complete the exercise in pairs. Check answers orally, eliciting examples as you go through, eg *What might emergency relief involve?*

Incorrect alternatives

1 timely (others refer to types of disasters – *timely* refers to something positive occurring at the right time)

2 help (others are forms of aid, or relief, which the charity provide – *help relief* is tautology)

3 staff (others are people working for the charity – *staff worker* is tautology)

4 humanitarian (others refer to diseases which the charity could work to prevent)

5 emergency (others describe ongoing work)

3 **2.19** This listening describes the work of one particular charity and gives specific examples of some local heroes.

Tell students that the listening is fairly long, so they will need to note down details. Play the recording. If you think students are losing concentration, pause it for them to compare notes thus far.

Suggested answers

1 He works for a charity that operates globally in countries where people face poverty and injustice; providing emergency relief and carrying out campaigns for long-term improvement.

2 floods in Pakistan, earthquake in Haiti, tsunami in Asia 2006, cyclone in Myanmar (Burma)

3 responding immediately with food, water, medical care, helping long term to rebuild

4 woman in Burma who didn't know where her son was and asked her mother to look for him while she joined the volunteer group in distributing relief supplies to local townships; man in Haiti whose family were buried under rubble for 24 hours and who joined the emergency team at the same time as trying to find them

2.19

A = Interviewer; **B** = Justin Byworth

A: So can you tell me a little bit about World Vision and the kind of work you do?

B: Well, World Vision works in nearly 100 countries in the world working with about 100 million people who face poverty and injustice, and we work through long-term community development, we work through humanitarian emergency relief and through campaigning for change in a situation of children's lives.

A: Can you tell me something about the kind of work that the charity has been doing recently?

B: So recently we've had several emergencies, several major emergencies, in Pakistan we've had floods affecting nearly 30 million people, in Haiti we've had an earthquake which brought, you know, huge amounts of death and devastation. But then we've got our work globally across the world through, you know, at community level where actually we're seeing some good things, some good news as well such as the number of children that die before their fifth birthday reduced from 8.8 million to 8.1 million a year, so every day 2,000 children less are dying of preventable diseases than they were this time last year and World Vision is a part of that, a small part of it, but we're part of that.

A: You mentioned disaster relief. Can you tell me a little bit more about what you do in disasters?

B: Well, because World Vision we are, you know, we work at community level in so many different countries in long-term development, when an emergency strikes, most places in the world we are working there already. So, you might remember the Tsunami in Asia back in 2006. Literally, within, within an hour in the south-east of India, community groups and local World Vision staff were responding, responding there with food, with water, with immediate medical care and things like that. So I think in an emergency situation, you know, one of the benefits of being a local organisation in those places is that you're there before and you're there after, kind of the media and the cameras come and go and so you can be there to help rebuild in the long term as well as providing immediate relief.

A: So you have staff locally? Or you have international staff?

B: World Vision has about 40,000 staff worldwide in nearly 100 countries of whom the vast majority are local to their own country, to their own communities, 95% or more. We do, of course, have some international staff going in, in some contexts as well … We also have thousands of volunteers that we work with.

A: And what sort of work do they do then?

B: Well, they're the kind of hands and feet of our work really. They are the people who often know best what the situation is whether it's an emergency or whether in longer-term development. And they often provide some of the most critical, you know, timely-critical, context-specific help and responses to, certainly to emergencies, but also to other things like, like diseases.

A: Can you give some examples of that?

B: Yes, one example from emergencies I'd say is, we had in Myanmar, Burma, a couple of years ago, a big cyclone, Cyclone Nargis which again, over 100,000 people died and thousands more were affected. Amazing. I heard from one of my colleagues there, a local volunteer there who had at the same time as her own house had collapsed, and in fact she didn't know where her six-year-old son was. He was out playing when the cyclone came or something like that and she sent her mum to go and look for her son while she went across town to go to the World Vision office, which opened things up there with the staff there and actually get relief supplies out to one of the townships nearby where World Vision works. So just extraordinary to hear someone putting the needs of others before their own needs at a time of real hardship.

Another example in Haiti recently we had our staff working there out of the car park by the office, because the office had collapsed, and many, many staff there had lost or, either lost loved ones in their family or didn't know where they were. We had, one family I know there, who his wife and two kids were buried in a building all night long, in fact more than, for 24 hours, while he was having to help get on with the emergency response at the same time as trying to find his own family. So really shocking stories of, kind of, heroism really in the midst of tragedy. But then there are thousands more across the whole of sub Saharan Africa, there's probably hundreds of thousands, if not millions, of just normal people, often women who go out and care for families, and particularly for orphans, and for families that have been devastated by disease, such as TB or AIDS, and who just bring care when they're ill, but also help with food or with local livelihoods and things. So there's an army of those from local churches, from other faith groups and from community groups.

4 In pairs, students compare notes. If appropriate, ask them to write a paragraph summarising what they heard about the charity using the four topic headings from exercise 3 to help: *World Vision is a charity which …*

TEACH GLOBAL THINK LOCAL Listening extra

The listening on *World Vision* is information-rich. If you would like your students to listen for specific information, put these numbers on the board (in the same order): *100 million; 30 million; 2,000; 2006; 40,000; 95%; 100,000; 6; 24*. Ask students to listen again and find out what these numbers refer to. If they are strong listeners, jumble up the numbers to make it more challenging.

5 Before talking, allow students a moment to think in silence about these two interesting questions. Encourage them to think of specific situations – perhaps something they heard about on the news, eg a fire, an accident, a natural disaster. Invite students to share some interesting answers with the whole class.

Vocabulary (SB page 56)

TEACH GLOBAL THINK LOCAL Mixed ability

If you anticipate that the words in exercise 1 will be quite challenging for your students, ask them to categorise them into three groups: *words I know / words I don't know / words I think I know, but need to check*. Students group their words independently, then compare their lists in groups. This way they peer teach each other.

1 Students work on their own, before comparing answers in pairs. At feedback stage, focus in on any problems relating to meaning and also pronunciation, eg *drought* /draʊt/, *famine* /ˈfæmɪn/, *flooding* /ˈflʌdɪŋ/. Write up the phonemics and word stress, if necessary, or ask students to use the dictionary to check.

1 epidemic
2 drought
3 hurricanes; tsunamis; volcanic eruptions
4 sanitation; health care; legal representation
5 corruption; debt
6 genocide; displacement

TEACH GLOBAL THINK LOCAL Writing extra

Ask students to transform the sentences from exercise 1. Write up these new sentence starters on the board:

1 *A major epidemic …*
2 *There is a severe drought …*
3 *Natural disasters …*
4 *Increased access …*
5 *Senior government figures …*
6 *Widespread migration …*

Do the first example together, eg *A major epidemic could develop from the recent outbreak of TB, experts fear* before students continue in pairs. There may be different alternatives. Monitor and assist before checking answers as a class.

2 Carefully group students into groups of three for this discussion, which should last several minutes. Tell them that they have exactly three minutes to plan what to say. As they are talking, monitor and take notes of any particular elements in their speaking which need work, eg how to disagree politely; how to give opinions convincingly.

Extend your vocabulary (SB page 57)

1 Put up three different abbreviations which you are sure your students will know. Ask them what they stand for. Students work together. (Nearly) all of them can be found in an Advanced monolingual dictionary, a feature which may be useful to highlight to students.

Association of South East Asian Nations
Brazil, Russia, India and China (economic grouping)
(The) International Monetary Fund
North Atlantic Treaty Organisation
Non-Governmental Organisation
Organisation of the Petroleum Exporting Countries
(The) United Nations
United Nations Educational, Scientific and Cultural Organisation
United Nations Children's Fund
(The) World Bank
(The) World Health Organisation (popularly, but not part of their official name)
(The) World Trade Organisation

2 In pairs, students should try to guess the pronunciation. They may be surprised to know that the pronunciation details are also included in the dictionary.

3 In pairs or groups of three, students share their knowledge. Alternatively, you could ask them to do some research for an info-sharing session next lesson!

Grammar (SB page 57)

TEACH GLOBAL THINK LOCAL Alternative procedure

The Grammar focus will be revision for most advanced students, so you could hand over to students to check the answers to exercise 1.

To do this, **in advance**, ask for two confident volunteers to take the role of teacher in the forthcoming class. Give them a grammar reference, if necessary, and the answers to exercise 1. They can prepare time-lines and questions for their peers. They should prepare to teach the others, in a 8–10 minute slot.

1 Tell students that they are going to see some present perfect and past simple examples taken from the listening. They study the pairs of sentences individually before discussing in pairs. While checking answers, ask probing concept questions, eg (h) *Do we know exactly how many?* (yes); (i) *Do we know if the hospital is completed?* (no).

a present perfect: has just happened + mentioned for first time, as in news announcement
b past simple: qualified by specific time reference + details given after initial announcement in news
c past simple passive: (action completed) – finished timescale
d present perfect passive: (action not yet completed) – unfinished timescale
e present perfect: timescale (her life) not yet complete – implication that this could go on
f past simple: timescale complete – implication that action will not go on
g present perfect continuous: duration emphasised; time period not yet complete
h present perfect simple: completed events; number of places visited stated (emphasised)
i present perfect continuous: action still continuing
j present perfect simple: action recently completed
k present perfect continuous: (continuous action emphasised) repeated activity
l present perfect simple: happened once, resulting situation emphasised

2 Students work in different pairs to respond to the task. Elicit some answers as a class. Be prepared to assist. See *Language note*.

1 have lived / have been living – often used interchangeably – continuous form is more common; arrived
2 have you known (stative verb)
3 hasn't rained (refers to event, not continuous aspect)
4 It's / It's been; were held or have been held

Language note

Sometimes the difference in use between the present perfect continuous and simple is minimal, eg *I've lived / been living here for three years.* However, they are often not interchangeable, eg *I've made / ~~been making~~ three large fruit cakes.* Usually if the amount, result or total is given, the simple form is preferred, as this embodies an idea of completion. If the action is a single one which cannot be extended or repeated, then the continuous, with its notion of duration or repetition, is not appropriate, eg *They've ~~been leaving~~ left for Australia.*

Perhaps surprisingly, the *it* + time period + *since*, takes the present simple or present perfect after *it*, eg *It's / It's been six months since I ate anything sugary*. The part after the time period – the subordinate clause – can either be in the past simple or the present perfect: *It's / It's been six months since I ate / I've eaten anything sugary*.

3 Focus students on the title and elicit what sort of genre this material is taken from (news bulletin / news on website / charity magazine). In pairs, students first read for content, referring back to the *Vocabulary* section as indicated, before they work on the grammar task (though some may prefer to do the two tasks the other way around). Monitor and take note of any problems. If students seem to be getting the majority right, put up the answers on the board for them to self-check. At the end, hold a whole-class feedback session to resolve any doubts on this grammar topic.

1 ~~have migrated~~ → migrated; ~~was distributed~~ → has been distributed
2 ~~decreased~~ → has decreased; ~~have not been treating~~ → have not treated
3 ~~has been digging~~ → has dug; ~~installing~~ → installed; ~~worked~~ → has worked / has been working
4 ~~was~~ → has been / is; ~~has been launched~~ → was launched
5 ~~has simply not been~~ → was simply not; (have encouraged / have been encouraging also possible); ~~increased~~ → has increased

G Grammar focus

Refer students to the language summary on present perfect simple and continuous on page 140.

You can use exercises 1–3 on page 141 for:
a) extra practice now, b) homework or c) review later on.

The answers are on page 163 of this Teacher's Book.

Writing (SB page 57)

1 Students should use the five short reports in the *Good news* text as a model. In pairs, they choose one of the four topics and elaborate on details, which can be totally fictitious.

2 Each pair of students swaps their report with another pair. After reading them, they should devise at least two direct questions relating to the actual content, eg *Why weren't medicines for the survivors bought with the aid money?*

Part 3

TEACH GLOBAL THINK LOCAL Lead-in

Put some of the following crimes from exercise 2 on the board: *arson, armed robbery, assault, fraud, manslaughter, treason, piracy*. Quickly check understanding. Students individually rate the three most serious crimes and the three least serious and discuss their answers in groups of three, giving their rationale.

Vocabulary and Speaking (SB page 58)

1 Ask students how punishments nowadays compare with 200 years ago. Provide dictionaries if necessary for students to do the task. Get them to peer teach any new lexis, and put it on the board, eg *flog (v); overturn / commute (v) a sentence; acquit (v) sb of a crime; be convicted of a crime; be tried for a crime; be hanged (passive v); raid (v).*

a Thomas Briggs was sentenced to death.
b Warren Kerr was jailed for six months.
c Mary Wade received the death penalty, but her sentence was commuted to transportation to Australia.
d Benjamin Goddard and Samuel Axtell were fined 20 pounds each and sentenced to six months' imprisonment.
e Ned Kelly was hanged.
f Stede Bonnet was hanged.

2 In pairs, students complete the discussion task. Discuss any points of interest with the whole class.

1 armed robbery (e); assault (c); blackmail (d); fraud (forgery) (a); murder (e); piracy (f); theft (b, c, e)
2 **Suggested answers:** less common in Western countries: blasphemy, piracy, treason

TEACH GLOBAL THINK LOCAL Extra activity

To focus students on the prepositions that go with the crime-related lexis, dictate the following, substituting the bracketed preposition for the word *thingamajig* - a useful filler or 'placeholder name':

Peter Marsh was accused (of) stealing a sheep in 1831. He was taken (to) court but was acquitted (of) that crime. Two years later he was again caught stealing livestock. He was tried (for) his crime in court and was instantly and unanimously found guilty (of) theft. As a result, he was sentenced (to) death (by) hanging. Luckily, his sentence was commuted (to) transportation to Australia, where he eventually became a very prosperous sheep farmer!

Reading (SB page 58)

1 Ask students to write down three associations with the word *pirate*. Elicit suggestions. Discuss the questions as a class.

2 Focus students on the map and the text heading. Ask *Have you heard of any recent incidents of piracy?* Discuss before they read and answer the questions individually. Then they compare answers before whole-class feedback.

1 Gulf of Aden in the Indian Ocean, off coast of Somalia
2 international fishing, merchant vessels and pleasure craft
3 board the vessel, take crew hostage and demand ransom payments
4 no internationally agreed legal system for prosecution

3 Students discuss these questions in small groups and then share some ideas with the whole class.

Listening and Speaking (SB page 58)

Both listenings talk about piracy but from very different points of view: first a captain's and then a pirate's.

1 **2.20** Let students read the statements before you play the recording. To raise interest and also focus students, you could elicit their predicted answers first. Write up the name of the ship: *Ellivita*. Students listen and then compare notes in pairs. Check answers as a whole class if you feel it is necessary.

1 T
2 T
3 F (… *the coalition warships that are meant to be patrolling the seas, warding off the pirates, are useless*.)
4 T
5 F (… *crews are also concerned that the next thing we'll be seeing are deaths, people being shot by pirates demanding ransoms*.)

2.20

No seaman has ever seen anything like this. It's a war zone out there and, quite simply, the situation is out of control. It's not like before when they'd come on board and rob you. These days they hijack ships, take the entire crew hostage and demand huge ransoms. It's very primitive and very frightening. I come from a seafaring family, my father and brother are both merchant seamen and I've been in this job for nine years, doing seven months at a stretch on the high seas. I can tell you I'm scared. I have a young family, a wife who is expecting a baby and rightly she is beside herself with worry.

This month we've had to go through the Gulf of Aden twice. The first time we were totally unprotected and I felt so alone, so responsible for my crew and cargo. The second time we were able to join a convoy that was being escorted by a Russian frigate, but when another merchant ship about 30 miles south of us was suddenly attacked, the warship had to leave. More often than not the coalition warships that are meant to be patrolling the seas, warding off the pirates, are useless. A lot of the time they don't respond to distress calls and, anyway, the pirates are so quick. I'm now more afraid of piracy than storms and cyclones.

When they attack you – and so far the *Ellivita* has been lucky – the game is up quickly. In five to ten minutes the pirates surround you in speedboats; then using ladders they board the vessel and from that moment there's nothing you can do. They're the ones with the weapons and they've taken the crew hostage.

We're mariners not military men and our job is not to use guns against other people. But I also think we have reached a point where to protect ships we have to have security teams, or weapons, on board. Right now it really does seem as if it can't get any worse. But crews are also concerned that the next thing we'll be seeing are deaths, people being shot by pirates demanding ransoms.

TEACH GLOBAL THINK LOCAL **Pre-listening**

To encourage students to consider both sides of a situation, ask them to roleplay an interview between a Somali pirate and an interviewer. They should do this **before** the listening in exercise 2 using the questions in exercise 2 to help structure their interview. Alternatively, they could do it **after** they have listened and checked their answers.

2 **2.21** Students listen, make notes and then compare answers in pairs. This time, let students check their answers against the audioscript in SB pages 158–9.

Suggested answers

1 university not possible so became fisherman; 1991 foreign fishing vessels started attacking Somali vessels so became pirate to protect himself
2 shoot near the ship, board with rope ladder
3 count crew and make ransom demand; don't harm hostages – only interested in money – when money delivered, let hostages go
4 heroes avoiding poverty; piracy like road tax

2.21

I'm 42 years old and have nine children. I'm a boss with boats operating in the Gulf of Aden and the Indian Ocean. I finished high school and wanted to go to university, but there was no money. So I became a fisherman like my father, even though I still dreamed of working for a company. That never happened as the Somali government was destroyed in 1991 and the country became unstable. In Somalia, there are no jobs, and no rule of law because of the conflict. At sea we were often confronted by foreign fishing vessels who didn't want us there to compete. They would destroy our boats and force us to flee for our lives. I started to hijack these fishing boats in 1998. For our first captured ship we got $300,000. With the money we bought Automatic rifles and small speedboats.

I don't know exactly how many ships I've captured since then, but I think it's about 60. To get their attention we shoot near the ship. If it doesn't stop we use a rope ladder to get on board. We count the crew and find out their nationalities. After checking the cargo we ask the captain to phone the owner and say that we've seized the ship and we'll keep it until the ransom is paid. We make friends with the hostages, telling them that we only want money, not to kill them. Sometimes we even eat rice, fish, pasta with them. When the money is delivered to our ship we count the dollars and let the hostages go.

Our community thinks we're pirates getting illegal money. But we consider ourselves heroes running away from poverty. We don't see the hijacking as a criminal act, but as a road tax because we have no central government to control our sea. But we're getting new boats and weapons. We won't stop until we have a central government that can control our sea.

3 Tell students that they have four minutes to think about these questions independently. Then they discuss them in groups. Finally a spokesperson for each group gives feedback later. Monitor and provide extra prompts if needed, eg *Do you see these Somali pirates as criminals or as victims of circumstance? If you were a local fisherman, would you encourage or try to prevent piracy?*

Pronunciation (SB page 59)

1 **2.22** This exercise focuses on word stress. Students work alone. Then play the recording for students to check their answers and ensure that they know how word stress is marked in dictionaries.

1	/ɪnˈkriːs/	in<u>crease</u>	3	/ɪˈskɔː(r)t/	es<u>cort</u>
2	/ˈɪŋkriːs/	<u>in</u>crease	4	/ˈeskɔː(r)t/	<u>es</u>cort

2 Students work in pairs. Check answers.

1 first	2 second

3 Say two of the words at random and ask students if each one is a noun or verb. Drill different forms, if necessary. Then students test each other.

4 You could handle this as a pair race to inject an element of fun. Explain the task, say *Ready, steady, go!* and ask them to put up their hand when they finish.

1 ob<u>ject</u>, <u>re</u>bels	2 pre<u>sent</u>ed, con<u>flict</u>ed/<u>con</u>flicts

5 In pairs, students write two (or more) sentences in the same way to test each other.

Part 4

TEACH GLOBAL THINK LOCAL Lead-in

Ask students to complete the questionnaire, answering *never, sometimes, occasionally* or *always* before discussing their responses in pairs. You could dictate it or put it on the board.

1 *I am a very calm person.*
2 *I have acted out of character in the past.*
3 *I can be aggressive.*
4 *I am good in a crisis.*
5 *I believe people are naturally cruel.*

Speaking (SB page 60)

1 Tell students that they are going to read about a rather bizarre, slightly frightening psychological experiment carried out in 1971. Ask them to read the introductory text first, and then to describe the picture, using the words given.

Suggested answer

The picture is of a prison inmate, handcuffed to the ceiling of the cell. It looks like he could be in solitary confinement, as there is no one else in view, but we don't know for sure.

2 After their pair discussion, invite students to share some of their ideas with the class.

Reading (SB page 60)

The text gives details of the psychological experiment, in particular, how the guards and prisoners reacted to the simulated conditions.

First, elicit what might normally happen in a prison, when a criminal first enters, eg *strip-search* (v) and *delouse* (v) (see *Glossary*). Elicit what guards would wear or hold, eg *truncheon* (n). This helps prepare them for this lexically-dense text. Do not let students use a dictionary.

1 After students read the text ask them if their predictions were correct, but keep the pace brisk.

2 Students read the text again to put the events in the correct order individually before checking their answers in pairs. Stronger students could try and order the events before reading a second time.

Correct order: d, h, a, f, b, e, g, c

3 Give students the opportunity to consider these words independently first, using the context to help. Let them confirm their answers by checking with a dictionary, then with one another.

1 causing confusion	3 obeyed	5 unpleasant but useful
2 treating badly	4 betrayed	

4 This is the first real opportunity for students to respond to this rather disturbing text. If they are interested and stimulated by it, let them talk for longer. Put these questions on the board for early finishers: *How do you think you would react as a) a prisoner b) a guard in this experiment? What would you find the most difficult aspect? What does it tell us, if anything, about human nature?* The last question leads into the next exercise.

5 Students work alone to choose the most logical conclusion, or to formulate a more comprehensive one of their own. Encourage them to think of comparable examples in real life. Elicit one or two responses, but do not comment at this point.

6 In small groups, students discuss one (or more) of the statements from exercise 5. Remind them to support their opinions with evidence. Monitor and have a class feedback session on any points of interest.

Extend your vocabulary (SB page 60)

TEACH GLOBAL THINK LOCAL

Extra activity

As a lead-in, books closed, two adjectives to describe people who behave badly. Then put up the words from *Extend your vocabulary* on the board, substituting the vowels with underscores, eg *b _ dly-b _ h _ v _ d* (badly behaved). In pairs, students work out what the other words are.

1 Students work on their own, using a dictionary if necessary, to complete the task. Early finishers can check the stress too. Check answers and drill the words, if necessary.

1	badly-behaved; naughty	5	brutal
2	evil; wicked	6	mischievous
3	infamous; notorious	7	sinful
4	corrupt		

2 In groups of three, students discuss characters from different genres. Elicit some examples.

Grammar (SB page 61)

1 Elicit the difference between a past participle and a present participle. Elicit an example of a present participle clause within a sentence – if necessary, refer students back to the text. Then students complete the task individually before comparing answers in pairs. Monitor and elicit the answers.

1 b 2 d 3 a 4 c

2 Students read the examples, then match up rules and examples in pairs. Conduct a feedback session.

a some participles have their own subject
b perfect participle to stress one action before another
c participle clauses after conjunctions
d *not* before participle
e participle clauses can be used to replace relative clauses

Language note

Participle clauses are examples of non-finite clauses. Students at this level are likely to use them only in a limited manner such as after some conjunctions, eg *While living in the suburbs …* or as a kind of reduced relative clause, *There were strange things happening around me and I started to feel afraid.* When students use them in their writing, it can raise the level of sophistication, something worth pointing out to advanced students.

One useful way of clarifying how they are used is to ask students to 'pad out' the sentences which include them by adding in extra words, eg exercise 1, sentence a: *At the next roll-call he told fellow inmates that there really was no escape, triggering genuine fear among them.* → *At the next roll-call … which triggered genuine fear …*

TEACH GLOBAL THINK LOCAL

Extra activity

In pairs, students finish these participle clause sentence starters. Point out the importance of the comma.

The lesson finished, …

Having completed the exam, …

After scoring so highly, …

Waving goodbye to the teacher, …

Truly surprised at …, the teacher/students …

3 Put students into AB pairs and refer them to their respective pages. Do the first example together, showing both A and B sentences on the board. Point out that not all of the gaps need a participle – just one is necessary per sentence. Let students work alone and then compare their sentences.

G Grammar focus

Refer students to the language summary on participle clauses on page 140.

You can use exercises 4 and 5 on page 141 for:
a) extra practice now, b) homework or c) review later on.

The answers are on page 163 of this Teacher's Book.

Function globally: managing conversations

These lessons in *Global* are designed to provide students with immediately useful functional language. They all follow a similar format.

Warm up (SB page 62)

Aim: to introduce the topic via a quick speaking task or picture work.

Tips:

- Do not over-correct here, especially in speaking activities.
- Encourage students to use as much variety of language as they can at this stage.
- If students enjoy the task, let them choose one more topic each to talk about.

TEACH GLOBAL THINK LOCAL **Alternative procedure**

If you think your students would rise to the challenge, then handle this activity as a 'Just a minute' game: each student has to talk for one minute exactly, with no hesitation, deviation from the topic or repetition at all. If the speaker does any of these, they have to start again from the beginning or lose their turn. (Listeners must call out *Hesitation!*, etc when the speaker does this.) Students should work in groups of three.

Ask a strong student to model this activity first, responding when he/she deviates, hesitates or repeats something.

Listening (SB page 62)

Aim: to present the functional language in context via a conversation or series of conversations.

Tips:

- Pause the recording after individual speakers, if your students look tired. (Tracks 2.23–2.28; 2.29–2.34)
- Monitor to see how they are doing after the first three parts. If students seem tired, ask them to compare answers so far with their partners.
- For fun at the end of this section, put students into groups of three and invite them to read out (some of) the dialogues. (Note that some of the conversations have fewer or more speakers so one person may need to read more than one part.)

1

1 h 2 c 3 i 4 j 5 a 6 g 7 e 8 b
9 f 10 d 11 k

2.23–2.28

1

A: So would anyone like some more coffee?

B: Oh I would love one thanks.

All: Yeah yeah.

B: Those cookies look nice.

C: Just the one sugar, please. Thanks.

B: It's very kind of you to invite us over and bake cookies …

D: They smell fantastic.

B: Speaking of being kind, something amazing happened to my daughter last week. She was due to fly back from Hong Kong, where she'd been teaching, and she missed her flight because she misread midnight for midday …

E: Oh no, I've done that, yeah …

B: … so she was …

2

B: … and he said oh I'll just … I'll buy you another ticket, you know, this could have been my daughter on the other side of the world …

D: That's so kind …

E: Seriously?

B: … and he bought her a ticket … um and …

E: To where she wanted to go?

B: Yes, back home.

E: Just like that?

B: Yeah.

E: That was it?

B: And apparently he insisted on paying for it and didn't want to be paid back or anything, wouldn't give her his name or address.

E: Oh that's really kind.

C: Sorry to interrupt, but do you know that reminds me of a time I was in, I was in Italy and I'd left all my bags in the car and the car was broken into. I didn't have any money or any ID, anything, and the people at the car hire company lent me some money just to get through the weekend …

3

B: … so we had to pay an extra £200 each to get back.

E: You've got to be very careful with these cheap flights really, because they're just not as cheap as you think they're going to be.

B: No, they have ways of getting you, don't they?

E: They do, they do.

B: Luggage yes, luggage costs extra. Yeah.

E: Oh luggage, that reminds me actually, once I was travelling abroad and I'd forgotten that we'd been for a picnic earlier in the day and I'd left my cutlery from the picnic at the bottom of my rucksack.

B: Oh no.

E: Yes, and it set off a big security alert and I was like no, I haven't got anything in here, I haven't got scissors, I haven't got a knife, nothing, I packed the bag myself, I swear, I swear. Completely forgetting about the picnic. And then …

4

B: We had a funny thing happen once going through security. Again I thought I'd taken everything out that shouldn't be going through and … um … and suddenly they stopped me and pointed to the X-ray and said what's that in your bag and I looked and it looked like there was this huge knife in my bag, like a flick knife. So they started unpacking my bag and it wasn't a flick knife of course it was two metal objects. It was a comb in a metal comb case next to a lipstick in a metal case and the lipstick looked like the handle and the comb looked like the blade.

E: Oh my goodness, yeah … On the subject of X-rays I had my results back, you know, for my knee operation.

D: Oh yes.

B: Is it all clear?

E: Yes, it's fine, it's just … och … that I'm going to have to go back and have another operation.

B: That's awful.

D: It's always happening, isn't it? It happened to my neighbour.

E: Yeah?

D: Yeah, that reminds me of my neighbour because he … he … he was going to have his hip operation today and they just phoned him up and said that they can't fit him in, they're going to have to … yeah … put him a week later.

E: It does affect your life …

C: Changing the subject completely though, you know, neighbours, I don't know how you get on with your neighbours but, you know, I hardly know my neighbours. I've lived there …

5

E: I live in a block of flats and … um … I don't know, it's very friendly, very communal, I mean, we don't go in and out of each other's houses, you know, it's nothing like that …

C: Sure.

E: … but we all speak on the stairs, we know where the other people work, that kind of thing. It's quite a nice community actually.

B: Yeah, people have been there a long time …

C: So do people help each other out and that kind of thing?

E: Yeah I guess so. I mean, if we're locked out we can …

D: Sorry, can I just say something …?

E: Sure.

D: … you're wanted on the phone, Alexandra, um …

B: Oh right OK.

D: Yes.

B: OK fine.

D: Sorry, do go on.

E: No no it's OK, no problem, no problem.

6

E: You know, I'm so pleased I'm a homeowner now and that I'm not renting flats. I would not want to go through that again, no way. It's so good to have the control.

D: Anyway, sorry, going back to my neighbour who's got this operation …

E: Aha. The hip one?

D: Yeah. The problem is he's probably going to have to go into hospital next week …

E: Right, right.

D: … and, um, he's asked me whether I can take him, but I can't because, um, my … my car's broken.

E: Take him to hospital?

D: Yeah.

B: I could probably help out if you like …

D: Oh could you?

B: … depends which day it is. Do you know which day it is?

3

1 *Speaking of being kind …*

2 *Sorry to interrupt, but do you know that reminds me of a time …*

3 *Oh, luggage, that reminds me actually …*

4 *On the subject of X-rays …; Yeah, that reminds me of …*

5 *Sorry, can I just say something …?*

6 *Anyway, sorry, going back to my neighbour …*

2.29–2.34

1

All: … Yeah yeah.

B: Those cookies look nice.

C: Just the one sugar, please. Thanks.

B: It's very kind of you to invite us over and bake cookies …

D: They smell fantastic.

B: Speaking of being kind, something amazing happened to my daughter last week. She was due to fly back …

2

B: … and apparently he insisted on paying for it and didn't want to be paid back or anything, wouldn't give her his name or address.

E: Oh that's really kind.

C: Sorry to interrupt, but do you know that reminds me of a time I was in, I was in Italy and I'd left all my bags in the car and the car was broken into. I didn't have any money or any ID, anything, and the people at the car hire company lent me some money just to get through the weekend …

3

B: … so we had to pay an extra £200 each to get back.

E: You've got to be very careful with these cheap flights really, because they're just not as cheap as you think they're going to be.

B: No, they have ways of getting you, don't they?

E: They do, they do.

B: Luggage yes, luggage costs extra. Yeah.

E: Oh, luggage, that reminds me actually, once I was travelling abroad and I'd forgotten that we'd been for a picnic earlier in the day …

4

B: … it wasn't a flick knife, of course, it was two metal objects. It was a comb in a metal comb case next to a lipstick in a metal case and the lipstick looked like the handle and the comb looked like the blade.

E: Oh my goodness, yeah … On the subject of X-rays I had my results back, you know, for my knee operation.

D: Oh yes.

B: Is it all clear?

E: Yes, it's fine, it's just … och … that I'm going to have to go back and have another operation. …

B: That's awful.

D: It's always happening, isn't it? It happened to my neighbour.

B: Yeah?

E: Yeah, that reminds me of my neighbour because he … he … he was going to have his hip operation today and they just phoned him up and said that they can't fit him in, they're going to have to … yeah … put him a week later. …

5

C: … So do people help each other out and that kind of thing?

E: Yeah I guess so. I mean, if we're locked out we can …

D: Sorry, can I just say something …?

E: Sure.

D: … you're wanted on the phone, Alexandra, um …

B: Oh right OK.

D: Yes.

B: OK fine.

D: Sorry, do go on.

E: No no it's OK, no problem, no problem …

6

E: … You know, I'm so pleased I'm a homeowner now and that I'm not renting flats. I would not want to go through that again, no way. It's so good to have the control.

D: Anyway, sorry, going back to my neighbour who's got this operation …

E: Aha. The hip one?

D: Yeah. … The problem is he's probably going to have to go into hospital next week …

Language focus (SB page 62)

Aim: to draw students' attention to the items of functional language.

Tips:

- Students work alone at first before comparing answers in pairs. Discuss any areas of ambiguity.
- If you need to raise the challenge, ask students to think of additional expressions to serve the same function, eg returning to the subject.
- Give students time to make a note of any new phrases they would like to remember.

1

1 c 2 a 3 b 4 e 5 f 6 d

2

We use them to be polite.

Other body language – lean forward, raised hand and eyebrows, open mouth to interrupt, hand up to hold turn

Pronunciation (SB page 62)

Aim: to focus students on a particular aspect of pronunciation of the target phrases.

Tips:

- Play the recording two or three times, if necessary. (Track 2.35)
- At this level, try to promote good all-round pronunciation including stress, intonation and linking. This also raises the challenge for students.
- Use students with exemplary pronunciation to act as models to help others in the class.

1 Sorry, say; interrupt
2 finish
3 do, on
4 Anyway, neighbour; saying
5 way, neighbours; Incidentally, operations; reminds, time, missed, flight
6 completely

Speaking (SB page 62)

Aim: to allow students an opportunity to use this language in a meaningful, real-world context.

Tips:

- Ask two or three students to model the beginning of the conversation, to motivate and clarify.
- Monitor but do not interrupt. Make a note of language aspects that you'd like to discuss at the end.
- Correct sensitively, paying attention to the target language especially.

- If time allows, ask students to repeat the task, but with a new partner.
- Invite one or two groups to share some examples with the whole class to round off the activity.

Global English

These lessons in *Global* have two main goals: 1) to give you and your students interesting information about English and language in general; 2) to provide practice in different kinds of reading comprehension tasks that they are likely to encounter in future study, for example in exams.

TEACH GLOBAL THINK LOCAL Lead-in

Ask students to do some creative categorisation, if you think this will appeal to your group. They have to decide if the following people / things are 'heroes' or 'villains' and why. Modify the list, if necessary.

- your English teacher
- your English school
- the person paying for your English course
- your English homework / exam
- the English language itself

Students then compare and discuss their choices.

Warm up (SB page 63)

Aim: to engage students with the topic, and highlight potentially difficult vocabulary in the text.

Tips:

- If students are really animated by the discussion, then let it continue.
- As students are talking, put up useful topic-related words or phrases on the board, to refer to later.

Reading (SB page 63)

Aim: to provide students with interesting information about English, and practise reading exam skills.

Tips:

- There are three tasks. The first focuses on the gist of the passage. The second and third are more difficult tasks, similar to that of a reading exam.
- Bear in mind that these texts may be quite challenging even for advanced learners so allow plenty of time, and also supply dictionaries, where appropriate.
- The third question raises students' awareness about a language feature.
- The language in this text is not tested or reviewed in future units, which means you have more flexibility with this material as to when and where you use it.

1

1 Neither; he is describing the term as used by other people.

2 Governments should develop a sensitive and intelligent language policy that recognises the two motivations for language use: intelligibility and identity.

2

1 c 2 b 3 c

3

1 language users
2 Bangla language
3 languages that have global presence
4 language villain
5 any government
6 people living within the borders of a country

TEACH GLOBAL THINK LOCAL Reading extra

If you would like your students to reread this information-rich text, then after exercise 3, ask them to work in pairs to try and recall the significance of the following events or references, taken from the text. Students can then check their answers in the text.

- International Mother Language Day
- People going on hunger strike
- Language power: bigger fish eating smaller ones
- Governments being perceived as villains
- The conflict between the need for intelligibility and the need to preserve identity
- The possibility of having no villains at all

Speaking (SB page 63)

Aim: for students to relate the material in the reading to their own language, culture and experiences.

Tips:

- Be sensitive to any possible conflicts that this discussion might produce within the class, especially if students come from different ethnic groups from within the same national state.
- Let students work on their own at first to reflect and decide on their answers (exercise 1).
- Remind students to justify their answers.
- Encourage students to refer to real incidents and policies related to the topic.
- Conduct a whole-class feedback session on any points of interest. You could try and encourage the class as a whole to select the two best ways to protect languages.

As you go through these *Global English* lessons in the book, don't be afraid to ask students' opinions and reactions to the information in the texts. Ask *Which do you find interesting? Do you know of similar experiences or facts in your language or other languages?*

Writing: a report

These lessons in *Global* are designed to provide extended writing practice. They all follow a similar format.

Reading (SB page 64)

Aim: to provide a sample text for students to analyse.

Tips:

- Exploit the visuals at the start – ensure that students are given time to digest them and to then discuss them.
- There are often two questions for these texts: one which focuses on gist and the other on specific details.
- For exercise 3, you could help by providing the axes on the board. Let students work in pairs if they wish to, as some learners tend to be less visual.

1

Figure 1: deprivation among children under five in rural and urban areas of Bangladesh

Figure 2: percentages of children under five living in urban and rural areas

Main conclusions: Most young children live in rural areas. Deprivation is generally greater in rural than in urban areas.

2

1 child poverty
2 a definition agreed at the 1995 World Summit for Social Development
3 food, safe drinking water, sanitation facilities, health, shelter, education, information and access to services
4 children under 18
5 lack of access to sanitation facilities
6 overcrowded housing
7 greater deprivation in rural areas
8 rise in economy growth rate, fall in population growth rate
9 rise in economy growth rate, fall in population growth rate

3

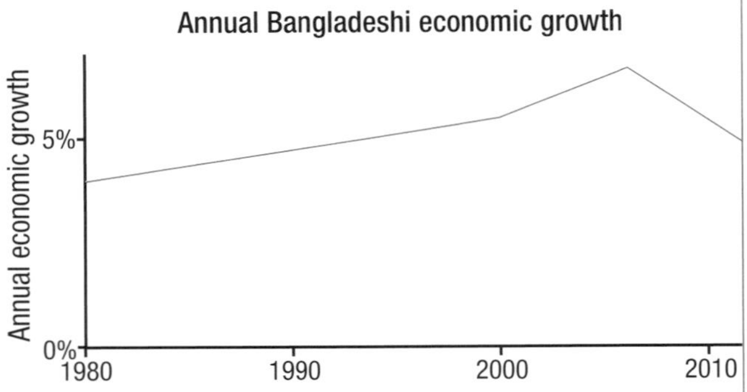

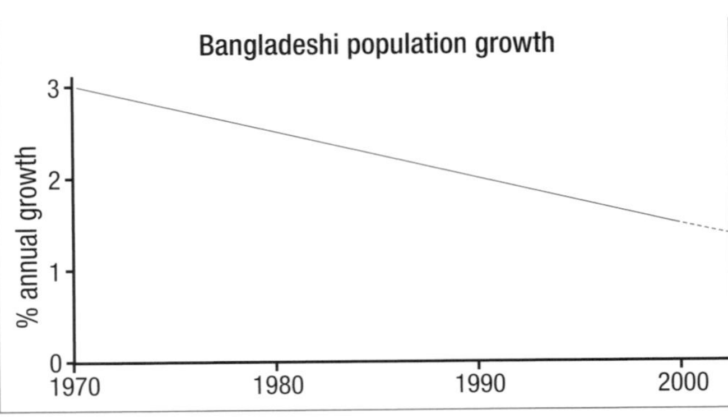

TEACH GLOBAL THINK LOCAL Extra activity

The activity described here encourages students to reread the report and to expand on graph-related language, which may be useful to some of your students.

Ask students to find and underline the examples of graph language, then to record them using the following categories: noun phrases, eg *a significant fall*; verb phrases, eg *increased steadily*; references to graphs, eg *Figure 1 shows …*

Writing skills: paragraph structure (SB page 64)

Aim: to give students a chance to develop their writing through various different micro skills.

Tips:

- If possible, project the paragraphs from the report, to facilitate the task.
- Clearly explain the focus and do an example of one of the text paragraphs together first before asking them to continue with exercises 2 and 3 on their own.
- Let students compare their answers in pairs or small groups before checking them in open class.
- Draw out some comparisons with students' first language(s), eg which conventions are similar or not.
- Ensure that students realise that these paragraph skills are useful in all sorts of writing genres, eg essays, letters, reports, reviews, etc.

TEACH GLOBAL THINK LOCAL Writing extra

If your students need a little more support at paragraph level before they write a full report, ask them to write a practice paragraph in pairs on a given topic, eg *effective writing in English,* or *the importance of attending a language course*. They should then use arrows / lines to label the function of each sentence within their paragraph, using the descriptions in exercise 2. Monitor while students write, checking that their paragraphs are both correctly labelled and coherent.

2

Paragraph 1

Sentence 2: elaboration; Sentence 3: a definition

Paragraph 3

Sentences 2, 3: an example / evidence

Sentence 4: a conclusion

3

Correct order: 5, 1, 4, 2, 3; Topic sentence: 5

Supporting evidence: 1: an example / evidence; 2: consequence; 3: conclusion; 4: reason

Preparing to write (SB page 65)

Aim: to give students time to gather ideas for the writing task.

Tips:

- Brainstorm / suggest possible topics on the board, eg *the economy, tourism, resources, education, health, travel, leisure, languages, crime or work trends*. They should ideally use some concrete data in the form of a graph, chart, etc, which they should include when submitting their report.
- Ask students to make notes here, but not to begin writing.
- Point out and encourage students to use the useful language under *Describing facts and figures*.
- Monitor and assist with planning. Encourage students to talk you through what they plan to write.
- Unless you have internet access in the classroom, allow students to continue their planning as homework.

Writing (SB page 65)

Aim: to give practice in more extended writing tasks.

Tips:

- This section can be done as homework.
- Remind students to refer back to the model text.
- Ask students to check their work carefully before they hand it in.
- Tell students that you will prioritise clear paragraph structure when assessing their work, as well as evaluating good interpretation of graph / statistics (if appropriate), accuracy and overall quality. (For example, you could assign total marks out of 50, with 20 for paragraphing and 10 each for the other aspects.)

Study skills

Register awareness (SB page 65)

TEACH GLOBAL THINK LOCAL

Pre-reading activity

Start the lesson by cheerily saying *Good morning* in different ways (if your lesson is at a different time, change the greetings accordingly): *I bid you good morning; Hi there; Good day my friends; Ciao!; Hello; Good morning; What's up?; Morning!* Ask students, in pairs, if they can remember the different forms you used. Ask *What was the basic difference between the greetings?* (style). *Do you have a similar range of options in your language?*

1 Ask students *Would you be so kind as to read this text?* followed by *Read this, please!* Elicit responses to the question in exercise 1.

2 In pairs, students discuss the sample sentences. They will probably be able to recognise whether they are written / spoken, but possibly not why. If necessary, give suggestions: the choice of words used, the length of sentences, use of contractions, complexity of structures used, etc. Elicit their responses.

1 written: high noun phrase content (*lack of access to education, high levels of illiteracy*)

2 spoken: contractions (*we've, we're*); spoken discourse marker (*actually*); general word (*things*)

3 spoken: filler (*like*); oral reported speech (*I was like* + direct speech); repetition; double negative (*haven't … nothing*)

4 written: formal written grammar (*the rebellion crushed*)

3 In pairs, ask students to look up the words in a dictionary, to see how the register is indicated there. Ask them to look for the list of style labels, usually found at the front or on the inside cover.

1 disapproving (*don't be … you're always + -ing*); informal (*-y* suffix)

2 informal (*-y* suffix). Disapproval is inherent in the meaning.

3 literary, old-fashioned (this is from the *Gilgamesh* extract)

4 legal, formal

4 Students discuss the questions and share suggestions about words with a special register. Invite students to share any personal examples of when they have used an inappropriate register, perhaps causing offence or a humorous reaction. Give any examples of use of inappropriate register that you are aware of, either written or spoken, eg students often write too informally in written genres.

Possible answers

clues: context (other words, ideas about type of text), punctuation

UNIT 6 Trade & Commerce

Coursebook			
Unit 6	**Language**	**Texts**	**Communication skills**
Part 1 SB page 66	Extend your vocabulary *change* and *exchange* Grammar The passive	Listening The Silk Road	Pronunciation List intonation
Part 2 SB page 68	Vocabulary Ways of looking	Reading *The Long Song*	Speaking Freedom and slavery
Part 3 SB page 70	Vocabulary Problems	Reading & Speaking *Bangalore* Listening Ideas for India's future	Speaking Tackling problems
Part 4 SB page 72	Extend your vocabulary *gold* and *golden* Grammar Cleft sentences	Reading *The new golden age*	Speaking Investments
Function globally SB page 74	Negotiating Listening to situations involving negotiations Negotiating and obtaining concessions		
Global voices SB page 75	Customer service Stance markers Discussing customer service questionnaires		
Writing SB page 76	Emails Writing skills: cohesion Linking ideas: clarification and emphasis A semi-formal email		
Study skills SB page 77	Learning language in context		

Additional resources	
eWorkbook	Interactive and printable grammar, vocabulary, listening and pronunciation practice Extra reading and writing practice Additional downloadable listening and video material
Teacher's Resource Disc	Communication activity worksheets to print and photocopy, review material, test, and video with worksheet
Go global Ideas for further research	**Trade** Ask students to research the history of one of the other major trade routes in the world, such as the Trans-Saharan trade route, or a particular feature, such as the Panama Canal or the Trans-Siberian railway. Using information from websites, students present details of why the route was established, what was traded and how it has changed over history. **Commerce** Ask students to follow up their work on industry and commerce by researching details of one of the sectors (finance, agriculture, fishing, IT, etc) that are important in their own countries. Using information from relevant websites, students give details of the importance of the sector, the leading countries, its location and worth to the economy.

Part 1

TEACH GLOBAL THINK LOCAL Lead-in

For a fun, sensory lead-in to the topic, bring in different spices such as cinnamon, nutmeg, ginger and cumin. Put these into unmarked boxes or envelopes, but make sure you know which one is which! Get students to smell the spices and to identify them. You could extend this further by putting pieces of cloth or clothing with different textures into a dark bag or box. Students have to put their hands in and identify the material, eg wool, velvet, linen, cotton, silk, leather, etc.

Listening (SB page 66)

1 If you suspect your students might be unsure of the information required in the first question, then try to do a little research beforehand and put alternatives up on the board, including some distractors: you could write up three countries, a selection of items and three different means of transportation. In pairs, students discuss the questions before sharing their ideas with the class.

2 **2.36–2.40** This listening is a description of the Silk Road in six parts by an expert. In the first five parts he discusses the historical development and the significance of this trade route from the first millennium BC.

Focus students' attention on the pictures. After listening, ask them to check, in pairs, what the five pictures represent. Write the answers on the board for students to quickly self-check.

Section 1: D	Section 4: B
Section 2: A	Section 5: E
Section 3: C	

2.36–2.40

1

The Silk Road was not, as the name suggests, a single road at all. It consisted of an extensive network of trade routes that criss-crossed China, parts of the Middle East and Europe, for almost 3,000 years from the first millennium BC until about 1500 AD. The starting point was in China, and the main land routes extended over a huge area of what is now modern day China, Turkey, Syria, Iraq, Iran, Afghanistan, Pakistan, India, Turkmenistan and Uzbekistan. And when goods arrived at the coast they were transported by sea to the major trading ports of Europe, northern Africa and Asia.

2

Since the transport capacity was limited, luxury goods were the only commodities that could be traded. As the name suggests, silk was the main commodity that was traded on the Silk Road. Silk was highly prized and in great demand in the west, and the silk-making process was a secret that was closely guarded for centuries under punishment of death. Silk was ideal for overland travel as it was light, easy to carry and took up little space. It was manufactured in China, and was intricately decorated and embroidered, and when it arrived in Europe it was made into luxury goods such as book coverings, wall hangings and clothes.

3

Silk was by no means the only commodity exchanged by traders, however. Perfumes, precious stones and metals, and foodstuffs were exchanged in both directions. There was also a lucrative trade in spices from east to west; in fact one European town is on record as selling as many as 288 different kinds. In the west, people had to keep meat for a long time until it turned rancid, and spices were very useful for disguising the flavour. Some of the most valuable ones – ginger, nutmeg, cinnamon and saffron – were actually worth more than their weight in gold. Pepper was also extremely valuable, and caravans that carried it were heavily armed.

4

In addition to silk and spices, Europeans were eager to import teas and porcelain from China as well as Persian carpets. The Chinese, for their part, particularly appreciated coloured glass from the Mediterranean, and also imported such commodities as fine tableware, wool and linen, horses and saddles. Many of these goods were bartered for others along the way, and objects often changed hands several times. And it was not only goods that were exchanged on the routes, but also many important scientific and technological innovations; the magnetic compass, the printing press, paper-making and gunpowder all originated in the East, not to mention important intellectual developments such as algebra and astronomy. And in return, the West taught the East about construction techniques, shipbuilding and wine-making.

5

Life for traders along the Silk Road was often hard. As well as having to trek over some of the world's most inhospitable terrain, they also faced the ever present threat of bandits, not to mention wars, plagues and natural disasters. Between towns and oases they would often sleep in yurts or under the stars, or else would stop for rest and refreshment at one of the several bustling oasis towns that sprang up along the routes. Here they would stay at caravanserais, places which offered free board and lodging, as well as stables for their camels or donkeys. The caravanserai became a rich melting pot of ideas, used as they were not only by traders and merchants, but also by pilgrims, missionaries, soldiers, nomads and urban dwellers from all over the region.

3 In pairs, students use the pictures as prompts to remind them what was said. Monitor to hear how much they picked up from the listening.

4 Before students discuss the origins of these items, ask them *Can you identify the one word which does not have stress on the first syllable?* (astronomy). Drill any words you anticipate may be tricky for your students, eg *algebra* /ˈældʒɪbrə/, *compass* /ˈkʌmpəs/, *ginger* /ˈdʒɪndʒə/, *porcelain* /ˈpɔːs(ə)lɪn/. When they have discussed what they can remember, students re-listen to sections 3 and 4. Keep feedback brisk by asking one student to read out the East to West list, and another the West to East list.

East to West: algebra, astronomy, compass, ginger, gunpowder, paper-making, porcelain, printing press, silk, spices

West to East: glass, linen, saddles, shipbuilding, wool

5 **2.41** This last part of the script discusses the long-term legacy of the Silk Road. In pairs, students read the questions and make logical predictions before listening to check their ideas.

1. music, arts, science, customs, ideas, religions and philosophies
2. so much cultural interchange over so many centuries that it is now often difficult to identify the origins of numerous traditions that our respective cultures take for granted – it was an early example of what we now call globalisation
3. tourism

2.41

By the end of the 14th century, as other trading routes were established, the importance of the Silk Road had greatly diminished. But it is no exaggeration to say that it had played a major part in establishing the foundations of the modern world. It had allowed the exchange not only of commodities, but also of music, arts, science, customs, ideas, religions and philosophies. In fact, there was so much cultural interchange over so many centuries that it is now often difficult to identify the origins of numerous traditions that our respective cultures take for granted. So we can say that, in its heyday the Silk Road was an early example of the political, economic and cultural integration that we know today as globalisation. And today, the Silk Road is again being used – not only by traders, but also for that most contemporary of international commodities – tourism.

6 Elicit students' response to the two questions as a whole class.

TEACH GLOBAL THINK LOCAL Listening extra

If you think your students would benefit from some intensive listening practice, then give out / show the following text, which has ten 'mistakes'. Remove the underlining for your students, to raise the challenge. They will need to listen very intensively to Section 1 of the audio to identify the minor differences. Do the first example together, pausing after the first sentence. Replay as often as necessary:

The Silk Road was not, as the name suggests, a single route at all. It comprised an extensive network of trade routes that crossed across China, parts of the Middle East and Europe, for most of 3,000 years from the first millennium BC until around 1500 AD. The starting place was in China, and the main land routes extended over a large area of what is now modern day China, Turkey, Syria, Iraq, Iran, Afghanistan, Pakistan, India, Turkmenistan and Kazakhstan. And when goods arrived at the coast they were transported by ship to the major trading ports of Europe, northern America and Asia.

Extend your vocabulary (SB page 66)

1 Write up the verb *exchange* on the board and elicit possible nouns which collocate with it. Students then work alone to complete the exercise. Encourage fast finishers to think of another noun that collocates with *change*, *swap* and *switch*, and also to identify the verb which collocates with the **incorrect** noun in the list, eg *change hair style*.

Incorrect alternatives

1. your hair style (change your hair style)
2. house (move house)
3. currency (exchange currency)
4. smiles (exchange smiles)

2 In pairs, students use the collocations to share information. Invite them to share some interesting experiences with the whole class.

TEACH GLOBAL THINK LOCAL Alternative procedure

You could adapt exercise 2 slightly to change it into an info gap activity. In pairs, students ask questions with *change* or *exchange* to find out three things that their partner has done recently and three things that they have never done, eg *Have you changed your hair style recently? / You've changed your hair style recently, haven't you? Have you ever exchanged smiles with somebody thinking they were someone different?*

Pronunciation (SB page 66)

1 This exercise highlights the falling tone at the end of a list. Students are unlikely to find this difficult at this level, but such activities do remind them of the significance of intonation. Let them compare their answers in pairs. Do not confirm any answers yet.

2 2.42 Students listen and then read aloud **with** the recording. Ask a student who sounds very natural to show the others.

> in all cases, voice goes down on the final items, and up on the others

TEACH GLOBAL THINK LOCAL

Extra activity

Pronunciation exercise 1 (SB page 66) also includes two very natural ways of adding emphasis: *not to mention* (in sentence 2) and *not only … but also* (in sentence 3). Books closed. Put up the two sentences on the board, with these phrases gapped. Elicit what the missing words are and what purpose they have in the sentences. Then encourage students to use these in exercise 3, if appropriate.

3 Do an example together using a different topic, eg topics you have studied so far this term on the English course. Then, in pairs, students make lists for two of the given categories; make sure they both write them down. Let them practise reading the lists aloud to each other at this stage, using the correct intonation.

4 Put students into groups of four to compare lists by reading them aloud. You could challenge them to read out their lists without looking at their papers!

Grammar (SB page 67)

1 Approach this by first dictating the first three sentences (a–c) but omitting the words in bold. Elicit what the missing words might be and in what form. Then students work alone to answer the language questions before comparing answers in pairs. Bear in mind that this will be revision for students at this level, so let them do all of the work!

> 1 active: a, e; passive: b, c, d, f
> 2 Use an active form when the focus is the doer.
> Use a passive form when the focus is the action / object.
> 3 appropriate form of the verb *be* + the past participle
> d (traders and merchants, pilgrims, missionaries, soldiers, nomads and urban dwellers) and f (traders)
> in sentences b and c: focus is on what was done rather than who did it

TEACH GLOBAL THINK LOCAL

Extra activity

If you have a monolingual group, and if you speak the students' first language, then get them to translate the six sentences into their first language. Then encourage them to discuss how the two languages differ in a) form and b) use / style.

TEACH GLOBAL THINK LOCAL

Language note

Given that this formal, rather academic description is about the Silk Route and the items traded, it is not surprising that the passive is frequently used here. It may be worth reminding students at this level that in more informal spoken English, *get* is often used in passive forms too. Although *be* and *get* are often interchangeable, *get* can sometimes convey an idea of a (lengthy or difficult) process, eg *after waiting for justice all those years, he finally got sent to jail; all my stuff got ruined in the rain.*

In the passive, the agent is not usually mentioned because a) it is not important or significant; b) it is obvious and/or c) it is intentionally omitted to be polite or discrete. Discoursally, it also depends on shared knowledge and on what has come before: in English we often place the new information at the end of the sentence to emphasise it, with familiar information coming before, eg *The house has been redecorated* (we know the house, but the redecorating is new information).

If it is important to mention the agent, it is placed in end position, after *by*, eg *All my lettuces were eaten by snails*. This is also used if the subject is very long: *I was denied entry by the people who were standing at the main entrance to the nightclub.*

2 Elicit what NAFTA and EU stand for (North American Free Trade Agreement and European Union). Do the first answer together, reminding students that they also have to select the appropriate tense. Then, in pairs, students discuss the remaining answers. Some of the verbs may be tempting for students to put into the passive, eg *consist*, *increase* and *disappear*, but a passive form can only be used with transitive verbs. If the topic is of interest to the students, after checking answers, let them discuss the content too. Ask *Do you agree? What do you think will happen in relation to future trade between countries?*

> 1 has been conducted
> 2 probably consisted
> 3 were exchanged
> 4 was introduced
> 5 has increased
> 6 have been established
> 7 is increasingly being carried out
> 8 may regulate
> 9 are usually imposed
> 10 may also be imposed
> 11 will ever be established
> 12 will completely disappear

TEACH GLOBAL THINK LOCAL

Extra activity

Exercise 2 contains some useful language related to trade: *trading* (n): *barter* (n/v), *tariff* (n), *taxation* (n), *exchange* (n/v) and collocations or compound nouns with *trade: conduct / promote / carry out; international trade, trade organisation, free trade, trade blocs, trade restrictions, trade quotas*. Allocate one of the above to each pair / individual and ask them to use it in a sentence. Give out dictionaries, if necessary, and monitor. Students should then read out their sentence for others to record if they want.

3 If your students are likely to need some help with ideas, dictate or put an example up on the board, eg *This product is exported from several hot countries and is a major source of income. It has been used for centuries and is said to be both good and bad for your health. It is picked from bushes and has to be roasted before it is used – it's nearly always bought already roasted. This product can be served in a variety of ways. (After this lesson, it will probably be used by some of us.)* (Answer: *coffee*.)

Ask students to complete the exercise in pairs, but first warn them what is going to happen in exercise 4, so that they are prepared and do not make it too simplistic. Monitor as they work, particularly with regard to the target language. Early finishers can choose an additional commodity.

Students' own answers.

4 Sit students in groups of four, opposite their new pairs. Invite them to read out their sentences and guess each others' mystery commodities.

5 Put students into groups of three. Give them about five minutes' preparation time and ask them to speak individually for between 90 seconds and two minutes on their chosen topic, to the rest of their group. Encourage students to ask follow-up questions.

TEACH GLOBAL THINK LOCAL Mixed ability

Depending on your students, they may benefit from having time to research these topics more fully first outside the class – if so, you can raise the profile slightly too: allow students to use a PowerPoint presentation and/or visuals if they like, for a three or four-minute presentation. Ask them to include details on a) what the 'contribution' is exactly; b) how it came about; c) how / if it has changed over time; d) what it is used for and e) how and why it has had such an impact.

G Grammar focus

Refer students to the language summary on the passive on page 142.

You can use exercises 1–3 on page 143 for:

a) extra practice now, b) homework or c) review later on.

The answers are on page 163 of this Teacher's Book.

Part 2

TEACH GLOBAL THINK LOCAL Lead-in

To motivate students on the topic of trade between countries, write out the following list of commodities and the main exporting country onto small, separate pieces of card / paper. Give the pieces out to students at the start of class and ask them to match the commodity to the principal exporter. Write some more if you have a large class.

mangoes	India
peanuts	US
cocoa	Ivory Coast, Africa
gold	South Africa
tobacco	China
tea	Kenya
rice	Thailand*
silk	China
paper	Canada
bananas	Ecuador
salt	US
oil	Saudi Arabia

* China is the largest producer

Speaking (SB page 68)

1 Put students into pairs to discuss the pictures. Invite students to share some reactions to the visuals with the whole class. Elicit what students know about slavery. You could put these prompts on the board, or dictate them, to find out how much they know: *where most of the slaves came from, when it happened, why the slave industry grew, why and when it was stopped*, etc. This prepares students for the next stage.

2 **2.43** In pairs, students attempt to complete the quotations. Let them refer to dictionaries, if necessary. Elicit one or two suggestions for several of the quotations in open class. Then play the recording for students to check. Clarify any quotations which they may not fully understand.

2 robots	5 others	8 attitude
3 opposition	6 oppressed	
4 right	7 armies	

3 Put students with a different partner to discuss their preferences and the relevance of the quotations. If students appear animated, encourage them to share some ideas with the rest of the class.

Reading (SB page 68)

This text is an extract from a novel, powerfully demonstrating the change in roles between slaves and their owners at the time of the abolition of slavery.

1 Read the first paragraph aloud to the class, without any comment. Then let students read the rest of the extract alone. Students compare and discuss their answers in pairs.

> Caroline is the master; Godfrey is the servant; July is another servant
>
> It is set during the emancipation. Caroline speaks to Godfrey as master to servant, but he rebels and asks for payment. Her attempt to punish him ends in humiliation for her, and she agrees to pay him.

2 This exercise will help to prepare students for exercise 4. If the words are new to students, they can look for support in the context. Let students attempt to work out their meaning in pairs first, referring to a dictionary, if necessary. Put up the new words on the board, in three columns, but keep the pace swift here: *facial expression, sounds, movement*. Elicit the answers and check students' understanding where necessary, visually, orally or by demonstrating.

> facial expression: *frowned*, *grimace*, *wince*
>
> sounds: *gasp*, *giggle*, *utter*, *sighed*
>
> movement: *scratching*, *seized*, *kneel*

3 In the same pairs, students try to work out the meaning of the highlighted words by looking at the context. Allow them a moment to compare their ideas with another pair before checking as a class.

> *valise*: a small travelling bag or suitcase
>
> *missus*: old-fashioned – the mistress of the house
>
> *gig*: old-fashioned – a cart with two wheels pulled by a horse
>
> *massa*: old-fashioned – the master of the house
>
> *bid*: old-fashioned – *Do as you are bid* means *Do as you are told*

4 Students work alone on this exercise which requires them to read the text closely to find the exact sentence or phrase. Students might enjoy exchanging ideas here, as there is more than one possible answer at times.

> 1 *'Godfrey, do not play the fool with me. You know I must go to town for my own safety until all this trouble is past.*
>
> *'Payment?', the missus repeated. She frowned upon Godfrey, then looked quizzically to July for some explanation of his behaviour.*
>
> 2 *July cupped her hands over her mouth so her gasp and giggle would not escape.*
>
> 3 *He then walked past the missus into the hall and sat himself down upon one of the massa's wooden chairs.*
>
> *'Then punish me, missus', he said as he lifted first one leg, and then the other, over the arms of the planter's seat and sat as if waiting for someone to remove his boots …*
>
> 4 *'Get up, get up!' Caroline jumped twice in her fury. 'Do as you are bid', then made to strike Godfrey with her closed fist.*
>
> 5 … Caroline Mortimer, quivering at his feet like a fish newly landed from the water, slowly lifted her head, wiped her snivelling nose upon the back of her hand, and quietly asked him, 'How much?'

5 Write the three names – *Caroline*, *Godfrey* and *July* – on the board. Give students five to ten minutes to work with a new partner, discussing which of the adjectives best describes which character. They then discuss the other two questions. Monitor to find out how much students have understood and empathised with the text and topic. Early finishers can think of other suitable adjectives to describe the characters. Conduct a whole-class feedback session, if necessary for your group.

> Caroline: aggressive, arrogant, controlling, self-confident, submissive
>
> Godfrey: controlling, defiant, self-confident
>
> July: loyal, submissive, timid
>
> 1 She is struggling in a new environment in which she is being controlled and is helpless.
>
> 2 Students' own answers.

TEACH GLOBAL THINK LOCAL

Speaking extra

If your students enjoyed the extract, put half of the class into 'Caroline and Walter' pairs. Caroline begins, telling her (imaginary) brother 'Walter' about the events of that day. Start like this: *Walter, you'll never guess what happened! I'm still reeling from the shock.* The other half of the class should instead roleplay July telling her cousin May. Start like this: *May, I'm never going to forget this day. I still can't believe it …* At the end, invite at least two different pairs to share their version of the events from Caroline's and then July's perspective.

Vocabulary (SB page 69)

1 In pairs, students discuss the two sentences. Check students understand *stare* (v) (n). Elicit their responses.

> *stared at*: literal
>
> *looking down on*: literal in text, but could also be metaphorical (double meaning implied)

2 Do the first example together. Encourage students to put the words in example sentences, to help them decide on the type of meaning. Let them use a dictionary after a few minutes in order to check and finish off their answers. Give students time to write down the example sentences from the dictionary for any new verbs / meanings. Check the answers in a feedback session.

look after: literal; metaphorical
look away: literal
look back on: metaphorical
look forward to: metaphorical
look into: literal; metaphorical
look on: literal; metaphorical
look out for: literal; metaphorical
look round: literal
look up: literal; metaphorical
look up to: literal; metaphorical

3 Draw a large eye on the board! Elicit some verbs related to different ways of looking, miming if necessary to prompt students, eg *stare*, *peer*, *glance*, *glare*, etc. Do the first example together. Don't worry if students find this exercise quite tricky – let them do the task with a dictionary and in pairs. If the words appear to be new, clarify their meaning when checking the answers by eliciting when or where one might look in this manner.

4 Clearly state the requirements of this writing task at the start: they need to include at least two 'looking' verbs or phrases, two descriptions of facial expressions and at least two pieces of direct speech. This and the following exercise can be done individually or in pairs depending on the level of challenge required.

TEACH GLOBAL THINK LOCAL

Alternative procedure

If students need more help in terms of ideas for exercise 4, then provide the following dialogue openers.

A She peered down the pipe. 'Give me the spanner!' she yelled irritably.

B She flicked through one of the magazines in the waiting room and caught sight of a young man staring at her intently.

C Joey caught sight of the girls laughing, and grimaced horribly.

5 Allow students, individually or in pairs, a few moments to practise reading their scene. Then put them into groups and encourage them to read their scene aloud with as much feeling as possible. Invite volunteers to share their work with the whole class.

Part 3

TEACH GLOBAL THINK LOCAL

Lead-in

To lead into the topic of major industries, put up the first and last letters from the industry words in the box in exercise 1, as shown below. Include the number of letters in brackets to help, if necessary. Put students in pairs or groups of three and handle it as a race.

A________e (11)	M________g (13)
F________e (7)	M________g (6)
F________g (7)	S________e I________y (7/8)
F________y (8)	T________m (7)

Reading and Speaking (SB page 70)

1 In pairs or small groups students discuss these points. You could do a little research beforehand, or ask students in advance to do it for you, in order to provide some concrete facts.

2 Show students where Bangalore is on a map. Elicit what they know about it. Ask them to read the three different descriptions (A–C). This is a genre-sensitisation task. As a guide, it might be useful to ask *Who is each text written for?* Let them discuss their ideas in pairs, then discuss their answers as a class.

A (extract from *The White Tiger* by Aravind Adiga, a novel about an Indian entrepreneur)
narrative (*When I drive down Hosur Main Road, when I turn into Electronics City Phase 1 and see the companies go past, I can't tell you how exciting it is to me.*)
descriptive (*Piles of mud everywhere. Piles of stones. Piles of bricks. The entire city is masked in smoke, smog, powder, cement dust.*)
fairly informal (*But you never know. It might turn out to be …*)

B (article in *Business India*, a magazine about business news in India)
descriptive, with lots of alliteration and repetition (*congenial, captivating, cosmopolitan confluence, software and shopping malls*)
more formal style: (*congenial, salubrious*)

C (extract from the *Encyclopaedia Britannica* entry on Bangalore)
factual, with long dense sentences with lots of noun phrases (*One of India's largest cities, Bangalore lies on an east-west ridge in the Karnataka Plateau in the south-eastern part of the state.*)

3 Let students work alone to complete the comprehension task. They then compare answers in pairs before whole-class feedback.

1 IT / electronics

2

A: exciting, lots of big companies (*I can't tell you how exciting it is to me.*)

B: captivating, friendly, cosmopolitan, nice climate, clean, modern but traditional, entertainment (*India's best city for business.*)

C: comfortable climate (*pleasant winters and tolerable summers make it a popular place of residence …*)

3 The author describes the city as being masked in smoke and dust, as if the city is under a veil. He also says the result may be a disaster or a decent city.

4 He is ambivalent about the result.

5 There is a lack of water. There is insufficient rainfall to provide water for the growing population and the increasing demands of industry.

4 Students quickly identify the parts of speech of words 1–6, and then find the synonyms. They compare their answers whilst you put the answers on the board for them to self-check. Point out that *congenial* (adj) and *salubrious* (adj) are low frequency.

1 turn out	3 sewage	5 captivating
2 slums	4 congenial	6 salubrious

5 In pairs, students discuss the questions. For question 2, ask them to think of at least four questions to ask, eg *What's the currency?* Elicit some of their questions.

TEACH GLOBAL THINK LOCAL **Writing extra**

Students imagine they are tourists to Bangalore. Ask them to write a postcard home. This also encourages them to re-focus on characteristics of a different written genre.

Listening (SB page 70)

This listening is an account of how the outsourcing industry in India has developed since the 1990s.

1 Books closed, read the definition aloud for students to guess what is being defined. Then, in small groups, they discuss the questions before sharing ideas with the class.

2 **2.44** Students listen to the audio once and answer the question. Check the answer as a class.

It has led to work being exported to cheaper countries.

2.44

For decades now as you know, large companies have been outsourcing information technology services as well as what we call 'back office services' – things like administrative duties and customer services. For companies, getting rid of these tasks, or passing on these office services, means lower costs, for one thing. But it also gives companies the chance to focus on their core business – manufacturing, sales, research, whatever business they're actually in. Up until the 1990s, American and British businesses tended to outsource these tasks to workers in their own country. But in the 1990s, company bosses realised that India had a large pool of technically literate workers who could work for a fraction of the cost. So many large companies started to take advantage of India's outsourcing companies in a big way.

The problem is that, now, India has just become too expensive. Firstly, there are no longer *enough* skilled English-speaking workers to cope with demand. So these workers have tended to move from company to company in search of the highest paid jobs. This has kept pushing up the cost of Indian salaries and therefore also pushed up the cost of outsourcing for American and British customers.

In addition, there's been a huge increase in property prices in cities such as Bangalore, Chennai and Pune. And infrastructure in these areas – things like transport and sanitation – has just not been able to keep pace with the growth of the outsourcing industry. Some Indian outsourcing companies have tried to move their businesses to rural locations in order to find a way round these issues. But, as you can imagine, there are usually fewer skilled workers in rural areas, so this isn't really a solution.

So basically, India has become a victim of its own success. What that means is that some American and British customers have started to outsource to lower-cost markets elsewhere instead – so places such as China, the Philippines, Brazil, Mexico, erm, eastern Europe. But there's also been a positive development and that is that some of the *Indian* companies which offer outsourcing services have begun to set up in business in other countries. So they're *re-exporting* outsourcing work to places with cheaper labour. Indian companies that used to be small firms providing services for global companies abroad have become important global companies themselves.

3 Students read the questions, then listen again to respond to these more in-depth comprehension questions. They compare answers before checking them as a class. Replay (part of) the recording, if necessary.

1 administrative duties and customer services

2 due to its technically literate workforce who could work for less money

3 a rise in salaries and property prices in cities

4 change their outsourcing destination

5 they are outsourcing their outsourcing work to other countries

4 Try to draw on students' own experiences here, or of people who they know, in relation to the use of English. Discuss these issues as a whole group.

Vocabulary (SB page 71)

1 Ask *What problem has the growth of outsourcing industry caused in Indian cities? How have some companies tried to resolve this? Has it been successful?* (The cities haven't had the capacity to grow at the same rate as the demand. Some Indian outsourcing companies have tried to shift to rural areas, but there is a skill shortage there, so it hasn't provided a solution.) Then, students complete the exercise in pairs. Check answers and any new phrases.

1 getting	3 pace	5 victim
2 pushing	4 way	

Phrases that refer to a problem: 2, 3, 5
Phrases that refer to dealing with a problem: 1, 4

2 Students complete the collocation task and record new phrases. Check answers as a class.

1 c 2 a 3 b 4 h 5 g 6 d 7 f 8 e

3 Students work together to complete the task. Check answers as a class.

1 major	4 alleviated	7 tackle
2 keeping pace	5 way round	8 pressing
3 solved	6 poses	9 exacerbated

Speaking (SB page 71)

1 Students select and reflect on three points. Monitor and assist.

2 In groups, students discuss the three questions. Monitor as they are talking and take notes on any points of interest to discuss as a class.

TEACH GLOBAL THINK LOCAL

Writing extra

Let students choose one area that interests them from Speaking exercise 1. Ask them to write either a report (see Unit 5 *Writing*) or an essay (see Unit 3 *Writing*), depending on their needs. To help them plan, they can use the following headings: *what the problem is and the main reasons why it has arisen*; *main risks or dangers, if relevant*; *ways the problems are being tackled and how successful these are*; *other possible solutions*.

Part 4

TEACH GLOBAL THINK LOCAL

Lead-in

Books closed. In groups of three, ask students to brainstorm what people can invest money in. Elicit an example at the start and then give them two or three minutes to discuss this. At the end, ask them to compare their lists with the box in exercise 1. Find out if they had any additional ones.

Speaking (SB page 72)

1 Ask students to work independently at first to rank the investments from 1–8. They should consider their rationale as they rank them.

2 Before students compare answers, refer them to *Useful phrases* and check any new words or phrases, eg *depreciate*, *be a safe bet*. Invite students to share some ideas with the class.

Reading (SB page 72)

This reading is a description of the historical popularity of gold.

1 First of all, elicit/pre-teach the meaning of *alchemist* and *alchemy*. Then students read *The new golden age* and decide on the best summary. Take a class vote before confirming the answer.

Gold is popular now, but it always has been for many reasons.

2 **Before** they look at the list of definitions 1–8, ask students to reread the text, identifying the word class and probable meaning of the words in bold.

1 mere	4 shooting up	7 turmoil
2 malleable	5 latter day	8 lust
3 commodities	6 mocking	

3 Students work independently initially. Some students are likely to need more time on this comprehension task, so have a couple of extra questions ready for fast finishers, eg *Gold is worth only as much as people think it is.* (T) (The text says: *Its value depends on how much people believe in it.*) *Gold can be mixed with other alloys to make it softer.* (F) (The text says: *When alloyed with other elements its density changes and you can get a whole range from reddish orange to white.*). Take feedback and clarify any problems with reference to the text.

1 T
2 T
3 DS
4 T
5 F (the reverse: *… turning base lead into noble gold, a transmutation …*)
6 T
7 DS

4 Students can discuss these questions in groups of three. If appropriate, add some further questions: *Which metal do you prefer, gold, silver or platinum? Why? What do you possess that is gold? Describe your (or someone else's) favourite gold item.*

Extend your vocabulary (SB page 72)

1 If you can, show something made of gold to the students, eg a ring, and elicit adjectives to describe it. Write *gold* and *golden* on the board. Elicit what the difference is and ask *Are there two different words in your language(s) too?* Then students complete the gapped sentences and check their answers in pairs before class feedback.

1 golden	2 gold	3 golden	4 golden

2 After students locate the correct collocations from the list, they can check their answers in a dictionary, including the actual meaning.

> no collocation with *golden*: address; dream; remark
>
> golden (wedding) anniversary: the day when people celebrate 50 years of marriage
>
> golden handshake: a large amount of money given to a senior manager when they leave their job
>
> golden oldie: something such as a film or piece of music that is old but still popular
>
> golden opportunity: a good chance to do or achieve something
>
> golden rule: an important basic principle that you should always obey

3 Students work in pairs to write sentences including two of the chosen items. Monitor as they are working. Invite students to share some nice examples with the whole class.

Grammar (SB page 73)

1 The following exercises focus on cleft sentences. After reading and answering the question with the class, ask students *What is interesting about the second sentence? Why do you think this clause structure is used?* Students will have seen and heard this language on many occasions, but (some) may not be using it yet, even at this level. See *Language note*.

> more than mere money

Language note

Cleft sentences are used to foreground information that is significant in a sentence. The structure *it is / was … that …* can be used to highlight different parts, eg *It was then that Mike finally told the truth. It was Mike who finally told the truth; It was the truth that Mike finally told.*

With cleft sentences with *what*, students often forget the main *be* verb, eg *What will be fascinating to see* **is** *what comes next.*

Another commonly used cleft sentence includes *the thing* or *the thing to do*, eg *The thing I like most is …; The (best) thing to do is to …*

When clarifying, give attention to pronunciation too, eg *What I love about English is the grammar*. The word *grammar* receives the most prominence, thereby matching the syntax.

2 Tell students before they start that the word in bold is not necessarily the starting word. Do the first example together and then let students work in pairs. Conduct a whole-class feedback session giving attention to accuracy and also to appropriate pronunciation.

> 1 It is gold that
> 2 What I really hate is
> 3 What he could never resist was
> 4 It was the price of gold that
> 5 What the alchemists did was experiment

3 Give a couple of true, personal examples using these sentence starters. Students then work individually to write three sentences. Monitor and check as they are writing. Put them into groups to compare and discuss sentences. Pick up on relevant pronunciation issues as they are talking. Invite students to share any interesting sentences with the class.

TEACH GLOBAL THINK LOCAL Extra practice

For fun, dictate the following sentence starters:

What I enjoyed about this lesson …

The thing that I'll probably remember most clearly about this class …

It is … that inspires me to carry on learning English.

What I'd really like to do now …

Ask them to complete the sentences and to pass their notebooks to their partner, who should read and write a brief reply. Elicit one or two examples to round off the class paying attention to correct intonation and emphasis at this point.

G Grammar focus

Refer students to the language summary on cleft sentences on page 142.

You can use exercises 4 and 5 on page 143 for:

a) extra practice now, b) homework or c) review a couple of lessons from now.

The answers are on page 163 of this Teacher's Book.

Function globally: negotiating

These lessons in *Global* are designed to provide students with immediately useful functional language. They all follow a similar format.

Warm up (SB page 74)

Aim: to introduce the topic via a quick speaking task.

Tips:

- Your students might benefit from a few minutes' thinking-time before they start talking.
- Encourage students to use as much variety of language as they can. Do not over-correct.
- Pick up on any points which students find interesting or tricky to raise as an issue for the whole class.
- Invite students to share personal examples with the class, eg when they last negotiated a price.

Listening (SB page 74)

Aim: to present the functional language in context via a conversation or series of conversations.

Tips:

- Play the recording all the way through for each task (there are always two tasks). (Tracks 2.45–2.48)
- Pause the recording after each conversation.
- Let students share their personal reactions to (some of) the situations from the listening.
- Encourage students to reread the audioscripts for homework, exploiting them for useful language.

TEACH GLOBAL THINK LOCAL Extra activity

After listening, pairs of students act out a conversation reading from the audioscript.

1

Conversation 1

buying a second-hand car: the customer leaves without buying the car

Conversation 2

bank charges: the penalty charge is waived, but the customer still has to pay interest

Conversation 3

fully booked plane: the customer is offered a seat on a later flight and negotiates an upgrade to club class and vouchers for a future flight

Conversation 4

manager of wholesale business: the retailer agrees to switch custom and stock five stores as the wholesaler lowers the price

2

1 conversation 2; the cheque
2 conversation 1; the car
3 conversation 4; the price of goods per kilo
4 conversation 2; the hours the account was overdrawn
5 conversation 1; price of car
6 conversation 4; the price of goods per kilo
7 conversation 1; extra insurance offered for car
8 conversation 3; seat on next flight

2.45–2.48

1

A: So is that really the best you can do?

B: I'm terribly sorry sir, that's the absolute best price we can do.

A: Well, I wasn't planning on paying that much, especially on a car that's done that mileage.

B: Yes, I appreciate that sir. We have an older vehicle here if you'd rather that one, that's slightly cheaper.

A: No, I'm not interested in the older one.

B: No?

A: This is the one I've got my eye on, but the price has to be …

B: I'm afraid that's absolutely the best we can do. We can throw in some cover if you'd like, but that's the best price we can offer.

A: And the car mats, you'll throw those in?

B: Absolutely, yes, but the price unfortunately is exactly the same.

A: You won't budge on that at all?

B: I'm afraid we can't sir. It wouldn't be worth my job.

A: Well, I'm going to have to think about it, to be honest.

B: OK, no problem, give me a call any time.

A: OK, thanks for your help.

2

A: Good afternoon.

B: Hello, Mr Akroyd. I just wanted to talk to you about the bank charges that I seem to have incurred. As far as I'm aware I was only … I only went beyond my overdraft limit for a matter of 12 hours really and as far as I was aware I actually … I put some money in at about quarter to five on the Wednesday.

A: Yes, after the bank closed I'm afraid so it didn't clear in time. So you did actually go into overdraft for, you're right, for a few hours.

B: Yes, but I mean, surely that … that … those few hours shouldn't have incurred such a hefty fine? I mean, I've been charged here £30.

A: Well, it's a combination of the fine for going into overdraft without authority and also the interest that accrued as a result, but we … I do understand it was for a short period of time so we could … in this case, I do have to charge the interest, but I could actually waive the penalty fee.

B: Thank you very much Mr Akroyd …

A: Is that all right?

B: … that's very kind.

A: Thanks. If in future though, you must bear in mind that if the cheque hasn't cleared by the end of the day it can't be credited to your account.

B: OK, thank you.

3

A: Sir, I'm afraid this, this flight is actually fully booked.

B: But I have a ticket.

A: I've just had a look at the computer and it's telling me, and I've just had it verified by my manager, that, um, this flight is fully booked and you will not be able to travel on this flight. I'm terribly sorry.

B: Right, so what do you suggest?

A: Um, well, there is another flight at 5.30 this afternoon …

B: That's too late for me, I have a meeting to get to.

A: There is availability on this flight sir. I mean, in terms of getting you there we can, yes it will be later.

B: But you do acknowledge that it's not my fault that I'm being bumped off this flight?

A: You are absolutely right about that sir. What I can do is I can offer you an upgrade on the 5.30 flight. Would that be acceptable?

B: To club class?

A: Just one second. Yes, there is a seat in club class and I can put you on that straight away.

B: Right, well, I mean … it will have to do I suppose, but it's not a good way to treat frequent fliers. Is there anything else you can do for me?

A: Sir, I could actually offer you a flight in the future if you wish and we can try to recompense you with vouchers for …

B: Well, I think that would be fair, don't you?

A: Well, as I said, we will get you on the 5.30, we'll get you a club class seat, and I will offer you, we will offer you some vouchers for [your] next flight, to any destination in Europe flying with us …

B: OK, well, let's do that then.

A: … and I hope you continue to fly with us …

B: We'll see.

4

A: So my company could sell to you at a much cheaper rate than you're getting now because we are literally two minutes down the road. So we'll make a huge saving in petrol, which we can pass on to you in the unit price.

B: Well, that does sound good, but we do have a long relationship with this other company. I mean, we'd, we'd need a pretty substantial discount in order to make it fiscally viable for us.

A: OK, your unit price at the moment?

B: It's about 70 per kilo.

A: OK, well, we could do 50.

B: Really?

A: Yeah.

B: OK, well, if you can do 50 … um … I'm actually … I actually run about four different stores so what I can do if you can get … tell you what … if you can get it down to 45 then I can guarantee we would do at least four stores for you, rather than just one.

A: OK, 45 is pushing it, but if we can make it at least five, I've got to get one more than four to make, to make that viable.

B: OK, OK, we'll do five, five for 45.

A: Yeah.

B: OK, we can definitely do that.

A: Fantastic, it's a deal.

Language focus (SB page 74)

Aim: to draw students' attention to the items of functional language.

Tips:

- Let students work alone at first on the exercises, before comparing answers in pairs.
- Students should be able to pronounce these phrases intelligibly so drill them, if necessary.
- Encourage students to make a note of new expressions which they would like to use.
- Ask students which alternative phrases they already use in English for the same functions.

1

1 What I can do; acceptable
2 If you can; then I can
3 prepared to
4 could; if you like
5 absolutely the best

2

1 c 2 a 3 b 4 a 5 c 6 a 7 c 8 b

Pronunciation (SB page 74)

Aim: to focus students on a particular aspect of pronunciation of the target phrases.

Tips:

- Play the recording two or three times, if necessary. (Tracks 2.49–2.50)
- Try to promote good all-round pronunciation including stress, intonation and linking. Ensure that they are stressing the auxiliary verb appropriately.
- Use students with exemplary pronunciation to act as models to help others in the class.

1 do acknowledge
2 did actually go
3 does sound
They are for emphasis.

 **2.49**

1 But you do acknowledge it's not my fault?
2 You did actually go into overdraft.
3 Well, that does sound good.

 **2.50**

You said you'd deliver them today.
You did say you'd deliver them today.
I understand.
I do understand.
It seems like a good deal.
It does seem like a good deal.
I think that would be fair, don't you?
I do think that would be fair, don't you?
Have a seat.
Do have a seat.
You promised me a discount.
You did promise me a discount.
That sounds tempting.
That does sound tempting.
I appreciate that.
I do appreciate that.

Speaking (SB page 74)

Aim: to allow students an opportunity to use this language in a meaningful, real-world context.

Tips:

- Give students time to prepare this activity. Circulate and monitor carefully whilst they are talking.
- Add one or two additional topics which you think will be of particular relevance to your learners, eg trying to obtain a discount in relation to language course fees.
- Correct sensitively, paying attention to the target language especially, and including pronunciation issues.

TEACH GLOBAL THINK LOCAL

Homework extra

If students have found this focus engaging, ask them to write up one of the conversations from *Speaking* for consolidation. They should use some of the new phrases, including the auxiliary verbs for emphasis. You could ask pairs of students to act out good examples.

Global voices

These lessons in *Global* are designed to provide students with exposure to authentic speakers of English from both native and non-native English backgrounds. They all follow a similar format.

Warm up (SB page 75)

Aim: to introduce the topic and highlight potentially difficult vocabulary the students will encounter.

Tips:

- Circulate and monitor any speaking task, but be careful not to over-correct.
- Note down any words or expressions relevant to the topic of customer service, to highlight at the end.

Listening (SB page 75)

Aim: to expose students to English spoken with a variety of accents.

Tips:

- Tell students you don't expect them to understand every word; some of it will be hard. This is because the text has not been scripted or graded in any way. It's what they would hear in 'the real world'. (Tracks 2.51–2.52)
- Let students give their own personal reactions to what people said after exercise 2. Ask *Can you relate to anything that the four speakers mentioned? What did you find interesting about their comments?*
- It may be tempting to hunt for specific pronunciation or language errors, but we recommend against this. In real-world communication not everyone speaks perfect English all the time, not even native speakers.

1 F (*… I think the difference between The Netherlands and England isn't very big …*)
2 T
3 F (*You literally walk inside the door and then you get five people come up to you all at once and ask do you need help.*)
4 T

 **2.51**

A = Marion; **B** = Scott

Marion (The Netherlands) and Scott (England)

A: I was in, um, I was in Holland over the weekend and went shopping with my mum and, um, it was really interesting because we went to, um ... generally I think the difference between The Netherlands and, and England isn't very big in terms of customer satisfaction or the way people meet and greet you in, in shops, um, but we were in a, a big department store and we were looking at children's socks and all of a sudden this woman came up to us and said 'Do you need help with anything?' and I thought 'We are in a department store', you know, 'looking at socks,' and it was just a really random sort of experience where she came up and said 'Do you need help with anything?' because they normally wouldn't do that.

B: I have had that experience in mobile phone shops before. You literally walk inside the door and then you get five people come up to you all at once and ask do you need help. You need a chance to actually look at the mobile phones to ascertain if you want to buy it or not so ...

A: Yes, and what you'd like.

B: ... a bit too intrusive I think, sometimes they need to stand back and let you decide on options ...

A: Let you decide.

B: ... before you want to buy.

A: Well, exactly, yes, absolutely.

B: I think certain industries are more intrusive ...

A: Yes.

B: ... when you go into ...

A: Yes, so ...

2

1 It doesn't extend to 'low-class citizens'.

2 an mp3 player; yes, but not insurance

3 Lilian

4 Sometimes she has to wait for service while two young girls are talking at the till, which doesn't happen in Poland, but she appreciates the politeness in England.

 **2.52**

A = Lillian; **B** = Dominika

Lillian (Kenya) and Dominika (Poland)

A: Well, um, Kenyans generally they are known for being hospitable and being nice to people, but sadly this is not extended to the, to the low-class citizens. You know, they just have to tolerate being not treated well. But I must compare it to the UK, I find the British pleasant, very pleasant. I just recall the other day I went into Currys to buy an mp3 player. Now I'm not good in this electronic guidance ...

B: Me neither ...

A: ... but the gentleman there was very helpful. He explained to me, you know, the technical products, you know, how, how many songs the mp3 can hold, and he went out of his way and he took me to the counter, processed the payment, talked to me about the insurance, and I almost bought it, but I didn't ...

B: I hope he got fantastic commission?

A: Yes, but he was really, really helpful and I walked away feeling wow, that was good.

B: Did you have to wait for any staff to approach you or ...?

A: Actually, no, he saw me, he saw me looking at the area where the mp3s were kept and he walked over to me and asked me if he can help me which I thought was really nice because he took a personal interest in me.

B: Very good. Sometimes I have to say that I have need to wait for people to serve me. It happens quite often that two very young girls are just busy chatting to each other over the till rather than ... that's, that's the common thing. And that's something that wouldn't happen in Poland really. But yes the manner and, you know, saying 'thank you' and 'Is there anything I can do for you?' is very good.

Language focus: stance markers (SB page 75)

Aim: to raise students' awareness of a particular piece of language present in the listening.

Tips:

- The objective of these exercises is primarily awareness-raising, not production. However, at this level they are likely to have heard the expressions and can experiment with using the language immediately.
- Drill the stance markers, if necessary.
- After exercise 3, ask students to choose three stance markers that they would like to experiment with, if possible before next lesson.

1

sadly: the speaker is unhappy about what follows

literally: the speaker is annoyed – this happens at an inappropriate moment

2

frankly – to be honest

basically – fundamentally

actually – in fact

thankfully – luckily

clearly – obviously

Speaking (SB page 75)

Aim: for students to discuss the same or similar questions as the speakers in the listening.

Tips:

- These speaking tasks are more open to allow students to explore the subject. Give them time to do this.
- Monitor as they are talking and note down good / problematic language to highlight later on.
- As you go through the book and the *Global voices* lessons, ask students for feedback on these listening activities and their potential use of English with other people.

TEACH GLOBAL THINK LOCAL **Writing extra**

Ask students to describe a negative customer service experience in a written complaint to a(n) (online) company / store, relating to seriously problematic services or faulty products. Students should write a formal email of complaint to the company's customer services department. Instruct them to be polite but firm and clear and to expect some sort of compensation or concession.

Writing: emails

These lessons in *Global* are designed to provide students with extended writing practice. They all follow a similar format.

Reading (SB page 76)

TEACH GLOBAL THINK LOCAL **Lead-in**

If you can, show some additional photos of Croatia. Elicit from students what they know about the country, and ask if the idea of a holiday there might appeal to them.

Aim: to provide a sample text for students to analyse.

Tips:

- Before starting, ask students if they have ever booked a holiday online. Invite them to share their experiences.
- The first exercise is a gist reading task.
- The retelling exercise (exercise 2) not only gives oral fluency practice, it also demonstrates how much they have understood of the text. Monitor carefully.
- Let students check their answers in pairs before whole-class feedback.

TEACH GLOBAL THINK LOCAL **Reading extra**

For a focus on style, highlight the way that the style of the emails change as the relationship between Anne and Ivana develops, becoming increasingly familiar. Elicit examples, eg *in the salutation and leave-taking; use of short forms; ellipsis; punctuation; choice of language,* etc.

1

1 Correct order: c, b, f, a, e, d

Anne booked a holiday in Villa Maria, Croatia for four adults and they all had a brilliant time.

2

1 two married couples, non-smokers, keen on water sports, especially snorkelling
2 available when they wanted, slightly more expensive than Villa Gemma, larger and recently refurbished
3 645 euros for one week, 15% deposit (96 euros) deposit payable in advance via internet or bank or by cheque, balance due on arrival
4 snorkelling possible at the local beaches, and many other beautiful beaches nearby
5 Ivana's husband Goran knows a lot about snorkelling, etc, unlike Ivana. They sound kind and hospitable.

Writing skills: cohesion (SB page 76)

Aim: to give students a chance to develop their writing through various different micro skills.

Tips:

- Clearly explain the focus and do an example together before asking them to continue on their own.
- Let students check their answers in pairs or small groups, then correct in open class.
- Ask students to make a note of any phrases they want to remember, or that they commonly get wrong.

1

a all these – local and nearby beaches
  such matters – snorkelling and water sports
b the former – Villa Gemma
  the period you mention – 19–26 July
  at that time – 19–26 July
  the accommodation – Villa Maria
e Further to our phone call – a phone call where the reservation was made (prior to this email)
  as discussed – a discussion they had earlier about the deposit arrangements (prior to this email)
f this apartment – Villa Maria

2

1 the latter
2 As promised; this
3 This
4 Further

Linking ideas: clarification and emphasis (SB page 77)

Aim: to highlight and focus on a particular aspect of language that students can use to improve their writing.

Tips:

- Sometimes this section serves as reinforcement of language that students have encountered passively before, for example in the reading texts. Make this link clear where possible.
- Let students check their answers in pairs or small groups, then correct in open class.
- For variety and efficiency, put some of the answers on the board for students to self-check, eg exercise 2.

1

a	not to mention	c	to be precise
b	namely; in other words	f	in particular; ideally

2 Incorrect alternatives

1	in particular	4	ie
2	in other words	5	precisely
3	or rather	6	ideally

Preparing to write (SB page 77)

Aim: to give students an opportunity to brainstorm ideas for the writing task.

Tips:

- Allow students to discuss ideas in pairs or small groups.
- Explain that ultimately they will write three or more emails, as part of the same transaction.
- Ask students to make notes at this stage, but not to begin writing the email.
- Refer students to the language in *A semi-formal email* and encourage them to integrate these into their forthcoming interaction.

Writing (SB page 77)

Aim: to give students practice in more extended writing tasks.

Tips:

- This section can either be done in class or students could email each other for real, for homework.
- Remind students to refer back to the model text and encourage them to experiment with some of the target language from this section.
- Ask students to check their work carefully before they hand it in.

TEACH GLOBAL THINK LOCAL **Homework extra**

In pairs, ask students to search the internet for details of a holiday rental property in a country of their choice. They should then write the imaginary email transaction between a 'holidaymaker' making queries and the 'owner of the property'. As potential holiday renters, they should stipulate two or three personal priorities, which are a reaction to previous negative experiences in similar rentals, eg cleanliness (last rental was filthy), noise, etc.

Study skills

Learning language in context (SB page 77)

1 Books closed. Write up this suggestion by a teacher trainer: *A good way to extend your knowledge of English at advanced level is …* Elicit some examples of how to finish the sentence. Then write up the remainder of the sentence: *… to study language as it occurs naturally in real (spoken or written) texts.* Ask students *How do you usually 'milk' a text, if at all, for useful vocabulary and phrases? How do you ensure that you understand and also remember this vocabulary?* Invite them to share their ideas with the class. Then students read the procedure and discuss it in pairs. Ask them *Are there any new strategies that you would like to try?*

2 Focus students' attention on the expressions in italics in exercise 1 and the two examples of vocabulary records. Ask them *How is this different from what you do? Do you usually store words as single items, or in a phrase/with a preposition or collocation? Do you usually give an example sentence?* It is this final point that is most significant here.

TEACH GLOBAL THINK LOCAL **Extra activity**

It might be useful for students to compare their current vocabulary records before they start exercise 3. If there is a good example of where a student has used clear example sentences, possibly showing collocations, show it to the class.

3 This exercise is particularly useful for those students who tend to be rather careless or superficial when recording new vocabulary items. See *Extra activity*. Students record at least three phrases in exercise 1 following the suggestions they consider best for them. If they don't have access to a collocations dictionary in class, they could do (part of) this task for homework. Encourage them to compare what they have written.

Possible answers

extend your knowledge: I try to extend my knowledge of prepositions by recording them in my vocabulary book.

on a regular basis: I go jogging on a regular basis.

the more often … the better: The more often I watch TV in English, the better my listening skills become.

UNIT 7 Hearts & Minds

Coursebook

Unit 7	Language	Texts	Communication skills
Part 1 SB page 78	Grammar Articles	Reading *The Beating Heart*	Pronunciation /ð/ and /θ/
Part 2 SB page 80	Extend your vocabulary Collocations with *heart* Grammar Unreal conditionals 1	Reading & Listening *Romeo and Juliet*: The balcony scene	Writing Advice
Part 3 SB page 82	Vocabulary *mind*	Reading *Mindfulness*	Speaking Concentration and daydreaming
Part 4 SB page 84	Speaking & Vocabulary Nature vs Nurture Reading & Grammar Gerund and infinitive	Listening & Pronunciation The developing brain /tʃ/ and /ʃ/ Reading & Grammar *Attachment theory*	Speaking & Vocabulary Nature vs Nurture
Function globally SB page 86	Dealing with difficult situations Listening to difficult requests and responses Roleplaying a difficult situation		
Global English SB page 87	Shakespeare: the best English teacher? Discussing experimenting with language		
Writing SB page 88	An argument Writing skills: structuring an argument Linking ideas: cause and consequence		
Study skills SB page 89	Improving your speaking skills		

Additional resources

eWorkbook	Interactive and printable grammar, vocabulary, listening and pronunciation practice Extra reading and writing practice Additional downloadable listening and video material
Teacher's Resource Disc	Communication activity worksheets to print and photocopy, review material, test, and video with worksheet
Go global Ideas for further research	**Hearts** There are a number of websites where students can find poetry linked to the heart by searching *poetry* + *heart*. Students find a poem that they like a lot (or dislike) and explain what it is that they like or don't like about it. **Minds** Websites such as www.self-guided.com/concentration-techniques.html and www.performanceprime.com offer a range of suggestions for how to improve your concentration. Students should compare several of these sites and explain the techniques they think would work well or not work.

Part 1

TEACH GLOBAL THINK LOCAL Lead-in

Read out the following sentences, slowly and steadily, pausing at the missing word each time. Inform students that the missing word is the same throughout. If they know what the answer is, they should write it down, not say it aloud. (Answer: *heart*.)

He spoke from his ______; He has a good ______; My ______ was in my mouth.; His ______ is in the right place.; His ______ wasn't in it.; She wears her ______ on her sleeve.; We had a ______ to ______; I learnt it by ______.

If necessary, repeat the expressions but give a little more context for each one, to make it simpler. Put up any of the expressions students like on the board, getting students to peer teach where possible.

Reading (SB page 78)

1 Give students two or three minutes to discuss these points.

1 heart located in the middle of the chest, between the lungs; pulse can be anywhere, but usually felt most strongly at the wrist
2 You can measure your heart rate by finding your pulse and counting. An easy way is to count the number of beats in 15 seconds and multiply by 4.

TEACH GLOBAL THINK LOCAL Extra activity

For fun, put students into groups and ask them to take each others' pulses. Find the person with the fastest / slowest rate!

2 In pairs, students discuss the two questions and predict the answers.

3 The reading describes similarities and differences in the hearts of three very different creatures.

Students read *The Beating Heart* and check if their predictions in exercise 2 were correct. Then ask them to complete the grid alone, before checking their answers in pairs. Ask an early finisher to write up the answers on the board for students to self-check.

2
1 according to the text the whale and the shrew have about the same
2 the shrew

3

	Whale	Shrew	Clam
weight	100,000 kg	2 g	–
heart rate	20	835–1511	2–20
lifespan (years)	100	1	–

4 Encourage students to match the words they know or can work out easily first. At the end, put up the more useful words on the board, eg *(my/his/her) prerogative* (n), *laid-back* (adj) and *lethargy* (n), *quota* (n), etc. Clarify their meaning and use, as necessary.

allowed number – *quota*	relaxed – *laid-back*
be careful – *mind*	right – *prerogative*
extreme laziness – *lethargy*	speed – *tempo*
one animal eating another – *predation*	wasteful – *profligate*

5 Invite one or two students to share their personal reactions to the text with the class. Ask *What did you find particularly interesting?* Then put students in pairs to discuss the two questions. Monitor while they are talking, picking up on any points which may be of interest to the whole class at the end.

1 Some animals use their heartbeats fast, eg animals at the lower end of the food chain have to live fast and furious to escape predators whereas animals at the higher end, we presume, are more laid-back and use the same number of heartbeats over a longer time.
2 Students' own answers.

TEACH GLOBAL THINK LOCAL Reading extra

If your students would benefit from a closer look at complex sentences, put this on the board:

There may have been some laid-back shrews out there once, but when you're that low in the food chain, living fast and furious is clearly the strategy of choice to ensure that you leave your mark, before succumbing to the pressures of predation.

Check students understand phrases like *strategy of choice, leave your mark* and *succumb to sth*. Highlight the first clause: *There* (or *she/they*, etc) + past modal … + (*once*), which usually precedes a *but* clause. (Comment on the fact that the modal, *may*, is stressed to show contrast.) Ask students to work in pairs to break this single sentence down into at least five smaller ones. Then hide the original sentence, and ask them to reconstruct it together.

TEACH GLOBAL THINK LOCAL Speaking extra

Ask students to play 'Fact Tennis' in pairs. Give them 20 seconds to reread the text, then to give one single fact each in turn about the text, without repetition, eg *Three animals were described: the whale, the shrew and the clam.* They should note how many facts they remember and go on as long as they can. The pair with the most facts wins.

Grammar (SB page 79)

This grammar focus is on articles. The amount of time you spend on this will depend on your learners' own difficulties with this area.

1 Students complete the task individually and quickly compare answers in pairs. This is unlikely to cause problems so keep feedback brisk.

Incorrect alternatives

1 singular
2 plural, uncountable
3 plural, uncountable

Language note

Articles are often used differently across languages. Because the indefinite and definite articles are invariably weak in terms of pronunciation, they are often not heard and this can contribute to (continued) inaccuracies in production. At advanced level, students should aim to be more conscious of article-use and their own usage.

The three rules about zero, indefinite and definite articles in Grammar exercise 1, **all** refer to generalisations, and this could be confusing for students. *The* is used in this way only when talking about something which is representative of its class, with singular countable nouns. This use therefore occurs with relative high frequency in scientific or technological genres, eg *the tiger, the computer, the heart.*

2 Draw students' attention at the start to the different alternatives: some use the (in)definite or zero article. Elicit why. If you think your students would relish discussing more controversial options, put up the following as additional alternatives on the board, if appropriate for your context: *Politicians or the police; men or women; crime and punishment; religion and science; a symptom or a cure* (in social/political terms).

In pairs, students write at least three sentences for their chosen topic(s), focusing on linguistic accuracy. Monitor as they work, giving attention primarily to article use. If necessary, collect the sentences in to look at more closely.

3 Give students time to hunt for examples in the text *The Beating Heart* on their own, then let them compare findings in pairs. Elicit some examples for each rule.

4 a tune; individuals; obsolescence
5 the notes; the tempo (of the previously mentioned tune)
6 the life (of an individual); the fact (that our bodies wear out at roughly the same rate); the automobiles (constructed for the mass market); the boom years (of the 1960s)
7 the animal kingdom; the mass market; the1960s
8 the same rate

G Grammar focus

Refer students to the language summary on articles on page 144.

You can use exercises 1 and 2 on page 145 for:
a) extra practice now, b) homework or c) review later on.

The answers are on page 163–4 of this Teacher's Book.

Pronunciation (SB page 79)

1 Students usually enjoy practising these two sounds. If they need the practice, put up the following noun-verb partners: *mouth – mouth, teeth – teethe, bath – bathe.* Drill the words and let students test each other in pairs, pointing at the words for each other to say.

tongue between teeth
/ð/ is voiced /θ/ is voiceless

2 **3.01** In pairs, ask students to practise the expressions. Then play the audio for them to check before eliciting the rules from students. Highlight the intrusive /j/ sound too, eg the /θi:ja:m/. Drill the words from the audio. Elicit other examples from students.

/ðə/: the heart / mouth / teeth / tongue (with following consonant sound)
/ði:/: the arm / eye (with following vowel sound)

3 After working individually, let students check their completed proverbs in pairs. Students discuss the three questions. Elicit some responses randomly, as a whole class. Ask *Are there any equivalent or similar proverbs in your language(s)?* It's often a nice idea to let them say it first in their own language too, for others to hear.

1 b 2 d 3 e 4 a 5 c

TEACH GLOBAL THINK LOCAL Vocabulary extra

Write up or dictate these commonly used English proverbs:

*Two **eyes** are better than one.*
*Beauty is in the **face** of the beholder.*
***Hair** is thicker than water.*
*Cold hands, warm **back**.*
*The best way to a man's heart is through his **ears**.*
*Walls have **mouths**.*
*Many **legs** make light work.*
*Don't cut off your **hand** to spite your face.*

Tell students that in each case the body part (in bold) is incorrect so they need to replace it with another. (Answers in order: *heads, eye, blood, heart, stomach, ears, hands, nose*) Ask students to discuss what they probably mean and then to put their hypotheses to you.

Part 2

TEACH GLOBAL THINK LOCAL Lead-in

Students work in pairs to think of well-known male-female couples in a successful or unsuccessful relationship. These can be real or fictional, dead or alive, historical or current, local or global. Elicit an example or two, eg *The Kennedys*. Students write a brief description of a couple, without saying their name, and read it out for others to guess.

Reading and Listening (SB page 80)

1 Books closed. Ask *Have you ever seen Shakespeare's* Romeo and Juliet*? What do you know about it?* In small groups, students briefly discuss these questions. Then ask them to read the text *Tragic Love* to confirm their ideas.

Background note

Romeo and Juliet is one of Shakespeare's best-known tragedies. It was written between 1591–1595. Although the original idea was not his own, Shakespeare's version succeeded in making Romeo and Juliet synonymous with the notion of doomed love. It has been made into films (the 1996 film starred Leonardo DiCaprio) and operas and adapted for TV. It has also been made into ballet and musicals, the best known of which are, respectively, Prokofiev's *Romeo and Juliet* and Bernstein's *West Side Story*.

2 Let students discuss the answers in pairs. Skip feedback on this exercise, unless there are any queries.

1 the sun, the moon and an angel
2 she questions why he has to have that (family) name and wishes he would change it; if not she will change hers if he swears love for her
3 because a rose would still smell sweet if it was called something else
4 they are from warring families (the Montagues and the Capulets)

3 **3.02** Explain to students that they will now hear part of the original Shakespearean version. Focus their attention on the *Glossary* and then have them follow the text as they listen. Students discuss the three questions. Silently write up some extra questions, for early finishers, eg *Are there famous writers from your own country who have had a similar impact? Have they been translated or modernised? What do you think about historic plays being adapted to suit a modern performance, eg the language used, the setting, the costumes? Do you personally know of any marriages between two individuals which made their relatives very unhappy or angry?*

TEACH GLOBAL THINK LOCAL Reading extra

If your students would be interested in reading the complete balcony scene as represented in the graphic novel, rather than just the extract, you may wish to supply the following extended text, which is also available from websites:

ROMEO:

But, soft! what light through yonder window breaks?
It is the east, and Juliet is the sun.
Arise, fair sun, and kill the envious moon,
Who is already sick and pale with grief,
That thou her maid art far more fair than she:
Be not her maid, since she is envious;
Her vestal livery is but sick and green
And none but fools do wear it; cast it off.
It is my lady, O, it is my love!
O, that she knew she were!
She speaks yet she says nothing: what of that?
Her eye discourses; I will answer it.
I am too bold, 'tis not to me she speaks:
Two of the fairest stars in all the heaven,
Having some business, do entreat her eyes
To twinkle in their spheres till they return.
What if her eyes were there, they in her head?
The brightness of her cheek would shame those stars,
As daylight doth a lamp; her eyes in heaven
Would through the airy region stream so bright
That birds would sing and think it were not night.
See, how she leans her cheek upon her hand!
O, that I were a glove upon that hand,
That I might touch that cheek!

JULIET:

Ay me!

ROMEO:

She speaks:
O, speak again, bright angel! for thou art
As glorious to this night, being o'er my head
As is a winged messenger of heaven
Unto the white-upturned wondering eyes
Of mortals that fall back to gaze on him
When he bestrides the lazy-pacing clouds
And sails upon the bosom of the air.

JULIET:

O Romeo, Romeo! wherefore art thou Romeo?
Deny thy father and refuse thy name;
Or, if thou wilt not, be but sworn my love,
And I'll no longer be a Capulet.

ROMEO:

[Aside] Shall I hear more, or shall I speak at this?

JULIET:

'Tis but thy name that is my enemy;
Thou art thyself, though not a Montague.
What's Montague? it is nor hand, nor foot,
Nor arm, nor face, nor any other part
Belonging to a man. O, be some other name!
What's in a name? that which we call a rose
By any other name would smell as sweet;

So Romeo would, were he not Romeo call'd,
Retain that dear perfection which he owes
Without that title. Romeo, doff thy name,
And for that name which is no part of thee
Take all myself.

Extend your vocabulary (SB page 81)

1 Write ______*-hearted* on the board and elicit a possible collocation. Then students find the odd one out.

Incorrect alternative
up

2 In pairs, students categorise the compound adjectives, consulting a dictionary if necessary.

character: cold-hearted; hard-hearted; kind-hearted; warm-hearted

sadness: broken-hearted; down-hearted

enthusiasm: whole-hearted

lack of enthusiasm: half-hearted

lack of seriousness: light-hearted

3 Give an example yourself first, eg *I spoke to my boss the other day and for some reason he was in a very light-hearted mood, laughing and joking. I found out later he was just about to go on holiday!* Give students two minutes to choose three compound adjectives and, if necessary, write down their sentences first. Then, in groups of three, students share their experiences.

Grammar (SB page 81)

1 Students read the examples. After a moment's reflection they discuss the two questions. Check answers in a whole-class feedback session.

1 imaginary
2 all four sentences about a rose mean the same; difference is in formality

were is more formal than *was*

if it were to be / were it to be – are more tentative, and also more formal

might: it's an uncertain result if the *if* clause is fulfilled

would: it's a certain result if the *if* clause is fulfilled

could: it's a possibility if the *if* clause is fulfilled

Language note

Although students will be familiar with the hypothetical conditional, the *were to* + verb form may be new. This is used to sound more tentative and therefore more polite, eg *If I were / was (by some chance) to marry him, how would you feel?*

At this point, you could also highlight the phrase *If it weren't / wasn't for* + noun phrase, which is similar, eg *If it weren't for the distance, I'd go there right now. If it weren't for the feud between the two families, there wouldn't be a problem.* The word *weren't* is generally stressed here when spoken.

2 Give students a few moments to complete the four sentences. Remind them that they can use other modals besides *would*, eg *might*, *could*. Monitor as they are working. For early finishers, give these extra sentence starters on the board: *If I was Juliet's mother, …*; *If I was Juliet's best friend, …*; *If I was Romeo's father, …* Let students compare ideas with at least one other person. If students are engaged in the topic and task, invite them to share some of their examples with the whole class. Finally, ask students how things would be different if this happened nowadays, rather than in the 16th century. This serves as a link with the next stage.

G Grammar focus

Refer students to the language summary on unreal conditionals on page 144.

You can use exercises 3 and 4 on page 145 for:
a) extra practice now, b) homework or c) review later on.

The answers are on page 164 of this Teacher's Book.

Writing (SB page 81)

1 Let students read the situations. Ask them if they know similar situations in real life – this can be discussed in pairs or as a whole class, depending on your students. If you wish, give them a useful letter starter, putting it on the board: *Dear XX, Your mother has told me what happened. I know that it must be very difficult for you at this time …* Before they start, highlight the sentences in *Useful phrases* and encourage students to integrate them in their writing. Give students 8–12 minutes to write one of the letters, indicating how much time they have and the length you expect at the start.

2 In groups of three, students read each of their letters aloud and select the most sensible and well-phrased advice. Invite some groups to share their nicest examples.

TEACH GLOBAL THINK LOCAL Homework extra

Ask students to choose one of the other situations and write the letter of advice to the niece/nephew as well as the reply from the niece/nephew. Ask them to include at least three conditional sentences in total.

Part 3

TEACH GLOBAL THINK LOCAL Lead-in

To lead into the topic of mindfulness, ask *What activities have you done in the last 48 hours which have demanded high concentration?* (*High concentration* here means where you are totally focused and unaware of passing time, and you might be startled if someone interrupts you.) Give a personal example before students discuss this in groups of three. Then ask students *Was there a time in the last 48 hours when you consciously tried to do the opposite – to empty your mind?*

If appropriate, ask students to sit in silence for 90 seconds and to try and empty their minds (ideally with eyes closed, or looking down). Then ask how easy or difficult they found it; whether they liked it or not; what the purpose might be, etc.

Speaking (SB page 82)

1 Let students reflect for two minutes on their own about these different activities before discussing this in groups of three and then with the whole class. Write up three activities that a majority of students feel demand high concentration.

2 Elicit some additional examples, adding the most interesting ones to the board.

3 Students work on their own to complete the sentences, before comparing them in pairs. While they are writing, write up on the board these commonly used phrases associated with the topic: *my mind starts wandering / wanders; stay focused (v); get distracted (v); daydream (v).*

Reading (SB page 82)

This reading comprises three factual descriptions of *mindfulness*.

1 Write up *mindfulness* on the board and ask students if they think they know what this is. Then they select the best definition. Do not confirm the answer at this point.

Background note

The term *mindfulness* has, rather confusingly, multiple shades of meaning.

Mindfulness is a key concept in Buddhism, where it relates to a calm awareness of self in the world and in the present moment: this is achieved by becoming conscious of physical – and usually unconscious – actions, such as breathing, entering a room, and so on. It involves giving non-judgemental and deliberate attention to things around you in the world. In aspiring to this, one can overcome delusions and anxieties about the self, reaching a state of awareness and wisdom.

In Western psychology, this approach is used to help cater for a variety of problems such as eating disorders, anxiety and depression, often integrated with cognitive therapy.

2 Students read *Mindfulness* to check their idea from exercise 1.

sentence 2

3 Draw two columns on the board with the headings: *Mindfulness* and *Opposite of mindfulness*. Do the first example together, then ask students to complete the task and to check their answers in pairs. Ask early finishers to fill in the table on the board, to provide a clear record.

mindfulness: alert, aware, non-judgementally, the present moment

opposite of mindfulness: brooding, critical thinking, monkey mind, tunnel vision

4 Ask students to work independently initially. Let them check their answers with a dictionary, but only at the end, so as to encourage them to make logical guesses.

1 sleep
2 trying to catch
3 stop it before it grows too large
4 stop
5 difficult to achieve
6 temporary existence

5 If your students seem very confident with the text, ask them to discuss the questions in pairs without referring back to the text at this point. Let them consult the text to check their idea at the end.

1 becoming aware of background noise that has been there for some time; waking up just before the alarm goes off
2 they are intensively focused on the present moment
3 we don't notice it; we are unable to assess the whole situation; we start treating our emotions as a problem to be solved; we think too much
4 we become aware of our moods; it teaches us to shift mental gears, focus on the present
5 to practise and have a good teacher
6 their mind wanders; need to accept thoughts, allow them to form and then disappear

6 Given the nature of the topic, it would be useful to provide a few moments in silence for students to consider these points before discussion. Monitor as they are talking, and later draw on any interesting points in a whole-class feedback session.

Vocabulary (SB page 83)

1 At the start, brainstorm any phrases with the word *mind* that students can think of. Give students a few seconds to think here, as they are sure to know some at this level; provide hints if necessary, eg *What do you say when …?* Students then complete the matching task.

1 c	2 b	3 f	4 g	5 e	6 a	7 d

2 In pairs, ask students to choose at least two of the exchanges from exercise 1 and to write a short dialogue. Encourage them to be interesting or amusing. As an example before they start, elicit suggestions to continue from 2b, writing the short dialogue on the board. Monitor as they are writing their exchanges. If possible, at the end, invite each pair to share one of their dialogues with the whole class.

Then ask students to underline the key phrases with *mind* from the exercise; volunteers should write the information on the board as a generalised vocabulary record, eg for sentence a: *crossed my mind* → *cross sb's mind* (in other words, they take the teacher's role).

3 Do the first example together, eliciting different alternatives of what might come **before** sentence 1, eg *I can't do this homework. I just don't feel like it and it's pointless and boring.* Check students understand sentences 3 and 5. In pairs, students choose two of the sentences and complete the exercise. Monitor to ensure that they have understood both the task and the target phrases. Elicit an example before you put them into groups of four to guess each others' sentences.

Possible answers

1 I know you don't feel very confident, but it's really not hard.
2 We both decided to buy the same present.
3 Why did I buy that pair of shoes?
4 I know I said I'd marry you.
5 There's no point in crying.
6 What shall we do this evening?
7 Careful!
8 I wish he wouldn't ask personal questions.

TEACH GLOBAL THINK LOCAL

Extra activity

After exercises 2 and 3, students could work in pairs to locate (some of) the phrases in an advanced learners' dictionary, both to practise their dictionary skills (locating idiomatic phrases in an entry) and to consolidate the new lexis.

Part 4

TEACH GLOBAL THINK LOCAL

Lead-in

Bring in some photos of yourself and your family. Show them to your students, telling them which family members you are like and which you are not like, both in terms of appearance and personality. As you speak, try to naturally integrate some of the phrases from exercise 1.

Speaking and Vocabulary (SB page 84)

1 Write up *nature* and *nurture* on the board. Elicit the difference. Refer students to the summary of the debate in exercise 1. Do the first example together and then let students complete the exercise in pairs. Clarify any new phrases in whole-class feedback, by asking students to rephrase or give examples as appropriate, eg *to be the spitting image of sb; X runs in the family; put sth down to X; to have an innate ability to do sth.* Put these phrases on the board.

1 nature	3 nature	5 nurture
2 nurture	4 nature	6 nature

2 Ask students to reflect for a moment, then discuss the questions in pairs. Remind them to try and use some of the new phrases where possible.

3 First of all, students read the three statements and decide if they agree or disagree. Then, in pairs, they choose one of the topics that interest them. You could also give additional ones that might motivate your particular group, eg *If you are born into a criminal family, you are going to be a criminal; If your parents are ill-educated, you are unlikely to be well-educated yourself,* etc.

Refer students to the *Useful phrases* and encourage them to use some of them in their discussion. Partners should adopt different stances and discuss the topic. Monitor and assist as needed.

4 Now put students into groups of four and encourage them to discuss their real views. Monitor again and pick up on any relevant lexical or topic-related issues to include in a whole-class feedback session at the end.

Listening and Pronunciation (SB page 84)

TEACH GLOBAL THINK LOCAL

Pre-listening activity

Ask students cheekily *How brainy are you?* Then fire questions about the brain at the whole class, eg *How big is an adult human brain?* (140 mm wide and 170 mm long) *How much does it weigh?* (1–1.5 kg) *What colour is it?* (grey / pink) *Can you survive if part of it is damaged?* (Yes) *Which part of the brain deals with language?* (generally the left).

Hearts & Minds

1 Students answer the questions in pairs. After a few moments, invite them to share their ideas with the class.

2 **3.03** This listening is an interview with a child development expert. She discusses the role of emotions, relationships and stress in a baby's development.

First ask students to read the six topic areas and, in pairs, discuss what they already know about these topics. Then play the audio while students listen and make notes; let them listen again, if they feel they need to. After students compare notes in pairs, conduct a whole-class feedback session on (some of) the topics, if necessary.

1 it doesn't develop automatically, but in response to other people
2 baby's brain is developing at its most rapid rate and emotion systems are being set up
3 stress response, soothing response, pre-frontal area which has a big impact on our emotions
4 it releases Cortisol to allow the stressful challenge to be met
5 Cortisol is toxic to other parts of the body, in particular the pre-frontal cortex and can hamper development of the pre-frontal cortex in babies
6 soothe the baby so that any stressful event is dealt with and the potentially damaging Cortisol is dispersed; focus on non-verbal communication such as holding the baby, tone of voice, eye contact, and especially help them put feelings into words

3.03

A = Interviewer; **B** = Sue Gerhardt

A: So can you say something about how a baby's brain develops?

B: Yes, I think the most amazing thing to remember is that the brain is actually a social organ so it doesn't develop automatically; it actually develops in response to other people, especially in the first couple of years when the baby's brain is actually developing at the most rapid rate that it will ever develop. And in particular what's happening in the first couple of years is that the emotion systems are getting set up. And what I call emotion systems are in particular the stress response, what I would call the soothing response, and the pre-frontal area of the brain, which is the first bit of the higher brain to develop and really has a big impact on our emotions.

A: Can you say a bit more about the stress response and the soothing response?

B: There's a whole system which we call the stress response which is about triggering off a response to stress that kind of energises and focuses an individual to deal with a problem, or a threat, or a challenge of some kind. This stress response works by releasing Cortisol so that a challenge can be met. And then in infancy you actually need parents to do the soothing and to put things right so that the whole thing can come to a kind of conclusion and the Cortisol can be dispersed, it is not needed anymore. Unfortunately, one of the things that's emerged from all this scientific research of recent years is that if a young child has too much stress and therefore too much Cortisol, this Cortisol has a very toxic effect on all sorts of other systems. It also has a very toxic effect on the pre-frontal cortex and so it actually hampers growth of the pathways there.

A: So what should parents do to regulate their baby's stress or emotions?

B: In very early infancy it's really got a lot to do with very basic non-verbal things like the way a parent holds the baby, it's a lot to do with touch, tone of voice, eye contact, the sort of musicality of turn-taking between the adult and the child. As the baby gets bigger it sort of widens out into helping the baby do more and more for himself, or herself, and then helping the baby to regulate himself more and more. And one of the main tools there is also, it's about putting feelings into words, and that's a really important tool to help your baby to manage feelings.

3 **3.04** Students read the task and listen to the second part of the interview. Check answers with the whole class.

We all have a genetic predisposition to certain types of behaviour, and how this is realised depends on our experiences; our genetic make-up will determine how we respond to particular genetic trigger. Her own children are completely different.

3.04

A: Do you think a baby's temperament is due mainly to nature or to nurture?

B: We have all sorts of genetic predispositions which may or may not get realised in actual life, depending on what happens to the person. Genes don't, don't determine our lives in any automatic sense. They are there as a kind of store that we draw on as we have to deal with all sorts of different environments and circumstances which trigger off a genetic expression of a particular gene.

I mean, I'm certainly aware that every baby is different. My own two children are completely different. One was very cheerful and bouncy and the other was very sensitive and cautious. So yes, we definitely come with a temperament, but it's, you know, what the people around us trigger off, what the circumstances of our lives trigger off, that really matters.

4 **3.05** In pairs, students discuss the question and then listen to the short, final extract to check that they were right. If your students are knowledgeable about parenting, ask them their own opinions on the subject.

focus on making the baby feel safe; give the baby attention, respond to its needs and be aware that the baby can't manage its own emotions

3.05

A: What advice would you give to parents on how to bring up babies, the best way to shape their brain?

B: Attachment theory has really stressed how important it is for development that babies feel safe. The crucial thing is really to give your baby attention and to really notice, to really respond, and to realise that the baby can't manage his or her own feelings or emotions, or meet his or her own needs. It's up to the parents to do this for them in the early stages of life and that will help them.

5 **3.06–3.07** Play the recording of track 3.06, asking students to focus on the two sounds. For question 1, ask them briefly to explain how each sound is made, then move quickly on to question 2, where the challenge is higher. In pairs, students say the words to each other as they work. Then they listen to track 3.07 and check.

Give students thinking time to reflect on how these words were used in the interview. Encourage them to discuss the interview, using some of the words from the pronunciation practice.

2 /tʃ/: atta<u>ch</u>ment; <u>ch</u>ildren; cul<u>ture</u>; na<u>ture</u>; nur<u>ture</u>
/ʃ/: atten<u>tion</u>; condi<u>tion</u>ed; cru<u>ci</u>al; emo<u>tion</u>; predisposi<u>tion</u>; rela<u>tion</u><u>sh</u>ip; so<u>ci</u>al

TEACH GLOBAL THINK LOCAL

Mixed ability

Your students may not have problems with the sounds /tʃ/ and /ʃ/. In this case, you could jump immediately to point 3 in exercise 5.

Reading and Grammar (SB page 85)

1 Students discuss, in pairs, what these things (1–9) might mean in terms of a baby's needs. Then ask students to read *Attachment theory* to check their predictions. Check answers as a class, referring back to the text as appropriate. Elicit students' personal responses to the text by asking *Is there anything you find surprising? Do you agree?*

1 a secure base: to develop emotionally, to help deal with distress
3 relationship: to learn to regulate own emotions
4 exploration: to attain independence
6 comforting: to set up internal working models (via emotional regulation)
7 an experience of loss: to be able to deal with later losses
9 secure attachment: to form healthy relationships in later life

2 Write up three columns on the board, with the headings: *to + infinitive, gerund* and *infinitive*. Ask students to search the text *Attachment theory* for examples of these patterns not only with verbs, but also with adjectives. Leave the mini focus on nouns until the end, to avoid overload. Give these examples and ask students where they go in the table: *a child* ***needs to learn*** (v + *to* + infinitive) and *such positive experiences* ***lead to the setting up*** … (v + gerund). See *Language note*. Let students work in pairs. Elicit answers to the board; clearly distinguishing word class within the columns, eg use different colours for adjective and verb phrases. At the end, write up *capacity (n)* and *ability (n)*. Students should locate these words in the text, and the pattern that follows them (n + *to* + infinitive).

1 needs to be (securely attached); ability to regulate; needs to learn; allows (him) to move; needs to be (protected); continue to operate; be able to manage; capacity to form; going on to develop; possible to compensate
2 essential to healthy functioning; dependent on (his) having; lead to (the) setting up; a result of having
3 help (him) deal with; develop (positive) relationships

Language note

When clarifying the patterns, maintain a clear distinction between *to* as part of the infinitive, and *to* as a preposition followed by a noun / gerund. In the following two examples *to* is a preposition (the noun phrases are underlined): *Relationships are as essential to <u>healthy functioning</u> as …* (adj + prep + noun); *Such positive experiences lead to <u>the setting up</u> of …* (verb + prep + noun).

3 Tell students they are going to do a second grammar search. You could manage this as a race in pairs to be first to find the answers. Do the first example together. Elicit answers at the end, clarifying any problems as necessary.

1 Learning to cope with loss is …
2 essential to healthy functioning; dependent on his having; lead to the setting up; without being overwhelmed; a result of having had; by going on
3 having had at least one secure attachment
4 being overwhelmed by anxiety
5 to be (securely) attached; to be protected
6 his having an attentive care-giver
7 the setting up of 'internal working models'
8 in order to develop emotionally; so as to attain independence

4 This exercise reminds students of other common patterns. Ask students to read the letter in 60 seconds to find out what Amelia has done wrong in the teacher's eyes. Elicit ideas as a class. Then ask students to work alone on the selection task and to compare their answers in pairs before whole-class feedback.

Incorrect alternatives
1 me to write
2 telling; tell
3 her miss
4 to not complete (*to not have completed* is a 'split infinitive' which is considered poor style but generally acceptable, especially in informal spoken English)
5 miss
6 explain
7 be told; having told
8 Not to
9 for catching up; for catch up
10 complete; having completed

5 Do the first verb together, reminding them that they may sometimes have to add additional words, eg *She advised me to work harder* (direct object). Explain that they may have to experiment with the verb patterns by putting them mentally in a made-up sentence. Let students use a dictionary to check their answers; if necessary, demonstrate how to use this resource effectively, using projected examples from an online dictionary, if possible. Encourage students to make a record of example sentences of those verbs and patterns which they are unfamiliar with. Discuss the trickier verbs in a whole-class feedback session.

When students are ready, ask them to work independently or in pairs to create a reply as if they were Amelia's mother or father. First of all, elicit how the parent might feel; what they are likely to say. Ask students to use at least two of the verbs from the box. Allocate a time for the writing task, eg 10–15 minutes, but monitor to see if students need longer. On completion, let them read one or two other letters by their peers. Take in the letters to mark.

1 gerund: appreciate; avoid; enjoy; prefer; suggest
infinitive: get used; let; make; would rather
either: advise; encourage

6 This exercise both extends students' knowledge of patterns after certain nouns and gives them the opportunity for oral fluency practice. First elicit what comes after *have difficulty* (gerund); *no point* (*in* + gerund); *no opportunity* (*to* + infinitive); *no intention* (*of* + gerund). Write the patterns up on the board. Students complete the sentence starters individually. Model the speaking task first, inviting a confident student to say what he/she had difficulty with, and you responding with one or two questions. Then monitor as students are talking.

TEACH GLOBAL THINK LOCAL

Extra practice

Your advanced students might benefit from further practice of the structure *the* + gerund / noun + *of* + noun, to make sophisticated, formal-sounding noun phrases (see *Reading and Grammar* exercise 3 rule 7). Look at the example again from the text: *the setting up of 'internal working models'*. Dictate the sentences below and ask students to transform them, using a noun / gerund to begin their new sentences. Do the first example together and, if necessary, give the first two words of each new sentence to help. Warn them that other parts of the sentence may need to be changed. Likely answers are included in brackets.

- *It's essential to establish clear rule boundaries to younger children. (The establishment of clear …)*
- *It is very important to make close friendships from a young age. (The making / The development of close relationships is very important …)*
- *Children need to be stimulated from birth to aid healthy brain development. (The stimulation of children is important from birth to aid …)*
- *As a parent you should foster good eating habits in a young child. (The fostering of good eating habits …)*
- *Most experts agree that it is crucial to give positive feedback to a child. (The giving of positive feedback …)*
- *Parents interact with their child from birth, long before speech emerges. This is essential for development. (The interaction of parents with their child …)*

Elicit possible answers, then you can have students discuss the opinions expressed by each of the sentences and whether they agree. Finally, elicit suitable genres for the use of this structure, eg *essay-writing, presentation-giving.*

G Grammar focus

Refer students to the language summary on gerund and infinitive on page 144.

You can use exercises 5 and 6 on page 145 for:
a) extra practice now, b) homework or c) review later on.

The answers are on pages 164 of this Teacher's Book.

Function globally: dealing with difficult situations

These lessons in *Global* are designed to provide students with immediately useful functional language. They all follow a similar format.

Warm up (SB page 86)

Aim: to introduce the topic via a quick speaking task or picture work.

Tips:

- Do not over-correct here, especially in speaking activities.
- Encourage students to use as much variety of language as they can at this stage.
- Invite students to share one or two nice roleplays with the whole class, if you think students will find it enjoyable / useful.
- Monitor and pick up on any personal examples of similar situations. If they are interesting, share the ideas with the whole class.

Listening (SB page 86)

Aim: to present the functional language in context via a conversation or series of conversations.

Tips:

- Let students read the task first.
- Play the recordings all the way through for the first task (there are always two tasks). For the second task, watch students writing – you may need to pause the recording occasionally. (Tracks 3.08–3.11)
- For multiple conversations pause the recording after each one.
- Encourage students to read and/or analyse the audioscripts for homework, especially if they are not living or working in an English-speaking environment.

1

Conversation 1

1 friends

2 one friend asks the other (Sarah) for a lift to a hospital appointment

3 Sarah can't do it because her car is being serviced.

Conversation 2

1 receptionist and patient / client (we learn in conversation 3 that Emily is a patient)

2 Emily wants to change the time of an appointment

3 success: the appointment is changed from 3.30 to 4pm

Conversation 3

1 same two friends as conversation 1

2 prescription wasn't ready so Emily asks Sarah to collect it tomorrow morning

3 success: Sarah agrees to collect it and it's not a problem for the hospital

Conversation 4

1 same friends as conversation 1

2 Sarah forgot to collect the prescription

3 she will collect it later the same day

2

1 I was wondering if you could …; Would it be possible to …; I don't suppose you could possibly …; Would that be possible?; Do you think it would be all right if … (in this situation she's asking permission)

2 I would if I could, but …

3 Yeah; that's not going to be a problem; no worries at all; I'm sure that'll be fine.

4 Sorry; I'm afraid …; I'm so sorry.

3.08–3.11

A = Emily; **B** = Sarah; **C** = Receptionist

1

A: Sarah, I was wondering if you could do me a favour?

B: Yeah.

A: The thing is you see I've got an appointment at the hospital this afternoon and I was wondering, is there any way you could give me a lift?

B: I would if I could, but I'm going to struggle this afternoon. The car is in for a service and I'm not entirely sure I'd be able to get back in time. Sorry.

A: Oh, OK, well, I just thought I'd ask.

2

C: Good afternoon, St Michael's, Julie speaking, how can I help?

A: Oh hello there. Um … I'm afraid there's a slight problem. I've got an appointment this afternoon at 3.30. Would it be possible to change the appointment?

C: What's your name, please?

A: My name's Emily Watkins.

C: OK. Ah yes, I see. Um … hmm … actually, let me just check something a minute.

A: OK, thank you.

C: Do you know, it's your lucky day. We've had a cancellation so that's not going to be a problem today.

A: Great.

C: So we will see you now at four o'clock.

A: OK, yes, I think that should be all right.

C: Will that be enough time?

A: Mmm … let's go for four o'clock, yes.

C: OK.

A: Thanks very much

C: We'll see you then.

A: OK, bye.

C: Bye bye.

3

A: Sarah, yes it all went fine actually. They saw me at four o'clock instead …

B: Great.

A: … and the only thing is … um … I don't suppose you could possibly pick up the prescription for me, it wasn't ready there and then, but they said it would be ready tomorrow morning. Would that be possible?

B: Um … yeah, no worries at all. And they're happy about me picking it up?

A: Yeah, yeah. I said that you might be able to do that so that was fine for them.

B: OK great.

A: Great, thank you.

4

B: I've got an apology to make. I'm so sorry. You know I said I'd pick up the prescription?

A: Yes.

B: I didn't. I completely forgot. I'm so sorry.

A: Oh no.

B: I … do you think it would be all right if I picked it up later this afternoon?

A: Yes, I'm sure that'll be fine. I'll give … I'll give the hospital a call.

B: Yeah, do that and I'll pick it up this afternoon. I'm so sorry.

A: That's OK.

Language focus (SB page 86)

Aim: to draw students' attention to the items of functional language.

Tips:

- Let students work alone at first, before comparing answers in pairs. Conduct a whole-class feedback session to discuss any areas of ambiguity.
- Give students time to make a note of any new phrases they would like to remember.
- You could let students continue some improvised dialogues, starting with the conversation openers in exercise 1.

1

1 apology	4 slight	7 about; thing
2 know	5 ask	8 make
3 trouble	6 do	9 word

2 Suggested answers

1 Would it be possible to change the appointment?

2 I was wondering if I could have a second opinion.

3 I don't suppose you could give me a lift to the hospital?

4 Is there any way you could pick up my prescription?

5 Would you mind if I used your phone?

6 Is it all right if I park outside?

Pronunciation (SB page 86)

Aim: to focus students on a particular aspect of pronunciation of the target phrases.

Tips:

- Do an example together as a model for exercise 1.
- Play the recording two or three times, if necessary, for exercise 2. (Track 3.12)
- Students should be able to pronounce these phrases intelligibly, so drill them, if necessary.
- At this level, try to promote good all-round pronunciation including stress, intonation and linking. This also raises the challenge for students.
- Use students with exemplary pronunciation to act as models to help others in the class.

1

a 1, 2, 5, 6, 8, 11, 12 b 7, 9 c 3, 4, 10

2

They are similar for similar ideas being expressed in the answer:

- being positive and friendly (1, 3, 4, 9, 10)
- expressing doubt (2, 5, 6, 11)
- being abrupt, not considering the speaker's feelings (8, 12)
- expressing surprise or alarm (7)

Speaking (SB page 86)

Aim: to allow students an opportunity to use this language in a meaningful, real-world context.

Tips:

- Give students time to prepare before they start talking. Let them first spend two or three minutes in silence looking back at the two *Language focus* exercises, and perhaps highlighting those phrases they would like to use.
- Circulate and monitor carefully whilst they are talking.
- Correct sensitively, paying attention to the target language especially. You may find that it's more efficient and appropriate to correct on the spot, particularly with pronunciation.
- If time allows, ask students to repeat the task, but with a new partner.
- Invite one or two pairs to share their roleplay with the whole class at the end, to round off the activity.

Global English

These lessons in *Global* have two main goals. The first is to give you and your students interesting information about English and language in general. The second goal is to provide students with practice in different kinds of reading comprehension tasks that they are likely to encounter in future study, for example, in exams.

TEACH GLOBAL THINK LOCAL **Lead-in**

Put the first question from the text on the board: *What does Shakespeare offer the English language learner?* Students work in pairs to try and think of at least two answers. Elicit some examples, including any humorous ones.

Warm up (SB page 87)

Aim: to engage students with the topic, and highlight potentially difficult vocabulary in the text.

Tips:

- First of all try and elicit any lines that students happen to know by Shakespeare.
- Let students work first in pairs, before you check the answers with the class.
- Ask pairs to 'translate' quotes 2, 5 and 6 into everyday English.

1 b 2 d 3 c 4 f 5 a 6 e

Reading (SB page 87)

Aim: to provide students with interesting information about English, and practice of reading exam skills.

Tips:

- There are two tasks. The first focuses on the gist of the passage. The second is a more difficult task, similar to that of a reading exam.
- The texts are dense, so let students compare answers after each stage, particularly if they are not too confident.
- This language is not tested or reviewed in future units, which means you have more flexibility with this material as to when and where you use it.

1

Correct order: b, a, d, c, e

2

1 T

2 F (*Some he coined himself; others he simply helped to popularise.*)

3 T

4 F (he used both: *his characters nose things as well as smell them; they ear things as well as hear them*)

5 T

6 F (*It is a sign of real fluency when learners can take a rule and adapt it to suit their purposes.*)

Speaking (SB page 87)

Aim: for students to relate the material in the reading to their own language, culture and experiences.

Tips:

- First ask students to look at the text to find examples of words which Shakespeare experimented with. If necessary, give examples for them to do the same with in their pairs, eg make verbs from nouns: *breakfast, vase, pencil, bus, foot*; make opposites: *clever, strict; no homework, no knife and fork, no dog*. They should discuss possibilities, then write some example sentences.
- Encourage students to think of their own words and to be inventive.
- Conduct a whole-class feedback session on any points of interest.

As you go through these *Global English* lessons in the book, don't be afraid to ask students' opinions and reactions to the information in the text. *Which do you find interesting? Do you know of similar experiences or facts in your language or other languages?* Some of your learners might be in your class because they are very interested in language, and these texts provide a great opportunity for you to capitalise on that motivation.

Writing: an argument

These lessons in *Global* are designed to provide students with extended writing practice. They all follow a similar format.

Reading (SB page 88)

Aim: to provide a sample text for students to analyse.

TEACH GLOBAL THINK LOCAL Pre-reading activity

Ask students to devise questions to ask someone in order to find out how fit and healthy they are, eg *How many portions of fruit and vegetables do you eat each day? Do you generally take the stairs or the lift?*, etc. Put students into pairs and give them eight minutes to think up at least seven good questions. Elicit some examples at the end, putting good ones up on the board. Then let students work with different partners to find out how fit and healthy their classmates are, asking and answering their questions.

Tips:

- If the *Pre-reading activity* wasn't used: before students open their books, ask them, in pairs, to discuss how fit and healthy they are.
- Encourage students to comment on the content and quality of the writing by asking *Is it clear? Is it well-written?*
- After doing exercise 2, raise any interesting points in a general discussion.
- Write up any useful words and phrases that come up onto the board.

1

Alex's ideas:

practising sport; following regular fitness routine / regular physical activity; special diet; preventive medicine; vitamins / nutritional supplements; regular routine; balanced lifestyle

2

Students' own ideas.

TEACH GLOBAL THINK LOCAL Reading extra

To encourage students to reread the text more closely, ask them to underline the topic sentence in each paragraph. Then, working in pairs, they should explain the function of the other sentences in the paragraph in relation to each topic sentence, eg to elaborate, to exemplify, to explain, etc. This acts as consolidation of *Writing* Unit 5 (SB page 64).

Writing skills: structuring an argument (SB page 88)

Aim: to give students a chance to develop their writing through various different micro skills.

Tips:

- Let students complete exercise 1 independently at first.
- In exercise 2, clearly explain the focus and do an example together first before asking students to continue on their own.
- Let students compare their answers in pairs or small groups, before checking them in open class.
- Draw out some comparisons with students' first language(s), eg which conventions are similar or not in the same genre. This helps raise awareness.

1 A

2 Suggested answers

introduction: 2; 4

conclusion: 5; 6

either: 1; 3

Linking ideas: cause and consequence (SB page 88)

Aim: to highlight and focus on a particular aspect of language that students can use to improve their writing.

Tips:

- Do the first example together, then let students work through the others in pairs.
- For exercise 1, invite students to share some suggestions with the whole class, **before** they check their answers in the text.
- Point out that these expressions and their prepositions are potentially useful for the essay genre.
- Ask students which of these cause and consequence expressions they already use in their writing. Encourage students to take a note of any words and prepositions which they sometimes avoid or misuse.
- When you are going through the answers, be careful to home in on problems, eg where students are muddling phrases which are similar. See *Language note*.

1

1 to	5 in	9 of
2 of	6 to	10 towards
3 to	7 to	
4 in	8 in	

Cause: 6; 7; 9

Consequence: 1; 2; 3; 4; 5; 8; 10

2

1 e	3 c / f	5 d
2 a	4 f	6 b / c

Language note

Students may need to be sensitised to the word class of the lexical items in *Linking Ideas* exercise 2, SB page 89 and their function in the sentence. For example, this example is incorrect in form, even though the meaning itself is appropriate: ~~*Because of a healthy diet is vital to health,*~~ *children should be educated … Because of* needs to be followed by a noun / noun phrase; a conjunction such as *given that* is needed in this sentence.

Preparing to write (SB page 89)

Aim: to give students an opportunity to gather ideas for the writing task.

Tips:

- Monitor as students are talking, to guide and assist with the planning as necessary.
- Encourage students to make notes on ideas that come up which might be useful in their essays.
- Ask students to make notes here, but not to begin writing.
- If students still need help with ideas at the end of the pair discussion, let them share their suggestions with other pairs.

Writing (SB page 89)

Aim: to give students practice in more extended writing tasks.

Tips:

- This section can be done as homework.
- Remind students to refer back to the model text when writing. Also point out that they should follow the structure plan in *Writing skills* exercise 1 on page 88.
- Point out and encourage students to use the sentence starters in *Useful language*.
- Ask students to check their work carefully before they hand it in.
- Tell students that you will be assessing their writing using the following criteria: clarity of organisation; range of grammar and syntax; appropriate range of relevant vocabulary and phrases, including 'cause and consequence' language; appropriacy of style; accuracy.

Study skills

Improving your speaking skills (SB page 89)

1 Ask students to think about whether speaking or writing is more difficult for them, and why. Encourage them to write down their responses in sentences. Invite them to share some of their comments with the class. Then students complete the task and refer to the back of the book to check their answers. To check comprehension, elicit from students the main points from page 131, using their own words.

TEACH GLOBAL THINK LOCAL **Extra activity**

Points 6 and 7 in exercise 1 relate to methodologies in teaching / learning. At this level, it can be useful to highlight these approaches to raise students' awareness of what goes on in the classroom and how it relates to their learning. Try to elicit examples of when these methodological approaches have been used in recent classes. Also elicit any other approaches used in class which, in their opinion, can help improve their speaking. This might be a good opportunity for discussion of alternative approaches, the role of correction and of peer teaching, analysis of authentic audioscripts, the place of drilling, etc.

1

1–5 F. (Native speakers normally rely on fixed expressions and a reduced range of language when speaking and frequently repeat themselves, use fillers and make false starts and grammatical errors. In many conversational situations it is not necessary to be precise, and even preferable to use general words and 'vague language'. Studying a transcript of real speech will soon confirm this!)

6–7 T. (It is hard to concentrate on content, accuracy, fluency and range of language at the same time, given the natural constraints of speaking in real time. Research suggests that both task rehearsal and task repetition can improve and enrich aspects of speaking by reducing what speakers have to concentrate on, especially if they can analyse their performance.)

2 Books closed. Ask students to reflect on the following question, which you can write up on the board: *If you could improve two or three aspects of your own speaking, what would it be?* After a couple of minutes, refer students to the list in exercise 2. Elicit any other aspects they would like to add to the list before they work individually to find the five most important. In pairs, students compare lists, then share some ideas in open class. At this point, choose one of the ideas, eg *fewer hesitations*, and elicit some possible strategies, in preparation for the ensuing exercise.

3 Ask students to read the procedure. Give them a few minutes to consider the first two bullet-pointed instructions. Go around the class and help individuals as necessary, checking that the task selected is appropriate for their speaking aims. Ask students to experiment with the suggested procedure at home.

TEACH GLOBAL THINK LOCAL **Extra activity**

Students could try and send you their recording electronically, if you have the facilities.

They should remind you (ideally on the recording itself), what their speaking aim is and send both of their recordings electronically (before and after analysis). There are many sites available for recording. At the time of publication, these include *Vocaroo* http://vocaroo.com/ or *Audioboo* http://audioboo.fm/boos/new.

If your individual students agree, it might be interesting and useful to hear a selection of students' recordings in class. Students can discuss how useful and enjoyable the exercise was.

If improving speaking is high on your students' priorities, consider doing more regular recordings, where students might focus on different speaking aims.

(Note that the publishers have no control over and are not responsible for, the content of third party websites. Please use care when accessing them.)

UNIT 8

Chance & Design

Coursebook

Unit 8	Language	Texts	Communication skills
Part 1 SB page 90	Extend your vocabulary *chance* Grammar Real conditionals	Reading *What are the chances?*	Speaking Probability
Part 2 SB page 92	Vocabulary & Speaking Verbs describing accidents Grammar & Pronunciation Unreal conditionals 2 *have*	Reading *The Idea of Perfection*	Speaking & Listening *The Idea of Perfection* Vocabulary & Speaking Awkward situations
Part 3 SB page 94	Vocabulary Describing reactions	Reading *Four highly controversial designs*	Listening & Speaking Buildings Speaking & Writing A short message or response about a building
Part 4 SB page 96	Grammar Passive reporting	Reading *Ruled by Design*	Speaking Conspiracy theories Writing Conspiracy theories
Function globally SB page 98	Giving a presentation Listening to a presentation about website design Giving an introduction to a presentation		
Global voices SB page 99	Places Language focus: incomplete sentences Discussing the design of different areas or public buildings		
Writing SB page 100	An article Writing skills: adding interest to your writing Linking ideas: attitude		
Study skills SB page 101	Extensive reading		

Additional resources

eWorkbook	Interactive and printable grammar, vocabulary, listening and pronunciation practice Extra reading and writing practice Additional downloadable listening and video material
Teacher's Resource Disc	Communication activity worksheets to print and photocopy, review material, test, and video with worksheet
Go global Ideas for further research	**Chance** Students research different ways of taking risks using websites. They prepare a short questionnaire listing five risks that people have taken and find out how many of these risks other students would take. **Design** Students find lists of conspiracy theories by searching online under 'conspiracy theories'. Which theory do they find most plausible, and why? Students report back to the class.

Part 1

TEACH GLOBAL THINK LOCAL Lead-in

You need a dice for each group of three. Ask students to take turns to throw the dice, going around the circle four times in a clockwise direction. Students should remember their own scores each time, eg 3, 5, 6, 1. At the end, find the student who was the luckiest in a) each group and b) the whole class, eg who got the most 6s!

Then dictate these points; in pairs, students should discuss whether this has happened to them:

1 *You get out of a car, wearing your favourite shoes. You step into a puddle.*

2 *You want to buy something special. You get the last one in the shop.*

3 *You leave some money in your trouser pocket and you put your trousers in the washing machine.*

4 *You win a prize in a raffle.*

5 *You finish a lot of work on the computer. Just before you save, the computer crashes.*

Reading (SB page 90)

1 Tell students an anecdote of yourself in one of the situations in the *Lead-in*. Try and make your story entertaining by embellishing it with details of your feelings or reactions. In pairs, students do the discussion task. Invite them to share any particularly amusing or frustrating stories. Take a show of hands to see if students consider themselves to be lucky / unlucky.

2 Before students read the text, elicit a definition of *luck*. (According to the dictionary, luck is *success that you have by chance and not because of anything that you do.*) Elicit from students possible reasons behind the 'slow queue' phenomenon. Then students read *What are the chances?* and discuss the questions. Check answers.

1 The author's conclusion is that you usually are in the slow queue, you don't just think you are.

2 It's nothing to do with luck, but the fact that there are more people in the slower lanes.

3 Students complete the summarising task initially on their own. Ask them to a) use their own words, and b) keep the answers in their head rather than writing them down. Then, in pairs, students finish the task together. If you think your students can manage, ask them to cover the text and do it from memory.

At the end, ask students to tell each other in their own words what these two sentences from paragraph 1 mean: *This situation is often known as Sod's Law … selective recording of evidence*. (The author means always being in the slow queue seems to be proof that the world is against you. Or it could be proof that people tend to think things are against them due to the fact that people only remember certain things.)

Possible answers

A When you're in a queue or a traffic lane, the other queues or lanes always seem to move faster.

B We usually remember coincidences, but forgot or don't notice all the non-coincidences that happen.

A The fact is that there are more people in slow lanes and queues.

B On average you are in the slower queue because this has more people, but not always.

A Being selective about what you choose or remember can have serious consequences for the analysis of data.

B If there is a bias of some kind, it can lead you to draw the wrong conclusion.

Language note

The phrase *It's Sod's Law*, is not really about a law at all, but simply refers to bad luck. It is the theory that *if something can go wrong it will*, referring to things that happen in a way you do not want. This phrase is commonly used in British English, eg *It's Sod's Law: the day before you go on holiday, someone offers you a job starting immediately!* It is often used as a comment on someone else's or your own predicament: *It's my wife's birthday and I was going to take her out tonight. But then my boss asked me to work late. (It's) Sod's Law*. It is a very informal phrase, and one that some people consider rude.

4 After students have discussed the two questions in pairs, invite them to share some real examples of scientific data that they consider to be unreliable or biased, eg related to health, the environment, etc.

TEACH GLOBAL THINK LOCAL Extra activity

Ask students, in groups of three, to consider possible causes for the following two pieces of 'bad luck': *1 If your toast falls it usually lands with the buttered side down; 2 A man in the US was struck by lightning seven times.*

Elicit suggestions and then confirm the answers. (*Toast is more likely to fall face down because it is heavier on that side; The normal probability of being hit by lightning is about 1:100,000 – the man in the US (Roy Sullivan) was a park ranger in Virginia, so to some extent he was more likely to be hit. Virginia also has a very high quota of thunderstorms.*)

Extend your vocabulary (SB page 90)

Do the first example together before students complete the task in pairs. Check answers with the class and ask students to make a note of the *chance* phrases, which are relatively high frequency phrases. Clarify meaning and elicit a possible context for each one – *off-chance* is probably the trickiest one. In pairs, ask one student to say a sentence randomly and their partner to respond spontaneously, where appropriate. Monitor as they are doing this to check they have understood how to use the target phrases. In a feedback session at the end, clarify any problems and elicit some nice examples.

1	fairly certain
2	fairly certain
3	uncertain
4	fairly certain it won't happen
5	uncertain (but hopeful)
6	uncertain (speaker's tone of voice determines whether hopeful or not)

Grammar (SB page 91)

This section focuses on 'real' conditionals, often called 'zero' and 'first' conditionals.

1 Do the first example together. Elicit what *line* refers to here (American English for *queue*). Let students check their answers in pairs before whole-class feedback. Ask students to look at examples a–h and to underline the verbs in both clauses, eg *When you consider …, you are more likely to be in the more crowded lines*. Then ask students to read quietly through the bulleted grammar points. The point about *will* and *should* being used in the *if* clause may be new to your students: ask them to work in pairs to think up additional examples. Invite them to share some examples with the class. Ensure that their pronunciation is also appropriate. See *Pronunciation note*.

a	general truth	f	prediction
b	general truth	g	suggestion
c	prediction	h	general truth / scientific fact
d	prediction		
e	instruction		

Pronunciation note

In the example *If you'll go to that checkout there, I'll open the till*, the underlined words are stressed, with the words *go*, *there* and *till* likely to receive the most prominence overall. Even at this level, it may be very helpful to drill students on such examples, ensuring that their intonation sounds polite. When students are practising, encourage them to raise their voice a little higher and to smile as they say it! In contrast, in the second example the stressed modal verb *will* shows clear irritation and exasperation: *If they will only have one checkout open, of course …* Explain to students that this is intended to sound very direct, but the greater the emphasis on the modal, the ruder it tends to sound.

2 Students tackle questions independently at first, then compare answers in pairs. Students are likely to be familiar with all of the conjunctions on a receptive level, but may very well avoid using them productively, eg *supposing*, *assuming*, *providing*.

1	when, unless, supposing (that), providing (that), assuming (that)
2	when the statement of the conditional clause is a fact or a general truth (zero conditional). (In predictions, *if* is used for something that might happen, *when* is used for something that will happen – first conditional.)
3	unless
4	providing (that)
5	supposing (that) / assuming (that)

3 Ask students to complete the text, but advise them to read it all through first. Do the first example together. Let students compare answers before class feedback.

1	unless	5	will
2	may / might / could	6	won't
3	will	7	should / if / assuming / supposing
4	Assuming / Supposing		

TEACH GLOBAL THINK LOCAL

Extra activity

If you think students need further practice with subordinating conjunctions, put these sentence starters on the board and let them work in pairs to finish them off, before sharing ideas with the class.

Providing we work really hard, …

As long as it doesn't rain tomorrow, …

Supposing the fire alarm goes off this lesson, …

Unless I eat something soon, …

Assuming the economic situation improves, …

G Grammar focus

Refer students to the language summary on real conditionals on page 146.

You can use exercise 1 on page 147 for:
a) extra practice now, b) homework or c) review later on.

The answers are on page 164 of this Teacher's Book.

Speaking (SB page 91)

1 Students read the puzzles and decide before comparing and discussing with a partner. Invite them to share some ideas, but do not respond, except perhaps with further questions. Students then read the answers and comment, if they wish.

1	No, the chance still remains 50% as each time you toss the coin there is a 50% chance it will be tails.
2	No. The proposition the host offers you is only at the stage where there are two remaining available choices: 1 or 2. Whether you choose door 1 or 2 the chance of winning at that point is still 50% for either door.

Part 2

TEACH GLOBAL THINK LOCAL Lead-in

Put up the verbs *watch*, *see* and *look at* on the board. Ask students to explain the difference in meaning to each other (When you 'see' something, you notice it with your eyes, although there are other meanings, such as 'meet' (*see friends*); when you 'watch' something, you look at it for a period of time – it's often something which is moving; when you 'look at' something, you direct your eyes towards it so that you can see it – it is usually something static).

Ask students to draw three columns one for each of the words. Read out this list of nouns to students, at a fairly fast pace. Ask students to put each word with its most likely collocating verb. Do the first example together: *TV, a painting, friends, an accident, the rain, a view, a football match, a play at the theatre, photos, somebody you know.* Students then discuss their answers. Bear in mind that there may be more than one possibility in each case, but that students should choose the most likely one.

Suggested answers

See: friends, an accident, a play at the theatre, somebody you know

Watch: TV, the rain, a football match

Look at: a painting, a view, photos

Speaking and Listening (SB page 92)

1 Write *watching* on the board. Ask students to say which of the following nouns does not collocate with *watching*: *weight*, *bird*, *clock*, *money* and *people* (money). Elicit the meaning of the others. Then students discuss the questions in pairs.

watching strangers, perhaps eavesdropping on their conversations, and imagining details of their lives

2 Let students reflect for a moment on the photos and questions, before discussing their ideas in pairs.

Students' own answers.

3 3.13 Give students a moment to read the questions for the listening, then play the recording. Students compare answers in pairs. Monitor and play audio again if necessary – the descriptive language makes the listening quite dense. In feedback, write up words that might be useful or appealing to students, eg *a ragged haircut*, *a salt of the earth type*, *Bless this Mess*.

1 He is standing at the bedroom window of his hotel, looking out onto the street. She is getting out of a car on the street in front of the hotel.

2 She is big, plain, tall and 'unlikely', with a ragged haircut and a white teeshirt. She is plainly dressed, confident in her appearance and unaccessorised. He imagines her having safe, secure, uncomplicated life on a farm.

3 Students' own answers.

3.13

The Idea of Perfection

Douglas stood at his bedroom window in the Caledonia Hotel, Karakarook, looking out at the street. After a long period of stillness an old brown car appeared at the end of the street, came slowly along and parked tentatively alongside the hotel. A woman got out and stood looking up and down the street with her hands on her hips. She was a big plain raw-boned person, tall and unlikely, with a ragged haircut and a white teeshirt coming unstitched along the shoulder. It was a long time since she'd been young and it was unlikely that she had ever been lovely. She was not accessorised. There was no collar, no scarf, no beads, no earrings. Her head just came up sternly out of the teeshirt saying, here I am, and who do you think you are?

Douglas stood with the curtain in his hand, watching her across the road as she looked at Parnassus Road exposed under the sky. A salt of the earth type. The way the woman stood with her hands on her hips, looking down the street as if she owned it, he could imagine her life, a proper life anchored solid to the ground. There would be a big cheerful husband, uncomplicated children, fat red-cheeked grandchildren calling her Nanna. He could imagine the kitchen out on the farm, with the radio going, and the fridge door covered with magnets that said things like Bless this Mess. He let the curtain fall and stepped back from the window. Then he stood in the dim room wondering why he had done that.

4 3.14 Motivate students by telling them that the two characters – Douglas and Harley – are about to meet, but in a rather interesting and unusual way. Students listen again and answer the questions. Play the recording again for them to check. Invite students to share and discuss their answers with the class.

1 in the doorway of the hotel as he is leaving and she is going in

2 They collide and both nearly fall. He is knocked backwards, throws out his arms and hits her on the shoulder. She grabs his arm to steady herself.

3 They are both embarrassed and apologetic.

4 physical contact between strangers; the thought that they were being observed by *the whole of Karakarook.* They don't know what to say.

3.14

Harley had seen him looking. She had seen him drop the curtain and move back from the window. She had forgotten how empty a country town could be, how closed, how you could feel looked-at and large. She walked further down the street and then, not looking where she was going, she walked straight into a man coming out of the doorway of the Caledonia. When they collided, he staggered backwards and nearly fell. She grabbed at a handful of his forearm, clutching at the fabric and the arm beneath, and he flailed out to steady himself, hitting her on the shoulder. Then they were both standing in the beer-smelling current of cool air from the doorway, apologising.

The man had a look of hysteria around the corners of his mouth. He wanted to blame himself.

My fault, he kept saying. Completely my fault. Stupid.

She had a feeling it was the man who had watched her from the window, but with his hat on it was hard to be sure.

Totally stupid. Not thinking at all.

So clumsy, Harley said. Me, I mean.

She did not look at him, but at the ground, where their shoes were arranged on the footpath like ballroom-dancing instructions.

Did I hurt you? Hitting you?

She looked at him, surprised.

Hurt me?

He pointed, but did not touch.

I hit you, he said, humbly. There.

No, no, she said, although now he had mentioned it, she could feel the place hurting.

She looked at her own hand, large and plain, that had clutched at him, and wondered if she should ask whether she had hurt him.

Well, he said, and laughed a meaningless laugh.

A moment extended itself into awkwardness.

Well, he said again, and she said it too at the same moment.

Their voices sounded loud together. Harley felt as if the whole of Karakarook, behind its windows, must be watching this event that had burst into their silent afternoon: two bodies hitting together, two people standing apologising.

5 Elicit the first line of the dialogue from the listening. Then, in pairs, students put the rest of the dialogue in order, before listening again to check.

Correct order: d, c, h, e, g, b, a/f, a/f

6 This exercise invites students to act in role and to use expression in their voices and faces. Decide how to pair your students up – if possible, put them in male / female pairs. Monitor and encourage full expression and natural-sounding intonation. Invite one or two pairs to perform their scene for the class to round off.

7 Ask *Did the characters behave in an odd or silly way?* In pairs, students discuss this question. Ask them *What would you do in this situation?* Monitor to see if they are using the 'second' conditional to talk about an unreal situation – the forthcoming grammar focus.

Vocabulary and Speaking (SB page 92)

1 Ask students *Have you ever had a similarly embarrassing incident with a stranger?* Students complete sentences 1–4, working alone. If possible, try to avoid giving dictionaries at this point. Let students compare their answers before checking as a class. At this point, just check the answers, without going into issues of meaning or form.

Correct alternatives

1 slip, stumble, trip
2 dented, scraped, scratched
3 cracked, shattered, smashed
4 crush, flatten, squash

2 In groups of three, ask students to peer teach the words from exercise 1. They should decide together what makes the words distinct, both in terms of meaning and form, eg how is *slip* different from *trip*? Let them use dictionaries if they need them. In feedback, clarify any words that students are unsure of by miming, asking questions or eliciting examples, eg *What might you trip over on the pavement? What might cause you to slip?* Write the infinitive on the board, as well as details of form, eg *slip (on sth)* (v).

Possible answers (refer to dictionary for meaning)

1 verbs are intransitive so require a preposition, eg slip on the ice, stumble into sb / through a doorway, trip over sth lying on the ground, tread carefully in a puddle
2 dent anything made of metal (also figurative: dent your pride / ego, etc); rip clothing or paper; scrape your knees when you fall; scratch yourself on a rose bush or scratch sb with your fingernails or scratch a CD
3 bump (intransitive) into sb / a car; crack a mirror (figurative: a smile); shatter glass (figurative: your confidence); smash a tennis ball / anything made of stone / glass / pottery
4 bang a drum / your head; crush your leg or other bone (figurative: your confidence / hopes); flatten a box / grass (by sitting on it); squash a can (to recycle it)

3 Do the first example together, asking two or three different students what they would do in one of these situations. Then students ask and answer the questions in pairs. Monitor to see if they are using the 'second' conditional for unreal situations. Encourage students to discuss other similar situations and invite them to share their interesting stories with the class.

TEACH GLOBAL THINK LOCAL Extra activity

If your students enjoy roleplaying, ask them to choose one of the situations in *Vocabulary and Speaking* exercise 1 and to act out a dialogue. Warn students that at the end, you will ask three pairs to perform their dialogue in front of the class.

Reading (SB page 93)

1 Students first read the two questions. Elicit what the first 'chance encounter' is, as they have already heard about this in the listening. Then students read the text. Elicit further examples of fortuitous events. Ask *What do you think will happen at the end in terms of the characters' relationship?* Elicit suggestions as to why Grenville gave her novel this title. (Possible answer: the couple had given up on the idea of perfection – the idea of love, and were both initially lacking in confidence; it's also a reference to the damaged bridge, which in the end can be repaired, not demolished). Invite responses to the extract. Ask *Would you be interested in reading the novel? Why / Why not?*

1 Douglas and Harley are walking in the same area of countryside and Harley is on hand to rescue him from the cows; Douglas notices Harley putting the quilt in the room, then later notices the smoke.

2 He overcomes his vertigo; they both become ready to love again.

TEACH GLOBAL THINK LOCAL Reading extra

Give students two minutes to reread *The Idea of Perfection*, then close their books. Put the following two lists on the board, or just read them out, jumbling the items in the 'noun' list (currently in the correct order). Then match the verb and the noun phrase, eg *earn money*, as they occurred in the text. Once they have finished, in pairs, students retell the story by elaborating on the collocations, adding any extra details they can remember.

VERBS: *set up, accept, demolish, work, bump into, walk, notice, rescue, give up, change, see*

NOUNS: *a museum, an invitation, a bridge, on small jobs, each other, in the countryside, smoke coming from the room, the quilt, on the idea of love, their minds, a way*

Grammar and Pronunciation (SB page 93)

1 Books closed. Put these words up on the board: *If Douglas* ________ *(look out) …, he … Harley*. Elicit possible ways to fill in the gaps, writing one or two on the board. Ask students what the grammar construction is (hypothetical past conditional, or 'third' conditional) before they complete exercise 1 on their own. Students compare answers for sentences a–e, then discuss the grammar questions 1–4 together. Check answers as a whole class. Ask *Which forms do you rarely or never use?* (Perhaps *But for* or the inversion *Had* + subject.)

Incorrect alternatives

a hadn't

b shouldn't

c If Douglas would have taken (but this is common in American English)

d What for

e would still have suffered

1 past: a, b, c, d
present consequences: e

2 *if* clause: past perfect simple and continuous; result clause: would(n't), could(n't), might (not)

3 noun phrase (*her interest in quilts*) or gerund (*meeting*)

4 more formal

2 3.15 In pairs, ask students to practise the sentences as fluently as they can. Draw out the features of pronunciation, especially the crushed *have* /əv/, but also word stress and linking. Drill one or two sentences, breaking them up into small parts if necessary, eg *he would have missed* → /hiːwʊdəv mɪst/. Then students try to say the other sentences equally fluently. Finally, students listen to the recording.

/əv/

Language note

Students might be interested to know that even native speakers make mistakes with the so-called 'third conditional' form. Today, British speakers often say 'ungrammatical' sentences: they might add an extra and unnecessary **'ve**: *If it hadn't 've been for her interest in quilts …* or *If she'd 've had more money …* Sometimes they might also say: *Harley would never of gone to Karakarook*, using *of* instead of *have*.

3 Let students work alone to complete the sentences about the story. Monitor to check on accuracy. Let them first mutter their sentences to themselves under their breath, focusing on natural-sounding pronunciation. Then ask them to compare sentences in pairs. Raise any potential problems as a whole class.

4 Encourage students to be imaginative here, but to use the conditional structures. In a whole-class feedback session discuss any points of interest, either linguistic or content-related.

5 Give an example of your own to start with. Then ask students to share their own experiences. Encourage listeners to ask questions such as: *So how would your life have been different if you hadn't …?* Monitor and respond to pronunciation issues on the spot, unless it is a common problem that is better discussed with the class. Also note down other form-related issues for later feedback.

TEACH GLOBAL THINK LOCAL

Extra activity

Advanced students often avoid using complicated conditional structures, managing to get around them in various ways. If your students would benefit from some extra practice in using past conditional or mixed conditional forms, then bring in one or two very recent newspapers, or project some online news headlines. Ask students to consider some recent global or more local events and to write some 'if' sentences in groups of three, eg *If the management of X corporation had listened more carefully to the workers, they wouldn't be / have gone on strike*. Encourage a class discussion if students are interested in the topics. Be sure to pick up on students' pronunciation, particularly in relation to the contraction of *would* (*'d*) and the crushed *have* /əv/.

G Grammar focus

Refer students to the language summary on unreal conditionals on page 146.

You can use exercises 2 and 3 on page 147 for:

a) extra practice now, b) homework or c) review later on.

The answers are on page 164 of this Teacher's Book.

Part 3

TEACH GLOBAL THINK LOCAL

Lead-in

Ask students to close their eyes and to try and visualise a building that they particularly like, either inside or outside, large or small, known or unknown. It should be a building they are fairly familiar with – ideally one they have seen in person rather than just from photos. Then ask students to describe their buildings in groups of three, saying what they find beautiful or impressive about it.

Listening and Speaking (SB page 94)

1 Students study and discuss the buildings in the photos and what they might all have in common.

2 **3.16–3.17** Ask students to read the questions before listening to the recording. Take immediate class feedback.

1 Pompidou Cultural Centre, Paris; positive

2 National Centre for the Performing Arts, Beijing; positive

3.16–3.17

1

I like the industrial look. It's sort of that kind of inside out, you know, unique style. And I like it because it's not like any other building that I've ever seen. So if someone showed me a picture of it, or a postcard, I would know exactly where it was and what it represented. And I think because it's a building that represents modern art, you know, that sort of industrial, very sort of … you know, those brightly coloured steel tubes, and that steel and glass, it's kind of modern, it's forward-thinking, it's a sign of our times you know, that's why I like it, because it reminds us of modern art.

2

Well, this building looks very modern, um, almost futuristic. It's like a giant dome which is half titanium and half glass with no straight lines, smooth and curved. Um, its nickname is the egg. It's surrounded by this man-made lake so that the light of the building reflects on the lake and makes it even seem bigger than it is. It's sort of silver in colour, but that can change depending on whether it's night or day and the light conditions. Um, it's a really amazing building. I love it.

3 Students listen again for more specific information, noting down the speakers' comments under the headings given. Let them compare their answers in pairs before whole-class feedback.

1 not like any other building that I've ever seen; represents modern art; industrial; brightly coloured steel tubes; steel and glass; modern, forward-thinking, a sign of our times

2 no straight lines; the light of the building reflects on the lake, making it look bigger than it is; modern, futuristic; shaped like a dome; silver

4 Let students discuss what they heard and whether they agree, before talking about the other two photos. Monitor and record any useful phrases that students are using to talk about the design of the buildings, eg *linear*, or phrases like *concrete box / blob*, etc.

5 Invite students to share their ideas in a class discussion which could also include other buildings that they would like to see.

Reading (SB page 94)

1 Write up the following phrases on the board: *the back of a fridge*, *a wedding cake*, *a car park* and *an egg*. Students in pairs discuss which description refers to which building. (In fact, The High Court, Chandigarh was used as a car park by the judges, rather than being described as such.) Students then read the list of phrases 1–6 and predict which phrase refers to which building, and why. Elicit just one or two suggestions, then ask them to read to check their predictions.

1	Pompidou Cultural Centre
2	Beehive, Pompidou Cultural Centre, NCPA
3	NCPA
4	NCPA
5	The Beehive
6	Pompidou Cultural Centre

2 Students work independently to guess the meaning from context rather than looking in a dictionary. Early finishers can write an example sentence for *a stone's throw* and *out of keeping*, which they can share at the end. Write the answers up on the board for students to self-check.

1	conceptual	4	very near
2	closeness	5	not in harmony with
3	emphasise		

3 Elicit the meaning of the expression *Beauty is in the eye of the beholder*. In pairs, students select their questions and share their ideas. Ask them to take notes, particularly on any differences of opinion, for feedback later.

Vocabulary (SB page 95)

1 First, in pairs, students mark the word stress on the adjectives provided. At the end, elicit which words are not stressed on their first syllable, eg *grotesque*, *impressive* and *unique*. Drill these and other potentially tricky words. Then students categorise the adjectives after doing one or two examples together to clarify. Ask an early finisher to write up the answers on the board.

Neutral: classic, innovative, modern, unique
Positive: awe-inspiring, impressive
Negative: dreary, grotesque, hideous, monstrous

2 This exercise requires students to decide between minor differences in meaning or to assess whether words collocate. Do the first example together, then students work independently before checking in pairs. At the end, ask students to circle up to five expressions that they would like to record from any part of this exercise, eg *Love or hate her, she …; it has its share of …*

1	provokes	4	greeted	7	divided
2	put	5	proved		
3	admirers	6	critical		

3 Encourage students to change the sentences as appropriate, eg *love or hate <u>it</u> …; the design of that <u>car</u> is just awful …* Ask students to write the sentences down before telling each other: this will help them to remember the phrases.

Speaking and Writing (SB page 95)

1 Ask students to work with a different partner. Together they decide which of the two designs they prefer; ideally they should both choose the same one. Invite them to find at least three reasons to justify their choice.

2 In the same pairs, students compose an email to the public relations department stating their preferences and rationale. Elicit from students how to start and end the email, eg *Dear Sir / Madam, I am writing with regard to the proposed … I hope you will consider the above points. Yours faithfully, [name]*. Indicate at the start how much time you will allocate for the task, eg 8–12 minutes. Ensure that they discuss what they are going to write together, so that both students are involved. Monitor and pick up on recurring issues worth highlighting in feedback, eg the tone of the email, the clarity of the points, etc.

3 Students read at least one other email. They should compare points and opinions as well as looking at the way others have expressed their ideas. Invite students to comment on any differences. If appropriate, take in the emails to look at in more detail.

TEACH GLOBAL THINK LOCAL **Extra activity**

For fun, ask students to draw a picture of a building that they have in their mind. It could be completely invented, or a mixture of parts from different buildings they know. Sit students back to back to draw each others' designs purely from their partners' verbal description; it is important that they do not look. At the end, they should compare pictures.

Part 4

TEACH GLOBAL THINK LOCAL Lead-in

Books closed. Write these different chunks from the words *conspiracy theory* up on the board:
spi con or racy y the.
Ask students to combine the mini chunks and make the two-word collocation.

Speaking (SB page 96)

1 Ask three different students to slowly read out one of the example conspiracy theories. Try to avoid letting students discuss what they think of the three conspiracy theories at this point. Write up the words *hoax* (n), *cover up* (v) and *shadowy* (adj) on the board, and elicit what they mean. In pairs, ask students to write the definition. Then refer them to the dictionary to check their definition.

2 Refer students to the *Useful phrases*, then ask them to discuss the two questions about the conspiracy theories. Monitor and note down any points of interest which can be raised in whole-class feedback.

Reading (SB page 96)

1 This text, *Ruled by Design*, summarises what all conspiracy theories have in common and details three principles which nearly always feature in these theories.

Write this sentence up on the board: *In essence, a conspiracy belief attempts to explain* ______. Elicit possible one-word answers from the class – they will see the answer in the text (evil). Then students read *Ruled by Design* to find out what such theories all have in common. Also ask *What kind of text is this?* (formal and academic, eg *in essence, albeit, hence*, etc).

Possible answer

All conspiracy theories try to explain evil or disastrous events. They believe: everything is done for a reason; there are no coincidences; you cannot trust anybody because everybody could be part of a conspiracy; all events are linked; everything is part of a pattern.

2 In pairs, ask students to look at the words 1–7 and try to guess the word class, using clues from the suffix endings, where appropriate. Then students refer back to the text to complete the matching task. Have them check answers in a dictionary, or simply put them up on the board for students to self-check.

1 d (noun)	5 b (adverb)
2 g (verb)	6 a (verb)
3 f (adjective)	7 e (adjective)
4 c (conjunction)	

3 Let students do this task alone and then compare answers. In a class discussion, ask students to justify their answers, using phrases like *It actually says …*, *According to the text / author …*, *It states …*

1 F (*… has often been left undefined, as though its meaning were self-evident.*)
2 F (*… acting secretly to achieve some malevolent end.*)
3 T
4 F (*… a world based on intentionality, from which accident and coincidence have been removed.*)
5 F (*… the appearance of innocence is considered no guarantee that an individual or group is benign.*)
6 T

TEACH GLOBAL THINK LOCAL Extra activity

If students have not already questioned or discussed the meaning of the title of the text on SB page 97, then ask them to close their books. See if anyone can actually remember the title: *Ruled by Design*. Put this up on the board. In pairs, students discuss what they think this title actually means. (*By design* is a formal way of saying *deliberately, not by accident*, so this refers to the fact that conspiracists believe events do not happen by accident, but deliberately.)

4 Allow students a few moments to reflect on these 'large' questions, then put them into groups of three to discuss the points. Ask the group to assign a 'scribe', to take notes and summarise their ideas at the end. Monitor and help students as necessary. Early finishers can discuss a particular conspiracy theory, such as the death of Princess Diana. At the end, ask *Did you all have similar opinions on the questions?*

TEACH GLOBAL THINK LOCAL Extra activity

Put these words on the board: *theorist, conspiracy, deceptive, randomness, coincidence, reassuring, definable, purpose*. Students work in pairs to decide on the word class and word stress of these words. Then they should add at least two words to each 'family', nouns, adjectives, verbs or adverbs, eg *essence* → *essential, essentially*. Towards the end, let students check in the dictionary. Early finishers could put some of the words in example sentences, to be checked by you.

Grammar (SB page 97)

1 This section focuses on common verbs used in passive structures to report information, both in speaking and writing.

Focus students initially by writing up the first statement: *Conspiracy theorists believe that pattern is everywhere*. Ask students to rephrase this using the passive – write up the first word in each case to help, if necessary, eg *Pattern* … and *It* … Write up the complete sentences. Then ask students to complete the rules in exercise 1.

1 b 2 c 3 a

2 Refer back to the passive examples on the board and elicit two or three other verbs that could be used instead of *believe*. Then students complete the task in pairs. When checking answers with the class, you could point out that *is regarded to be* and *is regarded that* are not commonly used in passive – *is regarded as* is more common.

Incorrect alternatives

comprehend, gossip

3 This exercise aims to clarify the difference between alternative infinitive forms which come after the passive structure. Students match the example with the description, then check in pairs. If appropriate, ask your students to translate the three options into their first language, to see how the same meaning is conveyed.

a to be working
b to work
c to have worked

4 Focus students' attention on the example. Elicit why the simple infinitive (*to be*) is used rather than the perfect infinitive (*to have been*) or the continuous infinitive (*to be being*). (Although it's a temporary / ongoing situation, *be* is a state verb.) Remind students to look at the tense of the original statements. In pairs, students work on the transformation task. At the end, take one example such as sentence 5, and ask *Why might a writer prefer one form over another?* Refer back to *Grammar* exercise 1 and the issue of placing the focus within the sentence.

2 The opposition party is alleged to belong to … / People allege that the opposition party belongs …
3 Large companies are claimed to be collecting … / It is claimed that large companies are …
4 The actor is believed to have worked … / People believe that the actor worked …
5 The head of state is rumoured to be … / It is rumoured that the head of state …

G Grammar focus

Refer students to the language summary on passive reporting on page 146.

You can use exercise 4 on page 147 for:
a) extra practice now, b) homework or c) review later on.

The answers are on page 164 of this Teacher's Book.

Language note

It would be worth pointing out to students that these reporting passive verbs are often very appropriate for academic writing, for example in essays, to introduce differing views and opinions or evidence. They are also commonly used when reporting news, both in written and spoken English and can be used as a distancing device between the reporter and the information reported, to avoid any sense of blame or responsibility.

Negative sentences, whilst possible, are often avoided as they can become rather over-complicated, eg *The head of state is rumoured not to be dead.* Often the meaning is expressed in a different way, eg *The head of state is (now) rumoured to be alive!*

Writing (SB page 97)

1 In pairs, students develop their own conspiracy theory. Remind them that they can use the ideas in *Grammar* exercise 4, if they wish, but give them a free rein to be creative. Other situations could involve politics, crime, power, language, war, espionage or money.

2 Students write their paragraph, beginning with a sentence like those in *Grammar* exercise 4 and following on with more details to support the theory. Monitor and support, paying particular attention to accuracy of the target language.

3 Put students into groups of four to share their ideas. Invite students to share one or two convincing examples with the class.

Function globally: giving a presentation

These lessons in *Global* are designed to provide students with immediately useful functional language. They all follow a similar format.

Warm up (SB page 98)

Aim: to introduce the topic via a quick speaking task or picture work.

Tips:

- Do not over-correct here, especially in speaking activities.
- Elicit a couple of examples for exercise 1, to start off.
- At the end of the *Warm up*, brainstorm some useful suggestions about good and bad presentations onto the board.

Suggested answers

Have a strong opening.
Start with an outline of your talk.
Follow a clear structure.
Do not give too much information.
Explain key terms.
Give examples.
Involve the audience.
Look at your audience.
Speak slowly and clearly.
Use humour.
Use visual aids.
Vary your intonation.
Keep an eye on your watch.
Rehearse and time your presentation.

Listening (SB page 98)

Aim: to present the functional language in context via a conversation or series of conversations.

Tips:

- Play the recording all the way through for each task (there are always two tasks). (Track 3.18)
- For exercise 1, you could ask students to design a mini poster presentation of their predictions, in pairs or groups of three. (If any of your students have had first-hand experience of website design, make sure the groups are mixed up.)
- Explain to students before they listen that the recording gives only part of the presentation.
- Let students compare their notes in pairs before checking answers as a class.
- Encourage students to read the audioscripts for homework, exploiting them for useful language.

3

1 T (*Head of IT at Ainsdale College*)
2 F (most of them *haven't a clue how to go about it*)
3 T (*… take the mystery out of designing a website*; *you don't need to be an IT expert to design a simple site.*)
4 F (*three parts*)
5 T (*Yes, spot on.*)
6 T (*If you'd like to take a look at the slide*; *I'll skip this slide*)
7 T (*Geoff is telling me it's time to stop.*)
8 F (*… designing a website is not rocket science …*)

 **3.18**

A = Geoff; **B** = Grant; **C** = Man; **D** = Woman

A: Right, right. OK, shall we start? I'd like to welcome our speaker today Grant Fisher, who has very kindly agreed to come and talk to us about how to design your own website, which I know many of you are extremely keen to do. Grant is Head of IT at Ainsdale College, and I know his talk is going to be very practical and useful. So without further ado, I'll hand over to Grant.

B: Thanks Geoff, and thanks for inviting me to come and talk to you. It's a great pleasure to be here today. Maybe I could start by asking if any of you already have your own website? Could you raise your hands? One, two, three of you. Well done. And now, how many would like to have your own website, but don't have one simply because you haven't a clue how to go about it? Could you raise your hands? So that's the majority of you.

Well, the topic of my talk today is website design, and my aim is to take the mystery out of designing a website and I hope that by the end of it, you'll all go away fired with enthusiasm to create your own site, and as you'll see, you don't need to be an IT expert to design a simple site.

So, there are three parts to my presentation. I'm going to start by outlining the steps you need to take to set up a website. Then I'll look at some features of a good website, and I'll illustrate that with some slides of good and bad website design. And finally, I'll focus on troubleshooting, what to do when problems occur, as they inevitably will. If anything is not clear, please feel free to interrupt me as we go along, otherwise if you have any questions, I'll do my best to answer them at the end.

OK, so, let's think about the process of setting up a website, step by step. Any ideas about the very first thing you have to do? Yes, the gentleman at the back?

C: Get permission.

B: Get permission. Well, no not quite. Anyone else? Yes, the lady over there.

D: Get a name.

B: Get a name. Yes, yes, spot on. The very first thing you need to do is get yourself a domain name. What do I mean by 'domain name'? Well, a domain name is the name given to your website, the one you put into your search engine when you want to access a site. For example, designers dot com, or creativedesign dot org. Perhaps I should point out that the name you choose should be …

Right, so, turning now to the features of a good website. If you'd like to take a look at the slide – can you all see there at the back? If not, there's a handout going round, I hope I've made enough. Well, as you can see on the slide, this is not a very user-friendly page. Just to elaborate on that, you can see that the graphics …

Well, I'll skip this slide as we're running out of time. Yes, Geoff is telling me it's time to stop. So, just to conclude, I hope I've demonstrated that designing a website is not rocket science, and that actually it can be quite fun as well. Well, that's it, and thanks for listening. Does anyone have any questions?

Language focus (SB page 98)

Aim: to draw students' attention to the items of functional language.

Tips:

- Ask students to work alone at first, and then compare their answers in pairs before you play the recording for them to check. (Track 3.19)
- Ask *Which of these expressions have you a) heard before and b) used yourselves in presentations?*
- Give students time to take a note of phrases they particularly like and want to incorporate into their repertoire.

1

1 great pleasure
2 topic
3 aim
4 divided
5 start by
6 go on to
7 illustrate
8 focus
9 feel free to
10 do my best

2

1 b 2 a 3 d 4 c

3.19

It's a great pleasure to be here today. The topic of my talk today is website design, and my aim is to take the mystery out of designing a website. So, my presentation will be divided into three parts. I'm going to start by outlining the steps you need to take to set up a website. I'll go on to mention some features of a good website, and I'll illustrate that with some slides. And finally, I'll focus on troubleshooting. If anything is not clear, feel free to interrupt me as we go along, otherwise if you have any questions, I'll do my best to answer them at the end.

Pronunciation (SB page 98)

Aim: to focus students on a particular aspect of pronunciation of the target phrases.

Tips:

- Play the recording two or three times, if necessary. (Track 3.20)
- At this level, try to promote good all-round pronunciation including stress, intonation and linking. This also raises the challenge for students.
- Provide rehearsal time for your students. Monitor and assist, as necessary. Try to hear all of them speak as you go around, even if it is just for one or two sentences.
- After feedback from their partners, ask students to read out the passage again to a different partner.

1

The first speaks with flat intonation, slight mumble, difficult to make out; the second with varied intonation, enthusiasm and good projection.

Speaking (SB page 98)

Aim: to allow students an opportunity to use this language in a meaningful, real-world context.

Tips:

- Give students time to prepare this activity. Encourage students to write notes only, although you may want to allow some students to write the introduction out word for word if they want to, especially those unused to writing presentations.
- Circulate and monitor carefully as they are writing their notes. Correct or upgrade their language as they write.
- As they are giving their introductions in groups, take notes on any problem areas, including pronunciation-related aspects.
- Before they start to work in groups, highlight the sentences in *Useful phrases* and encourage students to make use of them while questioning their partners.

Global voices

These lessons in *Global* are designed to provide students with exposure to authentic speakers of English from both native and non-native English backgrounds. They all follow a similar format.

Warm up (SB page 99)

Aim: to introduce the topic and highlight potentially difficult vocabulary the students will encounter.

Tips:

- Circulate and monitor any speaking task, but be careful not to over-correct.
- At the end, invite students to share information about some interesting places they have visited with the class.

Listening (SB page 99)

Aim: to expose students to English spoken with a variety of accents.

Tips:

- Students will need to hear the recording at least two or three times to be able to understand it.
- Tell students you don't expect them to understand every word; some of it will be hard. This is because the text has not been scripted or graded in any way. It's what they would hear in 'the real world'. (Tracks 3.21–3.22)
- The first task is easier and focuses on gist, the second task is more detailed.
- It may be tempting to hunt for specific pronunciation or language errors, but we recommend against this. In real-world communication not everyone speaks perfect English all the time, not even native speakers.
- Elicit personal responses. Ask *Are you familiar with these places? Have you been to any similar places?*

1

1 Tim: California: San Francisco, Los Angeles, Carmel
Beth: York

2 Tim: Yosemite National Park; Museum of Modern Art in San Francisco
Beth: York Minster (cathedral)

3 Tim thought San Francisco was superb; the people and the city were very warm; interesting architecture; museum was a beautiful building
Beth thought York Minster was beautiful and York itself was quite nice, with quite unique buildings.

2

Museum of Modern Art: 1, 4, 7

York Minster: 2, 3, 5

Buildings Tim saw: 6

 **3.21**

A = Beth; **B** = Tim

Beth (United States) and Tim (Northern Ireland)

A: Have you ever been to the States?

B: I have.

A: Have you? Where did you visit?

B: I visited San Francisco, Los Angeles, Carmel, places like that. In fact, Yosemite National Park.

A: Oh that's beautiful.

B: And I went there in 1995 for my honeymoon.

A: OK. What did you think of San Francisco?

B: Superb. I thought the people were very warm as well. The whole city had a nice warm feeling to it. Very interesting architecture in terms of earthquakes and so forth. Apparently, a lot of the buildings are built on huge ball bearings so that they move …

A: Really?

B: … the foundations move when there's an earthquake.

A: Interesting.

B: Yes, it is fascinating.

A: Was there any building in particular that you enjoyed?

B: Um, I think probably the Museum of Modern Art was a beautiful, beautiful building.

A: What did you like about it?

B: What did I like about it? I liked the openness of the inside, the whiteness of it, the Yoko Ono exhibition was quite interesting, and the outside, there is a huge circle with red bricks on the other side like a triangle with a circle in the middle. It is so long ago I can hardly remember, but I remember being impressed by the sense of space. It was almost like being in the open air.

A: Really?

B: Because it was so, so airy and spartan, apart from the artworks. Have you been to York?

A: I have.

B: And seen York Minster?

A: That's one of my favourites. That's beautiful, and outside is just as pretty as inside because some of the cathedrals, they are quite … just brick on the outside and there is not a lot … the decoration is more inside, but that one was … is both outside and inside are just full of sculptures and angles and arches and it's really pretty.

B: And what's the name of the window? There's a very famous window. I'm not going to remember the name of it.

A: I can't remember what it is …

B: But it's …

A: I do know what you are talking about.

B: Yes, it's all sort of greys and blues. It's not like your archetypical stained-glass multicoloured window. It's very, very subtle, very nice.

A: Yes, the whole … actually the town of York, all the buildings are quite nice. I thought that they were all quite unique.

B: Yeah.

3

1 air	4 reflections
2 light	5 ventilation
3 water	6 lighting

 **3.22**

A = Silvia; **B** = Evgenia

Silvia (Catalonia) and Evgenia (Belarus)

A: It is the Alhambra in Granada. And yeah, for like you said, as you said, it's also because of the air and the light and the water, these elements that make it a special place, like magic place.

B: What about water, how it works?

A: There are a lot of fountains and the reflections of the sun on the water and on the tiles, because it's very special for the tiles, Moorish style …

B: It's like a sunny place?

A: What do you mean …?

B: I mean, would you have a lot of sunshine there?

A: Yes, of course.

B: Because in Oxford it's like most buildings here are so beautiful, they are just beautiful, but when it's a sunny day, which is not that very often, especially in wintertime, it's just gorgeous. And it's like sunlight, just, you know, makes …

A: It makes a difference, yeah, and I think that is also why I like classical buildings because they really took into account the light and the air because there wasn't ventilation or artificial lighting so it was … they made the most of these elements. So, yeah.

Language focus: incomplete sentences (SB page 99)

Aim: to raise students' awareness of a particular piece of language present in the listening.

Tip:

- The objective of these exercises is awareness-raising, not production. Here the exercises highlight that native or fluent speakers are sometimes slightly incoherent: they adjust what they are saying as they go along, even if this means it is ungrammatical or repetitive.
- In exercise 3, ask students to reflect and discuss what they think the speaker does in each of the sentences from exercises 1 and 2.

1

Students' own answers.

2

1 b 2 c 3 d 4 e 5 a

3

rephrase an idea: 4e, 5a

change focus: 2c, 3d

pause because of an interruption: 1b

Speaking (SB page 99)

Aim: for students to discuss the same or similar questions as the speakers in the listening.

Tips:

- The speaking tasks here are more open to allow for students to explore the subject. Give them time to do this.
- If possible, in advance, ask students to bring in a photo or picture of their chosen place, to engage their partners.
- Monitor as they are talking and note down any good / problematic use of language. You can use this in feedback (oral or written) later on.
- As you go through the book and the *Global voices* lessons, ask students for feedback on these listening activities and their potential use of English with other people. *Are they very difficult? Have you used your English as a 'lingua franca' with other non-native English speakers? How did you find it? What tips do you have on understanding or making themselves understood in an international context?*

TEACH GLOBAL THINK LOCAL

Extra activity

If your students have just done the *Function globally* page (SB page 98) they might be interested in doing a mini presentation, which they could prepare outside class time, if necessary. Ask them to choose a place that they would recommend to tourists and prepare a two-to-four-minute presentation in which they should try to 'market' their place, as a good place to visit. If the place is already well known as a tourist hot spot, try to convince the audience that it could bring in far more revenue for the region/country. They should 'sell' their place, giving details such as historical and geographical information, then highlight what its main assets are as a tourist venue. They can then give their presentations in groups of three or four. Let students use PowerPoint presentations if you have the facilities.

Writing: an article

These lessons in *Global* are designed to provide students with extended writing practice. They all follow a similar format.

Reading (SB page 100)

Aim: to provide a sample text for students to analyse.

TEACH GLOBAL THINK LOCAL **Pre-reading activity**

Ask students *If you were offered a good, exciting job in a foreign country such as Nepal, would you go?* Encourage them to write down two reasons **for** going, and two reasons **against** going. Then students compare their responses. Ask *Which faraway country would you happily move to? Why?*

Tips:

- There are often two questions for these texts: one which focuses on gist and the other on specific details.
- Ask students to compare their ideas about exercise 1 in groups of three, then discuss some ideas as a class.
- Invite personal reactions to Chiara's article. Ask *Can you understand Chiara's dilemma? Have you ever done / could you ever do something similar?*
- If you did not do the *Pre-reading activity*, elicit suggestions on what would be a) wonderful and b) difficult about living in Nepal.
- Ask *Where might you find an article like this?* (on a blog, in a magazine article).

1

Chiara is imagining the consequences of having made a different decision from the one she actually did take.

2

1 T (*How can I abandon my boyfriend, my friends and my family to live in a country where the tap water is polluted and there is malaria? … travelling, exploring, maybe it would be exciting too … And so I accepted the invitation even though I felt homesick at the very thought.*)

2 T (*Deep down, I sensed that this invitation marked a radical change in direction … would have major implications for the rest of my life …* – and same evidence as above.)

3 T (*That visit proved to be a decisive turning point in my life.*)

4 F (*I would have got married, had children and cooked meals for my family.*)

5 T (*… the experience has opened my eyes to a great deal about the world … I have met a great many wonderful people on my travels …*)

6 F (*But do I regret it? No. Every path has both advantages and limitations …*)

Writing skills: adding interest to your writing (SB page 100)

Aim: to give students a chance to develop their writing through various different micro skills.

Tips:

- Ask students *Did you enjoy the article? Why?*
- Before doing the exercises, ask *What techniques do you think Chiara has used to make her writing interesting?*
- Do the first question in each exercise together with the students before asking them to continue on their own.
- Let students check their answers in pairs or small groups, then correct in open class.

1

1 have major implications for
2 find myself
3 bitter-sweet
4 my mind buzzing with doubts and confusion
5 opened my eyes to
6 intrigued
7 visualise
8 sensed

2

1 *I closed the door behind me, my mind buzzing with doubts and confusion.*

2 *… I think that any period of living abroad is a bitter-sweet experience … Every path has both advantages and limitations …*

3 *… my mind buzzing with doubts and confusion … a sort of wrench in my stomach … intrigued … I felt homesick at the very thought.*

4 *'But I don't even know where Nepal is! …'*

5 *… or would I? But do I regret it?*

6 *I closed the door behind me … a country where the tap water is polluted and there is malaria … I have been back ten times to do fieldwork … a job as a researcher in anthropology … I have lived in several different countries …*

7 *But do I regret it? No. … I cannot imagine myself without the experiences I have had, even the most painful ones.*

Linking ideas: attitude (SB page 100)

Aim: to highlight and focus on a particular aspect of language that students can use to improve their writing.

Tips:

- Let students compare their answers in pairs or small groups before you check them in open class.
- For variety and efficiency, put some of the answers on the board for students to self-check, eg exercise 3.

- Quickly ensure that students are pronouncing the words correctly, eg *oddly, thankfully, worryingly, predictably, ironically, inevitably.*

1

1 curiously 2 Naturally

2

1 oddly; surprisingly; strangely
2 clearly; obviously; of course

3

Incorrect alternatives

1 worryingly 3 Quite rightly
2 ironically 4 amazingly

TEACH GLOBAL THINK LOCAL **Extra activity**

To practise the other attitude markers, you could ask students to work in pairs and redo exercise 3. This time they should finish each sentence with the adverb that they deleted, eg *I had to go to hospital ~~but~~ and worryingly, there were no doctors available!* Do an example together and encourage them to use their imaginations. Elicit some examples.

Preparing to write (SB page 101)

Aim: to give students opportunity to brainstorm ideas for the writing task.

Tips:

- Let students reflect on the questions alone for a few minutes, before discussing them in pairs.
- Ask students to make notes at this stage, but not to begin writing – this stage is intended to provide ideas.
- Refer students to the language in *Looking back at the past*, which they might find useful both when talking and in their writing.

Writing (SB page 101)

Aim: to give students practice in more extended writing tasks.

Tips:

- This section can be done as homework.
- Remind students to refer back to the model text, and encourage them to experiment with some of the target language from this section. Stress the importance of making their article interesting for their reader(s).
- Ask students to check their work carefully before they hand it in.
- If your students are happy to share their personal information, let them read each others' writing in groups of three, and encourage them to comment and ask questions, where appropriate.
- You could ask students to rewrite their article, after oral or written feedback from you, if you wish.

Study skills

Extensive reading (SB page 101)

1 In pairs, encourage students to ask questions in order to find out more about their partner, eg *What kind of books have you read recently in your language / English? Why did you choose to read that?* Invite students to share information about their reading material in English with the rest of the class.

2 Give students a minute to tick the statements. If you have a less confident group, let them share their ideas in groups of three initially. Then conduct a whole-class feedback session, eliciting examples of what (some) students have ticked. Be prepared to give and/or elicit practical suggestions from peers for any students who have ticked one of the last three boxes in question 2.

3 Give students two minutes to read and digest the short text. In pairs, encourage them to say if they found anything surprising in the text. Then, in groups of three or four, students discuss the three questions. You could elicit examples of any novels featured in this Coursebook that they would like to read too.

TEACH GLOBAL THINK LOCAL **Alternative procedure**

To engage students more fully with the text, with their books closed, you could read it out pausing at various points to let them complete the sentences on their own: ask them to write only the missing word. Pause between each sentence, to let them go back and reflect, as necessary.

Research shows that extensive reading in a foreign language can not only improve reading skills and ______, but can also facilitate language acquisition and both spoken and ______ communication. You should choose texts related to your ______, and read for ______ as much as possible. You should not stop to ______ words, though you can, if you want, note down or mark words as you read to ______ later.

Students first compare their isolated words, then check with the original text in exercise 3, SB page 101.

4 Allow students time to identify suitable classmates and agree on an appropriate book. It is a good idea to define the practical details of this task as much as possible, eg who will get the book / article in the first place; who will read it first; when they intend to read it by; when they will share their thoughts and ideas on the material.

TEACH GLOBAL THINK LOCAL **Extra activity**

Now would be a good time to refer to library facilities, if you have them; if not, remind students of their local library, if appropriate. Another option is for students to bring in their own English reading matter and swap it within their group. Remind students that many of the classics are available online free of charge. If you have a small group, you could even organise a 'book group', where everyone reads the same book in a given time, eg two weeks, for discussion at a later point in a lesson.

UNIT 9

Time & Motion

Coursebook

Unit 9	Language	Texts	Communication skills
Part 1 SB page 102	Extend your vocabulary Collocations with *time* Grammar Unreal past time	Listening & Speaking Concepts of time	Speaking Time
Part 2 SB page 104	Vocabulary *get* Grammar Quantifiers	Reading & Speaking *Working Time Around The World*	Reading & Speaking *Working Time Around The World*
Part 3 SB page 106	Extend your vocabulary UK / US English Grammar Comparisons	Reading *Traffic*	Speaking Congestion problems
Part 4 SB page 108	Vocabulary Formal and informal language	Reading *The Secret Life of Bees* Listening The dance of the honeybees	Speaking Animal behaviour
Function globally SB page 110	Being interviewed Listening to a job interview Roleplaying an interview for a chosen job		
Global English SB page 111	Changing English Discussing how language changes over time		
Writing SB page 112	A proposal Linking ideas: results Writing skills: impersonal style		
Study skills SB page 113	Improving listening		

Additional resources

eWorkbook	Interactive and printable grammar, vocabulary, listening and pronunciation practice Extra reading and writing practice Additional downloadable listening and video material
Teacher's Resource Disc	Communication activity worksheets to print and photocopy, review material, test, and video with worksheet
Go global Ideas for further research	**Time** There are many professional organisations offering training in time management. Students look online to find details of some of these, and compare what they are offering, the fee, etc. They report some of their more interesting findings to the class and any suggested techniques they are able to download. **Motion** Students look online for details of traffic management schemes in their own countries and report them to the class. Alternatively, the http://think.direct.gov.uk/ site is an example of a series of road safety campaign information in the UK. Students could compare the campaign material with material they see in their own country, and discuss whether they consider the material successful and appropriate. Please be aware that that site does refer to drug and alcohol abuse.

UNIT 9 Time & Motion

Part 1

TEACH GLOBAL THINK LOCAL Lead-in

Assuming (most of) your students wear a watch, put them into groups of three to tell each other: a) where they got their watch b) how long they have had it c) why they chose that one d) where they keep it at home e) how many times they probably look at it a day f) if they feel comfortable without it. You can put these prompts on the board.

Speaking (SB page 102)

1 Introduce the topic of the lesson: time. In pairs, complete the poem, after reading the first example to see how the rhyming pattern works. Elicit some examples, but do not confirm answers at this point.

2 **3.23** Students listen to check their ideas. Then ask *What do you think the poem is saying about time?* (The older you get, the faster time seems to pass.) Elicit responses to the questions and any useful expressions to describe time, eg *you have all the time in the world; time flies; it's gone in a flash*, etc.

 **3.23**

When as a child, I laughed and wept,
Time crept.
When as a youth, I dreamt and talked,
Time walked.
When I became a full-grown man,
Time ran.
When older still I daily grew,
Time flew.
Soon I shall find when travelling on –
Time gone.

Listening and Speaking (SB page 102)

1 **3.24** This listening discusses two very different ways of perceiving time and the effect this has on individuals and on societies. Ask *Have you ever travelled to a place where time seemed to be viewed differently? In what way?* Invite them to share any personal examples with the class. Then give them an opportunity to label the diagrams before they listen, if they can. Finally students listen and complete the matching task and answer the question. Check answers.

1 & 3	monochronic; linear. Modern Western societies
2 & 4	cyclical; polychronic. Traditional agricultural societies and many parts of the non-Western world

3.24

What is time? Does it move forward in a line from the past to the future, or does it go round and round in endless cycles? And how can we break it up into different parts or units? Different societies have always provided varying answers to these fundamental questions of life.

In the West, time is typically conceived of as linear, moving forward relentlessly. Events occur and cannot be repeated. This view of time is associated with ideas of progress and evolution, and in fact it is the dominant paradigm in times of economic prosperity and national confidence. Modern Western time has also been described as 'monochronic' time. In a monochronic view, time is quantifiable. This is the time of schedules, clocks and organisations – some have called it 'male' or 'public' time. It is divided into fixed elements: seconds, minutes, hours, days, weeks, and so on – in other words, into blocks of time that can be organised and timetabled. And it is only possible to 'do one thing at a time', as time itself flows swiftly past. People who operate with this view of time love to plan in detail, make lists, keep track of their activities, and organise their time into a daily routine. Punctuality and time management are important. Switching back and forth from one activity to another is not only wasteful and distracting, it is also uncomfortable.

In traditional agricultural societies, on the other hand, time is often experienced as cyclical, or spiral, slowly advancing in an endless cycle of birth, death and rebirth. And we can see this reflected in the Buddhist and Hindu concept of reincarnation. This view of time has been called 'polychronic' and is common in many parts of the non-Western world. Time is experienced as continuous, with no particular structure. It is like a never-ending river, flowing from the infinite past, through the present, into the infinite future. Polychronic time has also been described as more 'private' or 'female'. The pace of life in polychronic societies is typically less frenetic and more relaxed. Tasks are completed only 'when the time is right' rather than according to a strict agenda, and people may engage in multitasking, changing from one activity to another as the mood takes them. In such cultures, it is not important to be punctual, or to meet deadlines and it is acceptable to interrupt someone who is busy.

2 Give students a moment to read the task, then replay the recording. Let students compare their answers, then conduct a whole-class feedback session.

1 a polychronic c monochronic e polychronic
b polychronic d monochronic f monochronic

2

monochronic: only possible to 'do one thing at a time'; punctuality and time management are important; like to plan in detail, make lists, keep track of their activities and organise their time into a daily routine; no switching back and forth polychronic: tasks are completed only 'when the time is right' rather than according to a strict agenda; acceptable to engage in multitasking; change from one activity to another; interrupt someone; not important to be punctual or to meet deadlines

3 Students read the questions and the *Useful phrases*. Encourage them to use this language in their discussion in pairs. Monitor and later discuss any points of interest.

Extend your vocabulary (SB page 102)

1 Ask the class to brainstorm any verbs which collocate with *time*, and invite a student to write them up on the board. Students complete the matching task, first alone and then in pairs. In feedback, clarify any phrases if necessary, eg *to fritter away time*.

1 b 2 a 3 e 4 f 5 d 6 c

2 Ask students to read the example. Then elicit four time-related questions, which they should direct at you, eg *Which aspect of your teaching takes up a lot of time?* Respond with genuine answers. Then invite students to think of four more questions to ask each other in groups. Monitor and check they are using the collocations appropriately.

TEACH GLOBAL THINK LOCAL

Homework extra

Any advanced learner's dictionary will give a very lengthy entry for *time*, as there are countless associated phrases. Ask students to find two example phrases that they like. Recommend that they look through the whole entry, so that they do not all select the same phrases from the beginning. Ask them to find or invent an example sentence to accompany each phrase, as well as using the definition. Ideally, they should write both the example and the definition out on computer, possibly with an associated visual, but warn them that this will be for a poster so that it should be of an appropriate size. The following lesson, you could collate these on a 'time' poster, to display in the classroom. If you have a large class, you could have several group posters.

Grammar (SB page 103)

1 This gives an overview of how the different past tenses are used. Ask students to complete the timeline matching task individually.

1 B 2 A 3 D 4 C

2 **3.25** Tell students they are going to listen to seven short dialogues and decide who's talking and what the situation is. Listen to the first extract together and discuss the answers. Then play the rest of the recording without pausing. At the end, let them compare answers before checking them as a class.

Possible answers

1 one colleague offering another a lift
2 guest asking host for permission to smoke
3 parent giving strong advice to teenager
4 one friend inviting another to birthday treat
5 two people discussing if a friend will be coming or not
6 boss asking worker to work late; worker wants to take the whole day off
7 one colleague complaining; another gives advice

3.25

1

A: Oh no, it's raining again! If only I didn't have to walk home.

B: I'm going home your way. Would you like me to give you a lift when I've finished these emails?

2

A: Do you mind if I smoke?

B: Actually, I'd rather you didn't, if you don't mind. It's a non-smoking household.

3

A: It's time you had a haircut.

B: Honestly! I'm old enough to decide for myself how I have my hair. I wish you wouldn't speak to me as if I were a child!

4

A: I was wondering if you'd like to go out tomorrow night – birthday treat.

B: Sounds great. What did you have in mind?

5

A: Is Caroline coming?

B: No, Stuart told me she went swimming on Tuesdays.

6

A: Would you mind working a couple of hours extra tomorrow?

B: Actually, I was hoping I could take tomorrow off. It's my daughter's school play and I really wanted to see it.

7

A: I wish I hadn't agreed to work overtime. Evie will be so disappointed.

B: Why don't you phone in sick? You need to be a bit more assertive, you know.

3 In the same pairs, students attempt to complete the gapped sentences. Do not give any hint about using past forms at this point. Play the recording for students to check their answers. Ask *What common feature in the answers for sentences 1–8 connects all of them?* (the past form). If students have any questions about the rules, ask them to wait until the next exercise.

1 didn't have to	4 I were	7 was hoping
2 didn't	5 was wondering	8 I hadn't
3 had	6 went	

4 Students match sentences from exercise 3 to the rules in the box. Do the first example together. Students discuss their answers in pairs, before whole-class feedback. Be ready to clarify as necessary. See *Language note*.

a 3 b 2 c 6 d 4 e 1; 4 f 5 g 8

Language note

The use of the past form in many cases here may feel rather odd, even to advanced learners, simply because there is no correlation between the past form and past time. Understandably, students are more likely to say things like: *~~I wish I have a better job~~*; *~~If only I don't have to walk home~~*. Often students find ways of avoiding such complex structures, eg *It's time to go* (also correct) rather than *It's time you went.*

With some of these forms, *would(n't)* or the past simple standard form are both possible, and often have very similar meanings, eg *I wish you wouldn't / didn't smoke; I'd rather you wouldn't / didn't do that; If only you'd talk less; talked less. Would(n't)* refers to a specific occasion such as *now*, whereas the past simple form refers to a state or repeated behaviour.

As if and *as though* are often followed by present forms, eg *You look as if you've had lots of fun!; You look as though you're enjoying it.* However, when you want to show that something is unreal, a past form is needed: *You treat me as though I was useless*. The present form is also possible, depending on how 'real' it feels to the speaker.

Work on guiding advanced students to a more general understanding of these alternative uses of the past form: to express unreality; to distance the speaker, and so on. Asking students to translate example sentences into their first language can help them to process the language at a deeper level.

5 Put up some of your own completed sentences on the board, trying to make them interesting. Let students ask you more questions about your sentences, if they wish, before they work on their own. Monitor carefully at this point, focusing on accuracy. Then students work in pairs to exchange their ideas, and give further comments.

TEACH GLOBAL THINK LOCAL Alternative procedure

Ask students to write their sentences in exercise 5 anonymously. Then put them into groups of four or five and shuffle up their papers so that they have someone else's sentences.They take turns to read out the sentences, for listeners to try and guess who wrote them. Afterwards, they can ask questions about any points of interest.

G Grammar focus

Refer students to the language summary on unreal past time on page 148.

You can use exercises 1 and 2 on page 149 for:
a) extra practice now, b) homework or c) review later on.

The answers are on page 164 of this Teacher's Book.

Part 2

TEACH GLOBAL THINK LOCAL Lead-in

Put up a list of countries on the board, ones which students will be able to relate to. Ask them to discuss in pairs who they think has the longest working hours and why, eg according to one report: *Korea, Mexico, Japan* (have long hours); *Australia, Spain, UK* (more average); *The Netherlands, France and Belgium* (shorter hours overall). If they are interested in knowing precise facts, ask them to research it for homework.

Reading and Speaking (SB page 104)

1 Before reading, ask students to discuss the questions in pairs. Monitor and have a class discussion about any major differences between students.

2 Students read the three texts and answer the questions in small groups. Prompts like *Which one sounds the most informal, both in language and in subject matter?* could help. If necessary, put up the three genres randomly on the board for them to match. Conduct a feedback session.

1 a lot of people all over the world (still) work long hours
2 internationally agreed maximum number of hours in the working week
3 Students' own answers. Actual sources:
A: press release from ILO (International Labour Office)
B: magazine article from *Forbes*® business
C: article on campaigning website *Four-hour Day*

3 Students in pairs discuss possible meanings of the underlined phrases in *Working Time Around The World*, referring to a dictionary if necessary. Encourage them to record any new phrases. Elicit some examples.

developing and transition countries: those with little industry or access to education, health care, etc, which are moving towards a more technologically developed state

the informal economy: working practices not governed by law

the average employee: worker whose life is similar to that of most people

bad form: behaviour which does not meet with official approval

hang around: wait, with nothing to do

the assembly line: system of manufacturing where each worker or machine is responsible for a particular part of the production process

drudgery: uninspiring work

exhausting recreation: working hard at playing / forcing ourselves to do recreational activities when we are tired

rat race: lifestyle in which people are too busy working to have time to relax and enjoy themselves

4 Students complete the task independently and compare answers in pairs. Take brisk feedback pointing out any useful phrases.

1 A: to make ends meet; B: to satisfy 'form' and gain promotion or salary increase
2 B: workers spend little time with family and hardly ever have a holiday; C: two-income families, both parents work so don't spend time with children
3 not getting promotion or salary rise
4 modern technology, such as computers should save us time and therefore reduce working hours
5 likely to fall into poverty
6 four hours a day, because a minority of workers can produce all we need

5 Students reread the text to locate the answers. In feedback, pick up on any pronunciation related issues, eg linkage in *one in five workers*; the consonant cluster in *fifths* /fɪfθs/; the schwa in 30 per /pə/ cent, and so on.

1 one in five workers	4 some 30 per cent
2 a considerable number	5 two per cent
3 three-fifths	6 thirty million or so

6 Students reflect on the questions alone at first, then discuss them in pairs or groups. Monitor and take notes on points of interest for feedback at the end.

Vocabulary (SB page 104)

1 Students find the eight uses of *get* in text B as quickly as they can, and put up their hand when they have done so. Elicit the answers quickly and then ask students, in pairs, to categorise them.

1 gets up; gets out (of)
2 gets dressed; gets interrupted
3 get to see
4 gets home; gets just three days; getting a promotion

2 In pairs, students match some of the uses of *get* with their one word equivalents. Ask early finishers to write up the answers on the board, and see if others agree.

arrive: get home	receive: get (three days' vacation / a promotion)
be: get (interrupted)	rise: get up
leave: get out	
manage: get to see	

3 Students complete the task and, after checking answers, add an extra ending to each sentence starter. Monitor as they are working and elicit one or two suggestions.

1 c 2 e 3 g 4 f 5 a 6 b 7 d

4 Encourage students to ask each other at least five questions, and to ask follow-on questions for at least three of them. Model an example with a confident student.

TEACH GLOBAL THINK LOCAL **Homework extra**

If your students were interested in the reading text B (SB page 105), they could write a similar description of themself or someone they know incorporating at least five different uses of *get*.

Grammar (SB page 105)

1 This section revises a variety of quantifiers, focusing primarily on form and register.

Start by writing this sentence on the board: *In our country, we tend to work ______ hours in comparison to people like Lee, in South Korea.* (Lee is the man described in text B.) Elicit different possible words that might fit here, eg *few, very few, a large number of.* Ask *Do you know what the grammatical term is for these groups of words?* (quantifiers).

Ask students to read the grammatical information and to answer questions 1–3 before comparing their answers in pairs. Have a class feedback session and write up the different options for question 3 on the board.

1 loads of; a bunch of (*lots of* and *a lot of* may be considered unsuitable too as they are imprecise)
2 all workers: unquantified – anyone who is a worker anywhere
all of the workers: all of a specific group of workers previously mentioned
most women: women is unquantified, so most of all women everywhere
most of the women: most of a specific group previously mentioned
3 huge, large, considerable, small, tiny, growing, significant

2 Do the first sentence as an example, asking students to explain why *several* does not fit grammatically. In pairs, students complete this task giving reasons for their answers. They should also discuss the issues of meaning / register. In feedback, check and pick up on any problems, eg the difference between *few* and *a few*, etc. Then students discuss whether each sentence is true, mixed nationality pairs, if possible.

Incorrect alternatives	
1 several	4 A huge number of
2 A large amount of	5 hardly
3 very much	6 Very little

Correct alternatives

1 *a great deal of*: formal; *loads of*: informal
2 *A great many / A considerable number of*: both formal
3 *lots of*: simple fact; *plenty of*: positive connotations of 'more than enough'
4 *Much*: formal; *A lot of*: informal
5 *virtually no* implies slightly less than *scarcely any*, though meanings are close
6 *Few*: not many at all – negative implication; *A few*: more than *few*, some but not many

Depending on where students live, most, if not all, the sentences are probably true.

Language note

Quantifiers belong to the class of determiners, giving details on quantity about the noun phrase which follows. They can also be used as pronouns, eg *They've got some; Jo has a few*, etc. They also act as pronouns when used with *of*, eg *I've had enough grapes* (*enough* = quantifier) vs *I've had enough of these grapes* (*enough* = pronoun). If another determiner is used, usually an 'of' structure is required with the quantifier, eg *A few of the people; most of my friends*; *either of these apples*. There are a few exceptions to this rule: *all*, *both* and *half*, eg *all (of) my friends; both (of) my cars*; *half (of) the guests*.

The choice of determiner depends on meaning, form / grammar (for example if the noun is countable or uncountable or if it is a question) and also style. The use of *many* or *much* at the start of a sentence / clause, for example, tends to sound fairly formal: *Many people attended the product launch*.

3 Put students into groups of three, in mixed nationality groups, if this is an option. Tell them *Look at the list of topics. Choose which three you wish to discuss*. Then give students five minutes to think about what they are going to say and make notes, if necessary. If you have confident students, then remind them to try and use different quantifiers as they are talking.

G Grammar focus

Refer students to the language summary on quantifiers on page 148.

You can use exercise 3 on page 149 for:
a) extra practice now, b) homework or c) review later on.

The answers are on page 164 of this Teacher's Book.

Part 3

TEACH GLOBAL THINK LOCAL Lead-in

Ask students to (silently) write the word that can precede each of the following words to make a compound noun. Then slowly write up the words on the board, pausing slightly between each one: *cone, island (BrE), warden, accident, lights* and *jam* (traffic).

Then read out the following statistics making notes on the board as you talk, to focus students.

- *The average American, in 2005, spent 38 hours annually stuck in traffic.*
- *In 1969, nearly half of American children walked or biked to school; now just 16 per cent do.*
- *From 1977 to 1995, the number of trips people made on foot dropped by nearly half.*

A recent joke states 'An American pedestrian is someone who has just parked their car.'

Ask students how these statistics compare with their own country; ask them if they often get stuck in traffic: where and when it is worse; what the main causes of congestion are.

Reading (SB page 106)

1 Students work alone and then compare and discuss their sentences in pairs.

2 The two reading texts, taken from the same book, outline the development and history of traffic problems in different parts of the world and some of its effects.

Elicit ideas about the first topic as a class. Then, in pairs, students discuss their predictions. At the end, elicit some ideas, but do not confirm they are right or not.

3 Put students into A/B pairs for them to read and complete the task. Warn them that they will not be able to look at the texts during the actual information exchange. When they are ready, ask students to close their books.

1 tracks only wide enough for one set of wheels, therefore they would be unable to pass
2 furiously driven carts and coaches
3 too fast, they spooked horses and they caused accidents
4 4 mph (about 6 kph)
5 traffic jams, many more people with cars, underground parking garages; the rich travelling by helicopter to avoid road congestion, increased road fatalities
6 political change; economic boom and cheap fuel leading to increased car ownership
7 commercial helicopter pilots; car jockeys – people who are paid to fill up cars in order to use car-pool lanes; road guides, who act as navigators
8 third-leading cause of death in the world

4 Give students time to read the other text and find the evidence. They check answers in pairs before feedback.

> *Traffic Problems* text:
> 1 *Traffic problems … are as old as traffic itself.*
> 2 *… society has struggled to catch up with the implications of mobility …*
> 3 *The larger the cities grew, and the more ways people devised to get around those cities, the more complicated traffic became, and the more difficult to manage.*
> 4 *… the last time the automobile existed at anything like human speed or scale … speeds beyond anything for which their evolutionary history had prepared them.*
>
> *Traffic: A Universal Condition* text:
> 5 *Traffic has become a universal condition …*
> 6 *… once tranquil Tibetan capital of Lhasa now has jams and underground parking garages.*
> 7 *… the wealthy shuttle between the city's more than three hundred helipads rather than brave the legendary traffic.*
> 8 *… the number of people being killed on the road every year is now greater than the total number of vehicles the country was manufacturing annually as recently as 1970.*

5 In pairs, students discuss their own views about their chosen statements. Monitor and discuss any interesting points as a whole class at the end.

Extend your vocabulary (SB page 106)

For a slightly higher challenge, you could do this with books closed. Simply read out the list of words in either British English or American English, whichever they are more familiar with. In pairs, students say the equivalent in the other version of English. Finally, complete the task in the book using a dictionary, if necessary.

car: automobile	number plate: license plate
caravan: trailer	pavement: sidewalk
car park: parking lot	petrol: gasoline
lorry: truck	windscreen: windshield
motorway: highway	

Grammar (SB page 107)

1 This focus looks at comparative structures, including qualifiers used with them.

Do the first example together, selecting the two words which cannot fit in the gap. Then students complete the task alone, before checking in pairs and as a class. Invite students, still in their pairs, to write some new sentences using the words they deleted, explaining why they deleted them, eg *It was **relatively** easy to do the exercise* (*relatively* is not used in comparisons). In feedback, discuss any interesting language points, such as the structure *the more …, the more …*, and the fact that, in sentence c, *by far* and *far and away* are the only ones that can be used with a superlative. See *Language note.*

> **Incorrect alternatives**
> a quite, relatively (*way* is correct in American English)
> b equally, rather
> c at all, far
> d more worse, worst
> e least, the less

2 Students reflect for a moment on the formality of the words. Discuss answers as a class.

> informal: *a bit, a lot, way*
> formal: *a great deal, considerably, infinitely*

3 Do the first sentence as an example. Encourage students to include a strengthening or softening adverb too, where appropriate, as a premodifier. (Sentence 1 already includes the word *far*.) In pairs, students find a suitable comparative structure in each case. Refer them back to exercise 1 to help. Monitor and assist, but highlight any widespread problems at the end, in open class.

> **Possible answers**
> 1 fewer
> 2 (much / far / a great deal, etc) worse, heavier
> 3 (just) as bad
> 4 (much / far, etc) higher than
> 5 the biggest / the greatest
> 6 more congested / more dangerous they will be

4 In pairs, students first add two extra items to each of the four lists. Then, elicit an example comparative for the first list; encourage them at this point to use some of the words from exercise 1, including adverbials such as *nowhere near*, *considerably*, etc. This will raise the challenge.

Language note

When using comparatives, there are many other ways of strengthening or softening the comparison, particularly in spoken English, eg *That car is loads / miles / tons faster than mine*. The most commonly used examples in everyday speech are *a bit* and *a lot*, eg *I'm a bit more relaxed now I've finished that test and I feel a lot happier (than before).*

You can use expressions like *by far* and *by miles* in a comparative, but only at the end of the structure: *the train is more popular (than the bus)* ***by far***. To intensify superlative forms, as well as *by far* and *far and away*, (see Grammar ex 1, SB page 107), you can also use *easily* and *simply*: *The south-western region is easily the most congested (of all).*

The grammar of the word is also a consideration, eg *There were far more students than I expected*. Instead of *far*, you could use *many*, *lots*, *loads*, *several*, etc, but not *much* because *students* is a countable noun. Similarly, for this reason you would say: *There are considerably fewer students*, not *less* students. Nowadays, however, many native English speakers overuse *less*, using it for both countable and uncountable nouns, eg ~~*There's less people here now (than earlier).*~~

G Grammar focus

Refer students to the language summary on comparisons on page 148.

You can use exercises 4 and 5 on page 149 for:
a) extra practice now, b) homework or c) review later on.

The answers are on page 164 of this Teacher's Book.

Speaking (SB page 107)

1 You could approach this speaking task as a brainstorm initially. Books closed, in groups of three, students think of different ways of solving or alleviating traffic problems. Elicit an example to start them off. After a few minutes, students pool their ideas, writing them on the board. Then ask them to compare their ideas with those in exercise 1. Students then work alone, selecting the five best solutions, with sound rationale; it might help if you contextualise the traffic problem first, for example, suggest a nearby city known to have serious traffic problems.

2 In pairs, students compare their ideas, justifying their choices. Remind them before they start to use the language of comparison, where appropriate. Then, they should discuss the three other questions.

TEACH GLOBAL THINK LOCAL Extra activity

Students might benefit from more practice with the expression *the more ..., the more ...*, eg *The more (things) you buy, the more (things) you want*. This structure can be followed by a noun phrase, a subject and verb, an adverb or an adjective, eg *The more you drive, the easier you('ll) find it*. The expression can be used to express insights and home truths (usually with the present simple), but also to give advice (typically with *will*). Ask students, in pairs, to complete four of the following starters. Monitor as they are working and focus on accuracy.

The harder you study, ...; The more English you listen to, ...; The more places you visit, ...; The more you get used to X, ...; The more exercise you do, ...; The more jobs you try, ...; The greater the pollution of our cities, ...

Invite students to share some examples with the whole class. Pay attention to natural pronunciation as they read their sentences. To round off, play a game using this expression. You start with: *The greater the pollution in our cities; the more people with asthma*. Indicate that a volunteer should try to continue, using the second part of the phrase, eg *The more people with asthma, the more cost to the state*, and so on. See how long you can keep the chain going!

Part 4

TEACH GLOBAL THINK LOCAL Lead-in

If possible, first project or show an image of a hive or a close-up of a honeybee (in addition to the photos in the book). Elicit one fact about this insect, eg *honeybees do not hibernate in winter.* Then divide the class into two teams, to play a game in which they receive a point for every correct fact. Give them three minutes to discuss what they know, and to check facts. Then, to start the game, one team gives just one fact about the honeybee. The other team does the same and so on, one fact for each team. The information should be true (as far as you know) and students need to listen carefully, to avoid repeating information and losing a point. The team with the most points wins. If necessary, as you are going along, write up any facts that need verifying; at the end ask for volunteers to check on these pieces of information at home.

Reading (SB page 108)

This reading is an extract from a novel, describing a close encounter with a hive of bees for Lily, one of the main characters.

1 In pairs, students try to describe what is happening in the photos, using the words in the box. If they ask you about any new vocabulary, use the photos to illustrate.

Suggested answer

The bees are working in the hive, filling the honeycomb with honey. The two beekeepers are inspecting one of the frames from the hive, probably to see how much honey there is. They are wearing hats with veils to protect their faces, though interestingly, no gloves.

Background note

Beekeeping is a highly marketable branch in many agricultural countries. It is practised on all continents except Antarctica. In the summer, there can be about 35,000 bees in a hive dropping to about 5,000 in the winter. There are three different types of bees in the hive: the queen bee, whose job it is to lay eggs; the male drone bees who fertilise the eggs, and the female worker bees who do all the jobs in the hive, including collecting pollen, nectar and water. These worker bees are responsible for the vital pollination of plants.

2 Ask students *Have you ever seen a hive close up? Would you like to see one? Why / Why not? Would you feel afraid in this situation?* After a brief discussion, invite students to read the information on Sue Monk Kidd and her novel, before reading the text and answering the comprehension questions 1–4. Let students compare answers in pairs. Discuss any discrepancies or queries as a whole class. Elicit responses to Lily's reaction, asking *Can you understand how she felt? Do you think you would react in the same way or not? What would you do?*

1 watching August examining the frames from the hives and taking out the honeycomb
2 to stay still and send the bees love; yes, she tells the bees silently that she loves them
3 fly around them and then begin to land on Lily's body
4 first she is paralysed with fear, but then relaxes

3 Write up two headings on the board: *Direction* and *Speed*. In pairs, ask students to look at the example sentences taken from the text, and to find a verb or phrase which fits with one of the headings, eg *rushing up* = *speed*. Check answers. Write up interesting verbs and any relevant prepositions on the board, if appropriate, eg *pour out (of a place); collide with sth; bump against / into*, etc.

1 rushing up, in spirals of chaos, straight at my forehead, spun around, began to light on
2 poured out, rushing up, flew, gathering strength till they made soft wind on our faces

4 Let students reflect for a minute on the questions, then put them into pairs or small groups, to discuss them. Encourage students to draw on any personal experiences, eg with pets. Monitor as they talk, and pick up on any points of interest to raise with the whole class at the end.

Listening (SB page 108)

1 Students look at the photos and, in pairs, try to work out why the bees are 'dancing'. If some of the students already know, ask them to listen to their partner's hypotheses first.

2 **3.26** Students listen and check their predictions, completing the information. Check answers with the class.

1 a worker bee that has returned to the honeycomb
2 where a food source is
3 distance and direction to the target food source

 **3.26**

Part 1

Honeybee dancing is one of the most intriguing aspects of bees' biology. The dances are performed by a worker bee that has returned to the honeycomb with pollen or nectar. In essence, the dances constitute a language that 'tells' other workers where the food source is.

When a bee returns to the colony with nectar or pollen that is sufficiently nutritious to warrant a return to the source, she performs a dance on the surface of the honeycomb. The dancer 'spells out' two items of information – distance and direction – to the target food source. Other workers then leave the hive to find the nectar or pollen.

3 **3.27** Refer students to the lines below the two photos in exercise 1. Ask them to listen and label the photos. Play the recording and check answers immediately together.

1 round dance 2 waggle dance

 **3.27**

Part 2

When a food source is very close to the hive, a bee performs a round dance. She does this by first running around in narrow circles and then suddenly reversing direction to her original course. She may repeat the round dance several times at the same location or she may move to another location on the honeycomb to repeat it. After the dance she often distributes food to the bees following her. A round dance, therefore, communicates *distance* ('close to the hive' in this example), but not *direction.*

The waggle dance is performed by bees which are foraging at food sources that are more than 150 metres from the hive. This dance, unlike the round dance, communicates both distance *and* direction. A bee performing a waggle dance runs straight ahead for a short distance, returns in a semicircle to the starting point and runs again through the straight course. Then the waggle dancer makes a semicircle in the opposite direction to complete a full figure of eight circuit. The bee's body, especially the abdomen, wags vigorously from side to side during the straight-line course of the dance. This vibration of the body produces a tail-wagging motion, and at the same time, the bee emits a buzzing sound.

Although the representation of *distance* in the waggle dance is relatively straightforward, the method of communicating *direction* is more complicated. The orientation of the dancing bee during the straight portion of her waggle dance is significant because it represents the angle of the Sun. This indicates to the other bees where the food source is, relative to the Sun.

4 Elicit the first collocation as an example. Then students complete the task independently, before checking in pairs. Elicit what the verb *wag* usually refers to (a dog's tail or someone's finger).

1 c 2 h 3 e 4 d 5 g 6 b 7 a 8 f

5 **3.27** Students listen to match the collocations to the appropriate dance. Ask them to write *W* (for *waggle*) or *R* (for *round*) next to each collocation. If necessary, play the recording once more, before students discuss the details in pairs, using the pictures and the collocations themselves.

round dance: 1c; 3e; 7a
waggle dance: 1c; 4d; 8f; 2h; 6b; 5g

Vocabulary (SB page 109)

1 Elicit what kind of listening genre the bee extracts were taken from (an academic lecture or talk). Tell students you are going to look at register. Refer students to extracts 1–4 and ask *Is this formal or informal language?* (formal). Do the first example together, before students complete the task on their own and then check their answers in pairs. Discuss any differences of opinion at the end. Encourage students to record any formal phrases they would like to experiment with, in their own writing or formal speaking; they should record both the formal version and the informal equivalent in their notebooks.

1 *items*: pieces
In essence: Basically
constitute: make up
2 *sufficiently*: enough
warrant: justify
3 *reversing*: changing
location: place
distributes: gives out
4 *orientation*: position
significant: important
represents: stands for
indicates: shows
relative to: compared with

2 Write up on the board: *Please ______ your shoes.* Ask *Where might you see this notice?* (perhaps at the entrance to someone's house). Elicit both the phrasal verb *take off* and the equivalent single word *remove*. Ask *What is the difference in style?* (the phrasal verb is generally more commonly used and less formal). Then students complete the exercise in pairs. Check answers.

Suggested answers

1 remove (more formal)
2 –
3 swell
4 tolerate / abide (more formal); stand (less formal)
5 discover
6 –
7 invent (more formal)
8 –

TEACH GLOBAL THINK LOCAL Speaking extra

For a lighter, fun activity, and also to consolidate work done in Part 3 on comparatives, invite students to do a *Name the Animal* quiz. In pairs, students write three sentences to describe their chosen animal, using at least one of the comparative forms. Read out an example and encourage students to guess the answer: *It's a very sure-footed animal, which is considerably bigger than a sheep, but nowhere near as big as a cow. It's got a relatively long neck, but it's nothing like as long as a giraffe. It's kept for its wool and meat, as well as for carrying. What is it?* (a llama). Have students do the same for two or more animals. Warn them not to make them too easy or too obscure. Ask both students to write the description down. When they are ready, split the pairs and put students into groups of three to describe their animals to the others.

Speaking (SB page 109)

1 Ask students to look at the three photos at the top of the page. In each case, elicit the animal and what they are doing. Explain that they are going to find out about how animals move and travel. Read the first example and elicit suggestions. Then let students discuss their answers in pairs. Don't confirm any ideas at this point.

2 Put students into AB pairs and refer them to their respective pages. Warn them that they should read and remember, as they will not be able to refer to the information when telling their partner later. Monitor and respond to any queries, and also have dictionaries to hand. When students are ready, ask them to close their books to relay the information. At the end, ask students which facts they found surprising.

Suggested answers

1 Kangaroos: feet too big, legs unsuited to walking, four toes, fourth toe propels them off ground, strong elastic tendons in legs, hop at 40–50 km an hour
2 Birds: migrate to find food, to breed in longer daylight, away from predators
3 Ants: store and activate memory images, poor eyesight, follow other ants' chemical trail
4 Bats: use sonar sound or 'echolocation', use voice box or click tongues and interpret resulting echoes, can hear minimal differences in sound
5 Snakes: muscles and scales push them off ground, four different types of movement using different parts of body – head, tail, belly
6 Salmon: ability to detect Earth's magnetic field, can sense direction, then use sense of smell when near target area

TEACH GLOBAL THINK LOCAL Homework extra

Ask students to pick one of the animals in Speaking exercise 1, or an animal of their choice, and do some research for homework, in preparation for a mini 'lecture' (two to four minutes long), like the honeybee talk (SB page 108). The details should focus on one or two aspects which they find particularly interesting, eg the way they move, their diet, habitat, any special adaptations (how they keep warm / cool, etc). Ask them to try and use a formal style, but to avoid just copying chunks from the internet. Next lesson, put them in groups of three or four to give their mini talks.

Function globally: being interviewed

These lessons in *Global* are designed to provide students with immediately useful functional language. They all follow a similar format.

Warm up (SB page 110)

Aim: to introduce the topic via a quick speaking task or picture work.

Tips:

- You could start by asking students to tell their partner about their last interview: *When / Where was it? Who was it with? What do you remember about it?*
- Do not over-correct here, especially in speaking activities.
- Decide which exercise in the *Warm up* you will do whole-class feedback on.
- Put any useful language which arises during the activities up on the board.

TEACH GLOBAL THINK LOCAL **Alternative procedure**

For exercise 3, exploit this task further by asking students to work in pairs or small groups and to select a job from the list which interests them. Then they decide on a list of qualities and skills ideally needed for that job. Tell them that they have six minutes to do so. Then students read out their choices to the class, if necessary giving justifications.

Listening (SB page 110)

Aim: to present the functional language in context via a conversation or series of conversations.

Tips:

- Play the recording all the way through for each task (there are always two tasks). (Tracks 3.28–3.29)
- Let students compare their notes in pairs before checking answers as a class.
- Encourage students to read the audioscripts for homework, exploiting them for useful language.
- In class feedback, elicit responses to exercise 3 about the interviewee, but also reflect on the performance of the interviewer: *Was it a good interview? What questions were missing?*
- Invite personal responses, if appropriate: *How did this example interview differ from one that you have had recently?*

1

1 receptionist in a medical institution of some kind (she mentions patients)

2 teacher

3 Students' own answers.

 **3.28**

1

Part 1

A: So, Mrs Blackburn, thanks very much for coming today. Would you just like to take a seat?

B: Thank you.

A: And … um … yes, perhaps you could start by saying why you're interested in the job?

B: Well, I wanted to do a job which meant being involved with people, dealing with people, their problems …

A: Yes.

B: … responding to people's needs and I thought this job was really ideal, and that, you know, I was ideally qualified for it really.

A: And what previous experience do you have of this kind of work?

B: Well, I haven't actually done a receptionist's job before, but … um …

A: Right.

B: … I've done similar kinds of jobs, I mean, I used to teach actually before I got married …

A: Aha.

B: … and then, you know, I wanted to get back into a job that meant I would be, you know, dealing with people, but I just felt I didn't want to actually have to go back into the classroom, I wanted to be just using my people skills in a different context.

A: Right, well, in that case can you perhaps tell me about a problem you solved, or, or something you achieved in your last job, when you were teaching?

B: Well, I … you'd often have to be very tactful with the parents, you know, you might be telling them something that they don't really want to hear. I did a lot of that and then obviously, you know, when you're a mum, you know, you have to also, you know, juggle a lot of things, you have to be good at paying attention to lots of different things going on at the same time and people all having demands to make at the same time and so on …

A: Yes, so multitasking basically.

B: Multitasking, but also you know paying attention to several different people simultaneously …

A: Very good.

B: … without alienating anybody …

A: Oh right.

B: … and making them feel that you are actually responding to their needs.

A: Well, that all sounds very good, multitasking and diplomacy and tact. What other qualities do you think you can bring to this position?

B: Well, I have quite good IT skills. I understand there's a bit of IT work. You have to enter things on the computer, look people's records up and so on …

A: Yes.

B: … and I'm quite good at that, I, you know, spent years doing freelance work involving those skills so I thought that would be interesting too, you know, mix the two things together …

A: Um, let me see. Could you perhaps tell me about your strengths and weaknesses, as a person?

B: Let's see, well, I think I've already described my strengths, you know, I'm quite good at multitasking and I'm good at dealing with people.

A: Of course, yes.

B: My weaknesses, um, I find it a little bit difficult I suppose if people get very aggressive …

A: Understandably.

B: Yes, so … um … so yes, I obviously, that might, that could be a problem if I had to deal with a very difficult patient who was … who was violent …

A: And just to finish off with, what are your career goals, I mean, where do you see yourself going?

B: Well, I'd like to get into human resource management ultimately actually, but I just think that a job like this would … um … hone my skills a bit, you know, be a good place to start.

2

1 F (*… we'll be giving you a call tomorrow morning to let you know if you've been successful.*)

2 T

3 T

4 F (*… we won't go over your 37.5 hours …*)

3.29

Part 2

A: Right, well, thank you very much, Mrs Blackburn. Are there any questions you'd like to ask me?

B: Um, yes, well, what's the next stage in the process? I mean, will I get feedback from you, will I hear from you quite soon?

A: Well, we're going to, um, make our decision by the end of today, basically, and we'll be giving you a call tomorrow morning to let you know if you've been successful.

B: Oh that's wonderful, yes. OK, and if I were to get the job, is there any kind of mentoring to sort of see me into the job?

A: Yes, well, our current receptionist isn't going to be leaving for a month …

B: Oh that's wonderful.

A: Yes, so it would be very helpful if you could come in and work with her, shadow her, for a week.

B: Right, yes. And in … in, what would you expect of me in the job, you know, in the first six months or so, what would you be wanting me to do?

A: Well, obviously you'll receive a full job description so … but we wouldn't throw you completely in at the deep end, … we'd like you to become familiar with the main tasks and duties and then we'll build it up from there. There'll be some additional duties after the first initial, let's say, first two or three months …

B: Right OK.

A: … we'll increase the amount of work that you have to do.

B: Great, OK.

A: But we won't go over your 37.5 hours, we promise.

B: Right, so, yes, yes …

Language focus (SB page 110)

Aim: to draw students' attention to the items of functional language.

Tips:

- Let students work alone at first, before comparing answers in pairs and listening to the recording to check. (Tracks 3.30–3.32)
- Give students time to make a note of any new phrases they particularly like and would like to incorporate into their repertoire.
- Drill some of the questions, to ensure students sound polite (which is essential, given the context), eg exercise 1, sentences 1, 3, 5 and exercise 2, sentences 2, 3, 6 and 8.

1

See audioscript below.

3.30

1

Perhaps you could start by saying why you are interested in the job?

2

What previous experience do you have of this kind of work?

3

Can you perhaps tell me about a problem you solved, or or, something you achieved in your last job?

4

What other qualities do you think you can bring to this position?

5

Could you perhaps tell me about your strengths and weaknesses, as a person?

6

Are there any questions you'd like to ask me?

2

Interviewer: 1, 5, 7 Interviewee: 2, 3, 4, 6, 8

3

Answer 1: question 5
Answer 2: question 1
Answer 3: question 7
Answer 4: question 2
Answer 5: question 8
Answer 6: question 6

3.31–3.32

A: So tell me a little bit about what you like to do outside of work. What are your outside interests?

B: Well, I have a close group of friends and we play golf on the weekend and I like to go swimming every morning before I come into work and seeing as this job starts in the afternoon I think that's … it's perfect for me there.

A: Why did you want to leave your present job?

B: Well, I just don't feel like it was … I think it was constricting me, holding me back from what I could really achieve so to come here I feel would just give me that extra push.

A: Good. And do you have any particular career goals, like can I ask you where you see yourself in ten years' time?

B: I don't really think that far along … after five or six years I'm sure I'll start to think about the next step, but other than that I'm more than happy coming into this job here.

A: Well, thank you very much and do you have any questions for me?

B: Yes, I was just wondering, what's the next stage in this process? Will I receive feedback from this interview I've just done?

A: Yes. Well, we have several more people to interview and we will definitely get back in touch with you either by email or letter. There may be a second interview if we decide that we are interested in what you have to offer.

B: And when I first start will I be given a mentor to oversee my development?

A: Yes, definitely, that usually happens for the first six months.

B: And in terms of the first six months, for those six months to a year, is there anything specific that will be expected of me?

A: Just to continue with the smooth running of the establishment and to make sure that staff and customers are happy.

Pronunciation (SB page 110)

Aim: to focus students on a particular aspect of pronunciation of the target phrases.

Tips:

- Play the recording two or three times, if necessary. (Track 3.33)
- At this level, try to promote good all-round pronunciation including stress, intonation and linking. This also raises the challenge for students.
- Use students with exemplary pronunciation to act as models to help others in the class.
- Elicit other possible examples from students, eg *Let me think*, *Oh, that's an interesting question.*

When we need time to think before answering a tricky question.

Speaking (SB page 110)

Aim: to allow students an opportunity to use this language in a meaningful, real-world context.

Tips:

- Give students time to prepare this activity; they could note down some possible questions before they start, referring back to the earlier exercises.
- Give students an idea of stage-timing: tell them they have three minutes for preparation, and four minutes for each interview.
- Before they start, elicit some suggestions for evaluating each others' interview performance, eg attitude, responses, suitability for the job.
- As students are roleplaying, monitor and make notes on any problem areas, including pronunciation-related aspects, for later group feedback.
- If time allows, ask students to repeat the task, but with a new partner.

Global English

These lessons in *Global* have two main goals: 1) to give you and your students interesting information about English and language in general; 2) to provide students with practice in different kinds of reading comprehension tasks that they are likely to encounter in future study, for example in exams.

TEACH GLOBAL THINK LOCAL **Lead-in**

Ask students to think of any examples of 'ungrammatical English' that they have heard or read, for example, the use of the apostrophe, the past simple instead of the past participle, eg *I've swam in that pool*. Invite them to share their examples with the whole class.

Warm up (SB page 111)

Aim: to engage students with the topic, and highlight potentially difficult vocabulary in the text.

Tips:

- Students discuss the questions in groups of three.
- For question 1, encourage students to try to justify their answers.
- Invite students to share suggestions with the class.

Reading (SB page 111)

Aim: to provide students with interesting information about English, and reading exam practice skills.

Tips:

- There are two tasks. The first focuses on the gist of the passage. The second is a more difficult task, similar to reading exam questions.
- The third exercise raises students' awareness about a language feature.
- After completing exercises 1 and 2, invite a personal reaction to the text. Ask *Did you find anything interesting or surprising?*
- After doing exercise 3, ask *Do you, as advanced speakers, feel you could use the present continuous in this way and sound sufficiently convincing? Or do you think you would sound as if you were 'making a mistake'?*
- Elicit any examples of the present continuous being used with state verbs, which students have personally heard or read.
- This language is not tested or reviewed in future units, which means you have more flexibility with this material as to when and where you use it.

1

1 Vocabulary 2 Pronunciation 3 Grammar

2

1 new words travel quickly, especially via the internet
2 by using corpora
3 both
4 use with state verbs, eg to describe states of mind
5 I'm knowing; I'm understanding

3

1 *feel*; *are feeling*: continuous
2 *love*; *'m loving*: either feels correct
3 *is*; *is being*: continuous
4 *have*; *are having*: continuous
5 *understand*; *'m understanding*: simple
6 *doesn't miss*; *isn't missing*: both

TEACH GLOBAL THINK LOCAL Reading extra

Ask students to scour the text and find examples of comparatives or of language showing contrast, *eg Pronunciation moves rather more slowly; And grammar moves slowest of all; … it became increasingly frequent; Fifty years on, we are more likely to hear …* Put them on the board and then ask students, in pairs, to think of alternative ways of saying the same thing; ask students to change or insert softeners or strengtheners too.

Speaking (SB page 111)

Aim: for students to relate the material in the reading to their own language, culture and experiences.

Tips:

- Put students into groups of three. If you have a mixed nationality class, then ensure that students with different languages are working together.
- For the last question, ensure that you have one or two meaningful examples ready, relating to your students' first language(s).
- Conduct a whole-class feedback session on any points of interest.

As you go through these *Global English* lessons in the book, don't be afraid to ask students' opinions and reactions to the information in the text: *Which do you find interesting? Do you know of similar experiences or facts in your language or other languages?*

Writing: a proposal

These lessons in *Global* are designed to provide students with extended writing practice. They all follow a similar format.

Reading (SB page 112)

Aim: to provide a sample text for students to analyse.

TEACH GLOBAL THINK LOCAL Pre-reading activity

Put the following pairs of words on the board. In pairs, ask students to discuss which element in each pair they associate with Beijing, the capital of China, giving reasons.

cars / bicycles	*red / black*	*historical / modern*
big / small	*quiet / bustling*	*interesting / uninteresting*
hot / cold		

Pick up on any points of interest. Find out if anyone has been to Beijing and if they would like to visit or not. Focus on how populated and busy it is (around 20 million people live there). Elicit problems associated with heavy urbanisation, eg *pollution, traffic problems*.

Tips:

- The first exercise focuses on gist and the others ask students to read individual parts more closely.
- Ask students to read the text and complete each exercise individually, before checking answers in pairs.
- Conduct a whole-class feedback session on each of the three exercises in turn. Write up the list of features of the proposal, in exercise 3, on the board, to focus students on the writing genre being studied.
- Ask *Have you ever written a proposal, either in English or in your first language? When / For what purpose / For whom did you write it?* Invite students to share their experiences with the class.

1

heading 2: A proposal for improving conditions for cyclists in Beijing.

2

1 c 2 a 3 b

3 Possible answers

Paragraph b

1 *Traffic conditions in Beijing are very dangerous … At present there is no legislation on the use of bicycle helmets, reflective vests or lights …*
2 *large population … neither feasible nor realistic for the city council to enforce* [use of safety equipment]
3 [The council] *could subsidise the purchase of such equipment … hold more educational events …*
4 [It would] *encourage more cyclists to invest in their own safety …* [and] *increase cyclists' awareness of traffic rules and the possible consequences of breaking them.*

Paragraph c

1 *Most current cycling lanes in Beijing are built alongside the traffic lanes … a dangerous environment for cyclists*
2 *space limitations* [in central urban areas], [need for] *funding and … resources*
3 *… the council should build special lanes for cyclists …*
4 [It would] *both promote the general safety of cyclists in Beijing and also encourage more people to choose a bicycle … Demand for private cars would thus decrease, and … Beijing would* [have] *a more pleasant environment for residents and tourists alike.*

Linking ideas: results (SB page 112)

Aim: to highlight and focus on a particular aspect of language that students can use to improve their writing.

Tips:

- Let students work in pairs or small groups, before you check answers in open class.
- Refer students to the *Language note*, with reference to the use of *thus*, *therefore* and *hence*.
- Highlight the use of the comma after some of the linkers, eg those used at the very beginning of a sentence such as *consequently*, *as a result*, etc.
- At the end, elicit the purpose of this focus on linkers within this genre of proposals: this language is often associated with problems and solutions.

1

1 Accordingly; As a result; Because of this; Consequently; For this reason
2 so
3 All of them are possible here.

only link expression: *so* (the only conjunction)

2

therefore (paragraph a)

hence; *and so*; *Consequently* (paragraph b)

thus; *whereas*; *In this way*; *and so*; *As a result* (paragraph c)

3 Possible answers

1 As a result, very few people cycle to work.
2 The council should therefore increase the number of street lights as a matter of urgency.
3 hence the increased number of accidents.
4 More people would thus be encouraged to abandon their cars and invest in a cycle.
5 thus creating a dangerous environment for cyclists.

Writing skills: impersonal style (SB page 113)

Aim: to give students a chance to develop their writing through various different micro skills.

Tips:

- Clearly explain the focus and do an example with the students before asking them to continue on their own.
- For exercise 1, give students time to locate the phrases and then to complete the task. You could help by writing up which paragraphs the answers can be found in.
- Let students check their answers in pairs or small groups, before you check answers in open class.
- After doing exercise 2, ask *Which of these 'depersonalising' strategies do you already use in your writing? Are these same techniques also used in your language?*

1

1 *it is vital that more should be done*

2 *Improving conditions for cyclists in Beijing should therefore be a high priority.*

3 *At present there is no legislation*

4 *the situation could certainly be improved in suburban areas or rural areas*

5 *Demand for private cars would thus decrease*

2

a 1, 4 b 3 c 1 d 2 e 5

Preparing to write (SB page 113)

Aim: to give students time to brainstorm ideas for the writing task.

Tips:

- Provide one or two additional, more localised topics too as options for the written proposal, if you can.
- Ask students to make notes here, but not to begin writing.
- Ask students to organise their notes using the framework: *problem, possible solutions, possible outcomes.*
- Monitor as students are discussing and taking notes, to see if they have sufficient ideas. If necessary, ask pairs to share their ideas with other pairs, to provide more material for their writing.
- Remind students to try and use the language in *Useful language*.
- Refer students back to the language of cause and consequence (SB page 88) which might also be useful.
- Remind students that they should endeavour to incorporate some of the language from Unit 9, such as unreal past, comparatives and quantifiers, eg *If there were more places available to walk safely, there would no doubt be considerably more pedestrians in our towns.*

Writing (SB page 113)

Aim: to give students practice in more extended writing tasks.

Tips:

- This section can be done as homework.
- Remind students to refer back to the model text when writing.
- Ask students to check their work carefully before they hand it in.
- Before students hand in their work, they should work in groups of three to show their work to one another. Ask readers to try and identify the problems, solutions and outcomes within the text.
- Tell students that you will be assessing their writing using the following criteria: clarity of organisation; range of grammar and syntax; appropriate range of relevant vocabulary and phrases, including comparatives and quantifiers; style; accuracy.

Study skills

Improving listening (SB page 113)

TEACH GLOBAL THINK LOCAL

Pre-speaking

As an introduction to the topic, ask students to listen to the following task: *Think of a recent time when you were listening to a native or fluent English speaker and you struggled to understand parts of what they were saying. Which of the following did you do: Did you pretend you understood? Did you use strategies to help yourself understand, such as the context? Did you directly ask the speaker to talk more slowly, to explain or repeat?*

Students discuss the incident and the strategies they used, in groups of three. Elicit some examples.

1 Ask students to read the statements and to tick the ones that are true for them. Then students compare answers in pairs. Elicit some of their listening difficulties as a whole class. When students have aired some common problems, ask them to read the advice in the box in exercise 1. Invite students to share their reactions to this with the class.

2 Books closed. Tell students that later they are going to read some concrete suggestions on how to improve and practise their listening skills. Elicit a couple of possible suggestions. Put them into groups of three and have them predict the kind of hints they are about to read: they should write down a list of at least five suggestions per group. Monitor and note down any strategies that seem interesting, particularly if they are not listed in exercise 2. Ask each group to share their two best hints with the whole class. Then students read and compare their own list with that given in exercise 2. At the end, encourage them to add any of their own to the list. Finally, ask *Which of these strategies have you already used at some point? Which ones might you try in the future?*

TEACH GLOBAL THINK LOCAL

Extra activity

You could ask students to reflect on the listenings in the last two or three units. Ask *Were there any you can remember as being difficult? Why did you feel that?*

Ask students if they would like to try the last suggestion given on the list as a whole class: *Listen to a very short piece …* Let students choose one of the listenings from the unit, deciding on whether they want a monologue or a dialogue, eg the lecture on different societies (SB page 102) or part of the job interview (SB page 110). A student could be put in charge of the audio equipment, playing and replaying as required by his/her peers.

At the end, ask students to share websites that could be exploited for this sort of 'dictation' exercise, where students can listen repeatedly if necessary, eg podcasts.

UNIT 10 Local & Global

Coursebook

Unit 10	Language	Texts	Communication skills
Part 1 SB page 114	Extend your vocabulary Collocations with *road*	Reading & Speaking *Isolarion*	Speaking Your neighbourhood Writing Your local journey
Part 2 SB page 116	Extend your vocabulary *have* Grammar & Pronunciation Plurals and number	Speaking & Reading *Why Eat Locally?* Listening Food choices	Speaking & Reading *Why Eat Locally?* Speaking Food debate Grammar & Pronunciation /s/ and /z/
Part 3 SB page 118	Grammar & Pronunciation Inversion Stress and rhythm	Listening Globalisation and football	Speaking & Vocabulary Globalisation Speaking The World Cup
Part 4 SB page 120	Vocabulary Using technology	Reading *A Treatise on the Astrolabe*	Speaking Technological inventions Writing A technical manual
Function globally SB page 122	Making proposals and suggestions Listening to a meeting to discuss proposed government cuts Roleplaying a meeting to discuss common interests		
Global voices SB page 123	Memories of places Language focus: *the thing is* Discussing local areas and how they have changed		
Writing SB page 124	A website entry Writing skills: register Linking ideas: alternatives and examples Describing a place		
Study skills SB page 125	Celebrating your achievements		

Additional resources

eWorkbook	Interactive and printable grammar, vocabulary, listening and pronunciation practice Extra reading and writing practice Additional downloadable listening and video material
Teacher's Resource Disc	Communication activity worksheets to print and photocopy, review material, test, and video with worksheet
Go global Ideas for further research	**Local** Students find the official website for their town or city. They report back to the class what information it contained, how easy it was to navigate around the site and its strengths and weaknesses. **Global** Students look at the www.fifa.com/worldcup official website, and report which global brand sponsors they found, and, in the news section they report back to the class on the latest news and what they found out in the *About FIFA* section. What are their views on the site?

Part 1

TEACH GLOBAL THINK LOCAL Lead-in

As a lead-in, and a follow-on from *Study skills, Improving listening* (SB page 113), give your students a picture dictation of an imaginary high street. Prior to the lesson, if possible, draw yourself a finished version to refer to, and script your description, as you may need to repeat parts of it. Draw a very basic sketch of this on the board, with just three or four places or landmarks already drawn and labelled, eg the butcher's (represented by a small square shape), a small park, a church (or other place of worship) and a bus stop. Ask students to first copy the unfinished map, then listen and draw the different places you describe, *eg In the middle of the park there is a historic fountain; Diagonally opposite the butcher's, going away from the church, is a health-food shop* … Decide whether or not to allow students to interrupt you to ask for clarification. At the end, students compare their maps in pairs. Ask one or two students to come to the board and complete the drawing, for students to check their own.

Speaking (SB page 114)

1 Books closed. Tell students you will read out a list of 13 different places to be found on a high street, which they should try and remember. When you finish, in pairs, students try and recall as many as possible before checking the list in exercise 1. Clarify vocabulary, if necesssary, eg *pawn shop*. Then students discuss the question about their own neighbourhood.

2 To raise interest, you could start by telling students about a local shop that you particularly like, giving reasons. Then let students continue the discussion in pairs. At the end, invite them to share information about any unusual-sounding shops with the whole class.

TEACH GLOBAL THINK LOCAL Language note

The rule regarding the possessive form in business and shops, eg *the butcher's (shop), the hairdresser's (salon), the doctor's (surgery)* is one of those which tends to be overlooked by some native speakers, who might write a note *Gone to the estate agents* instead of *Gone to the estate agent's.* However, this is regarded as grammatically incorrect by some.

Reading and Speaking (SB page 114)

1 This reading describes a very colourful street in Oxford, in the UK, which illustrates global influences on a local scale. To start off, you could show students some traditional scenes of Oxford, and elicit what they know about this historic city. Then students look at the title and the images in the text. Tell them that these pictures are actually from Oxford and elicit adjectives to describe them, eg *cultural, cosmopolitan, rich, lively*. Elicit their predictions about what the author will say about this area in his book.

2 Students read the text and, in pairs, discuss how it compares with their own neighbourhoods.

3 Refer students to phrases in a–f. Ask them to locate them in the text and try to work out what they mean, using the context to help, and dictionaries if necessary. Then do sentence 1 together, asking students to underline the italicised option which is closer to the meaning of the bulleted phrase, *in its heyday*. Students complete the task in pairs. Check answers in a whole-class feedback session. When you reach sentence 5, ask *Which institution do you think the author is referring to?* (the University of Oxford).

1 at its height
2 still attracts
3 personal
4 has not changed much
5 an extremely large number
6 mirrors

4 In pairs, students choose one of the questions to discuss. At the end, invite them to share any interesting points with the whole class. As students talk, write any useful phrases up on the board.

TEACH GLOBAL THINK LOCAL Reading extra

If your students enjoy memory tests, ask them to read the second half of the second paragraph in the text *Isolarian*, where the different types of shops are listed, starting from the words *sari shops*. Give them two minutes to read and try to remember the shops. Then, in pairs, with books closed, they should try and recall as many of the types of shops and outlets as they can, writing them down. The pair with the longest list wins! Let them check their answers with the book.

Extend your vocabulary (SB page 115)

1 Books closed. Ask students *What can branch into two, climb, cross, fork or lead to somewhere?* Invite them to raise their hand if they know the answer. Repeat the question slowly and, if necessary, add: *It can be bumpy, congested or winding* (a road). Then students complete the exercise on their own, before comparing answers in pairs. Check answers together. Check the pronunciation of *winding* /waɪndɪŋ/ and explain that windy /'waɪndi/ can also be used in British English.

1 goes up: climb
goes across: cross
goes to: lead
2 divides into two parts: fork
into two or more parts: branch
3 goes by the sea: coastal
there is lots of traffic: congested
4 it has a loose surface: dirt
isn't smooth: bumpy
isn't straight: winding

2 Do an example together, then ask students to work independently to complete the four sentences appropriately. Monitor as they are working and ensure that students are using the target words accurately, eg choosing appropriate prepositional phrases such as *The second road is a bumpy, coastal road which branches into two when it meets the sea.*

3 In pairs, students take turns to read their sentences out to each other. Their partner should select the road they would prefer to take giving reasons for their choice. Elicit some examples at the end.

TEACH GLOBAL THINK LOCAL

Extra activity

If you think your students might respond well, take one student's descriptions of the three roads and write them up on the board. Then ask students to do a 'psychoanalysis' interpretation in pairs: they should decide what each road represents in metaphoric terms, eg *a bumpy coastal road* is a road full of highs as well as lows. If you choose to do this activity, monitor it closely to ensure that it's kept at a light-hearted level, and that none of the descriptions get too personal or uncomfortable for the students.

Writing (SB page 115)

1 Ask students to draw a sketch of an interesting area nearby, and to label the key elements of interest. If they cannot think of anywhere local, they can select an alternative place that is familiar to them.

2 Give students sufficient time to write their descriptions or set the writing stage for homework. Encourage students to use a range of descriptive language to make their writing appealing and interesting to read.

3 In pairs, students read and comment on each others' descriptions, saying what they have learnt and what they would like to see. You could display their work around the classroom for the whole class to read.

Part 2

TEACH GLOBAL THINK LOCAL

Lead-in

Bring to class some labels from different food products, eg a tin of beans, a box of fish fillets. Give the labels out to pairs or groups of three. Ask them to read and find out as much information as they can about the product: *the ingredients, artificial additives; the sell-by date; the source country; the number of calories,* etc. At the end, ask students to summarise the main information to the class.

Speaking and Reading (SB page 116)

1 Encourage students, in pairs, to discuss the questions about a recent meal. Elicit any interesting answers.

2 Write the words *omnivore*, *carnivore* and *herbivore* up on the board. Elicit what they mean and clarify that the *-vore* suffix characterises 'eaters'. Slowly write up the word *locavore*, eliciting suggestions as to what this means. Students then read the questions and the text. They compare their answers in pairs before a whole-class feedback session. Ask *Is this information new to you? Did you find anything surprising?* At the end, you could quickly highlight that this is written in American English, inviting students to find the clues: *globalization* (*globalisation*) and *centers* (*centres*), *checkout counter* (*checkout* or *till*).

1 2,414 km
2 Food is often transported from the area where it is grown to distribution centres, and then sent back across the country to supermarkets.
3 Because when they buy food, people don't have to pay for things such as air pollution and loss of family farms.
4 Many children don't know where food comes from or how it is produced.

3 Put students into groups of three to discuss the questions. Early finishers can consider what sort of projects might help school children to reflect more on food sourcing and production, eg cooking, growing food themselves, analysis of food products in science, understanding food labels, etc.

Listening (SB page 116)

1 **3.34–3.38** This listening text comprises five monologues, in which speakers talk about their own food choices. Before listening, students, in pairs, take turns to briefly describe each of the people a–h in one or two sentences. Do the first one together. (*A vegan is a person who doesn't eat any food derived from animals, including milk, eggs, etc.*) After that, students listen to the recording and match them with the speakers. Ask a student to write the answers on the board, for students to self-check.

1 f 2 c 3 g 4 e 5 b

3.34–3.38

1

Yeah, it can be a bit of a hassle, eating, just because of my schedule with lectures, university and stuff, but I do a big shop at the supermarket once a week. Stock up on easy stuff really, ready meals and processed food, you know, pizza, lasagne and stuff. Stick it in the freezer. I do get some fruit, you know, just to nibble on between lectures, but I'm often on the move, moving from lecture to tutorial, so I'll eat on the move and just grab whatever I can really. I mean, I would like to eat more healthily, but just can't be bothered really sometimes.

2

I tend to buy my food from farmers' markets and local shops. I like to buy local and organic seasonal food from the area where I live. This can of course create problems sometimes because there's never enough data to actually tell you where the food was sourced from and also sometimes it can be difficult to stick to your principles, you know, when you're travelling, for instance, I was on a business trip recently and I had to, I had to buy … well, I didn't have to, but I did, I bought a coffee from a chain coffee shop and I had absolutely no choice really in the matter about where the coffee had come from and it had clearly travelled halfway around the world.

3

I'm not particularly picky about food. I mean, I eat most things, you know, like dairy and meat, but definitely no offal, I don't like offal. And all vegetables and fruit, well, most fruits, but not strawberries because I've got an allergy to them. I usually get a rash if I eat them and symptoms similar to a cold so like watery eyes and a runny nose. I mean, worst case scenario like my throat swells up if it's really bad and I have trouble breathing.

4

I haven't eaten meat or fish for over 20 years now and I love cooking. There's so much to choose from with vegetables and pulses. Not eating meat isn't a problem except when I'm travelling and I have to grab something quickly. That sometimes can be a bit problematic. I did consider becoming a vegan at one point, but that would have meant not eating cheese, milk, butter or any dairy and I didn't think I could go that far to be quite honest. I, at one point, toyed with the idea of not wearing any animal products, like wool from sheep for clothes, or leather for shoes. I even considered not eating any honey, but that I think is a little extreme so I'm quite happy as I am.

5

Absolutely, I mean, I agree that producers should get a better deal, be paid a fair price, to increase their standards of living and get more control over their lives. That's what I think. I've always thought that and that's why I never buy chocolate or coffee, bananas, anything that doesn't display a *Fair Trade* logo. Look, the *Fair Trade* it enables producers to invest in more environment-friendly practices and improve their lives so I want to be a part of that.

2 Do the first example together as a class – they do not need to listen again at this point but should simply refer back to exercise 1 and draw logical conclusions. Ask students to work alone and remind them that they will not need to use three of the statements. When they have finished, they compare answers in pairs before listening to the recording again.

1 e 2 f 3 h 4 a 5 c

3 This exercise requires students to listen very attentively for specific words uttered naturally and fluently. Encourage students, in pairs, to try and predict the missing words before listening. At the end, ask them to discuss how to say the words in a more formal way. Check answers in a whole-class feedback session.

1 hassle – problem
2 Stick – Put
3 grab – take and eat quickly
4 (I can't be) bothered; I'm too lazy to …

4 Ask students to reflect for a moment on their own food choices, either at this point in their lives or in the past. Point out that they could also talk about what they think they should do, even if they do not do it currently. As an example, tell students about your own food choices, or those of someone you know well. Ask *Do you agree or disagree with the speakers in exercises 1 and 2? In what way?*

Extend your vocabulary (SB page 116)

1 Challenge students to give you at least five or more food / drink expressions with *have*. Remind them to keep to collocations, eg *have some broccoli*.

Possible answers

have breakfast, a snack, a drink, lunch (dinner, etc)

2 First of all, ask students to read sentences 1–6 and underline the *have* expressions. Check students understand the expression *to have high hopes for sth or sb*, eliciting another possible sentence. Ask students to complete the sentences on their own before comparing them in pairs. Monitor and pick up on any errors of form or use, writing any relevant language on the board, eg *have a go at doing sth*.

TEACH GLOBAL THINK LOCAL

Speaking extra

Put up these questions on the board:

1) *Do you think your national diet is healthy or unhealthy?*
2) *Are food trends changing in your country?*
3) *What foods are grown and produced in your country?*
4) *Are there many diet-related health problems in your country, eg heart problems, obesity, diabetes?*

Put students into small groups to discuss the questions. Elicit any points of interest. Pick up on any food or diet-related words and phrases, which you can put on the board.

Grammar and Pronunciation (SB page 117)

1 Dictate a list of words at a fast pace and ask students to quickly write the plural: *horse, pig, deer, chicken, rabbit, sheep, tooth, person, problem, crisis, police, television, computer, data*. Check answers and put the irregular plural nouns on the board: *deer, sheep, teeth, people, crises, police, data*. Then focus students' attention on sentences a–e and have them answer the two questions at the start. Point out that they should read the bullet-pointed grammar notes to check their answers. Clarify any problems or queries.

1 *sheep* and *clothes* are plural nouns, no singular – we usually use *piece of clothing*
2 *data*: plural noun + singular verb; *family*: singular noun + plural verb; *percentage*: singular noun + plural verb

2 Do the first example together, eliciting the odd one out and the rule for plural formation of the other nouns. In pairs, students complete the exercise, always giving reasons for their choices. Discuss answers in a whole-class feedback session. See *Language note*.

1 pancake – the others don't change in the plural
2 products – the others don't have a singular form
3 lamb – the others have irregular plural forms
4 potato – the others form the plural only with *-s*
5 tennis – the others change from *-is* to *-es*

TEACH GLOBAL THINK LOCAL

Language note

The plural form *fishes* does exist, but *fish* is far more usual.

Lambs is the plural form of the countable noun *lamb* when referring to the animals. However, when referring to the meat, *lamb* is uncountable, and therefore has no plural form.

Newer words which end in *-o* do not add *e* (unlike older words such as *potato* or *tomato*). Such words are more recent additions to the English language and are usually borrowed from other languages. Nouns that end in *-o* preceded by a vowel do not add *e* either, eg *radios, zoos*.

3 Students quietly read through the task to themselves before saying the words to each other in pairs and answering the question. Confirm answers quickly.

words that end in *-oes* = /z/
-is words whose plural ends in *-es* = /z/
clothes, species, headquarters, premises, lambs = /z/
pancakes, products, works = /s/

TEACH GLOBAL THINK LOCAL

Language note

There are several food and drink items generally considered uncountable, which can sometimes be viewed as countable, and therefore have a plural form, such as *cheese / cheeses; wine / wines; fruit / fruits*, eg *I went to the food fair and there were loads of different cheeses that you could taste; There were also many fine wines on display.* The plural is used when the emphasis is on different kinds or varieties of the type.

G Grammar focus

Refer students to the language summary on plurals and number on page 150.

You can use exercises 1–3 on page 151 for:
a) extra practice now, b) homework or c) review later on.

The answers are on page 164 of this Teacher's Book.

Speaking (SB page 117)

1 Avoid doing an initial group example in this case. Ask students to complete the sentences on their own before they compare and discuss them in pairs. Conduct a whole-class feedback session and elicit the difference between the singular or plural choice of verb, referring students back to the third bullet point in *Grammar and Pronunciation*, exercise 1.

1 *says* (seen as unit) or *say* (individuals in group) (x 2)
2 *start*: *starts* more formal, less common
3 *shows*
4 *has released* (seen as unit) or *have released* (less formal, more common)
5 *throw* (individual supermarkets)

2 Let students first reread the sentences in exercise 1 then put them into groups of three and tell them that they have 6–10 minutes to discuss the five points. If any interesting issues come up, invite students to share them with the whole class.

TEACH GLOBAL THINK LOCAL

Homework extra

If students are interested in one of the food-related questions that arose in *Speaking*, exercise 1, you could ask them to write an argumentative / discursive essay on the topic, eg *Is it better to eat organic apples from abroad or local apples?*

Part 3

TEACH GLOBAL THINK LOCAL Lead-in

Ask students to look at the photo of the young boy. Elicit what he might be drinking and ask *Why is this interesting? What does it tell us about the 'global village' we live in?* (He looks like a Tibetan boy, yet he's drinking a global brand, or so it seems). Put the topics from exercise 1 on the board: *sport, drink, food, invention, type of music* and ask students to consider their personal 'favourites' of each category. They should write them down, then compare and discuss their answers in pairs, giving reasons.

Speaking and Vocabulary (SB page 118)

1 Students first work on their own to write a list (or adapt their list from the *Lead-in*) for each 'popular' category. Then they compare their answers in pairs, explaining their reasons, eg *I think the world's favourite sport is cricket, because it's popular in India and Pakistan, which are densely populated countries.*

TEACH GLOBAL THINK LOCAL Homework extra

Ask students to do some research to confirm or correct their ideas. You could give each student one category to investigate. Then, in the next lesson, give them a few moments to compare answers with classmates who investigated the same topic. Finally, invite each group to share their information with the rest of the class.

2 Write up the word *globalisation* on the board. In pairs, ask students to discuss what they understand by this term and to write a definition. Elicit some examples and after each version, briefly ask the class whether the writer's view seems to be in favour, against or neutral. Then ask students, still in pairs, to complete the exercise. Do the first example together, highlighting the fact that the italicised words are not necessarily in the right order. Check answers by putting them up on the board, and drill any difficult words, focusing on the word stress, eg *regional, dramatically, standardise, self-sufficiency*.

1 regional, communication
2 dramatically, investment
3 liberalisation, concentration
4 standardise, self-sufficiency
5 economic, understanding, majority

3 Do the first example together. Then students continue in pairs. Check the answers, asking students how they came to their decision – they will need to refer to the writers' choice of language and content.

in favour: 5 against: 3, 4 neutral: 1, 2

4 Ask students to look back at their list from exercise 1 and to discuss the questions in pairs or small groups. Encourage them to try and list some benefits and drawbacks of globalisation on their own first, before sharing their views. Be prepared to upgrade students' language when trying to express these complex ideas; write useful words or phrases on the board.

Listening (SB page 118)

1 This listening is a talk given by a football expert, in which he discusses football as a global sport.

Ask *Are you football fans? Do you sometimes watch international football?* In pairs, ask students to select and discuss three of the questions. Monitor and pick up on any interesting points, for later feedback.

TEACH GLOBAL THINK LOCAL Language note

The word *soccer* is American English for *football*, and is derived from its formal name, *Association Football*. What Americans refer to as *'football'*, most other English varieties call *American football*.

The rules of the modern game of football, as we know it today, date from 1863 and were agreed at a meeting to form the Football Association in England. This was the sport's first governing body. However, there are records of games similar to football throughout the Middle Ages in Europe and as far back as a military manual in China dating from the third century BC. In those versions, in addition to using the feet, the ball was often hit with different parts of the body, including the chest, back and shoulders.

[Info taken from Fifa.com]

2 **3.39** Ask students to read the statements and consider the probable answers before they listen. If students are very interested in the topic, let them compare their predictions in pairs before listening to the recording. Do not confirm any answers at this point.

3.39

Football isn't only the world's most popular sport, but it's also probably the most positive symbol of globalisation in the 21st century. Never before has a single activity captured the hearts and minds of so many people. The South African 2010 World Cup final drew an estimated television audience of over half a billion people across the entire planet.

This event, held every four years, is a celebration. A celebration of a happier globalisation than the one we all know. It's a time when the countries of the world come together for a healthy contest between neighbours in the global village, with no single nation in charge. Not for nothing is it called the 'beautiful game'.

Even the former secretary of the United Nations, Kofi Annan, said the World Cup made the UN 'green with envy'. In Kofi Annan's words soccer 'is one of the few phenomena as universal as the UN. You could say it's even more universal.'

Football shows in a very tangible way the benefits of cross-pollination between peoples and countries. It is inconceivable that Brazilian, Cameroonian or Japanese doctors, computer scientists, factory workers or teachers could move from one country to another as Brazilian, Cameroonian or Japanese football players do. The rich football clubs, usually European, will search the world over for the best players. Teams such as England's Chelsea or Arsenal, Spain's Barcelona or Real Madrid or Italy's Juventus or AC Milan have the top players in the world and it means the quality of the game increases.

Now, one could talk about this as a drain on the talent and resources of the nations that have lost these players to the richest clubs. But in fact, football shows us that this is not necessarily the case for two reasons.

First, free movement has meant that good players from small leagues improve much more than they would had they stayed at home. A good Australian or Serbian player improves much faster if he joins Manchester United or Barcelona. Secondly, that improvement returns to national teams thanks to the international federation of football FIFA's rule requiring players to play only for their national team in international competitions. The Cameroonian player Eto'o can play for any Spanish, Italian or English club, but in the national competitions, he can play only for Cameroon. In other words, FIFA has introduced an institutional rule that allows small countries (in the football sense) to capture some of the benefits of today's higher-quality game.

In addition, more and more national teams now welcome coaches from other countries. These bring new ways of thinking and playing to the game. Not only do these players and managers help bring skills and knowledge acquired abroad back to their country, they also become heroes in their adopted countries, helping, as Kofi Annan said 'to open hearts and minds'.

In short, everybody benefits and standards rise.

The same process could be applied to other activities. Free movement of skilled labour could be accompanied by international requirements that migrants from poor countries should spend, say, one year in five working in their countries of origin. They would bring home skills, technology and connections that are as valuable as the skills that Eto'o, Essien or Messi bring back to Cameroon, Ghana or Argentina. Job placement would remain a problem, but the principle is sound: the world should learn from its most popular sport.

Let me now move on to the benefits in terms of investment in a country that has hosted the World Cup. Looking at the last five nations that have …

3 Students listen again to check their answers and, in pairs, enlarge on the incorrect statements. Ask students if they would like to listen again – this time, give them the option of listening and reading the audioscript at the same time.

1 ✗ The number of people who watched the 2010 World Cup final on TV was amazing: over half a billion people.
2 ✗ Football is known as the 'beautiful game' because it brings people together.
3 ✓
4 ✗ Rich football clubs help players from other countries to improve more quickly. The players then take these skills back to their own countries.
5 ✗ FIFA's rule requiring players only to play for their own national team in international competitions.
6 ✓
7 ✗ Workers from poor countries should spend one year in five working in their countries of origin, so that they can bring home skills, technology and connections.

4 Read out the two questions and give students two minutes to think about their answers individually. Tell them at this point that they will have to discuss these questions in pairs for at least three minutes. If any pairs finish early, ask them to consider other sports which have an impact on the people in their own countries. Discuss any interesting points with the whole class.

Grammar and Pronunciation (SB page 119)

1 Books closed. Put the first sentence on the board, but jumbled up: *captured minds of before hearts many people and so never a has the activity single.* Challenge students to try to put it in the correct order in 60 seconds. Elicit some examples when the time is up. Then invite students to check their answers with exercise 1. Students then read the other examples and complete the task. At the end, ask students how they would rewrite the sentences in less formal English, eg Sentence a: *A single activity has never before captured* … Ask students what the difference in focus is between these two versions. (The inversion places emphasis on the negative at the start, and serves to create a slight sense of expectancy and even suspense in the listener. This is why it can be very powerful in speeches.)

1 *Never before / Not for nothing / Not only* – they are all adverbial phrases with a negative meaning (negative adverbials).
2 The subject and verb are inverted, ie the subject follows the verb as in questions.
3 The auxiliary *do* is used – as in present simple questions.
4 formal

2 **3.40** Ask students to listen to the sentences, to mark the stress and intonation. Discuss the answers as a class and then replay the recording before drilling the students on the example sentences: break each one into small components, if necessary.

sentence a: Never before

sentence b: Not for nothing

sentence c: Not only do these players and managers bring skills and knowledge back home (↗), // they also become heroes in their adopted countries (↘).

3 3.41 Ask students to work on their own to transform sentences 1–6, after doing the first example together. Monitor and assist with accuracy. When students have finished, suggest that they read their sentences aloud in their heads, paying attention to appropriate stress and intonation. Play the recording for students to check their answers.

See audioscript for answers.

3.41

1 Rarely do we find out how decisions are made by FIFA.
2 Only recently have Asian countries joined the top teams of football.
3 No sooner had the 2010 World Cup finished when preparations started for the next one.
4 Only by paying huge amounts of money to FIFA, can a country host the World Cup.
5 Never again should we allow countries to spend so much money on a sporting event.
6 Not only is winning the World Cup good for a country's self-esteem, it also boosts its economy.

4 Ask students to think of a sport event which they would like to win. For fun, you could write some different sports on slips of paper for students to randomly choose, eg *skiing*, *karate*, *golf*, *sumo wrestling*, etc. If necessary, do an example yourself first, uttering the words with genuine feeling and using an orator's pace and emphasis, eg *Rarely have I experienced such joy. This is an absolute surprise and honour. Never in my life have I won an award of this kind. At no time in the last few months did I expect to win this event and take the gold medal. Thank you, thank you.* Monitor as students are writing, helping with accuracy. Ask them to say the sentences in their heads, with emphasis and feeling, before reading to their partner. Elicit any good or entertaining examples.

G Grammar focus

Refer students to the language summary on inversion on page 150.

You can use exercises 4–6 on page 151 for:

a) extra practice now, b) homework or c) review later on.

The answers are on page 164 of this Teacher's Book.

Speaking (SB page 119)

TEACH GLOBAL THINK LOCAL **Extra activity**

If your students are interested in football, ask *Do you remember the last three places where the World Cup was held?* See how many they can remember, writing the dates on the board, eg *2010*, *2006*, *2002*, *1998*, etc. Ask *Where will the next two be held?* Then, in small groups, students discuss the following questions, which you can write up or dictate.

- *Why is it so good for a country to host a World Cup?*
- *What sort of criteria is used to evaluate a potential host country for the World Cup?*
- *Could your country host this event? Why / Why not?*
- *Can you think of a World Cup or similar top sporting event, which was held somewhere you felt to be unsuitable? Why?*

1 Divide the class into two equal groups, A and B. Subdivide each one into smaller groups of about four students. Try to mix football lovers with non-football lovers in each group, if possible. Ask the groups to read about their respective roles. Tell them roughly how long they have to prepare, eg 7–9 minutes. Encourage them all to take notes, as they will later work with different partners. Monitor and assist as necessary.

2 Shuffle students around, so that they are working in AB pairs. Elicit suggestions of how they could start their arguments, eg *Well, I'm wholeheartedly behind the idea of having the World Cup here in X. We are the ideal host country* … Suggest to students that they let each other speak, in turn, and ask any questions at the end. Monitor and check that students are using inversions.

3 Invite the whole class to discuss the two questions.

TEACH GLOBAL THINK LOCAL **Homework extra**

If students enjoyed the topic, ask them to write an article to a newspaper, either supporting or opposing the idea of hosting the next World Cup in their country.

TEACH GLOBAL THINK LOCAL **Extra activity**

Round off the lesson or topic by asking one or two students to make a spontaneous speech, as if they were the president of a newly-announced host country for the next World Cup, similar to what they did in *Grammar and Pronunciation* exercise 4, SB page 119. Give all students two minutes to think about what they would say before you randomly pick your 'presidents'. Invite them to stand up, and to give their speeches to the audience.

Part 4

TEACH GLOBAL THINK LOCAL Lead-in

Bring in a gadget that you personally rely on. It could be something serious, eg a mobile phone or a Sat Nav, or something slightly more humorous, eg some weighing scales, or a timer for cooking. Put it in a bag or cover it, then explain to students how and why you rely on this gadget – be a little obscure to make it interesting. At the end, elicit what it is, at which point you can reveal the gadget, removing it from the bag. Ask students to work in pairs to tell each other of a gadget important to them, in the same way.

Speaking (SB page 120)

1 Give students three or four minutes individually to think of at least eight important technological inventions that have had a major impact on society.

2 In pairs, ask students to discuss their lists and to select the three most significant objects between them, making notes to justify or explain their criteria, as implied by the examples given.

3 Put students into groups of four to explain their lists. At the end, invite students to say if they had similar or very different views and to share any interesting or novel inventions that students selected with the rest of the class.

Reading (SB page 120)

This reading is an extract from an ancient scientific manual describing an instrument called 'an astrolabe'. The manual itself was written by the 14th century English writer Geoffrey Chaucer, for his son. It was intended to help him understand the device.

1 Refer students to the photo of the instrument. In pairs, students discuss the questions before sharing some of their ideas with the class and finally checking their answers on the back covers of their books. Elicit how they think it is pronounced /ˈæstrəleɪb/.

According to the *Global* book cover, an astrolabe *is an ancient tool used for navigating the seas, studying the stars and calculating the time anywhere on the planet.*

2 Students read the text *A Treatise on the Astrolabe* on page 121 and then answer the questions about when, who for and why it was written. Let students compare their answers in pairs.

1391–92; apparently written for ten-year-old Lewis, Chaucer's son.

His son was good at science and numbers and interested in the astrolabe, so Chaucer wanted him to have an error-free manual for its use, suited to his son's age.

3 Draw students' attention to the six gaps in the text and do the first example together, eliciting the correct answer. Students then work independently before comparing answers in pairs. Ask an early finisher to put up the answers on the board, for students to self-correct. Focus on any discrepancies.

1 b 2 f 3 e 4 a 5 d 6 c

TEACH GLOBAL THINK LOCAL Extra activity

For interest and as a challenge, project up or write out the original first sentences of the treatise, written in Old English. Books closed. Ask students to work in pairs to endeavour to 'translate' it into modern English. At the end, let them compare their translation with the text on SB page 121.

Lyte Lowys my sone, I aperceyve wel by certeyne evydences thyn abilite to lerne sciences touching nombres and proporciouns; and as wel considre I thy besy praier in special to lerne the tretys of the Astrelabie.

Answer: *Little Lewis, my son, I see some evidence that you have the ability to learn science, number and proportions, and I recognise your special desire to learn about the astrolabe.*

4 Students complete the search for the geographical and astrological terms, describing what these words mean to their partner. Let them check their answers in a dictionary, if necessary.

1 longitudes, latitudes, meridian altitude
2 stars, Sun, celestial bodies, moon

5 Encourage students to reflect on the different purposes of the astrolabe, as defined by Chaucer. Then ask them to discuss the questions in pairs. Discuss any points of interest as a class.

TEACH GLOBAL THINK LOCAL Extra activity

Ask students to go back to the text *A Treatise on the Astrolabe* and to find four different words meaning book or document (*text, treatise, manuscript, manual*). Ask students, in pairs, to brainstorm other kinds of reading matter, eg *pamphlet, flier, leaflet, textbook, novel, brochure, catalogue, booklet, album, volume, e-book,* etc. Let the pair with the longest list read them out and write them on the board. Students can discuss the last time they read each of these items, giving details about the material and their purpose, eg *I read a mail order catalogue to try and find an outfit for a wedding I'm going to.* When they have finished, ask students to try and order the items in the list from thinnest to thickest, eg *flier, leaflet, …* It does not matter if students disagree slightly!

Vocabulary (SB page 120)

1 Books closed. First of all, you could write up the five words – *appliance, tool, gadget, device, instrument* – on the board and ask students to discuss in pairs how they differ in meaning. Then students check with the definitions in exercise 1 and select the two used in the text to refer to the astrolabe, checking by scanning the text itself. Elicit any other words that could be used from the list of five (near) synonyms.

device and *instrument*; *tool* could also be used

2 Students should work in pairs to think of at least one example for each of the words in exercise 1. Check answers to ensure that they have understood the parameters of meaning between each one.

3 Books closed. Prepare eight slips of paper, each one with the name of one of the objects from the list. Give eight students each one slip of paper; they should not disclose their object to anyone. Ask these students to describe their object to their peers, without saying what it is, eg *You use this to tell you where you are going if you haven't got a map* (GPS navigation). As students speak, note whether those students are using the correct verbs from exercise 3, as you may be able to refer back to this stage later.

Ask students to open their books and, as an example, elicit both the object described and the correct verb in sentence 1. Let students complete the task in pairs. Check answers and invite students to explain to their peers in open class the difference in meaning between the two verbs given in each case, eg *determine* and *evaluate*, *calculate* and *measure*. If there are any problem cases, refer students to their dictionaries.

1 GPS navigation; determine
2 CCTV; monitor
3 USB memory stick; access
4 robot vacuum cleaner; remove
5 ear thermometer; measure
6 bar code reader; scan
7 car alarm; discourage
8 mp3 player; decode

4 In pairs, ask students to say which of the devices they use, in what way and how often. They should decide together on the two gadgets which are the least useful, giving convincing reasons. Elicit students' choices and their justifications in a whole-class feedback session at the end.

Writing (SB page 121)

Students choose their preferred object from *Speaking* exercise 2. They should first make notes in response to the three bullet-pointed questions in point 1. Refer students back to Chaucer's example at this point. Allow at least ten minutes for students to write their introduction. Monitor and assist as students are writing. Then students exchange their texts with a partner and give oral feedback, in response to the two questions provided in point 2.

Function globally: making proposals and suggestions

These lessons in *Global* are designed to provide students with immediately useful functional language. They all follow a similar format.

Warm up (SB page 122)

Aim: to introduce the topic via a quick speaking task or picture work.

Tips:

- Encourage students to use as much variety of language as they can at this stage. Do not over-correct here, especially in speaking activities.
- As students are talking, write up any useful language that arises onto the board.
- Invite students to share some of their ideas with reference to the last bullet-pointed questions.

Listening (SB page 122)

Aim: to present the functional language in context via a conversation or series of conversations.

Tips:

- Play the recording all the way through for each task (there are always two tasks). (Track 3.42)
- Write up the words from exercise 2 on the board, if they are relevant to your students, eg *call a meeting; take issue with sth*, etc.
- Let students compare their notes in pairs before checking answers as a class.
- Encourage students to read the audioscripts for homework, exploiting them for useful language.

1

1 swimming pool

2 & 3 demonstrate: easy to organise, possible health and safety issue

reduce staffing levels: possible health and safety issue

reduce opening hours / days per week: weekends are paramount, need to ensure maximum time open

have a fundraising event: need organisers, Martin is suggested as a good contact

4 Wednesday 6.00

2

1 called	5 sidetracked
2 agenda	6 endorse
3 take issue	7 volunteer
4 clarify	8 wraps it up

3.42

A: … typical, that's the last thing I need …

B: OK, thank you, thanks for this bit of hush, thanks, thanks everyone for coming today. I appreciate you being here. Now I've called this meeting to discuss the local government spending cuts, but in particular what they are suggesting now is that they close our local swimming pool … so has everyone got a copy of the agenda by the way?

All: … yeah … yeah … didn't get one … makes frightening reading …

B: OK, well, let's … let's without further ado, let's get started. So moving to item 1 of the agenda, erm, what proposals can we give to the council to counter what seems like a fait accompli that they close the pool? Anybody want to start us off on that?

C: Well, we could demonstrate …

B: Yes …

A: I think that's a good idea …

D: Yes, a really good idea, you know, let them know how we feel about …

C: It's easy to organise on the internet …

D: Absolutely.

C: … everyone's emails …

D: … yeah yeah yeah … very important for the kids …

C: … kids involved … community … yeah … daytime demonstrations … preferably a Saturday morning … well, I …

A: involve the schools …

B: I would just take issue with that from a safety point of view. If you're getting children involved on demonstrations things can …

E: Can I just clarify something here? I mean, they're asking us to supply them with a proposal, so something concrete, something realistic, so we need to really think about what the options are. In terms of the financials, right?

B: That's a good idea, Jean. Yes …

A: Yeah, but I would like to take issue with what Nigel just said about the kids not getting involved, not in protesting and, you know, rioting, throwing rocks and stuff, but, you know, getting in touch with their friends on, you know, the social networks and that's … that's the way to spread the word.

B: I don't think we should get too sidetracked by the whole demonstration thing, although I do take Kate's point that we should show that we mean business here, but …

C: Actually, I would like to endorse what Nigel has just said about health and safety as well.

A: Yes, we have to keep it within the …

B: OK, so what other proposals could we make to the council?

E: Well, it might be an idea, um, to reduce staff levels?

D: Yeah, maybe.

E: Then again that's health and safety issues come to the fore …

C: What about less hours?

B: Fewer hours?

C: Perhaps only opening three days a week?

E: So open for schools on maybe two days of the week and open weekends for the public?

B: But I agree that weekends are paramount. We all want to make sure that it's open as often as it was before on the weekends, but maybe we can reduce hours …

E: In the week …

B: … some weekday mornings.

E: Yes, definitely.

C: What about, just thinking about sort of income, perhaps we could have like a fundraiser?

B: Yeah … who would be willing to volunteer for the fundraiser, I mean, can we have a show of hands?

C: Well, yes, I'll certainly help organise …

A: And I know people who would help.

B: Great.

E: I know Martin would do it for sure.

B: Martin's brilliant, yeah.

D: Yeah, he's very good.

E: Very good …

B: So are we in agreement on this then? Yeah …

All: Yeah … so far? … I think so.

A: Good. Well, could we perhaps move on to item 2 on the agenda. Nigel?

B: … OK, so I'm sorry to wrap this up. Any other business from anybody because there's another group waiting to come in?

C: Can we just set a meeting …

D: I think we should set a date …

B: Very good idea.

C: … next Tuesday everyone?

E: I would like to propose that we meet up …

D: Next Tuesday …

E: … on Wednesday …

B: Yes, because I can't do Tuesday either.

C: OK.

A: Wednesday at six o'clock?

B: Six o'clock Wednesday.

C: Same place.

A: Fine.

D: Brilliant.

C: Thanks Nigel.

B: Superb. OK, well, that wraps it up for today and see you all again on Wednesday at six.
E: Excellent.
D: Thank you.
A: Well, that seemed to go …
C: Yeah …
E: Anyone want a lift?

Language focus (SB page 122)

Aim: to draw students' attention to the items of functional language.

Tips:

- Let students work alone at first, before comparing answers in pairs.
- Ask *Which of the suggestions in exercise 1 have you heard before? Which ones have you used yourself?*
- Drill some examples in exercise 1, if appropriate for your class. Pay particular attention to intonation and stress (as a general rule, the modals are unstressed).
- Give students time to make a note of any phrases they would like to incorporate into their repertoire.

1

1 make	5 might be	9 that
2 would be	6 that we write	10 write
3 could	7 writing	
4 write	8 should	

2

a 2, 8, 10 b 3, 5, 7, 9 c 1, 4, 6

3 Suggested answers

1 That's a brilliant idea.
2 That's a good idea.
3 I suppose we could.
4 Yes, but the problem is …
5 With respect, I don't think that's feasible.
6 That's ridiculous.

Pronunciation (SB page 122)

Aim: to focus students on a particular aspect of pronunciation of the target phrases.

Tips:

- Play the recording two or three times, if necessary. (Track 3.43)
- At this level, try to promote good all-round pronunciation including stress, intonation and linking.

1

1 That's a good idea.
2 Yes, but the problem is …
3 That's ridiculous.
4 That's a brilliant idea.
5 I suppose we could.
6 With respect, I don't think that's feasible.

TEACH GLOBAL THINK LOCAL

Speaking extra

Put students in AB pairs. Explain that Student A should randomly choose three of the phrases from *Language focus* exercise 3, eg *I suppose we could.* They need to think of a way of making Student B choose that particular response without actually telling them which one it is, eg Student A: *Shall we do our homework before we go out?* Student B: *I suppose we could*. If Student B uses a different response from the list, then Student A needs to make another suggestion, until they give the right response! They need to do three of these each. Model the task first with a strong student: ask the student to stand with his/her back to the board. Write the answer you have chosen on the board (so the rest of the class can see which response you are looking for), then demonstrate the activity.

Speaking (SB page 122)

Aim: to allow students an opportunity to use this language in a meaningful, real-world context.

Tips:

- Give students time to reflect on what they are going to say before starting. You could brainstorm some initial ideas together first.
- Refer students to the *Useful phrases* and encourage students to make use of them in their discussion.
- Point out to the chairperson from each group that he/she should manage the meeting, eg invite everyone to speak, calm people down, summarise, etc. At the very beginning, elicit how the chairperson can start the meeting.
- As students are having their meetings, take notes on any interesting language points – either good or problematic – for delayed feedback. Do not interrupt.
- At the end, encourage students to reflect on the activity. Ask *How useful was it? Did you enjoy it? What, if anything, would you say differently another time?*

Global voices

These lessons in *Global* are designed to provide students with exposure to authentic speakers of English from both native and non-native English backgrounds. They all follow a similar format.

Warm up (SB page 123)

TEACH GLOBAL THINK LOCAL Lead-in

Ask students to close their eyes and picture their English classes at secondary school. If they didn't study English, they should try to visualise another language lesson they had. Ask them to picture the classroom, the teacher, the desks, the books used (if possible) and then to imagine the kind of tasks they typically used to do. Then ask students to work in groups of three to tell each other about their English classes, and how it was different from the lessons they have now.

Aim: to introduce the topic and highlight potentially difficult vocabulary the students will encounter.

Tips:

- Focus students' attention on the photo of Evgenia and elicit where Belarus is.
- Let them listen to the recording twice if they need to. (Track 3.44)
- Invite students to share their responses related to different approaches to learning and teaching.

3.44

Evgenia, Belarus

I am sorry, I am laughing because when you start to learn English like in Belarus there are like topics you are learning, or texts you are memorising, and one of the topics is, like, 'my native town' and you also have to prepare it for an exam. And it's like, you know, this text that you remember and write down, and it took ages and then learn and then repeat and I even suspect I had it in an exam because when you asked that the first thing was like this, there's the beginning of this text, like Vitebsk is found on the banks of three rivers and it is just like, you know, there, like a learned thing. I am feeling like I am back to school.

Listening (SB page 123)

Aim: to expose students to English spoken with a variety of accents.

Tips:

- Students may need to hear the recording twice in order to understand it. Tell students you don't expect them to understand every word.
- It may be tempting to hunt for specific pronunciation or language errors, but we recommend against this. In real-world communication not everyone speaks perfect English all the time, not even native speakers.
- Give students the opportunity to read the sentences in exercise 1 before listening. (Track 3.45–3.46)
- Monitor as students are retelling the stories in exercise 2, to find out how much they understood. If necessary, play the recording again, before they do the retelling.
- After they have completed exercise 3, ask students to discuss in pairs whether Jiawei's and Harshula's comments are relevant to their own countries. (Track 3.47–3.48)

TEACH GLOBAL THINK LOCAL Extra activity

After completing the three listening tasks, if your students would benefit from a quick revision of *used to* and *would* – for talking about memories – then exploit the audioscript. First ask them to locate examples, eg *What my father would do, is he would put me on top of that structure*. Elicit the difference between the two forms. (*Would* is not usually used to talk about states and situations, but for past repeated actions and habits. *Used to* can be used for both.) Ask students to think of a similarly strong memory from their own childhood and to talk about it in pairs. Make sure they focus on an activity, rather than a place.

1

1 J 2 H 3 H 4 H 5 J 6 H 7 J

2

Students' own answers.

3.45–3.46

Harshula, Sri Lanka

Similarly, when I grew up, when I was growing up, I started schooling in the capital Colombo, but whenever I had holidays I used to visit Ratnapura because that was where I used to get the proper break and I remember whenever my parents asked where, what I wanted to do during the summer vacation or holidays I always used to say I want to go to my cousin's place in Ratnapura because that's where I rejuvenate and where I feel like I am living life because that was the proper break for me with the tea estates, the birds, the people, and even today when I am here in Oxford studying for my Masters in Law there are so many opportunities for me to stay back here and work for a London law firm, but I have decided very strongly to go back home. That is because of the experience I got from my home town I suppose, with the close, closeness I have with my people, the villagers, and the fact that I feel that I should do something for the community. So that's a very strong feeling.

Jiawei, China

My childhood memory is, as I mentioned earlier, my family used to live in, on the eastern side of the river, which is called Pudong these days. So I remember … so when we were living on the eastern side, which is the not so developed part, so my father always take me to visit the western side like the central Shanghai area on weekends. At that time there runs a ferry, a very, very cheap ferry. When I remember it. The ferry was very old styled and it has this front of the boat like totally exposed to the weather. But at the front of the boat there is this, um, it's like a round structure, I would think that's almost like a part of the engine, but it's covered, totally covered, so it almost make a perfect sitting surface. So what I remember … what my father would do, is he would put me on top of that structure, which was about three or four foot tall. So when my father put me on that, and when I was sitting there, my father was just able to stand beside me, but his head, I remember, is at my eye level so we could continue talking, my father and I would ride back and forth on the same ferry, so we don't need to pay for the multiple trips, but we get to enjoy the view of the river, and also the architecture, the fantastic architecture, on the waterfront side, yeah. So that … because I guess it cost so little, but it gave me such immense happiness as a little child, it becomes a very fond memory of mine. Because nowadays I am sure Shanghai, like other parts of the world, or other parts of China, because of the economic development, people also got more materialised.

3

1 not many politicians came from the area, and any who did were not involved in local politics
2 the admission fee made it feel commercial and lacking simplicity ('simpleness')

 **3.47–3.48**

Harshula, Sri Lanka

Well, the town centre, I have noticed that it hasn't changed very much compared to other cities in the country because politically the town, and Ratnapura as a district, was neglected due to not many politicians coming up from the area. And even when they did come up to the national level, they were more involved in national level politics than the local politics so I would really say that Ratnapura as a district and as a major town in Sri Lanka has been neglected for two, three decades.

Jiawei, China

A lot of things have changed, like last year when I was back in China they had this Shanghai Expo, but the thing is they charge admission fee, right, and so it becomes a little bit different, it becomes like a commercial, it no longer … I think previously all the lighting, all the ferry boat in some way it feels like a public good, you know, you could enjoy it because it's almost free, but now like everything seems to have a price tag associated with it. Yes, like China is growing a lot, but I think in some way it lost that kind of simpleness that was previously associated with the city in, at least locals' mind. Yeah. Of course, the greater economic development, that is for everybody to see, yeah.

Language focus: *the thing is* (SB page 123)

Aim: to raise students' awareness of a particular piece of language present in the listening.

Tips:

- Ask students if they use this phrase already when speaking English. You could ask them if there is a similar expression in their first language.
- Let students compare their answers to exercise 2 in pairs before sharing some examples with the class.
- Give attention to pronunciation of the phrase *the thing is*. The word *thing* is stressed, and there is often a slight pause after *is* (or *was*, if used in the past). Drill one or two example sentences.

1

2 – to focus attention on a problem

2

Students' own answers.

Speaking (SB page 123)

Aim: for students to discuss the same or similar questions as the speakers in the listening.

Tips:

- The speaking tasks are more open to allow students to explore the subject. Give them time to do this.
- Let students have a couple of moments to think about the place from their youth and to mentally reflect on the questions before talking.
- Monitor as they are talking and note down good / problematic language to highlight in feedback (oral or written) later on.
- Invite one or two students to share any interesting or unusual descriptions with the whole class, at the end.
- As you go through the book and the *Global voices* lessons, ask students for feedback on these listening activities and their potential use of English with other people.

Writing: a website entry

These lessons in *Global* are designed to provide students with extended writing practice. They all follow a similar format.

Reading (SB page 124)

Aim: to provide a sample text for students to analyse.

TEACH GLOBAL THINK LOCAL **Lead-in**

Ask *When was the last time you looked up a website entry to find out about a place – a town, region or country?* Ask students to raise their hands if they can remember. Put students into pairs or small groups each including at least one person who raised their hand. Instruct students to ask questions to find out more details, eg *Where was the place? Why were you looking at it? Did you find a positive description? What did you find out about it? What did you do as a result?* If necessary, write a few prompts on the board.

Tips:

- There are often two questions for these texts: one which focuses on gist and the other on specific details.
- Before starting, ask students to look at the photo and elicit where the village might be.
- Let students check their answers to exercise 2 in pairs. Monitor as they work and decide if a whole-class feedback session is necessary or not.

1 Possible answers

1 Travel / Getting there
2 The village / Mirabello
3 Things to do / Visitor attractions
4 Eating out
5 Cultural events

2 Possible answers

1 Where (exactly) / Whereabouts is Mirabello (situated)?
2 How can you / I get there?
3 Why should I / anyone visit Mirabello?
4 What is the countryside like?
5 What is the population / How many inhabitants are there?
6 What is there to do there?
7 Where is the best place to eat?
8 Are there any festivals or special events in / during the year?

Writing skills: register (SB page 124)

Aim: to give students a chance to develop their writing through various different micro skills.

Tips:

- Clearly explain the focus and do an example together first before asking them to continue on their own.
- Let students check their answers in pairs or small groups, then correct in open class.
- As you check the answers to exercise 2, ask students to give you examples of the formal characteristics from the text, eg complex sentences, noun phrases instead of verbs, precise details.
- Draw students' attention to the *Language note* at the top of page 125, that provides a general rule about the use of words with Latin derivations.

1

1 (It) is situated
2 it is easily reachable
3 leaving
4 the village boasts
5 no reservation is required
6 sporting activities are also well provided for
7 attract a large number of tourists
8 a hugely enjoyable occasion

2

complex sentences; noun phrases instead of verbs; passive verbs; precise details

TEACH GLOBAL THINK LOCAL **Writing extra**

Ask students to underline positive sounding words and phrases in the sample text which help to 'market' the place to potential visitors. Such language is very typical of the genre, (*easily reachable, a perfect place to XX, spectacular, steeped in history, boasts, well provided for, strongly recommend, delicious, several cultural events, attract, notable, hugely enjoyable*). In addition, language such as *can be visited* and *no X is required* also give a sense of opportunity and scope.

Linking ideas: alternatives and examples (SB page 125)

Aim: to highlight and focus on a particular aspect of language that students can use to improve their writing.

Tips:

- Encourage students to work alone at first, then check their answers in pairs or small groups.
- Ask students to reflect on why these words and phrases are particularly useful for this genre (because the writer aims to transmit the scope of everything that the place can offer).
- Monitor and make a note of any problematic words or phrases for feedback later.
- Point out relevant issues relating to punctuation and syntax too, eg *alternatively* can also go at the start of a sentence; *whether* is a conjunction and therefore needs to be in a sentence with two clauses, etc.

1

1 alternatively; equally; likewise; otherwise; similarly; whether … or
2 eg; for example; for instance; including; like; such as

2 Possible answers

1 … *such as* carbonara and *pastel de choclo*.
2 … *equally*, you can travel to the nearby town to go sightseeing.
3 … *alternatively*, there are a number of cheaper bed and breakfast options.
4 … *including* canoeing, trekking and whitewater rafting.
5 … *or* a romantic getaway.
6 Cities *like* London and Oxford are …
7 … *similarly*, there are plenty of activities for children to enjoy.

3

1 for example; for instance; including; like
2 alternatively; likewise
3 equally; likewise
4 for example; for instance; like; such as
5 –
6 such as
7 equally; likewise

Preparing to write (SB page 125)

Aim: to give students time to brainstorm ideas for the writing task.

Tips:

- Ensure students choose a place which they feel positively about.
- To motivate students and provide an example, model the task with a strong student who should respond to the questions which you and the other students ask from Reading exercise 2.
- Refer students to the language in *Describing a place* and encourage them to try to incorporate some of these phrases into their writing.
- Ask students to make notes at this stage, but not to begin writing.

Writing (SB page 125)

Aim: to give practice in more extended writing tasks.

Tips:

- This section can be done as homework.
- Remind students to refer back to the model text and encourage them to experiment with some of the target language from this section.
- Ask students to check their work carefully before they hand it in.
- Before they hand their writing in, students should ask their partner to read and critique their entry by asking *Does it make the place sound appealing and attractive?*

TEACH GLOBAL THINK LOCAL Writing extra

For fun and further practice, you could ask your students to think of a town or region which is not particularly attractive, which they should nevertheless try to promote to visitors in a website entry. Tell them that they cannot lie about the place, but they can disguise the truth a little, eg *It's a historic town.* (It's old, but not very old; the old buildings have practically disappeared.) They could also write euphemistically, eg *It's a lively, bustling town.* (It's crowded and horribly congested.) Ideally, let students do this work during class time in pairs or groups of three, as long as they are all familiar with the place being described.

Study skills

Celebrating your achievements (SB page 125)

TEACH GLOBAL THINK LOCAL Lead-in

Write up the word *Congratulations* on the board. Write it slowly, one letter at a time, pausing between each letter for students to guess the word before you finish writing it. Ask *Why have I written this?* Tell students that you are going to attempt to draw a metaphoric expression which you say when congratulating someone for their hard work and effort. Try to draw a graphic representation of: *Give yourself a pat on the back.* Don't worry if your artistic skills are limited. When students have guessed what it is, elicit phrases which have a similar meaning, eg *You should be proud of yourself.*

1 Ask students *How do you feel now that you have finished* Global Advanced*?* Then ask *Do you feel like an advanced student now? Does finishing an advanced coursebook make you advanced? Do you feel that you have improved?* Let them reply in detail if they wish, but these are primarily rhetorical questions. Students then read the list of skills and abilities, ticking the ones that apply to themselves and adding at least two more 'can do' statements about their skills and abilities, not specific language points.

2 Encourage students to compare their list with a partner, commenting on each others' additional points. Then ask them to write down a few of the highlights from the course. These could be directly or indirectly related to language learning in the class. Invite them to share some examples.

3 In groups of three students think of at least six ways to keep up their English now the course has finished. Elicit one example as an example before they start. At the end, invite students to share any ideas which they feel are unusual or adventurous.

TEACH GLOBAL THINK LOCAL Extra activity

Now is a good opportunity to ask students for feedback on the course. One way of doing this is to use one of the appropriate forms on the Teacher's Resource Disc: *Letter to a student in the next class*, or *My English at the end of the course*. Alternatively, you could ask students the questions below. Whichever way you choose, ask students to do this individually (and anonymously, if they wish). However, it is possible to do it in pairs if students prefer. Encourage them to take it seriously and to proffer information which realistically can be of use to you and future learners.

What did you enjoy most about the course?

What do you think you made the most progress in?

What lesson or language item(s) do you think you'll remember from the course?

What techniques / activities did you particularly like in the lessons?

Do you have any helpful suggestions for your teacher, to help him/her plan the next Advanced course?

Grammar focus answer key

Unit 1

1 **1** I'm speaking **2** It's getting
3 is happening **4** tells
5 are closing down **6** is changing

2 both options possible: 1, 3, 4, 6, 7

3 **1** b **2** a **3** c **4** b **5** c **6** a

4 Suggested answers
1 B: No, I don't (feel like it).
2 B: No, I don't think so.
3 B: Yes, I think I will (take one) too.
4 B: No, I can't afford it / one / to.

5 Least likely alternative
1 I'll retire **2** thinking **3** I play
4 has the film arranged to start
5 do you do **6** I'll

Unit 2

1 Possible answers
1 bound / certain **2** unlikely **3** would
4 might / may / could **5** will
6 chance / likelihood / possibility

2 Possible answers
1 This book will probably win the prize.
2 There's no way this painting will sell for a million.
3 Solar power is bound to replace other forms of domestic power.
4 There's a strong likelihood that she will win the Nobel Prize for Literature.
5 Scientists may / might / could well discover a new way of producing energy.
6 It's highly unlikely that people will learn to use less electricity.

3 **1** will be giving
2 will have finished
3 will have completed
4 will be waiting
5 will have already started

4 **1** wanted; hadn't brought; would accept
2 went out; started
3 had visited; hadn't forgotten
4 didn't arrive; had had
5 opened; was blowing; had packed
6 glanced; was sleeping; was sitting
7 was going to accept
8 were on the verge of building

5 Possible answers
1 was standing; began; had come; was staring
2 was growing; was now dripping; opened; started; realised; had left
3 woke up; was coming; were shouting; were hooting; tried; was he doing; had he slept; had he ended up
4 noticed; was walking / walked; had been carrying; had dropped / dropped; had noticed / noticed; had put / put; picked; looked; seemed; was thinking; realised

Unit 3

1 **1 – 2** whose (mother …) **3** k
4 who (are …) **5** (for) whom (one …)
6 which (was …) **7** who (have …)
8 which (was …)

2 **1** My teachers gave me some good advice, which helped me to decide my future.
2 She met an enthusiastic publisher who believed she had talent as a novelist.
3 The main character, whose parents died when he was young, was brought up by his sister.
4 At the end of the book Pip works to pay back the money which the convict had given him.
5 There are many interesting characters in the book, some of whom are comic characters.
6 Dickens wrote two different endings for the book, which makes it more interesting.
7 There are five Great Lakes in North America, of which the largest is Lake Superior.

3 **1** Esther is the person Pip is in love with.
2 Everyone needs something they can believe in.
3 He is someone Pip has great respect for.
4 It's a book I was impressed with.
5 Is this someone you are related to?
6 She is someone you can rely on.

4 **1** shop windows (most likely), the windows of shops (possible)
2 bottle of water
3 end of the lesson
4 tennis court
5 rubbish bin
6 office phone number
7 kitchen knife
8 bus stop
9 yesterday's newspaper
10 the president's children

5 **1** computer program **2** bookshelf
3 evening paper **4** trouser pocket
5 doorbell **6** check-in desk
7 fashion show **8** shop assistant
9 guide dog **10** paintbox

6 Incorrect alternatives
1 agent **2** truck **3** cost
4 travel **5** operator **6** library

Unit 4

1 Possible answers
1 can / could / will / would **2** Shall
3 won't **4** should **5** will
6 may / might **7** must / should / have to **8** could / might / should
9 won't **10** should / ought to

2 Possible answers
1 I'll finish the work by Friday.
2 Can / Could / May I leave my bike here?
3 Shall we take the bus?
4 I'll do the washing-up.
5 You should take a holiday.
6 She just won't listen to anyone!
7 Could / Would / Can you open the window, please?
8 She just won't pay for anything!

3 Possible answers
1 You mustn't eat in the classroom.
2 You shouldn't eat too much late at night.
3 You can't park here.
4 You don't have to / needn't wear a tie.
5 You can / may bring two guests free of charge.
6 You / We ought to / should get there early.
7 You have to drive on the right.
8 My doctor told me I must lose weight.

4 Possible answers
1 The journey didn't take long, so we didn't have to so early.
2 I should have discussed it with her.
3 She had to show the police officer her licence.
4 I needn't have worried, as she phoned me soon afterwards.
5 I didn't need to / didn't have to pay an extra charge.
6 I shouldn't have argued with her.
7 In the end, they were able to rescue her from the burning building.
8 We could have stayed an extra day, but we didn't.

5 **1** correct **2** incorrect: We didn't have any training. **3** correct **4** incorrect: The children play well with each other. **5** incorrect: The government has introduced a programme to eliminate drug addiction.
6 correct **7** incorrect: I didn't enjoy either concert / either of the concerts. **8** correct **9** correct
10 incorrect: Neither student / Neither of the students has conducted an orchestra before. **11** correct

Unit 5

1 **1** stole; have been carrying out
2 has increased; have been patrolling
3 finished; sentenced
4 have seized; have received
5 came; grabbed; had
6 have been reading; haven't found
7 is; last flooded

2 **1** finished; has been looking for (*has looked for* is possible but less likely); hasn't had
2 has ever discovered; buried; have been searching / have searched
3 has been; happened
4 have been thinking; said; have changed
5 has recently sent; caused
6 didn't attend; have been having / have had; went

3 **1** have been waiting; have you been doing
2 has been running; has won
3 have been looking; Have you found
4 have known; have only been going out
5 have just stopped; have been studying; haven't finished
6 has been rising; has reached
7 haven't read
8 have had

4 **1** After inspecting the damage, the team reported their findings.
2 There were three people in the boat waving flags.
3 Having lost her wallet, she was unable to pay for the ticket.
4 With both legs broken, he was unable to move.
5 While robbing the bank, he shot and killed two people.
6 The fire having gone out, the rescuers were able to search the ruins of the house.
7 On seeing the fire, he immediately phoned the fire brigade.
8 Not having anything to eat, she was forced to beg.
9 It rained heavily causing extensive flooding.

5 **1** Opening the box, she looked inside.
2 Having repaired the building, they opened it as a health clinic.
3 With the bank surrounded by police, the robbers were forced to surrender.
4 There was a long line of people waiting to see the doctor.
5 With the level of the water rising, the villagers were unable to cross the river.
6 Since appearing in a TV documentary, she has become well known.

Unit 6

1 **1** All the slaves were given their freedom by their masters.
2 A documentary about the Silk Road is being made by a French film company.
3 A new business park has been built by the local authority.
4 Responsibility for the bank's debts should have been taken over by the government.
5 Small farmers were being exploited by some large supermarket chains.
6 The problem of modern slavery will be highlighted in a UN report next week.

2 **Possible answers**
1 The number of employees (in the company) is going to be cut by 20%.
2 It has been suggested that the banks have not been telling the truth.
3 Camels have been used by nomads for centuries for carrying goods.
4 The bars of gold should be kept deep below ground in secure rooms.
5 These fish are caught off the shores of the south island.
6 Shells might have been used as currency.
7 The classroom will be painted next week.
8 Children should be taught in school how to manage their money.

3 **1** All the rooms have been taken / are taken.
2 The name of the company has been changed.
3 This bank was taken over by the government in 2008.
4 The Silk Road has been used as a trade route for centuries.
5 The village was abandoned after the earthquake in 2011.
6 An investigation into slavery is currently being carried out.

4 **1** It is **2** What; is **3** The reason; was
4 What; did; was **5** It was when
6 All / What **7** The thing **8** It is

5 **1** It is the cost of transporting the goods that adds to the price.
2 What adds to the price is the cost of transporting the goods.
3 It was after I looked more closely that I saw the difference.
4 What surprised me was the speed of the camels.
5 What the government did was (to) stop the ships which transported the slaves.
6 It is the length of the Silk Road that is surprising.
7 What happened was that sales rose to record levels.

Unit 7

1 **1** –; the; –
2 the; the; an
3 The; an / the; the; the
4 The; the; the
5 A; a; the
6 the; a / the; the
7 –; an; –
8 a; a; the; the
9 The; the
10 A; a

2 **The** World's first heart transplantation was carried out by Christiaan Barnard in 1967, on 53-year-old Lewis Washkansky. **The** operation was a success; however, **the** medications that were given to **the** patient to prevent his immune system from attacking **the** new heart also supressed his body's ability to fight off other illnesses and 18 days after **the** operation, Washkansky died of double pneumonia. Since then, scientists have been trying to develop an artificial heart that can completely replace **the** functions of **the** human heart. In August 2010, Angelo Tigano had his failing heart removed and replaced with a totally artificial heart after a five-hour operation conducted at **the** Heart Transplant Unit at St Vincent's Hospital in Sydney. This was **the** first case of an artificial heart being implanted into a living human in **the** southern hemisphere. In many countries, **the** cost of a heart transplant is too high for **the** majority of patients, so **the** use of an artificial heart could be a way of reducing **the** costs involved in such operations

3 **Incorrect alternatives**
1 would give; could
2 were to be; may
3 Did; would offer
4 Would he be; couldn't

4 **1** If he were to have the operation, it might save his life.
2 Were you to apply for this post, we would support your application.
3 If I were you, I'd take more exercise.
4 If he were to ask me to marry him, I would say no.

5 **1** pretending **2** to inform **3** helping
4 to speak **5** to have been
6 Being taken **7** Leaving **8** seeing
9 taking **10** go **11** to be taken left behind **12** study; apply

6 **1** of **2** as; to **3** been **4** having; been
5 my / me waking **6** to **7** to; being
8 order; to **9** being **10** not; having
11 to; getting / **12** him / his

Unit 8

1 **1** incorrect: Supposing nobody turns up to your party, what will you do?
2 incorrect: Unless you explain how the machine works, I won't be able to use it.
3 incorrect: If it rains tomorrow, we may not go for a picnic after all.
4 correct
5 correct
6 correct
7 correct
8 correct
9 incorrect: Should you begin to feel tired, take a 15-minute break.
10 incorrect: If you get into difficulties, I'll help you.
11 incorrect: I'll lend you my key on condition that you don't lose it.
12 correct

2 **Possible answers**
1 If they hadn't searched the room, they wouldn't have found the missing money.
2 If she hadn't taken the 5.00 train, she wouldn't have met him.
3 If the storm hadn't been so powerful, the bridge wouldn't have collapsed.
4 If she'd been looking where she was going, she wouldn't have fallen over.
5 If she hadn't felt / been feeling stressed, she wouldn't have driven / been driving dangerously.
6 If I'd been able to speak Italian, I would have been able to explain what had happened.
7 If he hadn't reacted quickly, there would have been an accident.
8 Had she looked carefully at him, she would have recognised him.
9 If I'd been able to get a flight, I would have attended the meeting.
10 Had the architect not changed the plans, the building may not have survived the earthquake.

3 **1** had saved up; would be able
2 NO
3 hadn't decided; would have
4 had managed; wouldn't need
5 NO
6 hadn't argued; would still be working
7 hadn't lied; would believe
8 NO

4 **1** She is believed to be one of the richest women in the country.
2 It is reported that the President has resigned.
3 The architect is said to have earned more than $2 million.
4 The council is understood to have refused planning permission.
5 It is thought that the prisoner has escaped.
6 The weather is thought to have been the worst for a decade.
7 The police are known to be looking for two men.
8 It is rumoured that bank officials stole the money.
9 Marilyn Monroe is alleged to have been murdered.
10 Interest rates are expected to rise.

Unit 9

1 **1** time **2** rather **3** were
4 was /were **5** If **6** didn't
7 knew **8** wondering **9** had
10 did **11** did **12** was

2 **1** He acts as if he was / were the boss.
2 If only we hadn't forgotten the map!
3 It's time you went home now.
4 I wish I didn't have to work tomorrow.
5 If only he hadn't lost the keys!
6 I'd rather you didn't sit there.

3 **1** correct
2 incorrect: Unemployment is a problem in a great / large number of countries.
3 incorrect: Most economists claim that the economy is recovering.
4 incorrect: The majority of commuters use the train to get to work.
5 correct
6 incorrect: When the police found the security van, most of the money was still inside.
7 correct
8 incorrect: A considerable number of new jobs have been created in the private sector.
9 incorrect: I'm sorry but there are (very) few seats available of that flight.
10 incorrect: There are hardly any / very few really good restaurants open in this area.
11 incorrect: Most people in this area have casual jobs.
12 correct

4 **1** more **2** much / far / considerably
3 nearly **4** than **5** as **6** lot
7 most considerably **8** slightly
9 nowhere **10** bit

5 **Possible answers**
1 I used to spend less time on my work.
2 This is the hardest job I've ever done.
3 Travelling by bus is much cheaper than travelling by train.
4 This is by far the largest company in Oman.
5 My journey to work is a great deal shorter than it once was.
6 The roads are nothing like as crowded as they were.
7 Cycling is far and away the cheapest form of commuting.
8 The buses here are just as crowded as the trains.

Unit 10

1 **1** is **2** receives **3** is **4** is / are
5 is **6** owns / own **7** suggests
8 devotes **9** is; is **10** are
11 moved

2 **1** year **2** their **3** pair **4** neither
5 their **6** passers-by **7** either
8 minute **9** is **10** are

3 **1** tomatoes **2** crises **3** – **4** –
5 P **6** kilos **7** – **8** phenomena
9 – **10** – **11** coffees **12** P

4 **1** No sooner; than **2** when / after; did
3 Such; that **4** until; did **5** So; that
6 Little; did **7** Rarely; does / Never; has
8 Never; again

5 **1** The plane had hardly started to take off when there was an explosion.
2 I have rarely seen such a range of exotic fruit and vegetables!
3 We didn't realise what a lovely street it was until we moved here.
4 Under no circumstances will spectators be allowed on the pitch.
5 So popular was the restaurant that you could wait a couple of hours for a table.
6 Only when I visited Delhi did I realise how much I liked Indian food.

6 **1** Never before has there been such a violent match.
2 Seldom does a new product sell so many examples in so short a time.
3 Scarcely had the power been turned on when the fire began.
4 Little did we know what was in store for us at the new French restaurant!
5 Rarely has there been such a universally popular appliance.
6 Such was the interest / was people's interest in the new phones that they sold out very rapidly.
7 Not only is she a professional violinist, but she also sings beautifully.
8 So exciting was the match that we sat glued to the screen all evening.

Global Teacher's Resource Disc

The *Global* Teacher's Resource Disc includes a comprehensive range of resources.

The Communication activities section contains a number of photocopiable worksheets for classroom use provided as printable PDFs. There are two worksheets directly linked with the content of each of the units in the Coursebook. In addition, there are generic worksheets appropriate for different points of the course (eg beginning of the year).

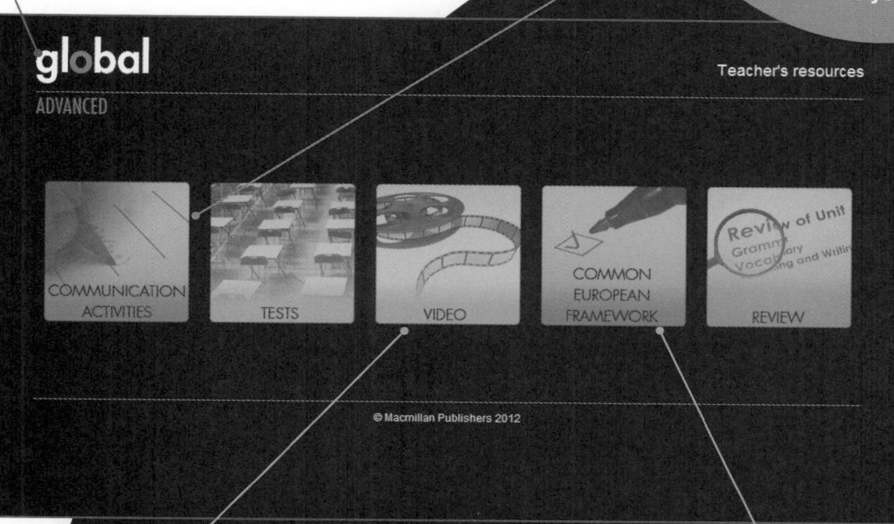

Also included are video clips for classroom use, with their corresponding worksheets and teacher's notes provided as printable PDFs.

Each level of *Global* is mapped against the corresponding level in the Common European Framework.

global
ADVANCED
home
Tests
DIAGNOSTIC TESTS
UNIT TESTS
PROGRESS TESTS
END-OF-YEAR TEST
© Macmillan Publishers 2012

The Teacher's Resource Disc also contains numerous *Global*-related tests for use in class.